Destructive Turfgrass Insects

Biology, Diagnosis, and Control

Daniel A. Potter
University of Kentucky

Ann Arbor Press
Chelsea, Michigan

Library of Congress Cataloging-in-Publication Data
Potter, Daniel A.
    Destructive turfgrass insects : biology, diagnosis, and control / by Daniel A. Potter.
        p.   cm.
    Includes bibliographical references and index.
    ISBN 1-57504-023-9
    1. Turfgrasses--Diseases and pests. 2. Insect pests. 3. Turfgrasses--Diseases and pests--United States. 4. Turfgrasses--Diseases and pests--Canada. 5. Insect pests--United States. 6. Insect pests--Canada.   I. Title.
    SB608.T87P68   1998
    635.9′64197--dc21   97-22727
                                                                                                                                    CIP

Front cover: Mole cricket photo courtesy of David J. Shetlar
            Additional photos courtesy of Monte P. Johnson
Back cover: Photos by the author

ISBN 1-57504-023-9

ANN ARBOR PRESS, INC.
121 South Main Street, Chelsea, Michigan 48118
Ann Arbor Press is an imprint of Sleeping Bear Press

PRINTED IN THE UNITED STATES OF AMERICA
10 9 8 7 6 5 4 3 2 1

Dedicated to

Terri, my dear wife and best friend
Benjamin and Joseph, our sons
Professor Norman and Adele Potter, my parents

About the Author

 **Daniel A. Potter** is a professor of entomology at the University of Kentucky, where he has taught courses and conducted research on turfgrass insects since 1979. He received his B.S. degree from Cornell University in 1974, and his Ph.D. from Ohio State University in 1978. Dr. Potter is a worldwide authority on insect pests of turf and woody landscape plants, and his research on white grubs, cutworms, and other pests has been widely noted by the green industry. He has published well over 100 scientific papers and book chapters, and dozens of trade journal articles. Dr. Potter has been a Keynote Speaker at the International Turfgrass Research Conference, and has lectured in Africa, Australia, Canada, Europe, and throughout the United States. His research has been funded by the U.S. Golf Association, the O.J. Noer Turfgrass Research Foundation, and the U.S. Department of Agriculture. Dr. Potter has received several professional awards for service to the green industry, as well as the Distinguished Achievement Award in Urban Entomology from the Entomological Society of America.

Series Preface

Destructive Turfgrass Insects by Dr. Daniel A. Potter is a comprehensive, authoritative source of information on insect problems in turfgrass environments that is specifically oriented to the turfgrass manager's needs. The author has called upon his many years of experience in research and teaching to prepare this practical text. Diagnosis and biology of all important insect and mite pests of turfgrasses in the United States and southern Canada are covered. Included, too, is discussion of beneficial insect species, stinging and biting pests, as well as moles and other destructive vertebrates in turfgrass settings. Emphasis is placed on environmentally sensitive management, including effective use of conventional insecticides, strengths and weaknesses of alternative tactics, and the use of selective treatments for specific pests. This book is a welcome, key addition to the *Turfgrass Science and Practice Series.*

Dr. James B Beard

Preface

This book was written as a practical reference for turfgrass professionals, including golf course superintendents, lawn care specialists, grounds managers, seed and sod growers, landscapers, and others interested in maintaining high-quality turf. There are several excellent books available on biology of turfgrass insects, but a practical handbook was needed that integrates diagnostic and biological information with specific guidelines for managing these pests. The text is written in everyday language, with a minimum of entomological jargon. This book should also be useful to students and teachers of turf management, turfgrass consultants, county and state extension personnel, garden center personnel, home lawn enthusiasts, and representatives of agribusinesses that serve the green industry.

Turfgrasses continue to increase in importance in the United States and worldwide. Healthy turf enhances the quality of our lives at work, at home, and at play. With society's emphasis on leisure time and recreation, the growing popularity of golf, and the high value placed on lawns and landscapes, demand for quality turfgrass will remain high. At the same time, there is heightened concern over environmental safety, and growing awareness of the problems that overuse of insecticides may cause. Today's turf managers thus face the dual challenge of growing healthy, attractive turf, but doing so with reduced reliance on conventional pesticides.

High-quality lawns, golf courses, and other fine turfs don't just happen; they require careful attention and skillful management. Accurate identification, and knowledge of pest life cycles and habits, are essential, regardless of the control tactics used. This book contains the technical and practical information needed to diagnose and resolve turfgrass insect problems in a safe and cost-effective manner, with minimal adverse side effects.

The book covers all of the important insects and related pests that are destructive to turfgrasses in the United States and southern Canada, as well as many of the less common ones. Beneficial and nuisance species, biting and stinging insects, and vertebrate pests commonly encountered in turfgrass settings are also discussed. The early chapters provide a brief overview of insect biology and integrated pest management, including tactics for detecting and monitoring particular pests. Recognizing that pesticides often play a key role in turf management, I have provided in Chapters 4 through 6 an up-to-date account of conventional and so-called biorational insecticides, with guidelines for their safe handling and effective use. Chapter 7 addresses environmental side effects of insecticides, including means for safeguarding wildlife and beneficial species. The remaining chapters group the pests by the type of injury that they cause. For each pest, the distinguishing characteristics, symptoms of damage, and life cycle and habits are described or explained. Guidelines for preventive or curative control are outlined. Means of alleviating pest problems through cultural or biological tactics (e.g., resistant grasses, cultivation, modified irrigation) are emphasized wherever applicable.

For quick reference, a glossary of scientific terms appears near the end of the book. Most of these words appear in bold type when first introduced in the text. Four appendices provide further information for turf professionals. Appendix 1 contains a list of land-grant universities and State Agricultural Experiment Stations from which local information or pesticide certification training can be obtained. Appendix 2 lists some additional reference books, as well as periodicals that run occasional articles about turfgrass insects. Sources for entomological supplies, protective clothing, and other pest management equipment are given in Appendix 3. Appendix 4 is a table of weights and measures, with conversions between the metric and English units. It will prove useful to those who must calibrate application equipment or calculate application rates of pesticides or fertilizers.

Various life history charts, distribution maps, and other illustrations appear throughout the text. The full-page color plates, which depict commonly encountered life stages and damage symptoms for practically all of the important turfgrass insects found in the United States and southern Canada, should be especially useful for identifying turfgrass insects and for promoting understanding of their habits.

Many people have helped me in the writing of this book. First and foremost, I thank my parents, Norman and Adele B. Potter, for their love and encouragement, and for their many sacrifices that allowed me to pursue my interest in insects. Thanks, too, to my brother Mike, for helping to keep me focused on the important questions.

I am especially grateful to David J. Shetlar (Ohio State University), who shared scanned images of USDA drawings, saving me countless hours of work, and for making available his collection of superb, original color slides. Others who shared reprints, extension bulletins, or slides used for preparing the color plates or figures include: Frederick P. Baxendale (University of Nebraska), S. Kristine Braman (University of Georgia), Rick L. Brandenburg (North Carolina State University), Patricia P. Cobb (Auburn University), Whitney S. Cranshaw (Colorado State University), Robert L. Crocker (Texas A&M University), Bastiaan M. Drees (Texas A&M University), Kenneth F. Haynes (University of Kentucky), Monte P. Johnson (University of Kentucky), Milton E. Kageyama (O.M. Scott & Sons), Jim Kalisch (University of Nebraska), Michael Klein (USDA–ARS, Wooster, Ohio), Michael E. Merchant (Texas Agricultural Extension Service), William Mesner (University of Kentucky), Thomas V. Myers (All-Rite Pest Control, Lexington, Kentucky), Timothy D. Paine (University of California), Michael F. Potter (University of Kentucky), James A. Reinert (Texas A&M University), Gwen K. Stahnke (Washington State University), Haruo Tashiro (Cornell University), Michael P. Tolley (Dow–Elanco, Indianapolis, Indiana), Michael G. Villani (Cornell University), and David F. Williams (USDA–ARS, Gainesville, Florida). I also thank the many companies and individuals that have permitted reproduction of photographs and illustrations used in this book.

I am grateful to many colleagues who reviewed drafts of various chapters and were responsible for many improvements but none of the mistakes. Reviewers from outside the University of Kentucky included Frederick P. Baxendale, S. Kristine Braman, Rick L. Brandenburg, Patricia P. Cobb, Whitney S. Cranshaw, James A. Reinert, David J. Shetlar, and Michael G. Villani. I also wish to thank colleagues at the University of Kentucky who provided advice and reviews. They include Ricardo T. Bessin, Kenneth F. Haynes, Andrew J. Powell, David Williams, Lee H. Townsend, Jr., R. Chris Williamson, and Kenneth V. Yeargan. Special thanks to my brother Mike, who read much of the book and provided many helpful suggestions.

Aaron Anderson (University of Kentucky) was a wizard with the computer and scanners. His skill in compositing figures, scanning slides, and managing files turned chaos into order and allowed me to concentrate on the writing. I wish to thank Andrew J. Powell (Department of Agronomy) for teaching me much of what I know about turf management, Bobby C. Pass (Chair, Department of Entomology) for his continued encouragement, and Kenneth F. Haynes for his friendship. Others who have inspired me in my career include my former mentors, George C. Eickwort (deceased), Donald G. Johnston (deceased), and Dana L. Wrensch. I also acknowledge the many graduate students and technicians who have enriched my career, and whose work has enhanced my knowledge of turfgrass insects. Thanks, too, to James Beard for encouraging me to write this book, and to the folks at Ann Arbor Press for their help in processing the manuscript.

Finally, a heartfelt thanks to my very special wife, Terri, and sons, Benjamin and Joseph, for their patience and understanding during the long hours that I neglected them while writing this book. My task was made much easier because of their love and support.

Photograph Credits

I gratefully acknowledge the many colleagues who loaned the color slides used in compiling the photographic plates. This book would not have been possible without their cooperation. The list below reflects the sources of these slides. The original photographer is credited, unless unknown.

Arthur L. Antonelli (Western Washington Research and Extension Center, Puyallup): Plate 2B

Frederick P. Baxendale (University of Nebraska, Lincoln): Plates 5H; 8B

Rick L. Brandenburg (North Carolina State University, Raleigh): Plates 2H; 3F; 4A,C,E,F

Leland R. Brown (University of California, Riverside; loaned by Timothy D. Paine): Plates 14E–G

R. Scott Cameron (from New York State Agricultural Experiment Station [NYSAES], Cornell University, Geneva; loaned by M.G. Villani): Plate 15C

John L. Capinera (University of Florida, Gainesville; from the Gillette Entomology Club Slide Collection; loaned by Whitney Cranshaw): Plates 18F; 24F

Gertrude Catlin (from NYSAES, Cornell University, Geneva; loaned by M.G. Villani): Plates 9D,E; 15D

Shiu-Ling Chung (from NYSAES, Cornell University, Geneva; loaned by M.G. Villani): Plate 9C

Patricia P. Cobb (Auburn University, Auburn, Alabama): Plates 2F; 4B,G; 10F; 20F,G

Whitney S. Cranshaw (Colorado State University, Ft. Collins, Colorado): Plates 17E; 21C,F,G; 26B; 31A

Robert L. Crocker (Texas A&M Agricultural Research and Extension Center, Dallas): Plates 4H; 10B,E; 12G,H; 18H

Ken Gray Slide Collection (Oregon State University, Corvallis; loaned by G. Stahnke): Plate 2A

Kenneth F. Haynes (University of Kentucky, Lexington): Plate 13C

Monte P. Johnson (University of Kentucky, Lexington): Plates 5D,F; 8C; 10A,C,G; 11A; 12A,D; 16B; 24C; 26F; 30E; 31C,D,F,G

O.M. Scott & Sons (Marysville, Ohio; loaned by Milton Kageyama): Plates 11H; 14C; 15A,F; 16G; 18B; 32E

James Kalisch (University of Nebraska, Lincoln): Plates 16A; 21A,B; 22D,E; 23C,D; 24H; 25B,F; 29E; 30B,C

David L. Keith (University of Nebraska, Lincoln; loaned by F.P. Baxendale): Plate 23F

Michael G. Klein (U.S. Department of Agriculture at the Ohio Agricultural Research and Development Center, Wooster): Plate 11E

Philip Koehler (University of Florida, Gainesville; loaned by M.F. Potter): Plate 29F

James Larner (from NYSAES, Cornell University, Geneva; loaned by M.G. Villani): Plate 9B

Michael E. Merchant (Texas A&M Agricultural Extension Service, Dallas): Plate 28D

William Mesner (University of Kentucky, Lexington): Plates 5E; 11F; 12E; 13A,D,F; 19B,F; 25D

Charles L. Murdoch (University of Hawaii, Honolulu; loaned by M.G. Villani): Plate 27H

Thomas V. Myers (All-Rite Pest Control, Lexington, Kentucky): Plates 29A,G,H

John Ogrodnick (from NYSAES, Cornell University, Geneva; loaned by M.G. Villani): Plate 7D

Frank Peairs (Colorado State University, Fort Collins; loaned by W.S. Cranshaw): Plate 21H

Daniel A. Potter (University of Kentucky, Lexington): Plates 5A–C; 10D; 11C,D; 13H; 16F; 19C–E; 24D; 26D; 29D; 30G; 31H; 32G,H

Michael F. Potter (University of Kentucky, Lexington): Plate 29C

Andrew J. Powell (University of Kentucky, Lexington): Plates 13G; 16E; 28H; 32A

James A. Reinert (Texas A&M Agricultural Research and Extension Center, Dallas): Plates 3E,G; 14H; 22F; 28G; 30F

David J. Shetlar (Ohio State University, Columbus): Plates 1A,B; 2E,G; 3A–D; 4D; 5G; 7A–C,E,G; 8D; 9A,F; 11G; 12B; 13E; 16C; 17A–D; 18A,C,D,G; 19A; 20A,C–E,H; 21D; 22B; 23A,B,E,G; 24A,B,E,G; 25A,C,E; 26A,C,E; 27A–C,E,F; 28E,F; 30A,H; 31E; 32F

John Shoulders (loaned by M.P. Tolley): Plate 1F

Gwen K. Stahnke (Washington State University, Puyallup): Plates 2C,D

Haruo Tashiro (NYSAES, Cornell University, Geneva; loaned by M.G. Villani): Plates 6A–F; 7F; 8A,E; 11B; 12C,F; 13B; 14A,B,D; 15E,G; 16D; 17F; 18E; 20B; 21E; 22A,C; 23H; 25G,H; 27D; 28A,B; 30I; 32B–D

Michael P. Tolley (Dow–Elanco, Indianapolis, Indiana): Plates 1C–E

D.M. Tsuda (from NYSAES Collection, loaned by M.G. Villani): Plate 27G

U.S. EPA: Plates 29B; 30D; 31B

David F. Williams (USDA–ARS, Gainesville, Florida): Plate 28C

Contents

Managing Insect Pests
of Turf

INTRODUCTION

This book was written as a practical reference for golf course superintendents, lawn care specialists, grounds managers, seed and sod growers, consultants, extension agents, turfgrass educators and students, and others concerned with maintaining high-quality turf. It will help you to identify insects and related pests that damage turfgrasses, and to better understand their biology and control. It provides specific guidelines for resolving pest problems effectively, economically, and safely. Today, more than ever, this knowledge is important for all turfgrass professionals.

Citizen concern about the potential risks of pesticides to human health and the environment has led to ever tighter regulations that affect the day-to-day operation of golf courses and the landscape maintenance industry. Many communities have enacted laws requiring posting of signs in areas where pesticides have been used. Several states require written notification to neighbors or pesticide-sensitive persons living near application sites. Protecting groundwater and surface water from chemical pollutants is a national initiative. Professional applicators face increasing scrutiny and a complex web of compliance issues that regulate all aspects of pesticide usage (Figure 1.1). At the same time, the public continues to have high expectations for "picture perfect" lawns and uniform playing surfaces on golf courses. Turf care professionals thus face the dual challenge of growing healthy, attractive turf, but doing so with reduced use of chemical pesticides.

Maintaining dense, uniform, attractive turf isn't easy. Turfgrasses are subjected to stress from the environment, intensive use, diseases, and weeds. Grass foliage, stems, thatch and roots provide a bountiful habitat for a host of insects and related arthropods. Some of these pests damage the turf by devouring leaves, stems, crowns, or roots. Others suck juices from leaves and stems, weakening and discoloring the plants. Within every region, there are several major pests that pose a perennial threat (e.g., white grubs in the Northeast and mole crickets in the South). Other pests are sporadic, but may be locally abundant and destructive in a given year. Large numbers of beneficial and innocuous insects also occur in every turfgrass stand. Turf care professionals need to be able to distinguish between the beneficials and the pests, and

Figure 1.1. *Professionalism, environmental stewardship, and communication skills are essential for turfgrass managers who use insecticides in the public's view.*

to recognize the symptoms of pest presence before the damage gets out of hand. They must understand insect life cycles in order to target the life stages that are most vulnerable to control.

A substantial part of the pesticide budget for golf courses and lawn care goes for insect and mite control. Managing insect problems requires more knowledge today than it did a generation ago. In the 1960s, turf managers simply applied a long-residual soil insecticide such as chlordane and didn't worry about insect pests. The lawn service industry was built during the 1970s and 1980s on the "one treatment fits all" approach: the promise of a perfect lawn was provided by calendar-based applications of pesticides regardless of whether or not an infestation was present. Times have changed. Many of today's insecticides are shorter-lived, more selective, and require greater skill to use successfully. Turf managers must understand, and be able to select from, a growing number of insect control alternatives (e.g., parasitic nematodes, resistant grasses, insect growth regulators, and so on). Today there is heightened awareness of the problems caused by overuse of pesticides. There is close scrutiny by regulators, environmentalists, and the media. As the green industry evolves in response to these pressures, success will come to those who have the desire to learn, and are willing to adapt.

VALUE AND BENEFITS OF TURF

The turfgrass maintenance industry has grown rapidly since the 1960s. Use of turf skyrocketed as large tracts of land were developed to accommodate the growing suburban population. Turfgrasses now cover more than 30 million acres (12.2 million hectares) in the United States, more than the combined area of the New England states. Most of this acreage is subdivided into more than 50 million lawns; the remainder is in golf courses, parks, athletic fields, cemeteries, sod farms, and other sites.

According to the Lawn Institute (Roberts and Roberts, 1988), a typical U.S. community of 170,000 citizens has:

- 45,200 single-family homes on 3,495 acres (1415 ha) of lawns, costing more than $9 million per year to maintain
- 19,600 multiple-family residences located on 987 acres (400 ha) of lawns, costing nearly $400,000 a year for lawn maintenance
- 50 city parks, 3 cemeteries, 56 schools, 2 colleges, 195 churches, and 350 factories located on 1,338 acres (542 ha) of turf, employing 126 maintenance workers and costing $1.5 million a year for turf maintenance
- Six golf courses, occupying another 600 acres (243 ha), with annual maintenance costs of about $1.3 million

In total, this 6,400 acres (2592 ha) of turf requires 166 professionals and more than $13 million per year to maintain. These figures don't include the value of the substantial time homeowners spend maintaining their own lawns.

Although many citizens enjoy working on their lawn and landscape, they may not realize the economic value and environmental benefits of their efforts. These same benefits are provided by golf courses where the combination of mowed turf, woody plants, and natural areas provides a diverse environment for people and wildlife. Turfgrass also provides a low-cost, safe recreational surface. The enjoyment and the benefits of improved physical and mental health derived from sports and leisure activities on turfgrass are vital to the quality of life in contemporary society, especially in densely populated urban areas.

Turfgrasses contribute substantially to the national economy. Consider the following facts:

- Turfgrass culture, in its many forms, is estimated to be a $45 billion per year industry in the United States. Hundreds of thousands of people make their living directly from the care and maintenance of turf.
- An attractive, well-maintained landscape adds about 15% to the selling price of a home.
- Commercial lawn care receipts increased at an average annual rate of 22% from 1977 to 1984.
- U.S. golf course facilities impact the economy at an estimated $18 billion each year. Golf courses are often the main attraction that brings vacationers to a community.
- Today, more than 24.5 million men, women, and youth spend 2.4 billion hours outside each year, playing on more than 14,500 golf courses. Over 78% of these rounds are played on public courses.

Turfgrasses provide substantial environmental, recreational, and aesthetic benefits. Here are some of the benefits provided by lush, healthy turf:

Turfgrasses control water and wind erosion of soil. Well-maintained turfgrass acts as a vegetative filter that captures and slows surface water runoff. During heavy rainstorms, there is considerable loss of soil from bare ground and tilled cropland, but almost no erosion from areas covered by healthy turf. This is very important in reducing dust and mud problems around homes, schools, and businesses. From an environmental standpoint, reduced erosion means conservation of valuable and nonreplaceable topsoil and less sediment pollution of streams, rivers, and lakes.

Turfgrass captures and cleans runoff water from urban areas. Rain is a major source of clean groundwater, which supplies much of our drinking water. During heavy rainstorms, excess surface water may run off parking lots, streets, and bare ground, carrying sediments, wastes, and pollutants into streams and lakes. Rainwater lost as surface runoff can't move through the soil to replenish the groundwater. Turfgrass absorbs and retains rainwater and surface runoff so that it does not enter storm sewers or waterways. As the water percolates through the grass, thatch, and soil below, it is filtered and cleansed by microorganisms that may digest and degrade trapped organic chemicals or pollutants. Thus, turfgrass can reduce the risk of groundwater contamination.

Turfgrass provides soil improvement and restoration. As turfgrass grows, it enriches the soil with organic matter. Many communities have found that planting perennial turfgrasses is an excellent way to restore highly eroded or clear-cut areas, or sites where landfills, quarries, or strip mines once stood. These areas can then be developed as parks, golf courses, or recreational areas.

Turfgrass moderates temperature and improves air quality. Through the cooling process of transpiration, turfgrasses greatly reduce the temperatures in urban areas. Synthetic turf can be much hotter than green, living grass, and asphalt is even hotter. Green grass and landscapes actually reduce the energy needed for air-conditioning of adjacent homes and offices. As plants carry out photosynthesis, they absorb carbon dioxide and release oxygen. A landscape of turf and woody plants, about 2000 ft^2 (186 m^2) in area, generates enough oxygen for one person for a year. Certain turfgrasses, such as tall fescue, can even absorb carbon monoxide from the urban environment.

Turfgrass reduces noise and glare. Turfgrass reduces undesirable noise levels by as much as 20–30%. Living grass absorbs sounds better than a heavy carpet on a felt pad, and much better than hard surfaces such as pavement or bare ground. Turf also reduces the glare of bright sunlight better than buildings, concrete, or glass.

Turfgrass reduces pests, pollen, and human disease exposure. Dense, closely mowed turf helps to reduce the weeds that produce allergy-related pollens. Closely mowed residential lawns also discourage nuisance pests such as rodents and snakes. As these undesirable creatures seek refuge in more distant higher grass and brush, they are less likely to invade homes. Well-maintained turf also discourages arthropod pests, such as chiggers and ticks, which thrive in unmowed tall grass and brushy habitats. Reducing exposure to ticks helps reduce the threat of Lyme disease in suburban areas.

Properly designed urban green areas, such as golf courses, parks, and backyards create good wildlife habitats. More than 70% of golf course acreage consists of rough and natural habitats, such as woodlands, ponds, and wetlands. This integrated landscape supports a diverse wildlife population, even to the extent that many golf courses can be described as wildlife sanctuaries.

Turfgrass improves the physical and mental health of the urban population. Turf provides a low-cost, safe recreational surface. The unique cushioning effect of turfgrass reduces injuries on athletic fields. Home lawn care, gardening, golf, and other leisure activities on turf provide benefits of both physical exercise and therapeutic relaxation from stresses of the workplace. Cities can be bleak without outdoor landscapes and vegetation. Open spaces with grass and

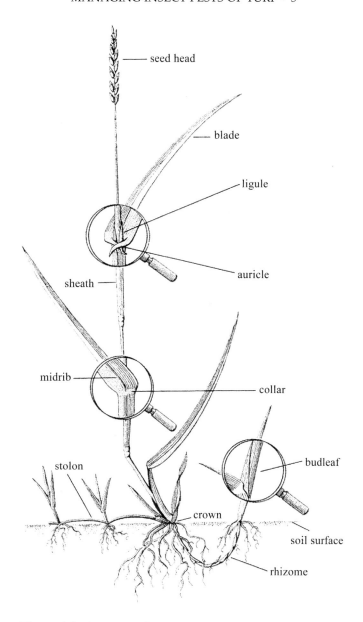

Figure 1.2. Structure of a grass plant (from Bruneau, 1993).

trees provide a pleasant environment in which to live, work, or play. Such aesthetic benefits are increasingly important to the mental well-being of city dwellers.

TURFGRASS STRUCTURE AND ADAPTATION

Structure of Grasses

Turf is composed of many individual grass plants growing in close association. Each plant consists of a shoot, a root system, a crown, and lateral stems (Figure 1.2). Variation in the form of these vegetative parts is used in distinguishing one grass species from another. Familiarity with the basic structure of a grass plant is helpful in understanding where insects hide and lay their eggs, and how they damage the turf.

A typical vegetative (nonflowering) grass plant has a **crown** located at or near the soil surface. The crown is the most important part of the plant because it contains the **meristematic tissue** from which roots, lateral shoots, and leaves are initiated. Grasses can withstand all types of injury, including loss of leaves and roots, so long as the crown survives. A fibrous, multibranched **root system** originates at the bottom of the crown and permeates the surface soil, anchoring the plant and absorbing nutrients and water. Roots may also originate from lateral stems (see below). The **shoot** consists of leaves and an associated short stem. The internodes of most turfgrasses do not elongate during vegetative growth; thus, the stem consists of a series of nodes separated by unelongated internodes. Each leaf consists of a flattened upper **blade** and a lower **sheath** that encircles the stem. The sheath is shaped like a hollow cylinder that is split down one side. The leaves formed on individual shoots arise from buds on the nodes of crowns and lateral stems. Because leaf growth occurs from the base of the plant, turf can be mowed without severe damage to the grass. If allowed to grow naturally, without mowing, the plant will form a **seedhead** — an elongated stem with a flower at its apex. Seedhead production usually occurs in late spring and early summer for cool-season grasses and during the summer and early fall for warm-season grasses.

Some turfgrasses produce lateral stems, which arise from the crown and extend out horizontally. These are called **rhizomes** if their formation is underground, or **stolons** if they grow mostly aboveground. Both can produce new roots and shoots from each node along their length. Stolons and rhizomes are formed when young, vegetative shoots grow outside the basal leaf sheath by penetrating through the sheath. This process, called **extravaginal growth**, results in a **spreading or creeping growth habit**. This type of growth is important because it allows certain grasses to fill in bare spots, including areas that have been damaged by insects. Extravaginal growth occurs in Kentucky bluegrass, creeping bentgrass, red fescue, and most warm-season turfgrasses.

Certain turfgrasses, such as ryegrass, chewings fescue, colonial bentgrass, tall fescue, and bahiagrass, do not develop significant lateral stems. These grasses achieve dense turf by development of **tillers** — erect vegetative shoots that arise from the crown and grow next to the original shoot. This type of growth, called **intravaginal growth**, results in a tufted or **bunch-type growth habit**. Bunch-type grasses usually do not recover from insect damage as well as those that produce rhizomes and stolons.

Leaves contain **chlorophyll**, the green pigment that carries out photosynthesis to produce carbohydrates, the food for growth and recuperation. Pests such as cutworms, armyworms, and webworms that consume these tissues reduce the area available for photosynthesis. They may also expose the crown to lethal environmental temperatures. Sucking insects and mites drain chlorophyll and carbohydrate-rich sap. Some also inject toxins that clog the vascular system, impeding translocation of water and nutrients within the plant. White grubs and other root-feeding pests reduce the plant's ability to absorb water and nutrients, particularly under drought stress. Billbugs damage the crown and may kill the plant outright.

Cultural practices greatly affect the ability of turf to tolerate and recover from insect injury. Healthy turf will be quick to recuperate from damage by foliage- or root-feeding insects by means of vegetative regrowth from buds on the crowns and lateral stems. Grasses with vigorous rhizome and/or stolon development generally have the best recuperative potential. High carbohydrate reserves also are needed. Recuperative potential is enhanced by higher-than-usual cutting heights, moderate nitrogen fertility, deep watering, good soil aeration, and other cultural practices that promote a deep, healthy root system.

Climatic Adaptations of Grasses and Insects

Different turfgrasses are adapted to grow best under particular climatic conditions. Perennial **cool-season turfgrasses**, which include bluegrasses, bentgrasses, fescues, and ryegrasses,

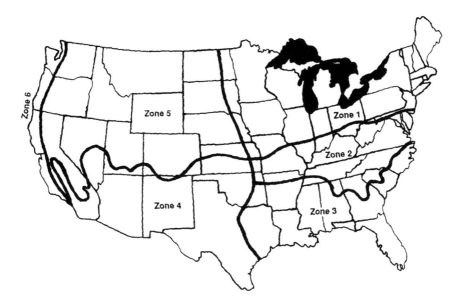

Figure 1.3. *Turfgrass adaptation zones in the United States (adapted from Emmons, 1995).*

are adapted to the temperate, northern two-thirds of the United States. These grasses grow best at temperatures of 60–75°F (16–24°C). They are able to withstand low winter temperatures, but may become partially dormant during the hot summer months. In contrast, **warm-season turfgrasses**, including bermudagrass, St. Augustinegrass, zoysiagrass, bahiagrass, and centipedegrass, are adapted to the southern United States. As a general rule, these subtropical grasses grow best when temperatures are above 80°F (27°C). They are intolerant of cold weather and may be killed by low winter temperatures or late spring frosts. These grasses usually become dormant when the temperature drops to below 50°F (10°C).

The United States can be roughly divided into northern and southern **turfgrass adaptation zones** based on temperature (Figure 1.3). These zones can be further divided on the basis of rainfall and climate. Zones 1 and 5 have severe winters and are most suitable for the cool-season turfgrasses. Consequently, they are designated as cool-season zones. Zones 3 and 4 have a moderate to subtropical climate where the warm-season grasses grow best. They compose the warm-season zones. Zones 4 and 5 are characterized by semiarid or arid climate. In the drier areas of these regions, quality turfgrass can be maintained only with irrigation. Where irrigation is not available, native dryland species such as crested wheatgrass, buffalograss, and blue gramagrass make acceptable low-maintenance turfs. Zone 6 has a cool, oceanic climate in the north, and a moderate to subtropical climate in southern California. Keep in mind that the boundary lines between zones and regions represent transitional areas rather than discrete divisions of climate and turfgrass species.

The major insect and mite pests also differ to a large extent between the different zones, mainly reflecting preference for either cool- or warm-season grasses. Environmental constraints also restrict many insects to particular regions. Japanese beetles, for example, are unlikely to expand their range into the arid parts of the Great Plains (Zones 4 and 5) because soil conditions are too dry to allow survival of eggs and larvae.

Kentucky bluegrass, creeping bentgrass, perennial ryegrass, fine-leaf fescues, and tall fescue are the main turfgrasses cultivated in the cool-season zones. Major insect pests in Zone 1 are introduced white grubs (e.g., Japanese beetle, European chafer), native white grubs (e.g., masked chafers, May beetles), bluegrass billbug, hairy chinch bug, black cutworm, and sod webworms. Important insect pests in Zone 5 include native white grubs, sod webworms, armyworms, cutworms, and billbugs. Sod webworms and European crane fly are important pests in the northern half of Zone 6.

Bermudagrass and zoysiagrass are widely cultivated in Zones 3 and 4. **Cool-season grasses**, such as Kentucky bluegrass, tall fescue, fine-leaf fescues, perennial ryegrass, and creeping bentgrass, are grown along the northern edge of these zones. Zone 3 has a subtropical climate along the Gulf of Mexico and in Florida. Here, bahiagrass, St. Augustinegrass, centipedegrass, and carpetgrass are grown, along with bermudagrass and zoysiagrass. Major insect and mite pests in Zone 3 include mole crickets, southern chinch bug, tropical sod webworm, army-worm, fall armyworm, cutworms, ground pearls, hunting billbug, two-lined spittlebug, bermudagrass mite, bermudagrass scale, and Rhodesgrass mealybug. White grubs are also important in Zone 3. Red imported fire ant is a problem from the southern half of Zone 3 to the Gulf. Hawaii has a climate similar to Zone 3. Turfgrasses cultivated there are nearly the same as in southern Florida, except for bahiagrass. Hawaii has a relatively unique pest fauna that includes grass webworm, lawn armyworm, and fiery skipper.

Zone 4 extends from central Texas and Oklahoma across to southern California. Summers are hot and dry, with low humidity. Bermudagrass is widely cultivated throughout this region, with or without irrigation. Zoysiagrass is also common, and St. Augustinegrass, centipedegrass, and dichondra are used in southern California. Irrigation is generally necessary for good quality turf. Major insect and mite pests include white grubs (mostly masked chafers), cutworms and armyworms, fiery skipper, southern chinch bug, Phoenix and hunting billbugs, sod webworms, bermudagrass scale, and bermudagrass mite on grasses; and dichondra flea beetle and veg-etable weevil on dichondra.

Climatic conditions in areas near the boundary separating the northern and southern grass adaptation regions are not ideal for either cool-season or warm-season turfgrasses. Winters may be too cold for warm-season species, and summer too hot for cool-season species. These areas immediately north and south of the warm-season/cool-season zone boundary are referred to as the **transition zone** (Zone 2). Kentucky bluegrass, perennial ryegrass, tall fescue, creep-ing bentgrass, bermudagrass, and zoysiagrass are the most frequently used grasses in this zone. Tall fescue is generally well-adapted to the transition zone.

COMMON TURFGRASSES FROM AN ENTOMOLOGICAL PERSPECTIVE

Cool-Season Grasses

The major cool-season turfgrasses cultivated in the northern two-thirds of the United States are grouped into four genera: the bluegrasses (*Poa* spp.), bentgrasses (*Agrotis* spp.), ryegrasses (*Lolium* spp.), and fescues (*Festuca* spp.). All of these grasses are relatively tolerant of low temperatures, although this varies among species and cultivars. The bluegrasses and bentgrasses can tolerate the severe Canadian winters, whereas tall fescue and perennial ryegrass are better adapted to those portions of the cool-season zones where winter temperatures are not extreme. Heat tolerance generally is poor to fair. Cool-season grasses generally require irrigation when grown in Zone 5. Tall fescue, creeping bentgrass, perennial ryegrass, and Kentucky bluegrass can be grown in the transition zone.

Kentucky bluegrass (*Poa pratensis* L.) is the most important and widely cultivated cool-season turfgrass. Dozens of cultivars are available, with more being developed all the time. The genus *Poa* is distinguished by having a boat-shaped leaf tip. Kentucky bluegrass is medium green in color with medium-textured blades. Its spreading, creeping growth habit allows it to fill in patches of insect-damaged turf. Kentucky bluegrass may become brown and inactive (dormant) during extended hot, dry periods in summer. When this occurs, early damage by hairy chinch bugs or sod webworms may be masked by the general droughty appearance of the dormant turf. Healthy bluegrass will recover quickly from summer dormancy when moisture and temperature conditions become favorable. Only then do the patches of insect-damaged turf become obvious. Kentucky bluegrass seems to have little natural resistance to insects. It is susceptible to white grubs, bluegrass billbug, hairy chinch bug, sod webworms, greenbug, and other pests.

Annual bluegrass (*Poa annua* L.), called simply "Poa" by many turf managers, is considered a weed in most turfs. Annual bluegrass invades turf that is heavily irrigated, such as golf greens, fairways, and high-quality lawns. Because it is persistent and hard to control, turf managers often have to live with it. In fact, many golf courses in the Northeast maintain *Poa annua* var. *reptans* as a perennial grass. It forms a very dense, stoloniferous turf under close mowing. Clumps of annual bluegrass are easily spotted during spring or early summer by the presence of seed heads which disrupt the uniformity of turf. Another problem is its tendency to die out during the hotter, drier parts of the summer, resulting in dead, brown patches throughout the turf. Daily irrigation is often necessary to prevent this problem. Annual bluegrass weevil is a major insect pest of this grass on golf courses in the Northeast.

Creeping bentgrass (*Agrostis stolonifera* L.) is the standard grass on U.S. golf course putting greens except in the Deep South. Its low growth habit allows it to tolerate extremely close mowing. It is also used on fairways, tees, bowling greens, and grass tennis courts, and is sometimes used for high-quality lawns. Creeping bentgrass produces a fine-textured, soft, extremely dense, carpet-like sod. It spreads by aggressive growth of stolons, which enables it to recuperate rapidly from insect damage. At higher cutting heights this growth habit results in excessive thatch formation. Coring, topdressing, and vertical cutting are used to reduce thatch buildup. Creeping bentgrass is very cold tolerant, but quite susceptible to fungal diseases. It does not grow well on compacted soils. To alleviate compaction, soil mixes for bentgrass putting greens usually contain high percentages of sand, and are mechanically aerated. Most cultivars of creeping bentgrass (e.g., Penncross) are established from seed, but some of the older cultivars were vegetatively propagated. Major insect pests include black cutworms, white grubs (including black turfgrass ataenius), and hairy chinch bug.

Colonial bentgrass (*Agrostis capillaris* L.) is a fine-textured, bunch-type to weakly creeping grass that is occasionally used on golf fairways and tees. Its poor heat and drought tolerance limit its use to coastal regions of New England, and in the Pacific Northwest. Insect pests are the same as for creeping bentgrass.

Perennial ryegrass (*Lolium perenne* L.) is often used in seed mixtures with slower-germinating grasses (e.g., Kentucky bluegrass) because of its ability to establish quickly and prevent soil and the remaining seed from washing away. It is a noncreeping, bunch-type grass with fine-textured leaf blades that are heavily veined on the upper surface and glossy underneath. Perennial ryegrass is often used on golf fairways, tees, and athletic fields because it can be mowed relatively short, and is resistant to wear. Improved turf-type cultivars can be blended with bluegrass for use in intense traffic areas. Perennial ryegrass is used for overseeding dormant, warm-season turfs for winter play and color, and for repairing damaged grasses. It may also be planted as a temporary ground cover in the cool-season zones. Planted alone, the improved turf-type cultivars will form a durable lawn under sun or semishade conditions. Nonendophytic cultivars are especially susceptible to billbugs, sod webworms, chinch bugs, and white grubs. Endophyte-infected cultivars are relatively resistant to many foliage- and stem-feeding insects, but are susceptible to grubs.

Annual ryegrass (*Lolium multiflorum* Lam.) is also called Italian ryegrass. This annual plant is used for quick, temporary coverage, and in cheap seed mixes. Within one year, most of the annual ryegrass dies and hopefully is replaced by more desirable grass species in the mix.

Tall fescue (*Festuca arundinacea* Schreb.) has the best heat and drought tolerance of the cool-season grasses, making it well-suited for use in the transition zone. It is susceptible to low-temperature injury, however, making it a poor choice for the northernmost parts of the United States. Tall fescue grows well in sun or semishade, and withstands the abuse of intense traffic. The older, coarse-leafed cultivars, such as Kentucky 31, are used on low-maintenance sites or for home lawns that require little care. The newer, turf-type tall fescues have leaves that are more dense, darker green, and finer-textured than the older type. These will provide a high-quality lawn under proper cultivation. Because of its deep, sturdy root system, tall fescue is more tolerant of white grubs than are other cool season grasses. Sod webworms, fall army-worms, billbugs, and greenbug also attack tall fescue, but seldom cause much damage. The inclusion of endophytes in tall fescue cultivars improves drought hardiness and resistance to some insects and diseases.

Fine-leaf fescues include several *Festuca* species and subspecies that have fine-textured, bristle-like leaf blades. The most widely used ones are **creeping red fescue** (*Festuca rubra* L.), **chewings fescue** (*Festuca rubra* var. *commutata* Gaud.), and **hard fescue** (*Festuca longifolia* Thuill). Fine-leaf fescues tolerate moderately low light intensities, making them the best of the fine-textured cool-season grasses for shaded sites. For this reason they are often blended with Kentucky bluegrass and perennial ryegrass in general purpose seed mixtures. They are fairly drought tolerant, and well-adapted to acidic, low-fertility soils. Fine-leaf fes-cues perform especially well under low maintenance. They spread by tillers or by short, creeping rhizomes, forming a dense, low-growing turf. Fine-leaf fescues are especially sus-ceptible to sod webworms and hairy chinch bug. They are also damaged by white grubs, armyworms, and cutworms. Some cultivars have fungal endophytes that enhance resistance to leaf- and stem-feeding insects.

Warm-Season Grasses

The warm-season turfgrasses are tolerant of close mowing, and withstand heat, drought, and traffic better than the cool-season grasses. Low-temperature hardiness varies among the species and cultivars. Some cultivars of zoysiagrass and bermudagrass can be cultivated as far north as the southern edge of the cool-season zone. St. Augustinegrass, bahiagrass, centipede-grass, and carpetgrass, however, are usually grown only in the warmest regions of the South.

Bahiagrass (*Paspalum notatum* Flugge.) is ideally suited to low-maintenance areas. It forms a very coarse, upright, open turf that thrives in sun or shade and can withstand drought and heavy traffic. Bahiagrass is often used for playgrounds, roadsides, and similar sites. It spreads by short stolons and rhizomes. It is a prolific seed producer, forming numerous tall, unsightly seed heads that require frequent mowing to remove. It is best adapted to south Florida and along the Gulf coast. Propagation is mainly by seed. In spite of its poor turf quality, this species is becoming more popular as a lawn grass because it is relatively resistant to pests. Mole crickets are the main insect problem.

Dactylon bermudagrass (*Cynodon dactylon* [L.] Pers.), also called couchgrass, is the most widely used turfgrass in the southern United States. Bermudagrass tolerates a wide range of soil conditions, but it is the least shade tolerant of the warm-season grasses. Breed-ing efforts have produced hybrid cultivars (*C. dactylon* × *C. transvaalensis*) with improved disease resistance, density, color, and cold tolerance. Some of these improved cultivars are cold-hardy enough to be used in the transition zone. Bermudagrass produces a fine-textured, low, dense, dark green turf that is used for lawns, athletic fields, parks, and golf course tees, fairways, and putting greens. It spreads quickly by creeping stolons and rhizomes, giving it excellent recuperative potential. Except for common bermudagrass and a few recently re-leased seeded cultivars, most cultivars are propagated vegetatively from sprigs, plugs, or sod. Bermudagrass seems to have little natural resistance to insects. Problems are caused by mole crickets, fall armyworm, tropical sod webworm, bermudagrass scale, bermudagrass mite, Rhodesgrass mealybug, two-lined spittlebug, southern chinch bug, striped grassworm, and cutworms. In Hawaii, bermudagrass is attacked by the lawn armyworm, grass web-worm, and fiery skipper.

Buffalograss (*Buchloë dactyloides* [Nutt.] Engelm.) is an important rangeland grass adapted to the dry, semiarid regions of the North American Great Plains. This perennial, warm-season species is well-suited for use on unirrigated lawns, fairways, parks, athletic fields, and roadsides in the transitional and warm, semiarid regions of the United States. It forms a low growing, fine textured, soft, gray-green turf with fair shoot density. It tolerates high temperatures and is more cold-hardy than other warm-season grasses. Shade tolerance is poor. Buffalograss has relatively few insect problems other than mealybugs and mites.

Centipedegrass (*Eremochloa ophiuroides* [Munro.] Hack.) is used on low-maintenance lawns and similar sites. It forms a turf of acceptable quality with a minimum of care. Centipedegrass spreads slowly by creeping, thick, leafy stolons forming a low growing, dark green turf. However, it is very sensitive to iron deficiency, producing a yellow, chlorotic appearance. Drought tolerance is poor because of its shallow root system. It will not withstand traffic, and recovers slowly when damaged. Shade tolerance is fair, and salt tolerance is poor. Cold hardiness is poor — slightly better than St. Augustinegrass, but not as good as bermudagrass. Establishment is mainly by sprigs, plugs, or sod. Centipedegrass is especially susceptible to ground pearls. It is also damaged by mole crickets, tropical sod webworm, two-lined spittlebug, hunting billbug, and Rhodesgrass mealybug. In Hawaii, it is susceptible to the grass webworm.

St. Augustinegrass (*Stenotaphrum secundatum* [Walt.] Kutze) is a popular lawn grass in Florida, around the Gulf coast, and in California. It establishes easily, tolerates shade and salt spray, and produces an attractive, dense, mat-like cover. It adapts well to a wide range of soil types and conditions. However, it is the least cold-hardy of the warm-season grasses. Propagation is vegetative by sprigs or sod. St. Augustinegrass is coarse in texture and spreads by means of long, thick stolons. This aggressive growth habit gives it good recuperative capability, but makes it prone to buildup of thatch. Southern chinch bug is the most important pest of St. Augustinegrass. Rhodesgrass mealybug, hunting billbug, Banks grass mite, tropical sod webworm, striped grassworms, and mole crickets cause occasional damage.

Zoysiagrass (*Zoysia* species) is used for lawns, tees, and fairways throughout much of the warm-season and transition zones. The two most common species are Japanese or Korean lawngrass (*Zoysia japonica* Steud.) and manilagrass (*Zoysia matrella* [L.] Merr.). Zoysiagrass spreads and develops slowly, but eventually forms a very dense, low-growing turf. It wears very well, has good salt tolerance, and moderate drought tolerance. Except for a few recently released cultivars, improved zoysia cultivars are propagated vegetatively by sprigs, plugs, or sod. Japanese lawngrass has the best low temperature tolerance of the warm-season grasses, but it has a short growing season in the northern zone. It turns a straw color after the first heavy frost and is slow to green up in the spring. Recuperative potential is poor because of the slow spreading rate. Zoysiagrass is somewhat more resistant to insects than most other warm-season grasses. Hunting billbugs are common pests, and tropical sod webworms, fall armyworms, and mole crickets cause occasional problems. Lawn armyworm attacks zoysiagrass in Hawaii.

Dichondra

Although not a grass, dichondra is a low-growing broadleaf plant that produces an attractive, dense ground cover. It is best-suited to the warm, mild climate of southern California and Arizona, where it is used mainly on lawns. Disease problems limit its use in the southeastern states. Dichondra has soft, bright green, round or kidney-shaped leaves that arise along creeping stems. It spreads by creeping stolons and underground rhizomes. It has poor wear resistance, and regular watering is necessary. Dichondra is attacked by dichondra flea beetle, vegetable weevil, cutworms and armyworms, lucerne moth larvae, spider mites, slugs, and snails.

INTEGRATED PEST MANAGEMENT

Integrated pest management (or **IPM**) is an effective and environmentally responsible approach to plant protection. IPM relies on a combination of preventive and corrective measures to keep pest densities below levels that would cause unacceptable damage. Its goal is to manage pests effectively, economically, and with minimal risks to people and the environment.

Turfgrass IPM is not a fancy new concept invented by university professors — it's been around for as long as there have been skilled turf managers. When a golf superintendent walks the course regularly to monitor conditions, keeps track of weather patterns, gets down on hands and knees to check for pests, and uses cultural practices to correct problems wherever possible, he or she is following the tenets of IPM. It occurs when a grounds manager scouts a landscape to evaluate the status of pests, modifies cultural practices (mulching, watering, etc.) to enhance plant vigor, and withholds sprays unless they are truly warranted. There has been so much misunderstanding about IPM that a brief look at what this approach is, and is not, is helpful in understanding the concept.

- *IPM does not preclude the use of insecticides.* IPM recognizes that an insecticide may be the only practical solution when a pest problem gets out of hand. The emphasis, however, is on selective intervention rather than calendar-based cover sprays. We try to limit use of insecticides to situations in which pests reach, or threaten to reach, damaging levels. Relatively less toxic, environmentally friendly products are used when practical. When successful, IPM usually reduces the turf manager's dependence on pesticides.
- *IPM recognizes that the mere presence of a pest does not necessarily justify chemical control.* Some pests will always be present, and to try to eradicate them all is impractical and unnecessary. With IPM, we manage the turf system so that pest densities remain below levels that will cause unacceptable damage.
- *IPM is not a biological or organic pest control program*, though biological controls or organic materials may be preferred if they are effective.
- *IPM does not necessarily mean* "I Pay More." The investment in monitoring, sampling, and employee training is offset by reduced pesticide costs and better long-term health of the turfgrass stand. Reduced liability, increased professionalism, and environmental stewardship are additional benefits.
- *IPM is a decision-making process*, not just a reaction (e.g., applying an insecticide) to mere presence of pests.

This process of integrated pest management involves the following steps:

Sampling and Monitoring. Inspecting turf areas regularly throughout the growing season allows you to detect pests early, before they reach damaging levels. By monitoring, you can assess the need for action, evaluate how well control tactics have worked, and develop site history information that helps in anticipating future problems.

Pest Identification. Correct identification is needed before one can understand the habits and life cycle of an insect, and when and how it can best be managed. Professionals must be able to distinguish incidental and beneficial insects from serious pests.

Decision-Making. In IPM, management decisions are guided by **action thresholds** — flexible guidelines based on the level of insect abundance or damage that justifies a treatment or other intervention (see Chapter 3). The cost of the treatment, as well as any social or environmental consequences, is factored into the decision.

Appropriate Intervention. IPM goes beyond routine preventive or curative applications of insecticides. Rather, the turf manager tries to determine why a pest outbreak has occurred, and if cultural practices can be adjusted to reduce damage and the risk of future infestations. All appropriate management options are considered. Insecticides are applied only as necessary. Relatively less toxic products are used when practical.

Followup. By continued monitoring, the turf manager can evaluate how well a control tactic has worked, and assess the need for further action.

Record-Keeping. Effective record-keeping allows a professional to know when and where to expect certain pest problems and to plan ahead to deal with them. Certain neighborhoods or areas of the golf course may be perennial "hot spots" for particular pests. Record-keeping also helps you to evaluate which management practices are effective and which need to be modified in the future.

Employee and Client Education. Communication is a key part of successful IPM. It involves educating lawn care customers, club members, the Greens Committee, and most importantly, your employees. Developing an ongoing training program that focuses on pest recognition and agronomic factors assures that technicians have the knowledge to make sound management decisions. Send your staff to educational workshops, and ask them to share what they have learned. Employees who are trained to recognize and monitor pest problems and make informed decisions are more valuable than just laborers. The investment in training and higher salaries will be offset by less turnover of employees, costs saved by using less pesticides, better quality turf, and more satisfied clients. Professionalism and environmental stewardship are increased. Trained employees will work more safely and effectively. They can do the labor, but they are also able to communicate with the public.

Lawn service customers who are accustomed to paying for calendar-based, "pay-for-spray" may need convincing that an inspect and treat-as-needed program is better. Clients may feel that they have not received full value for their dollar unless the whole lawn is treated. That makes as much sense as not wanting to pay your doctor because your annual exam for prostate cancer turned out negative! Customers must be reminded that they are paying for professional management, not just for someone to show up once a month to drench the premises with insecticides. Still, if they are paying for a management program, they need to see something tangible. Soil tests, aerifying, dethatching, fertilization, weed control, tree and shrub care, landscaping, consultations, and written reports fill this need. Good communication with clients will help you to provide safe, environmentally responsible lawn care. Lawn care companies that have adopted this approach report a high degree of customer satisfaction, low cancellations and service calls, improved retention of employees, reduced pesticide usage and costs, and higher profits.

CONTROL OPTIONS IN IPM

Cultural Control

Cultural control involves suppressing pests or reducing their damage by normal or slightly modified management practices. In agriculture, cultural control includes such practices as sanitation (e.g., plowing under corn stubble after a growing season), crop rotation, tillage, planting resistant cultivars, physical or mechanical destruction of pests, quarantine, or other tactics. Skilled turf managers know that cultural practices significantly affect the development of diseases. What follows is a brief overview of how these practices affect insect pests. More specific suggestions for cultural control are listed in the individual pest sections.

Fertility. High nitrogen fertility levels result in rapid, succulent growth, and may substantially increase the chance of damage from insects. Excessive fertilization, coupled with improper mowing and watering, encourages accumulation of a thick, spongy thatch layer in some grasses that is good habitat for chinch bugs, billbugs, and sod webworms. Heavy fertilization of cool-season turfgrasses in the spring stimulates rapid, succulent shoot growth at the expense of developing a deep, healthy root system. This results in weak, shallow-rooted plants that are less able to recuperate from insect damage. Fertilization can stimulate the insect pests themselves. Like other animals, insects and mites have high dietary nitrogen requirements. This is because nitrogen is a key component of amino acids, the building blocks of proteins. Plant tissues are composed mostly of carbohydrates and have a relatively low nitrogen content. This fact limits the rate at which plant-feeding insects can grow and reproduce. Research has shown that many foliage-feeding and sucking insects grow faster, survive better, and lay more eggs on heavily fertilized plants.

On the other hand, a balanced fertility program provides controlled shoot growth, a deep, extensive root system, and good recuperative potential. Light fertilization, coupled with irrigation, can promote more rapid recovery from light to moderate insect damage. Your local cooperative extension office can provide fertility recommendations for your area.

Irrigation. Irrigation can have positive or negative effects from the standpoint of insect injury. Many root-feeding insects, especially white grubs, require moist soil for survival of eggs and young larvae. Hot weather and dry soil conditions cause the adult beetles to seek out moist areas in which to lay eggs. If fairways or lawns are irrigated while surrounding turf areas go into summer dormancy, egg-laying females will be attracted to the moist, lush turf. Some species, such as Japanese beetles, may fly as far as a half mile (0.8 km) in search of suitable egg-laying sites. Turf that is irrigated during peak beetle flight should be watched closely for grub problems in late summer. Once grubs have hatched and begun to feed, however, the practical consequences of irrigation are reversed. Well-watered turf will tolerate much higher densities of white grubs before showing damage. Irrigation or rainfall in late summer alleviates plant stress, masks the effects of white grubs, and encourages recuperation from root loss. Irrigation may also mask damage from billbugs, sod webworms, and other pests.

Irrigation has variable effects on thatch-dwelling or foliage-inhabiting pests. Chinch bugs, for example, require hot dry conditions for optimum survival and reproduction. Watering during spring and early summer can drown the nymphs and encourage spread of a lethal fungus, *Beauveria* spp. In contrast, two-lined spittlebug nymphs seem to survive better in irrigated turf. Responses of other pests to irrigation, and suggestions for favorable manipulations, are discussed in the individual pest sections. In general, sound irrigation to encourage a deep, vigorous root system helps turf to recover more quickly from foliar damage.

Mowing. Excessively close mowing or scalping drastically reduces root growth, carbohydrate reserves, and plant vigor, while decreasing tolerance to environmental stresses. Close-cut turf generally shows greater damage from grubs and other pests. Proper mowing practices (e.g., using a sharp blade; removing no more than a third of the grass blade at each mowing) will make a turf more tolerant of insect damage. Mowing may remove eggs of some pests, such as black cutworms (see Chapter 11).

Sanitation. Sanitation involves practices to avoid introducing insects or mites into noninfested sites, as well as cleanup of debris that serves as hiding or overwintering sites for pests. Inspect beforehand to avoid shipping or using sod that may be infested with billbugs, grubs, or chinch bugs. Large numbers of greenbugs may be transferred from lawn to lawn on wet clippings adhering to mowers or boots of lawn applicators. Cleaning up mulch or other hiding places around the foundation often alleviates problems with nuisance pests such as millipedes or earwigs entering homes.

Thatch Management. Thatch is an accumulation of tightly-knit dead and living stems and roots that builds up between the zone of green vegetation and the soil surface. Problems associated with excessive thatch are discussed in Chapters 6 and 14. Thatch removal is a form of sanitation because thatch is a prime habitat for insect pests. Thatch also acts as a barrier to penetration of soil insecticides, reducing their effectiveness. The best preventive biological control for thatch is an active earthworm population. Earthworms and microorganisms that decompose thatch can be conserved by avoiding use of certain pesticides (Chapter 7), maintaining a soil pH between 6 and 7, and cultivating by coring or slicing to enhance soil oxygen levels. A light topdressing also encourages breakdown of thatch. Excessive thatch can be removed by vertical cutting.

Good Turf Management. As with any pest problem, sound cultural practices that promote vigor will help a turf survive insect attacks and recover quickly. Vigorous turf often can withstand several times the normal threshold population of insects that would destroy a weak, moisture-stressed, starved turf.

Insect-Resistant Turfgrasses

Insect-resistant grasses can be a valuable tool for IPM. Start with selecting turfgrass species or cultivars that are best suited for local soil conditions and climate. Well-adapted turfgrasses are better able to withstand stress and will be better able to tolerate and outgrow damage from insects. Blends of improved, adapted turfgrasses will usually be more insect-resistant than stands planted with a single cultivar. Information on locally adapted turfgrasses is available from cooperative extension offices, university turf agronomists, and knowledgeable local seed dealers. Skillful management to grow vigorous, healthy turf is one of the best IPM tactics.

Different turfgrass species vary in susceptibility to particular insect pests. Southern chinch bugs, for example, are especially troublesome on St. Augustinegrass. Bluegrass billbugs clearly prefer bluegrass and ryegrass over tall fescue. Such differences should be considered when establishing lawns or renovating insect-damaged turf. Feeding preferences of particular pests are discussed in the individual pest sections.

Within some turfgrass species, researchers have found cultivars which have varying degrees of genetic resistance to particular pests such as billbugs or greenbugs. Resistance may take the form of greater recuperative potential, or the grass itself may produce toxins that poison the insect, or be otherwise unsuitable as food. Unfortunately, genetic resistance is rather specific; e.g., a cultivar with resistance to greenbugs may be quite susceptible to webworms. In reality, turfgrass breeding and cultivar selection are usually driven more by traits such as color, texture, growth form, and cold-hardiness than by insect resistance. Many of the cultivars in which resistance has been found are no longer marketed, having been replaced by newer cultivars. Notable exceptions are the St. Augustinegrass cultivars "Floratam" and "Floralawn" which are resistant to southern chinch bug, the major pest of lawns in Florida.

Using **endophyte-infected turfgrasses** is one means of growing quality turf that can persist with reduced use of pesticides. **Endophytes** are fungi (e.g., *Neotyphodium* spp.) that live within healthy grass plants (Figure 1.4) but have no pathogenic (adverse) effects. So far, they are known to occur only in certain species of turfgrasses, notably perennial ryegrass, tall fescue, and fine-leaf fescues. In a mature plant, the fungus grows into the flower stem and seeds, but does not penetrate into the roots. The presence of endophyte confers, among other things, enhanced resistance to certain insect pests. This resistance comes from production of toxins, called alkaloids, by the fungus. The alkaloids do not harm the plant, but they are deterrent or toxic to insects that feed on stems, leaves, and leaf sheaths.

Perennial ryegrass cultivars hosting the endophyte are generally resistant to billbugs, sod webworms, hairy chinch bugs, and greenbugs (Figure 1.5). Partial resistance to fall armyworms has also been reported. Endophyte-infected fine-leaf fescues are relatively resistant to hairy chinch bug and, to some extent, fall armyworm. Tall fescue with endophyte is somewhat resistant to fall armyworms, leafhoppers, and possibly other foliage-feeding pests. Thus, endophytes provide rather broad-based resistance against various surface-feeding insects. Unfortunately, they don't provide significant protection against root-feeding pests, such as white grubs. This may be because the fungi do not grow within the root system, and little of the protective alkaloids is translocated into the roots.

Besides having enhanced resistance to insects, endophyte-infected plants may have improved stress tolerance and enhanced resistance to some diseases (e.g., dollar spot on fine-leaf fescues). However, endophytes are not a "silver bullet" that will solve all insect problems.

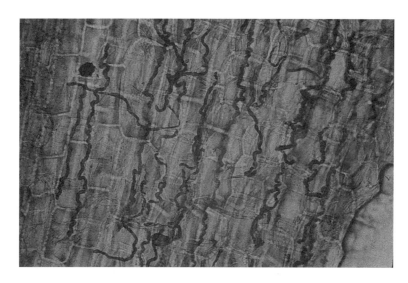

Figure 1.4. Hyphae of the endophytic fungus Neotyphodium lolii *growing intracellularly within a perennial ryegrass leaf sheath (photo courtesy R. Funk).*

There are no endophytic cultivars of Kentucky bluegrass or creeping bentgrass, nor do endophytes occur in the common warm-season turfgrasses. Methods of incorporating endophytes into these grasses by tissue culture, seedling inoculation, or genetic engineering are being investigated.

Endophytes are transmitted maternally, through the seed. Within a seed lot or turfgrass stand, the level of endophyte is often expressed as the percentage of seeds or plants that are infected. Endophyte-infected seed must be stored under cold, dry conditions (32–40°F, or 0–5°C). Viability of the endophyte declines rapidly under warm, humid seed storage conditions. Make sure that the seed that you purchase has been stored properly. Planting or renovating with endophytic cultivars can provide long-term protection against surface-feeding insect pests.

Biological Control

Biological control is the use of **predators**, **parasitoids**, and disease-causing microbes, or **pathogens**, to suppress pest populations. One form of biological control involves purposeful **importation and release** of exotic natural enemies to control a foreign pest that was accidentally introduced into a new area. The premise is to establish some of the natural agents that suppress the pest in its native land. Several such programs have been carried out by the U.S. Department of Agriculture and state agencies to introduce natural enemies of the Japanese beetle, mole crickets, Rhodesgrass mealybug, and a few other exotic turfgrass pests. These area-wide programs have met with varying degrees of success.

Another form of biological control involves purchase and release of predators or parasitoids for the purpose of controlling pests at a specific site. This approach, called **augmentation**, has been used with some success in greenhouses, orchards, and interior plantscapes, and its use is increasing against some pests of woody ornamentals. Unfortunately, the types of natural enemies that can be purchased commercially (e.g., lady beetles, aphid-lions, predatory mites) generally have little or no impact on major turfgrass pests. Furthermore, this approach is prohibitively expensive for lawns or golf courses. To date, there has been little research on how such released natural enemies might best be deployed. In the broad sense, use of microbial insecticides such as milky disease spore powder or *Bacillus thuringiensis* is a form of biological control. These products are discussed in Chapter 5.

Figure 1.5. Advertisement for ryegrass seed containing endophyte showing greater damage to noninfected plots (courtesy Turf-Seed, Inc.).

The most practical form of biological control for professional turf managers is **conservation of natural enemies**. Healthy turf supports a multitude of naturally occurring predators and parasites that help to keep pest populations in check. Choosing insecticides with reduced impact on natural enemies, and treating only when and where pests are getting the upper hand will pay off by conserving these natural buffers (see Chapters 7, 14).

Insecticides

Used selectively and responsibly, insecticides are important tools in an overall pest management program. Properties, safe handling, and use of insecticides are discussed in Chapters 4 through 6. Tactics for controlling particular pests are listed in the individual pest sections.

IS INTEGRATED PEST MANAGEMENT A REALISTIC GOAL?

The components of IPM — setting reasonable tolerances for pest populations, monitoring and sampling instead of assuming the need for treatment, and selecting controls that are relatively less hazardous and least disruptive to beneficial species and the environment — are clearly sensible approaches. Still, various reasons are often given for not adopting IPM for professionally managed turf:

- Preventive or blanket applications provide needed "insurance" against damage. Injury from sudden or unexpected pest outbreaks could jeopardize a golf superintendent's standing with the Greens Committee, or cause a lawn service company to lose customers.
- Some insecticides must be applied early, before the extent of the infestation is known.
- Many people are unwilling to accept higher risk of turf damage in exchange for reduced pesticides, especially when *their* lawn or golf course is affected.
- Lawn care customers have become accustomed to "pay-for-spray." They equate "value" with number of applications, and will not pay unless a treatment is applied. Having consistent cash flow throughout the year is a means of company survival.
- The number of lawns to be serviced or the area to be managed is too large to allow sampling and monitoring and still make a profit.
- Less training is needed by the applicator to apply a predetermined pesticide at a scheduled time than to monitor and spot-treat as needed.
- Golfers and Greens Committees don't want to see anything but perfect turf.

These are legitimate issues, most of which were addressed in the preceding sections. With the steady increase in environmental concerns, however, it is not really a question of *whether* the turf and landscape industry will have to reduce its reliance on pesticides, but only a matter of *when*. Wise King Solomon stated it thus: "A prudent man foresees evil and hides himself, but the simple pass on, and are punished." Prepare yourself and your organization now.

SELECTED REFERENCES

Anonymous. 1979. *Scott's information manual for lawns*. O.M. Scott & Sons Co., Marysville, OH.

Anonymous. 1994. *Golf and the environment*. United States Golf Assoc., Far Hills, NJ.

Beard, J.B. 1973. *Turfgrass: Science and culture*. Prentice-Hall, Inc., Englewood Cliffs, NJ.

Beard, J.B. 1979. *How to have a beautiful lawn* (2nd ed.). Beard Books, College Station, TX.

Beard, J.B and R.L. Green. 1979. The role of turfgrasses in environmental protection and their benefits to humans. *J. Environ. Qual.* 23:452–460.

Bruneau, A.H. (Ed.). 1993. *Turfgrass pest management manual*. North Carolina Cooperative Extension Service Bull. AG 348. Raleigh, NC.

Emmons, R.D. 1995. *Turfgrass science and management* (2nd ed). Delmar Publ., Albany, NY.

Leslie, A.R. (Ed.). 1994. *Handbook of integrated pest management for turf and ornamentals*. Lewis Publishers, Boca Raton, FL.

Roberts, E.C. and B.C. Roberts. 1988. *Lawn and sports turf benefits*. The Lawn Institute. Pleasant Hill, TN.

Turgeon, A.J. 1996. *Turfgrass management* (4th ed.). Prentice Hall, Upper Saddle River, NJ.

2

INSECT BIOLOGY AND IDENTIFICATION

INTRODUCTION

Whether fully aware of it or not, we are immersed in a world of insects. They buzz around our heads, watch us from every tree and flower, and tunnel the earth beneath our feet. Their sheer abundance is staggering. About a million species are known, and probably several times that number are yet to be discovered. There are about three times as many kinds of insects as of all other animals combined. It is estimated that at every instant there are about 40 million insects for every acre of land surface on earth.

In their many forms, insects are adapted for almost any specific way of life. They are by far the leading consumers of plants. We do well to hold our own in the face of the constant pressure that insects exert on our crops, forests, and urban landscapes. Some insects transmit important diseases; others feed on our houses, stored food, and belongings, or annoy us through painful bites or stings. Of course, not all insects are pests. Many are beneficial, from our self-centered perspective. Without pollination by insects, there would be little for us to eat besides grain crops. Predatory and parasitic insects are the main enemies of the plant-feeding pests. Insects partially decompose plant litter and carrion, turn the soil, and serve as food for fish, birds, and other vertebrates. Indeed, without insects, the world as we know it would cease to exist.

Among the millions of species of insects are a few dozen or so that are pests of turfgrasses. Some others that live in the turf environment are a nuisance because of their biting or stinging habit, or when they accidentally invade our homes. Because of their potential to damage or destroy lawns and golf courses, insects are of great concern to turf care professionals.

Turf managers must be able to identify the common pests and beneficial insects that they encounter in order to select the appropriate course of action. To manage insects effectively, one needs to know a bit about their way of life. This chapter provides a brief overview of the anatomy and habits of insects — how they feed, grow, and reproduce, what life stages are most damaging, where they go in winter, and so on.

USING THE RIGHT WORDS

Like any field of study, entomology requires some specialized vocabulary. Throughout this book, scientific jargon is kept to a minimum. Still, some technical words are necessary to understand the biology of insects. Most folks are familiar with words like arthritis, bacteria, carburetor, polyurethane, and rhododendron. These technical terms are derived from Greek or Latin words just as are most of the special terms used in entomology. Entomological terms are no harder to understand or remember than these. Once they become familiar, words like "nymph," "metamorphosis," or "pheromone" will also become a part of your regular vocabulary. A glossary near the end of the book will help with definitions of any unfamiliar terms.

INSECT PARTS LIST AND ASSEMBLY INSTRUCTIONS

A general knowledge of insect structure is important to understand the descriptions of particular pests, how different groups are distinguished, as well as the habits of insects and the basis for their control.

The insect body is basically an elongated tube with appendages such as legs, wings, mouthparts, and antennae arising from either side. Like humans, insects have **bilateral symmetry**, that is, the left side of the body is a mirror image of the right. The body is segmented, or jointed, with segments being grouped into three distinct regions: the **head**, **thorax**, and **abdomen** (Figure 2.1). Each body region is specialized for different functions: the head for sensory reception and food intake, the thorax for locomotion, and the abdomen for digestion and reproduction. Most appendages on the insect body also are segmented.

An insect's skeleton is on the outside of its body, and is called an **exoskeleton**. The exoskeleton, which is lighter and stronger than bone, serves as a suit of armor that protects the internal organs. The insect's muscles are attached to the inside wall of the exoskeleton, stretched across hinged joints. This arrangement makes it possible for insects to have remarkable strength in relation to their size. The exoskeleton is formed from hardened plates, called **sclerites**. The sclerites are joined together by membranes which allow flexibility and movement. If you have eaten a lobster or crab, the hard, jointed shell was the animal's exoskeleton, and the meat was the muscles.

The exoskeleton is composed of two principal layers, a hard outer wall called the **cuticle** and the underlying layer of cells, the **epidermis**, that secretes the cuticle (Figure 2.2). The epidermis also contains specialized cells that give rise to surface hairs, called **setae** (singular = seta), or gland cells that produce defensive secretions and other substances. The cuticle itself consists of three layers. The **endocuticle** and **exocuticle** are hardened and darkened, providing rigidity and color. The **epicuticle** is a very thin, outermost layer. It contains waxes which help to "waterproof" the insect, and a hard, lacquer-like coating which gives the surface of the exoskeleton its sheen. Insecticides that kill by contact must be able to penetrate this protective outer layer.

The Head

The typical insect head is a capsule, resembling a football helmet, formed from five or six segments that are fused together. The head includes the eyes, antennae, and mouthparts. The hardened head capsule encloses and protects the insect's brain.

Insects usually have two kinds of eyes, compound and simple. Most adults and some immature insects have a pair of large **compound eyes**. Each eye is composed of many facets, each with its own lens. All of the lenses combine so that the insect sees a mosaic image. Insects have color vision, but they see farther into the ultraviolet range than we do, and less far into the red range of the spectrum. Most insects also have one to three **simple eyes** (ocelli) located on the upper front part of the head. These simple eyes do not perceive images, but are sensitive to

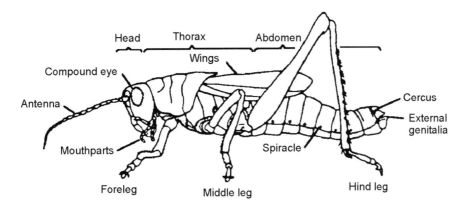

Figure 2.1. General body plan of a grasshopper, a typical insect (adapted from Turpin, 1992; with permission).

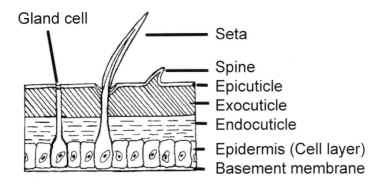

Figure 2.2. Cross section of the insect exoskeleton (from Wilson et al., 1977; with permission).

sudden changes in light intensity (e.g., an approaching shadow) which may trigger alarm reactions such as running or flight.

Insects have two **antennae** between their compound eyes. These are movable and contain sensory receptors that are used to detect odors, tastes, vibrations, and other stimuli. Antennae vary greatly in form; their size and shape is often used to distinguish among different species of insects, and between sexes of the same species.

Insect Mouthparts

Mouthparts are a set of structures used for feeding. These structures surround the actual mouth, which is merely an opening in the head. The structures comprising the mouthparts vary greatly in shape and function. Many insects have toothed jaws for biting off and chewing pieces of leaf, stem, or root, or for ripping apart their prey. Others have mouthparts modified into an elongate beak for piercing plant tissues and sucking out sap, for piercing skin and sucking blood, or for spearing and draining insect victims. Butterflies and some moths have delicate, coiled tubes for siphoning nectar from flowers, and many flies have sponging mouthparts for sopping up exposed liquids. Most turfgrass pests have either chewing or piercing-sucking type mouthparts.

Chewing Type. Chewing insects include white grubs, mole crickets, cutworms, sod webworms, beetles, ants, and many others. These insects have two powerful grinding jaws called **mandibles** (Figure 2.3). The mandibles, which in most species are lined with tooth-like projec-

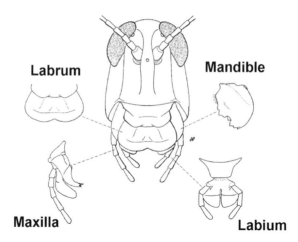

Figure 2.3. *Chewing mouthparts, as typically found in grasshoppers, beetles, and caterpillars (adapted from Wilson et al., 1977; with permission).*

tions, work sideways, not up and down as ours do. The insect uses these jaws for biting or tearing off plant material, as well as chewing. A second pair of less powerful jaws, called **maxillae**, operates just behind the mandibles. They also move sideways, and are used for handling food and pushing it down the throat. Each maxilla has a small feeler-like structure, called a **palp**, that has receptors for taste, touch, and smell. Chewing insects have two lips. The upper lip, or **labrum**, is a simple flap that hangs down over the mandibles much like our upper lip covers the upper teeth. The lower lip, called the **labium**, covers the mouth from behind. It bears a second pair of feeler-like palps. Inside the mouth is a fleshy, tongue-like structure called the **hypopharynx**.

Piercing-Sucking Type. In some insects the mouthparts have become adapted to piercing plants or animals and then sucking up the juices or blood (Figure 2.4). Chinch bugs, greenbugs, leafhoppers, and spittlebugs have the **labium** modified into a long, grooved beak. Four slender piercing structures called **stylets** lie in the groove. When the insect feeds, the stylets penetrate a leaf or stem while the sheath-like labium folds out of the way. The inner surfaces of the stylets are double-grooved and, when held together, form food and salivary channels. Saliva injected through the salivary channel helps to predigest the plant tissues; the plant juices are then sucked up through the food channel. The saliva may contain toxins that discolor or kill the plant tissues around the feeding site. Mosquitoes and predatory bugs feed in much the same manner, except that their food is blood or insect body fluids.

The Thorax

The **thorax** is a rigid "box" composed of three fused segments. Its walls serve as a base for attachment of powerful muscles that operate the legs and wings. On either side of the thorax are usually two pairs of small, slit-like openings called **spiracles** (Figure 2.1), which are external openings of the respiratory system. In adult insects, each segment of the thorax bears a pair of jointed legs, and usually the second and third segments each have a pair of wings.

Legs. Insect legs are jointed and consist of five segments: coxa, trochanter, femur, tibia, and tarsus (Figure 2.5). The **coxa** and **trochanter** are small segments which connect the leg to the main body. The powerful **femur** corresponds more or less to the thigh in humans, and the elongate **tibia** to our lower leg. The **tarsus**, or foot, consists of several segments. It usually terminates in a pair of claws, and often there is a pad or lobe between the claws. These structures enable the insect to cling to rough bark or smooth plant leaves. The legs may be modified

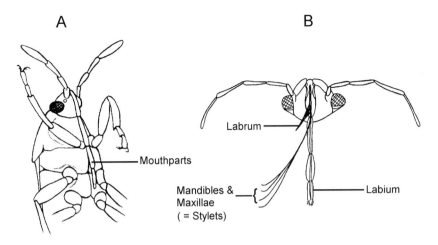

Figure 2.4. *Sucking mouthparts, as found in chinch bugs, greenbugs, spittlebugs, and leafhoppers (Figure A, courtesy of Entomological Society of America).*

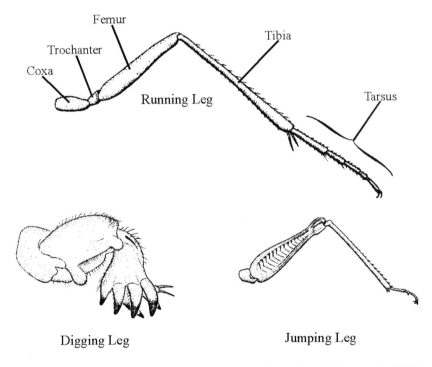

Figure 2.5. *Some modifications of insect legs (redrawn from Wilson et al., 1977).*

for running, jumping, digging, or grasping prey. Leg characteristics can give a good indication of the habits of the insect. Some immature insects such as white grubs and mole cricket nymphs have three pairs of jointed legs; others, such as billbug larvae, are legless.

Wings. Insects are the only extant animals other than birds and bats to have wings. Most adult insects have two pairs of wings, but true flies have only one pair, and some adult insects (e.g., worker ants) are wingless. Most insect wings are thin and membranous; in some groups, such as beetles, the front wings are thickened and leathery, or hard. The size, shape, texture, arrangement of veins, and position of the wings are used in identification of insects. Immature insects lack functional wings, although older nymphs may have visible, developing wing pads.

The Abdomen

An insect's abdomen (Figure 2.1) consists of 10 or 11 segments connected by flexible membranes. These membranes make it possible for the abdomen to expand when it is full of food or swollen with eggs. Many insects have a pair of jointed feelers, called **cerci**, on the last abdominal segment. The external reproductive structures are attached to the eighth and ninth segments of the abdomen. Females of many species have an **ovipositor**, or egg-laying tool, used to insert the eggs into plant tissues, soil, or in the case of parasites, the bodies of other insects. Males have a copulatory organ (penis) called the **aedeagus**. The shape and size of the aedeagus often is used to identify insect species. There is a small hole on either side of each of the first seven or eight abdominal segments. These are the **spiracles** through which oxygen enters, and carbon dioxide exits, the internal respiratory system. Near the end of the abdomen is an opening, the **anus**, through which wastes pass from the insect's body.

BLOOD AND GUTS (INTERNAL ANATOMY)

The internal body plan of an insect is a compact masterpiece of functional design. Although insects are small, they are able to perform the essential functions of life as efficiently as we do. A brief study of their internal anatomy provides insight into the habits of insects that will help turf professionals in solving insect problems.

Digestive System

The digestive system, or gut, is an elongate tube which runs from the mouth to the anus with various parts modified to help the insect digest its particular type of food (Figure 2.6). The gut is divided into three main regions — the foregut, midgut and hindgut — with valves controlling passage of food between regions. The **foregut** is concerned with intake, storage, and grinding of the food. As food enters the mouth, it passes through a muscular **pharynx**, which may be modified into a sucking pump in sap-feeding insects. The food then passes down a narrow tube, the **esophagus**, and enters a sac-like storage organ called the **crop**. Having a crop allows the insect to take a large meal, and then to pursue other activities (mating, egg-laying) while the food is digested. Insects that chew plant material may have a grinding organ, the **proventriculus** (or gizzard) at the end of the foregut. There are usually **salivary glands** in the area of the mouth that secrete saliva. In caterpillars, such as sod webworms, these glands are modified to produce silk, which is used in making larval nests and cocoons. The middle region, or **midgut**, is where most of the actual digestion occurs. Here digestive enzymes are secreted and nutrients are absorbed. The midgut may have several out pockets, called **gastric caecae**, which are areas of high digestive activity. After passing through the midgut, the remains of the food enter the **hindgut**. Here water, salts, and other valuable substances are absorbed from the fecal matter before it is eliminated through the anus.

Caterpillars and other insects that chew foliage or roots produce relatively dry fecal matter in the form of small pellets called **frass**. Piles of greenish or brown frass at the base of chewed grass leaves or stems indicate that sod webworms or cutworms have fed there. Many sap-feeding insects, such as greenbugs and mealybugs, discharge a sugary liquid called **honeydew** from the anus. When excreted, the sticky honeydew coats the surface of leaves, attracting ants and encouraging growth of an unsightly black fungus called **sooty mold**. Regardless of their other food preferences, all insects require water. Many insects will drink free water from dew or rainfall, while others obtain sufficient water from the plants upon which they feed.

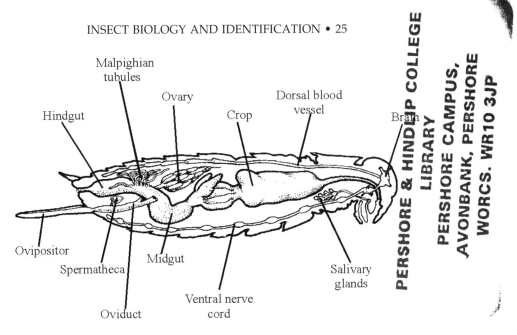

Figure 2.6. General internal anatomy of insects (adapted from Pfadt, 1985; with permission).

Excretory System

Excretion is the process of eliminating waste products from the body. Instead of kidneys, insects have special organs called **Malpighian tubules** which are attached at the juncture of the mid- and hindgut (Figure 2.6). The tubules float free in the body cavity, absorbing waste materials from the blood and discharging them into the hindgut, where they are passed out with the feces.

Circulatory System

An insect's blood does not flow through veins and arteries as does ours. Blood fills the whole body cavity, and bathes all the organs and muscles. The blood is circulated by a tube, the **dorsal blood vessel**, that lies just under the exoskeleton along the back. This tube picks up blood from the rear of the abdomen and pumps it forward, dumping it into the head. From there, it sloshes back around the internal organs to the rear where it is picked up and pumped forward again. Because the blood moves through the body cavity in an open manner, insects are said to have an **open circulatory system**. An insect's blood, like ours, carries food and waste products to and from the cells of the body. But unlike our blood, it is not involved in bringing oxygen to the cells. Insect blood is greenish, yellowish, or clear because it lacks hemoglobin, the red respiratory pigment. In soft-bodied insects such as caterpillars, the body form is maintained in part by internal pressure of the blood. This hydraulic pressure is especially important when growing insects have to shed their old exoskeleton and produce a new, larger one.

Respiratory System

Like humans, insects must obtain oxygen from their environment and eliminate carbon dioxide respired by their cells. An insect breathes by means of tiny holes, called **spiracles**, along the sides of its body (Figure 2.1). Each hole leads to a large tube called a **trachea**. The large tubes divide into small tubes, which in turn divide into still smaller tubes that branch out to all the cells of the body. This system of branched tubes carries oxygen to the cells and takes away carbon dioxide. Many insects can increase movement of oxygen through the tracheae by rhythmically expanding and contracting their body wall. The spiracles usually can be closed, thus conserving water vapor when air is not being taken up. Horticultural spray oils kill insects by clogging their spiracles and suffocating them.

Nervous System

The central nervous system of an insect is capable of receiving a stimulus and coordinating a response in a fraction of a second. To be convinced of this, one need only try to snatch a fly between one's thumb and forefinger. The central nervous system consists of a **brain**, located in the head, and a double **ventral nerve cord** that lies along the floor of the thorax and abdomen. The brain receives information from the eyes and antennae, and helps to coordinate the insect's body activities as a whole. The nerve cord is expanded into masses of nerve cells called **ganglia** within each main body segment. Each ganglion acts as a sort of little brain that coordinates the activities of that segment. A network of nerve cells or **neurons** carries impulses throughout the body much like the wiring of a house. These neurons receive stimuli from sensory receptors, relay them to the central nervous system, and then transmit impulses to muscles and glands. Sensory structures and their associated nerve endings are particularly concentrated on the antennae, mouthparts, and feet. Most modern insecticides owe their toxicity to their ability to disrupt the normal functioning of the nervous system.

Muscular System

Insects have a well-developed muscular system with several hundred to as many as 2,000 small but very strong muscles. The powerful **skeletal muscles** attach to the inside of the exoskeleton and are stretched across hinged joints to allow walking, biting, flying, and mating. Other muscles occur in sheets or layers surrounding various organs; these **visceral muscles** move materials within the organs (such as food within the gut) and seldom are attached to the exoskeleton.

Reproductive System

The internal reproductive organs of insects are not unlike those of humans. Males have a pair of **testes** which lie in the abdomen. Sperm from the testes are passed down ducts to pouches, called **seminal vesicles**, where they are stored until mating. A pair of **accessory glands** supplies seminal fluid that acts as a medium to carry and protect the sperm. At copulation the sperm are introduced directly into the female's body by means of the aedeagus (penis). Females have a pair of **ovaries** in which eggs are produced. The eggs pass down tubes called oviducts that lead into the vagina, where fertilization occurs. Sperm received by the female during mating are stored in a pouch, the **spermatheca**. Later, the sperm are released to fertilize each egg as it is laid. In many insects, a pair of **accessory glands** produces secretions that are used to glue the eggs to plants or other objects.

Most insects reproduce sexually, but some are parthenogenetic (females reproduce without being fertilized by a male). The latter mode of reproduction is common in aphids, weevils, and some parasitic wasps.

HOW INSECTS GROW

All insects begin life as an egg. In most species, the young hatch from an egg after it has been laid; however, in a few insects the young are born alive from eggs which have developed inside the female's body. Insect eggs usually are rounded or oval, and are covered with a shell that varies in color and surface texture from one species to another. Eggs may be laid singly, in small clusters, or in masses containing hundreds of eggs. The female usually lays her eggs in protected locations on or near food plants which the young feed upon when they hatch. Some turf pests, such as sod webworms, simply drop their eggs into the thatch. Others, such as scarab beetles and mole crickets, lay their eggs in the soil. Eggs of cutworms and armyworms are glued to grass blades or other objects, while those of billbugs are inserted into grass stems. Females of some insect species lay only a few dozen eggs in their lifetime. Others may lay hundreds or even thousands of eggs.

After hatching, the insect begins to feed and grow. Some turf insects, such as greenbugs, reach adulthood after only a few days, whereas others, such as May beetles, require two years or longer. Growth of insects occurs through a series of steps, called **molts**. Between molts, increase in size is constrained because the exoskeleton does not grow with the insect, as do the bones of a child. Thus, the exoskeleton must be periodically shed and renewed, a process called **molting**. During molting, the insect lays down a new exoskeleton beneath the old one. The old body wall splits down the back and the insect wriggles out. The new exoskeleton is pale and soft, so the insect gulps air to stretch and enlarge it before the cuticle hardens and darkens. Most insects molt four to eight times before reaching adulthood. The form of the insect between molts is called an **instar**. Thus, a young insect that has just hatched from an egg is a **first insta**r. After it goes through a molt it is a second instar, and then a third instar, and so on.

Most insects change not only in size but also in form as they develop into adults. Thus, young insects often look very different from their parents, with different food and habits. This change in body form is called **metamorphosis**. Insects associated with turfgrass go through one of two types of metamorphosis, either gradual or complete.

Gradual metamorphosis occurs in such insects as mole crickets, chinch bugs, greenbugs, leafhoppers, and spittlebugs (Figure 2.7). With this type of development, the active immature stages are called **nymphs**. Nymphs generally look much like their parents, except that they are smaller and lack wings. They usually have legs, antennae, compound eyes, and multi-segmented tarsi. The wings first appear as pads after the insect has molted several times. The wing pads enlarge with each further molt until the adult emerges with full-sized wings. Nymphs have the same type of mouthparts, usually live in the same places, and eat the same food as adults.

Most species of insects undergo **complete metamorphosis**. Such insects go through four life stages: egg, larva (with several instars), pupa, and adult (Figure 2.8). **Larvae** (plural of **larva**) are generally worm-like and look quite different from their parents. They lack compound eyes and any external evidence of wings. They may or may not have the same type of mouthparts as the adults. Often, larvae live in different places, have different habits, and eat different kinds of foods than the adults. A cutworm, for example, has mouthparts adapted for chewing grass foliage, whereas the adult cutworm moth has a coiled sucking tube for sipping nectar from flowers. Larvae of moths and beetles, including armyworms, cutworms, sod webworms, billbugs, and white grubs, always have typical chewing mouthparts. Larvae of many flies (e.g., frit flies) have a greatly reduced head and no true jaws, although they often have a pair of mouth hooks which enable them to lacerate plant tissue.

Larvae of butterflies and moths are called **caterpillars**, those of beetles or wasps, **grubs**, and those of flies, **maggots**. Some larvae (e.g., billbugs) are legless; others have jointed legs on the thorax. Caterpillars have additional fleshy, leg-like structures, called **prolegs**, on the abdomen.

Larvae do little more than eat and grow. Indeed, a cutworm or armyworm may consume several times its weight in foliage in a single day. Not surprisingly, many turfgrass pests do the greatest damage in the larval stage. Turf care professionals need to be able to recognize larvae and adults, and to know the habits of both stages in order to effectively manage insect infestations.

After molting several times and completing its growth, the larva stops eating and prepares to become a **pupa**. Some larvae spin a protective cocoon, others burrow into the thatch, and some excavate an earthen cell in which to **pupate**. Most pupae lie quietly and appear lifeless, but

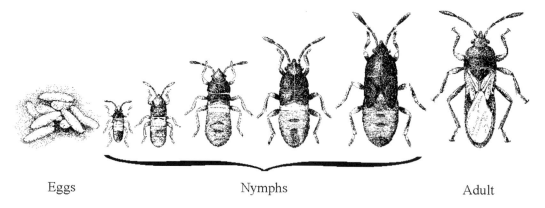

Eggs   Nymphs   Adult

Figure 2.7. Chinch bug life cycle — an example of gradual metamorphosis (from USDA).

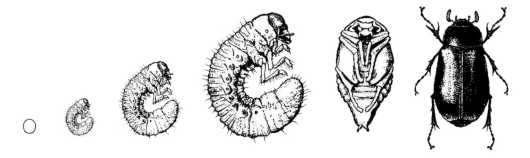

Figure 2.8. May beetle life cycle — an example of complete metamorphosis. Life stages (left to right) are egg, 1st instar, 2nd instar, 3rd instar larva, pupa, adult (from USDA).

inside there are great changes taking place. The larval structures are being broken down and the tissues reorganized into adult organs. The legs, wings, antennae, and reproductive structures become fully formed. After the change is complete, the pupal skin cracks and the new adult wriggles out.

Two important hormones regulate the processes of molting and metamorphosis in insects. These hormones are secreted by glands and carried in the blood. Release of **ecdysone**, the **molting hormone**, "commands" the insect to molt. *What* life stage it molts into is determined by levels of a second hormone, the **juvenile hormone**. If the titre of juvenile hormone is high, the insect molts to a larva or nymph. A lower titre of juvenile hormone results in a pupa, and when the glands stop producing it altogether, an adult is produced. A new class of insecticides called **insect growth regulators** (IGRs) works by mimicking or disrupting one or the other of these hormones. Because the targeted hormonal system is unique to insects and their relatives, IGRs are thought to be very safe for humans and other vertebrate animals.

THE HABITS OF INSECTS

Insects respond to their surroundings in a largely automatic manner. There is no conscious thinking involved in their reactions. The insect's behavior patterns are inherited and built firmly into its nervous system, so that members of a given species will all react in the same manner. Many of an insect's reactions are toward or away from such stimuli as light, moisture, temperature, or gravity. For example, black cutworm moths fly toward light, while their larvae avoid it. White grubs move up or down in the soil profile in response to moisture and temperature. Most insects lay eggs in certain places, feed in a characteristic manner, live in a particular type of environment, and spend the winter in a particular life stage and location.

There is good reason why turf managers should understand the habits of the pests they deal with. Insects are only capable of learning or modifying their behavior to a small degree. Thus, understanding the behavior of insects will help professionals to "fine-tune" their control tactics, and to anticipate where and when infestations will occur.

Mate-Finding

Insects attract mates in various ways. Females of many species release a chemical odor, or **sex pheromone**, to attract males. Some of these sex pheromones have been identified and synthesized, and can be used in sticky traps to monitor the adult flight periods for timing controls. Male mole crickets "sing" to attract mates; this behavior has been exploited in sound traps for these pests (see Mole Crickets — Management). Leafhoppers communicate by drumming the abdomen on the leaf surface. The vibrations produced bring the sexes together. The flashing of fireflies is a kind of Morse code by which the sexes locate one another for lovemaking.

Hibernation and Migration

Insects are intolerant of freezing temperatures. Most insects survive the cold winter months by undergoing a state of prolonged dormancy called **diapause**. During diapause, bodily functions such as heartbeat and breathing are nearly halted. In autumn, the diapause of most overwintering insects is triggered by the progressively shorter day lengths. Depending on the species of insect, diapause may occur in any stage of life. In insects that overwinter as eggs, nymphs, larvae, or pupae, the diapause is an interruption of growth and development; in adults, the diapause is a period of no reproduction. The stage at which diapause occurs is genetically determined for each species, but whether it will occur or not may be influenced by environmental conditions, e.g., temperature. Development resumes in the spring when temperatures become warmer. Other factors, such as the availability of water, may also be important in stimulating termination of diapause. Thus, the local population is synchronized in growth by environmental conditions in the spring.

Some insects can reduce their water content and elevate concentrations of glycerol (a kind of antifreeze) in their blood to resist freezing. White grubs go deep in the soil to overwinter below the frost line. Other species, such as the fall armyworm, migrate southward each fall, overwintering only in the southern states. Offspring of these moths migrate northward again in spring, laying eggs as they go.

CLASSIFICATION OF INSECTS

With millions of different species of animals in the world, scientists need some system of arranging them into groups, or classifying them. Classification is based mainly on structural characteristics; animals with similar characteristics are classified together; those with other features are placed into other groups. Thus, the animal kingdom is divided into a dozen or so major groups called **phyla** (singular = phylum). Members of each phylum share characteristics that distinguish them from other types of animals.

Insects belong to the phylum **Arthropoda**, by far the largest group in the animal kingdom. Members of this phylum are called **arthropods** and include spiders, mites, ticks, scorpions, centipedes, millipedes, crabs, lobsters, sowbugs, and other animals that have a segmented body, an exoskeleton, and other features in common with insects. Each phylum is further subdivided into groups called **classes**. Insects make up the class **Insecta** and have certain characteristics that distinguish them from other arthropods. Classes are further subdivided into **orders**, orders into **families**, families into **genera** (singular = genus), and genera into **species**. The classifications of a Japanese beetle and humans can be compared as follows:

Classification	Japanese Beetle	Human
Kingdom	Animalia	Animalia
Phylum	Arthropoda	Chordata
Class	Insecta	Mammalia
Order	Coleoptera	Primates
Family	Scarabaeidae	Hominidae
Genus	*Popillia*	*Homo*
Species	*japonica*	*sapiens*

When a particular insect is referred to by its scientific name, both the genus and species names are listed, written in italics (i.e., *Popillia japonica*). The scientific name is often followed by a person's name, sometimes abbreviated or in parentheses. This individual first named, described, and classified the insect.

Several classes of arthropods are encountered in turfgrasses (Figure 2.9). These are listed below; a few examples of turf-inhabiting types are indicated in parentheses. Management of non-insect arthropods as nuisance pests is discussed in Chapter 13. Plant-feeding mites, ticks, and spiders are covered in Chapters 10, 12, and 13, respectively. Scientific classification of important pests and beneficial species covered in this book is summarized in Table 2.1.

Arachnida (spiders, mites, ticks, "daddy long-legs")

Most members of this large and diverse group are predators, but some (e.g., ticks) are blood-feeders, and a few others feed on plants. Arachnids have two main body regions: a cephalothorax (fused head and thorax) and abdomen. They have no antennae. Adult arachnids have four pairs of legs, but immature mites and ticks may have only three pairs of legs. Arachnids encountered in the turfgrass environment include ticks, chiggers, spiders, and such pests as clover mites, winter grain mites, and bermudagrass mites.

Crustacea (crayfish, sowbugs)

Most crustaceans, which also include lobsters, crabs, shrimp, and barnacles, are marine. Crustaceans breathe by means of gills and so must either live in water or else in very moist habitats. Most have two pairs of antennae and 10 or more legs. Outside of a seafood restaurant, sowbugs, and crayfish are the only crustaceans which turfgrass managers are likely to encounter.

Diplopoda (millipedes)

Millipedes, or "thousand-leggers," are elongate, slow-moving creatures with short antennae. Most species are cylindrical, the body being composed of many ring-like segments, all of which are alike except for the head. Each body segment has two pairs of legs. Some species roll into a ball when disturbed. Millipedes feed mainly on decaying organic matter.

Chilopoda (centipedes)

Members of this class are elongate and multi-segmented. They differ from millipedes in having long antennae, only one pair of legs per body segment, and a somewhat more flattened body form. Centipedes are fast-moving creatures, as befits their predatory habits. If handled, some species can inflict a painful bite.

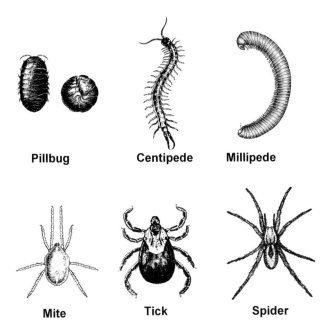

Figure 2.9. *Classes of non-insect arthropods: pillbug (Class Crustacea); centipede (Chilopoda); milli-pede (Diplopoda); mite (Arachnida); tick (Arachnida); spider (Arachnida) (from USDA).*

Insecta (insects)

Insects are characterized by having three body regions (head, thorax, abdomen), one pair of antennae, usually one or two pairs of wings as adults, and three pairs of legs. Most entomologists group insects into 28 orders. Only 11 of these are commonly encountered in the turf environment, and only seven of those contain important pests of turf. Knowledge of the distinguishing characteristics of these important orders is useful in beginning the identification process. The following are brief descriptions of the main orders of insects that have turf-infesting species. Examples of types that are common in or around turf are underlined (Figures 2.10, 2.11).

Collembola (springtails)

These very small, wingless insects are abundant in thatch and soil. They feed mainly on decaying organic matter, helping to recycle plant litter and nutrients. Springtails have chewing mouthparts. Many species have a forked, springing organ on the abdomen with which they jump.

Orthoptera (mole crickets; also grasshoppers, crickets, katydids)

These medium to large insects have chewing mouthparts and usually two pairs of wings. Most species are plant-feeders. The front wings are narrow and leathery; the hind wings are broad and membranous and are folded like a fan under the front wings when at rest. They have gradual metamorphosis. Many species, including mole crickets, communicate by sounds.

Hemiptera (chinch bugs, big-eyed bugs; other true bugs)

True bugs have piercing-sucking mouthparts and gradual metamorphosis. They may be plant-feeding or predatory. There are usually four wings, which are held flat over the back with the

Table 2.1. Scientific Classification of Insects, Mites, and Vertebrates Associated with Turfgrass.

Phylum Arthropoda
  Class Arachnida
    Order Acari (mites and ticks)
      Family Eriophyidae
        Bermudagrass mite
        Buffalograss mite
        Zoysiagrass mite
      Family Ixodidae
        Ticks (hard ticks)
      Family Penthaleidae
        Winter grain mite
      Family Tetranychidae
        Banks grass mite
        Brown wheat mite
        Clover mite
      Family Trombiculidae
        Chiggers
    Order Araneida
      Spiders
  Class Crustacea
    Order Decapoda
      Crayfish
    Order Isopoda
      Sowbugs and pillbugs
  Class Chilopoda
    Centipedes
  Class Diplopoda
    Millipedes
  Class Insecta
    Order Collembola
      Springtails
    Order Orthoptera (crickets and relatives)
      Family Gryllidae
        Short-tailed cricket
      Family Gryllotalpidae
        Mole crickets
    Order Dermaptera
      Earwigs
    Order Homoptera
      Family Aphididae
        Greenbug
      Family Cercopidae
        Two-lined spittlebug
      Family Cicadidae
        Cicadas
      Family Cicadellidae
        Leafhoppers
      Family Diaspididae
        Bermudagrass scale
      Family Margarodidae
        Ground pearls
      Family Pseudococcidae
        Buffalograss mealybug
        Rhodesgrass mealybug

Phylum Arthropoda (continued)
  Class Insecta (continued)
    Order Hemiptera (true bugs)
      Family Lygaeidae
        Big-eyed bugs
        Hairy chinch bug
        Southern chinch bug
    Order Neuroptera (lacewings)
      Family Chrysopidae
        Green lacewings
    Order Diptera (true flies)
      Family Bibionidae
        March flies
      Family Chloropidae
        Frit flies
      Family Stratiomyiidae
        Australian sod fly
      Family Tipulidae
        Crane flies
    Order Hymenoptera (bees, wasps, ants)
      Family Formicidae
        Harvester ants
        Red imported fire ant
      Family Scoliidae
        Scoliid wasps
      Family Sphecidae
        Cicada killers and sand wasps
      Family Tiphiidae
        Tiphia wasps
      Family Vespidae
        Paper wasps, hornets, yellow-jackets
    Order Lepidoptera (moths, butterflies, skippers)
      Family Acrolophidae
        Burrowing sod webworm
      Family Hesperiidae
        Fiery skipper
    Order Lepidoptera
      Family Noctuidae
        Armyworms
        Cutworms
        Fall armyworm
        Striped grassworm
      Family Pyralidae
        Grass webworm
        Lucerne moth
        Sod webworms
        Tropical sod webworm
    Order Siphonaptera (common fleas)
      Family Pulicidae
        Dog and cat fleas
    Order Coleoptera (beetles)
      Family Carabidae
        Ground beetles

Table 2.1. Scientific Classification of Insects, Mites, and Vertebrates Associated with Turfgrass (Continued).

Phylum Arthropoda (continued)	Phylum Animalia (continued)
Class Insecta (continued)	Class Aves (continued)
Family Cicindellidae	Family Sturnidae
Tiger beetles	Starling
Family Chrysomelidae	Order Anseriformes
Dichondra flea beetle	Family Anatidae
Family Coccinellidae	Canada goose
Lady beetles	Class Mammalia
Family Curculionidae	Order Carnivora
Annual bluegrass weevil	Family Mustelidae
Billbugs	Skunks
Vegetable weevil	Family Procyonidae
Family Scarabaeidae	Raccoon
Aphodius grubs	Order Edentata
Asiatic garden beetle	Family Dasypodidae
Black turfgrass ataenius	Nine-banded armadillo
European chafer	Order Insectivora
Green June beetle	Family Soricidae
Japanese beetle	Shrews
Masked chafers	Family Talpidae
May and June beetles	Moles
Oriental beetle	Order Marsupialia
Family Staphylinidae	Family Didelphidae
Rove beetles	Opossum
Phylum Animalia	Order Rodentia
Class Aves	Family Cricetidae
Order Passeriformes	Voles
Family Corvidae	Family Geomyidae
American crow	Pocket gophers
Family Icteridae	Family Sciuridae
Common grackle, blackbirds	Chipmunks

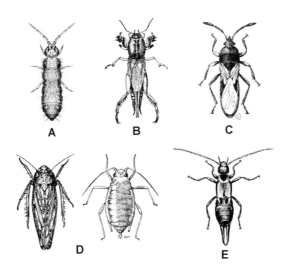

Figure 2.10. *Some common orders of insects found in turf (not drawn to scale): (A) Collembola; (B) Orthoptera; (C) Hemiptera; (D) Homoptera; (E) Dermaptera (from USDA).*

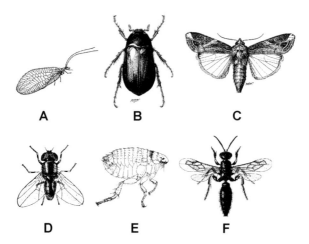

Figure 2.11. *Other common orders of insects found in turf (not drawn to scale): (A) Neuroptera; (B) Coleoptera; (C) Lepidoptera; (D) Diptera; (E) Siphonaptera; (F) Hymenoptera (from USDA).*

tips overlapping. The front wings are thickened and leathery at their base and thin and membranous at the tip. The hind wings are membranous and are folded under the front wings when the insect is not flying.

Homoptera (<u>greenbug</u>, <u>ground pearls</u>, <u>scale insects</u>, <u>mealybugs</u>, <u>spittlebugs</u>, <u>leafhoppers</u>; other aphids, planthoppers, cicadas)

Except for the robust cicadas, these are mostly small insects. All are plant-feeders with piercing-sucking mouthparts. Metamorphosis is gradual. Some Homoptera have two pairs of wings; others are wingless. When wings are present they are of uniform thickness throughout and are held roof-like over the body when at rest. Two groups, the scale insects and ground pearls, are so highly modified that they look more like abnormal plant growths than insects.

Dermaptera (<u>earwigs</u>)

Earwigs are predators or scavengers that live under mulch or other moist debris in the turfgrass environment. Their distinguishing feature is a pair of large, pincer-like cerci at the end of the abdomen. They have chewing mouthparts and gradual metamorphosis. They may be wingless or have two pairs of wings. Front wings, when present, are very short and leathery; the large, membranous hind wings fold under the front wings when the earwig is at rest.

Coleoptera (beetles, including <u>white grubs</u>, <u>billbugs</u>, <u>weevils</u>, <u>flea beetles</u>)

Beetles are the largest order of insects, and include some of the most important turf pests. A distinctive feature of beetles is their hard, shell-like front wings, called **elytra**, which meet in a straight line down the back when the beetle is at rest. The hind wings are membranous and are folded under the front wings when the insect is not flying. Beetles have chewing mouthparts and complete metamorphosis. Beetle larvae, called grubs, have a dark-colored head capsule with chewing mouthparts. Some species have six jointed legs; others are legless.

Lepidoptera (moths and butterflies, including <u>sod webworms,</u> <u>cutworms,</u> <u>armyworms,</u> <u>skippers</u>)

Most Lepidoptera have four broad wings which are membranous and covered with tiny, shingle-like scales that provide coloration. The adult mouthparts of many species form a long, coiled tube that can be extended for sucking flower nectar. Metamorphosis is complete. Larvae have chewing mouthparts and are called caterpillars. In addition to three pairs of jointed walking legs, caterpillars have distinctive, fleshy leg-like appendages called **prolegs** on the underside of the abdomen (Figure 2.12).

Diptera (true flies, including <u>frit fly</u>, <u>European crane fly</u>, <u>March fly</u>)

Adult flies have only two wings. The hind wings are replaced by a pair of stalked, knob-like structures called **halteres** which are used as balancing organs during flight. Flies have mouthparts adapted for piercing and sucking or for sponging up food. Metamorphosis is complete. Larvae of many flies are legless and worm-like, with a greatly reduced head bearing a pair of mouth hooks which operate vertically, like tiny scythes. Such fly larvae are called maggots.

Siphonaptera (<u>fleas</u>)

Fleas do not harm turfgrasses, but their populations sometimes build up in lawns where pets reside. Fleas are small, wingless, blood-sucking parasites of warm-blooded animals. The body is flattened from side to side, and there are long hind legs adapted for jumping. Adults have piercing-sucking mouthparts, and metamorphosis is complete. Flea larvae are tiny, whitish, and legless. They often occur in wild animal dens, or in carpets or upholstery frequented by cats or dogs.

Hymenoptera (<u>ants</u>, <u>wasps</u>, <u>bees</u>)

Most Hymenoptera have four membranous wings, but some, such as worker ants, are wingless. The front pair of wings is larger than the hind pair. The mouthparts are adapted for chewing, or for both chewing and lapping up nectar. They have complete metamorphosis. Many species have the abdomen constricted into a narrow "waist" where it joins the thorax. Hymenoptera develop by complete metamorphosis. Larvae of some species resemble small, hairless caterpillars; others have whitish, legless, grub-like larvae. Many species of Hymenoptera live in colonies and have social behavior.

DIAGNOSIS AND IDENTIFICATION

Accurate diagnosis is the first step in effective pest management. Fortunately, only a handful of pest species usually accounts for most of the problems in a given region. As one gains experience, it becomes easier to identify the more common pests on sight. The identity of an unknown pest can usually be narrowed down by considering the nature of its feeding injury (e.g., root-feeding, chews leaves and stems, etc.) and where in the turf profile (leaves, stems, thatch, or soil) it is found. The **diagnostic key** at the end of this chapter groups the more commonly encountered pests by the type of injury they cause. By referring to this key and then comparing the specimen or its damage symptoms with the color plates, diagrams, and descriptions, you should be able to identify most pests that are encountered.

Insects can produce symptoms that resemble those caused by drought, disease, gasoline spills, or other agents. Close examination by the "hands and knees method" may be the only way to

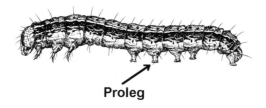

Proleg

Figure 2.12. *Larvae of Lepidoptera, called caterpillars, have fleshy, unsegmented prolegs on the underside of the abdomen. This group includes the sod webworms, armyworms, and cutworms.*

get a correct diagnosis. If insects are the cause, careful inspection usually reveals either the pests themselves, or telltale signs of their presence. Look for chewed leaves, greenish fecal pellets, silken tubes or webbing, stem tunneling, turf that feels spongy underfoot or pulls free from the soil, holes, or mounds in the turf. Flocks of birds foraging in the turf, and tunneling or digging by moles, skunks, or raccoons is often evidence of an insect infestation. Likewise, swarms of masked chafers or sod webworm moths flying over the turf at dusk, or adult billbugs crawling over sidewalks and driveways, may signal the potential for a damaging infestation. Again, the ability to "trouble-shoot" such problems comes from keen observation and experience. Chapter 3 discusses additional means of sampling and monitoring insect pests.

Turf managers can get help with identifying insects from county agents employed by the **Cooperative Extension Service**, and from extension entomologists at state land-grant universities and agricultural experiment stations (Appendix 1). These services are free, and they are usually the most reliable source of local information. Be wary of diagnoses and recommendations by clerks at garden centers, feed or hardware stores, or pesticide dealers. Consult an expert before launching into a management program without knowing for sure what pest you are dealing with.

There is a right way and a wrong way to submit specimens to a specialist for identification. Adult moths (e.g., cutworm, armyworm, or sod webworm moths) should be sent dry. Moths can be disabled or killed by sharply pinching the thorax between thumb and forefinger, or by placing them in the freezer overnight. Try to keep the wings, legs, and antennae intact. The moth can then be placed in a small envelope or folded paper, and packed in a box between sheets of tissue paper or cotton for padding. If possible, submit several representative specimens. Include information on when and where the insects were collected, the species of grass, and the type of damage.

Immature or soft-bodied specimens (grubs, billbug larvae, webworms, cutworms, armyworms, mole cricket nymphs, greenbugs, mites, spiders, etc.) should be sent in a leak-proof bottle or vial containing 70% ethyl alcohol (preferred), rubbing alcohol, or even vodka. Ship the vial in a well-protected container, and include a note or label with collection information as above. Inexpensive vials can be obtained from vendors of entomological supplies (Appendix 3). Many insect larvae will turn black after a few days if placed directly into alcohol. More natural color will be retained if they are first killed by dropping them into boiling water for about 15 seconds before pickling them in alcohol. Hard-bodied adult insects such as beetles, adult mole crickets, wasps, ants, and adult chinch bugs can be sent either dry or in alcohol-filled vials.

DIAGNOSTIC KEY TO COMMON INSECTS AND RELATED PESTS OF TURF

A. Insects that feed on roots of turfgrasses; turf dies in irregular patches

1. Small or large patches of dead or dying grass; roots pruned so that sod can be pulled up or rolled back like a loose carpet; numerous C-shaped whitish larvae with brown head in

upper soil; turf may be damaged by mammals or birds digging for grubs; adults are scarab beetles, including Japanese beetle, masked chafers, June beetles, European chafer, etc.

White grubs, Chapter 8.

2. Narrow, meandering raised ridges on soil surface; 1/2 in. (1.25 cm) diameter tunnels in root zone; brown to grayish-brown crickets with spade-like front feet for digging; pests of southern turfgrasses.

Mole crickets, Chapter 8.

3. Numerous small patches of dead or dying grass; a "tug test" reveals that stems break off easily at crown and are tunneled and packed with sawdust-like frass. Small, legless white larva with brown head feeding within stem, or more often on crown or roots; fine, white frass often in vicinity of larva.

Billbugs, Chapter 9.

4. Tiny (1/16 to 1/8 in. [1–3 mm] diameter) pearl-like, yellow to purple spheres attached to roots of grass; pest of southern turfgrasses.

Ground pearls, Chapter 8.

B. Insects that burrow in stems or crown of turfgrasses; turf dies in scattered patches

1. Numerous small patches of dead or dying grass; a "tug test" reveals that stems break off easily at crown and are tunneled and packed with sawdust-like frass. Small, legless white larva with brown head feeding within stem, or more often on crown or roots; fine, white frass often in vicinity of larva.

Billbugs, Chapter 9.

2. Small yellow-brown spots on close-cut annual bluegrass that may coalesce into dead patches; notches or holes in leaf blades; stems severed from plant; small, white legless grub with brown head feeding on crown.

Annual bluegrass weevil, Chapter 9.

3. Tiny, light yellow maggots tunnel into stems of grasses or injure crown, causing stem to die. Small, shiny black flies, 1/16 in. (1.5 mm) long with yellow on legs attracted to white surfaces such as golf balls. Pest of cool-season grasses, especially bentgrass.

Frit fly, Chapter 9.

C. Insects and mites that suck juices from leaves and stems of grasses; discolor foliage

1. Turf appears drought-stressed, may be killed in irregular spots, especially in sunny areas of thatchy lawns; numerous small winged or wingless bugs up to 1/5 in. (5 mm) long present; adults black with white wings folded across back, some may have short wings; young nymphs red with white band across middle.

Chinch bugs, Chapter 10.

2. Cool-season turfgrasses, especially bluegrass, show burnt-orange or yellow discoloration, usually under shade of trees or beside buildings (but sometimes in open areas); small, green, soft-bodied aphids on grass blades of living turf at perimeter of damaged patches.

Greenbug, Chapter 10.

3. Grass foliage discolored, appearing yellowed, blanched, silvery or frosted, but is not chewed; tiny eight-legged mites on leaf blades. Mainly on cool-season turfgrasses.

   Clover mite, winter grain mite, or other non-eriophyid mites, Chapter 10.

4. Bermudagrass, zoysiagrass, or buffalograss becomes thin, yellowed, with shortened internodes; leaves and buds become bushy and curled, producing rosetted or tufted growth; microscopic banana-shaped mites under leaf sheaths.

   Bermudagrass mite or other eriophyid mites, Chapter 10.

5. Bermudagrass or St. Augustinegrass weakened, wilted, gradually turning brown; masses of white, cottony material at crown, nodes, or leaf axils; **or** small, globular insects covered with whitish, shell-like cover attached to nodes of bermudagrass stems so that infested grass appears covered with mold.

   Rhodesgrass mealybug; Bermudagrass scale, Chapter 10.

6. Turf wilted, yellow or brown; masses of white, frothy spittle on leaf blades or at base of stems; pale-colored insect inside spittle mass; mainly on bermudagrass and other southern turfgrasses.

   Two-lined spittlebug, Chapter 10.

D. Insects that chew on leaves and stems of grasses; turf sparse, with irregular brown or dead areas with missing leaves or stems, or ragged leaves

1. Grass chewed off close to crown; greenish to beige-brown caterpillars, usually with brownish circular spots, live in silk-lined burrows in thatch. Adult moths often seen flying erratically over turf at dusk; moths are beige or grayish-white, have snout-like projection and roll wings around body when at rest; foraging birds may be attracted to turf.

   Sod webworms, Chapter 11.

2. Leaves and stems chewed, ragged-looking, or cut off close to crown; numerous dark-colored caterpillars with lighter stripes visible crawling in grass or thatch; birds frequenting turf.

   Armyworms, Chapter 11.

3. "Pockmarks" chewed on golf greens, tees, or fairways; thick-bodied, dark-colored caterpillars, with pale or contrasting stripes; typically curl up when disturbed; hide in coring holes or burrows by day and feed at night; chew off grass close to crown.

   Cutworms, Chapter 11.

E. Pests that produce mounds or holes in turf

1. Mounds of granular soil with ants present; mounds may be rounded or somewhat conical and 6 in. to 2 ft (15–60 cm) in diameter (red imported fire ants), low and 1–3 ft (30–90 cm) across, with foliage cleared around nest (harvester ants); or resemble a small volcano 1–3 in. (2.5–7.5 cm) in diameter (field ants).

   Ants, Chapters 12,13,14.

2. Mounds consist of pile of loose soil, 1–3 in. (2.5–7.5 cm) across; adjacent to a large, 1/4–1/2 in. (6–12 mm) open, vertical hole.

   Green June beetle grubs, Chapter 8; or ***Cicada killer wasps***, Chapter 12.

3. Turf feels lumpy underfoot; small mounds of soil glued together in compact mass (***earthworm castings***), or mounds 1–3 in. (2.5–7.5 cm) in diameter in turf canopy and thatch which have leaves, thatch, and turf stems incorporated.

   Earthworms or nightcrawlers, Chapter 13,14.

4. Mounds built upward with mud, without turf leaves or stems incorporated; opening 1–2 in. (2.5–5 cm) across; usually near waterways or poorly drained areas.

Crayfish, Chapter 14.

5. Many holes about 1/2 in. (13 mm) in diameter, especially under trees. Brown, shed skins of insects attached to nearby tree trunks, fence posts, or other objects. Robust, dark-bodied insects having clear wings marked with green or orange making shrill "singing" in trees.

Cicadas, Chapter 14.

F. Pests of dichondra lawns

1. Dichondra with crescent-shaped holes chewed in leaves; leaves turn brown and die; small, 1/16 in. (1.5–1.8 mm), oval, dark-colored beetles may be present on foliage; elongate, whitish larvae feed on roots and crown.

Dichondra flea beetle, Chapter 8.

2. Leaves of dichondra with small holes, skeletonized, or completely removed; grayish brown to dull black "snout" beetles, greenish, legless grubs with brown head hide in soil around plants by day, feeding at night.

Vegetable weevil, Chapter 9.

G. Arthropods which do not damage grass, but which may bite, sting, or annoy people using the turf

1. Small, flat-sided, reddish-brown wingless insects, jump when disturbed; not usually associated with turf except in yards where dogs and cats are kept.

Fleas, Chapter 12.

2. Microscopic mites whose bites cause itchy red welts, especially around ankles, waistline, or other areas where clothing fits tightly against the skin. Not usually abundant in turf, but high populations may reside in high grass, weeds, or brush bordering lawns or golf roughs.

Chiggers, Chapter 12.

3. Small, flattened, 8-legged arthropods that attach themselves by their mouthparts to skin of humans or pets; feed on blood and may transmit diseases; seldom a problem in turf but may infest edges bordered by tall grass and weeds.

Ticks, Chapter 12.

4. Yellow and black wasps about 1/2 in. (13 mm) long with wings folded lengthwise when at rest; live in large colonies that nest in underground cavities or sometimes in sheds, bushes, or trees; wasps forage for food around outdoor concession or picnic areas and trash cans; stings painful, life-threatening if allergic.

Yellowjackets, Chapter 12.

5. Very large (1-1/4 in. [30 mm]) black and yellow wasps resembling oversized hornets or yellowjackets; buzz-bomb and upset homeowners and golfers; wasp makes burrows with unsightly mounds.

Cicada killer wasps, Chapter 12.

H. Nuisance pests that often live in or around turf but do little or no feeding damage to grass

1. Elongate, slender, brown insects, 5/8–7/8 in. (16–22 mm) long; pair of large, forceps-like "pinchers" at tip of abdomen.

Earwigs, Chapter 14.

2. Flattened, oval, grayish or gray-brown animals; up to 1/2 in. (12.5 mm) long; with seven pairs of legs; sides of body extend over place where legs attach.

Sowbugs and Pillbugs, Chapter 14.

3. Elongate, worm-like animals with 30 or more pairs of legs, two pairs of legs per body segment; short antennae; slow moving; body cylindrical or slightly flattened; numerous in damp areas; may invade homes after heavy rains.

Millipedes, Chapter 14.

4. Elongate, flattened animals with 15 or more pairs of legs, one pair of legs per body segment; long antennae; fast-moving, usually brown or reddish brown.

Centipedes, Chapter 14.

SELECTED REFERENCES

Borror, D.J., C.A. Triplehorn, and N.F. Johnson. 1989. *An introduction to the study of insects* (6th ed.). Harcourt Brace College Publ., Orlando, FL.

Borror, D.J. and R.E. White. 1970. *A field guide to the insects*. Houghton Mifflin Co., Boston.

Elzinga, R.J. 1997. *Fundamentals of entomology* (4th ed.). Prentice-Hall, Inc., Englewood Cliffs, NJ.

Pfadt, R.E. 1985. *Fundamentals of applied entomology* (3rd ed.). Macmillan Publishing Co., New York, NY.

Romoser, W.S. and J.G. Stoffolano, Jr. 1994. *The science of entomology*. Wm. C. Brown., Dubuque, IA.

Turpin, F.T. 1992. *The insect appreciation digest*. The Entomological Foundation, Lanham, MD.

Watt, W.B. 1994. Insects. *The world book encyclopedia*. World Book, Inc., Chicago, IL.

Wilson, C.W., D.B. Broersma, and A.W. Provonsha. 1977. *Fundamentals of applied entomology*. Waveland Press, Inc., Prospect Heights, IL.

3

DETECTION AND MONITORING OF INSECT PESTS

WHY SAMPLE AND MONITOR?

Sampling and **monitoring** are keys to successful pest management. By understanding the biology of insects and mites attacking turf, you'll know when to expect damaging life stages or infestations to occur. You can then periodically inspect or monitor the turf to see if potential pests are present and whether they are reaching levels that are high enough to warrant control. For example, lots of adult billbugs crawling on sidewalks or driveways in the spring or fall should provide warning of a possible infestation of larvae in nearby turf during July and August. Periodic inspections allow you to detect pest infestations early, before significant damage has been done. Most insects can then be dealt with on a reactive, or as-needed basis. Sampling before and after control actions helps in evaluating treatment effectiveness.

Whereas certain annual weeds (e.g., crabgrass) and many turfgrass diseases are best controlled preventively, most insects can be adequately controlled on a curative basis, after they are detected but before significant damage has occurred. Insect outbreaks tend to be sporadic and rarely occur uniformly over whole lawns or golf courses. Applying insecticides wall-to-wall, whether needed or not, is wasteful and reduces the professional status of the turf manager. By sampling and monitoring, you can reduce the risks of getting "burned" by an unexpected pest outbreak, lower your insecticide costs, and increase the effectiveness of curative treatments. Reducing nonessential insecticide applications is important in this era of increasing concerns about safety and the environment.

Certain insecticides (e.g., imidacloprid for grub control) are more effective when used preventively. Unfortunately, such products also have greater potential for excessive use, because they must be applied before the damage potential of the insect population is known. Monitoring and sampling, together with good record-keeping, can help you to identify those lawns, fairways, or other sites that are at greatest risk. When making preventive applications, concentrating on these high-risk sites is wiser than going wall-to-wall with the insecticide. In this manner, preventive treatments can be used within the context of IPM.

WHERE TO SAMPLE AND MONITOR

Turf managers often do not monitor and sample for insect pests because they view these practices as being too time-consuming and complicated. This need not be true. Various techniques can be used to monitor particular lawns, large golf courses, or even whole neighborhoods. These range from quick visual inspections to more specific tactics such as using traps or accumulated degree-days to pinpoint the occurrence of vulnerable life stages. Understanding insect life cycles and knowing which pests to concentrate on in your area helps to narrow the time period for scouting.

One way to make monitoring more efficient is to concentrate on areas where pests are most likely to occur. Hairy chinch bugs, for example, seem to prefer sunny, perennial ryegrass or fine-leaf fescue lawns with thick thatch. Golf superintendents may know that certain putting greens are prone to damage by cutworms, while others are rarely infested. For reasons not well understood, some sites have just the right combination of turf type, soil characteristics, and site topography to make them magnets for pests. Sites that have had problems in the past are often the most likely to be reinfested. Keeping a map or record of these high-risk or **key locations** helps to identify sites that are most likely to need attention.

Pest Mapping

Pest mapping is well-suited to golf courses because the superintendent is on the site daily. Keep historical records of problem spots, and train your employees to watch for symptoms of cutworms, white grubs, or mole cricket damage. Designate a "sampling team" to scout the turf for early signs of insect damage (e.g., flocks of birds attracted to certain sites). Infestations of grub or mole crickets are usually patchy, so that treating all fairways is rarely warranted. Systematic sampling can reveal where the perennial "hot-spots" are located. Once you develop good maps (Figure 3.1), it's quicker, cheaper, and easier on the environment to target those areas with recurring problems than to treat wall-to-wall. Tips for mapping grubs, mole crickets, and other pests are given in the particular pest sections.

Pest mapping also helps lawn care applicators to keep track of accounts or neighborhoods with a history of insect problems. Obtain a large city map and mark the locations of infested lawns with pushpins, color-coding them to the particular types of pests found. In newer subdivisions, the developer often will have obtained seed or sod from a single source, so that most of the lawns will consist of the same types of grasses. If the lawns are predominantly nonendophytic perennial ryegrasses and fine-leaf fescues, then sod webworms, chinch bugs, and billbugs may be present. If Kentucky bluegrass was used, then billbugs and white grubs may predominate. Tall fescue lawns usually have relatively few insect problems. Lawns that are irrigated frequently during midsummer may attract egg-laying Japanese beetles, masked chafers, or other scarabs. By mapping locations of lawns with similar characteristics and pest problems, lawn service applicators can gain a sense of which pests are most common in particular neighborhoods. Service routes can then be adjusted to give first priority to neighborhoods at highest risk from particular pests.

HOW TO SAMPLE AND MONITOR

Various tactics can be used to detect and monitor for turfgrass insects, or to assess the effectiveness of treatments. Sweep nets, hand lenses, pheromone traps, and other equipment discussed in this section can be purchased from entomological supply houses (see Appendix 3).

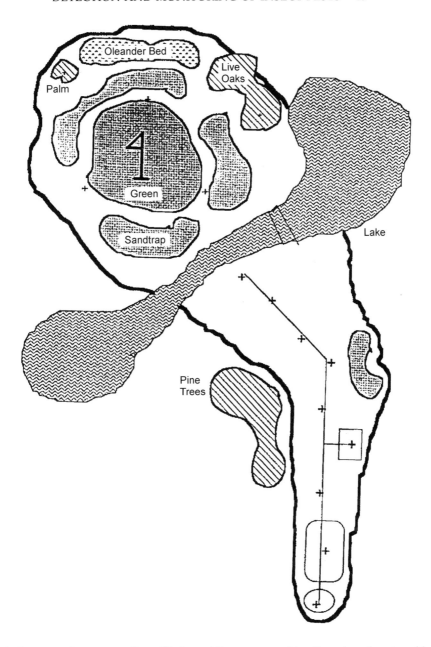

Figure 3.1. *Computer-drawn map of a golf hole enabling a scout to identify and mark pest problem areas (adapted from McCarty and Elliott, 1994).*

Visual Inspection

Frequent and careful observation is the best method for detecting insect problems in turf. Be alert for off-color foliage, gradual thinning, isolated patches of dying grass, or any other signs of deterioration. Injury caused by insects is often confused with damage from disease, localized dry spot, pH imbalance, poor nutrition, or other causes. Close examination by the "hands-and-knees method" will help you to make the correct diagnosis. Examine the foliage, poke around in the grass and thatch, and dig below the surface to see if pests are there. Damaged turf may no longer be harboring the pests themselves because the insects may have moved to fresher food, gone down to pupate, or dispersed as adults. Examine the boundary zone between green, apparently healthy turf, and damaged or dead areas. Look for by-products of insect activity: silk-lined burrows or piles of dried frass from sod webworms, hollowed stems caused by billbug larvae, or pockmarks on golf greens caused by night-feeding cutworms. Heavy activity of adults can foretell problems with grubs, billbugs, or caterpillars later on in the growing season. For example, swarms of brown beetles or small moths flying over the turf at dusk means that sod webworms or masked chafer grubs will be present a few weeks later. High bird activity often signals a caterpillar or grub infestation, whereas turf torn up by skunks or raccoons usually indicates white grubs. Signs and symptoms of damage caused by particular insects are discussed in the individual pest sections.

A 10x to 15x **hand lens** (Figure 3.2) is a useful tool for examining rastral patterns of white grubs and on-site identification of other insects encountered in the landscape. Use of such a tool conveys a professional image to clients and employees. An adequate hand lens can be purchased for about $15. Don't be without one.

Soil Pest Sampling

Sampling the soil is the only way to accurately estimate densities of white grubs, billbug larvae, and other root-feeding insects. Grubs of Japanese beetles and masked chafers tend to concentrate in the upper 2 in. (5 cm) of soil during their feeding periods in late summer through fall, and in the spring. These grubs become harder to sample in late fall as they move deeper for hibernation, and in early spring before they've returned to the root zone. European chafers, oriental beetles, and green June beetle grubs tend to move up or down in the soil profile in response to moisture gradients, so they may require more extensive digging.

The standard **golf course hole cutter** (Figure 3.3), or an oversized 6 in. (15 cm) diameter hole cutter ("turf mender") are useful for sampling for white grubs. With care, sampling can be done with minimal damage to the turf. Once removed, samples can be broken up and examined on the spot. Place the crumbled soil back in the hole made by the cutter, replace the sod cap, and irrigate to promote recovery. Record the numbers of pests present and the predominate life stages on a data sheet or map. Examining samples in a grid pattern helps to delineate areas that are infested. An experienced person can cut and examine about 20 samples in an hour. The standard hole cutter is 4-1/4 in. (11 cm) in diameter. To convert the number of insects found per hole cutter sample to number per square foot (0.1 m²), multiply each sample by 10.15.

Another method of sampling for soil insects is to cut and examine sections of sod using a **flat-blade spade**. Cut a square-foot (0.1 m²) sample on three sides to a depth of 3–4 in. (7–10 cm) and then turn back the sod as if it were a flap. The soil is then broken up and the grubs counted. Return the soil to the hole, tamp down the sod flap, and irrigate to promote recovery. If done carefully, this procedure allows many of the grass plants to keep their root systems intact. Be sure to examine several samples to get an estimate of grub densities in different areas. A **motorized sod cutter** can also be used to sample for white grubs.

Irritant Sampling

Sod webworms, cutworms, mole crickets, billbug adults, vegetable weevils, chinch bugs, and other pests inhabiting the thatch and soil can be flushed out by applying an irritating drench (sometimes called a **disclosing solution**). Mow the grass beforehand so the insects will be easier to spot. Mix one ounce, or 2 tablespoons (30 mL) of liquid dishwashing soap in 2 gal (7.6 L) of water and sprinkle or pour the solution over 1 yd² (0.8 m²) of turf (Figure 3.4). One tablespoon (15 mL) of pyrethrin (e.g., Pyrenone 6% EC) or a couple of drops of a synthetic pyrethroid insecticide in 2 gal of water will also do the job. Any caterpillars or mole cricket nymphs that are present should come to the surface within a few minutes. Soap flush sampling

Figure 3.2. A hand lens is useful for diagnosing pest problems.

Figure 3.3. Standard golf hole cutter (4.25 in.) and oversized "turf mender" (6 in. diameter) can be used to sample for grubs or other soil insects.

for mole crickets is most effective in summer, during periods when the soil is warm and moist, and the nymphs are burrowing and feeding close to the surface. It generally works best when applied after rains or irrigation. During cooler periods in spring and fall, or during extended dry spells, most of the crickets may be too deep in the soil to be reached by the drench. At such times, mole cricket adults may require two flushings and still be difficult to bring up.

Detergents vary in concentration and ingredients; test them beforehand to determine the soap-to-water ratio that flushes out the target insects without discoloring the turf. Irrigate the sampled area afterward to reduce any chance of sun scalding. This sampling method will not bring root-feeding pests such as grubs or billbug larvae to the surface.

Flotation Sampling

This technique is mainly used in sampling for chinch bugs. Remove the bottom from a large, empty coffee can or similar metal cylinder and cut off one rim with tinsnips to produce a sharp edge. Push the can about 1 in. (2.5 cm) into the turf in the area to be sampled. Fill the can to the brim with water, and add more if the water recedes (Figure 3.5). Any chinch bugs that are

Figure 3.4. *Sampling for cutworms with a soap disclosing solution.*

Figure 3.5. *Flotation sampling for chinch bugs.*

present should float to the surface within 5–10 minutes. An alternative technique is to cut turf cores with a golf cup cutter and submerge them in a bucket of water for the same amount of time. See Chinch Bugs — Management, for additional details.

Sweep Net

With a sweep net, you can quickly check the turf for presence of greenbugs, chinch bugs, or other small pests that are up on the grass blades during the day. A sweep net is like a standard butterfly net, but it has a sturdier frame and a net bag made from muslin or other heavy, tear-resistant cloth. Hold the net as you would a long-handled broom when sweeping off a sidewalk (Figure 3.6). While walking slowly, sweep the net back and forth across the turf so the rim just brushes the foliage. After 10 or 20 sweeps, turn the net bag inside out and examine the contents. If foliage-dwelling pests are present, they'll be easily spotted.

Pitfall Traps

Pitfall traps are cups or cans set in the ground to detect and monitor for billbug adults, mole crickets, and other crawling pests. The concept is simple: insects walking through the turf drop

Figure 3.6. Using a sweep net to sample for foliage-dwelling insects.

into the trap and are unable to crawl out. Large plastic picnic cups used for cold drinks make ideal billbug traps. One design (Figure 3.7) uses a Solo® 16 oz (470 mL) cup (#P-16). The large cup can be used alone, or with smaller cups to serve as a funnel (Solo #806A 7 oz coffee cup liner with the bottom cut out) and sample receptacle (Solo 4 oz, #P400). Traps can be set in the ground by removing a core with a standard golf cup cutter. The lip of the trap should be just below the soil surface. A rain shield (e.g., a board on two stones) can be placed over the top, or pin holes can be punched in the bottom to allow rainwater to drain. Pitfall traps are useful for monitoring spring activity of adult billbugs for timing of insecticide treatments (see Bill-bugs — Management). The pests can be easily counted by inspecting the traps several times a week. Place the traps in turf along flowerbeds or other out-of-the-way sites.

Some entomology texts recommend using antifreeze (ethylene glycol) in the bottom of pit-fall traps as a preservative for specimens. However, this may be hazardous in turfgrass settings because antifreeze is quite toxic to dogs and cats. Large mesh wire screen, placed flat over the pitfall trap and staked to the ground, allows insects to enter while excluding pets and wildlife.

A special type of pitfall trap is sometimes used to monitor mole crickets on southern golf courses. A small wading pool, partially filled with water, and an electric calling device sus-pended over the pool are used to attract female crickets. Attracted females fly to amplified, synthetic male "love calls" and collect on the water surface. These traps give a general indica-tion of cricket activity, but they have little value for reducing populations or predicting damage at particular sites (see Mole Crickets — Management).

Pheromone or Floral Lure Traps

Sex pheromones are chemicals produced by insects to attract mates. Sex pheromones are usually released into the air from glands in the female's abdomen. Males detect the pheromone with specialized receptors on their antennae, and then search upwind, following the odor plume of the female. Entomologists were quick to recognize the usefulness of these substances in IPM, particularly for monitoring insects for the purpose of spray timing. The chemical struc-tures of hundreds of insect sex pheromones have been determined, and many companies are involved in producing synthetic insect sex pheromones. Although most of the identified phero-mones are for agricultural pests not associated with turf, synthetic lures for black cutworm, variegated cutworm, true armyworm, fall armyworm, cranberry girdler, and bluegrass web-worm are presently on the market. Each lure is specific for males of a particular species.

Figure 3.7. Pitfall traps can be made from standard 16 oz drink cups, with or without smaller cups to serve as a funnel and sample receptacle (see text for details).

Cardboard sticky traps baited with pheromone lures (Figure 3.8) can be used to fine-tune management schedules for those pests. For example, a golf superintendent who hangs a few black cutworm traps in the early spring can determine when the first moths are present. Capture of moths indicates that egg-laying has begun; cutworm damage may begin showing up on putting greens about 2 weeks later. Continued monitoring helps in tracking flight peaks for successive summer generations (see Black Cutworm — Management). Pheromone traps can reveal whether a particular pest is early or late relative to its normal seasonal occurrence. Use of these traps will not result in greater pest injury because only males are attracted (male moths don't feed or lay eggs). This monitoring tool will become more useful when additional pheromone lures are developed for turf-infesting insects. Sources from which traps and lures can be purchased are listed in Appendix 3.

Japanese beetle traps are a widely used type of insect trap in landscape settings. This trap uses a combination of female sex pheromone and a potent floral lure. Potential problems with use of these traps are discussed later (see Japanese Beetles — Management).

Black Light Trap

Light traps use a 15-watt ultraviolet or fluorescent "black light" tube that is highly attractive to night-flying insects. The lamp is mounted between baffles that deflect the attracted insects into a container (Figure 3.9). The trap is supported by a tripod and usually operated on 110 volt AC current using an outdoor extension cord. Some models of traps can be operated on a 12 volt car battery. These have a photocell switch that conserves battery life during the day. Battery-powered traps allow more flexibility in location but cost more to operate. Light traps attract night-active scarabs, such as black turfgrass ataenius, northern and southern masked chafers, European chafers, Asiatic garden beetles, and May beetles (*Phyllophaga* spp.). Annual bluegrass weevils, and moths of cutworms, armyworms, and sod webworms are also captured. Like pheromone traps, light traps provide information about flight periods of adult insects. On the downside, light traps may catch thousands of different insects in a single summer night. Sorting through this huge pile of "bugs" is tedious and time-consuming, and it may take an expert to identify and interpret the material collected. Another drawback is the price of the traps — more than $400 for a store-bought model.

Figure 3.8. A cardboard sticky trap baited with pheromone lure for monitoring moths of turf-infesting caterpillars (courtesy Gempler's, Inc.).

Figure 3.9. A black light trap used for monitoring night-flying insects (courtesy Gempler's, Inc.).

WHEN IS THE BEST TIME TO TREAT?

Effective control of insect pests usually requires that action be directed against a particular life stage. Often, as for white grubs, webworms, or chinch bugs, the most vulnerable stage is the young larvae or nymphs. In other cases (e.g., annual bluegrass weevil, black turfgrass ataenius) the newly emerged adults may be vulnerable before they can lay eggs. Turf managers should cultivate a good working knowledge of the seasonal cycles of key pests in their area. Specific recommendations for which life stages to target are given in the sections dealing with individual pests.

Even when the most vulnerable life stage is known, timing of controls is complicated by the fact that seasonal development of insects varies from year to year. This is because insects, like trees and flowers, are cold-blooded, so their development is affected by temperature. Yearly temperature and weather variations cause pests to hatch, grow, or become active at a different rate each spring. For this reason, timing of control measures by **calendar date** alone is often inaccurate — the target date for a particular pest can be several weeks earlier or later than average in a warm or cool year. This is one reason why visual inspections, monitoring, and sampling are important — they help you to adjust the timing of control actions to local conditions.

Indicator or Signal Plants

Phenology is the practice of relating seasonally recurring biological events, such as flowering, to climate and other events that are happening at the same time. Phenology involves keeping track of events in nature and using them to time certain activities. For example, Native Americans taught early European immigrants to plant corn when young oak leaves are about the size of a mouse's ear. Fishermen know that crappies are biting when lilac leaves begin to expand. In turf and grounds maintenance, phenology can help you to time pest control actions.

One way to accomplish this is to relate the seasonal occurrence of insects to the development of **indicator or signal plants** in the landscape. The seasonal occurrence of pests and signal plants is correlated because the same weather patterns affecting pests also influence plant growth. The best signal plants are easily recognizable, and have showy developmental stages that coincide with occurrence of vulnerable life stages of the insect pests. Flowering trees and shrubs make good springtime indicator plants. For example, annual bluegrass weevils emerge from overwintering sites and become active on golf courses when *Forsythia* is approaching full bloom. Egg laying begins just before flowering dogwood (*Cornus florida*) is in full bloom (full bract). Thus, applications made between these two phenological events will intercept the adults before they can lay eggs in the turf. Other examples of signal plants associated with particular pests are given in the separate pest sections.

You can make the observations necessary to set up a **phenology calendar** for your own region. First, select a number of suitable indicator plants. These should be plants with easily recognizable developmental stages that are encountered in your daily rounds. Once you have your indicator plants, observe pest activity and correlate it with plant growth stages such as bud break, leaf expansion, first bloom, full bloom, or petal drop. Concentrate on the major pests in your region, and keep good records. You'll need to monitor pest activity and plant development for several growing seasons to ensure that you have accurate correlations. The time you invest in developing a phenology calendar will be repaid many times over in improved timing, better insect control, and reduced insecticide costs.

Degree-Day Accumulations

Using **degree-day accumulations** is another method for timing the occurrence of insect pests. Below a certain temperature, insects are essentially dormant, and growth and physiological development are stopped. This temperature is called a **lower threshold temperature** and for most insects it is about 50°F (10°C). Above the lower threshold, the rate of growth and development increases with temperature in an almost straight-line fashion. All insects also have an upper threshold at which development begins to deteriorate because of heat shock. If its temperature rises too far above this threshold, the insect will die. In nature, insects usually seek environments (shade, moist thatch, soil, nighttime) that enable them to avoid lethal extremes of temperature.

Degree-day accumulation is a measure of the total number of degrees that each day's temperature is above the lower threshold. In forecasting systems based on degree-days, the lower threshold is often referred to as the **base temperature**. The simplest way to calculate degree-days is to determine the average temperature for each day, subtract the base temperature, and then total the number of degree-days accumulated from a predetermined starting date. Table 3.1 shows how it works. After so many degree-days have accumulated, the insect should be at a certain stage of development. Degree-days are usually accumulated from a January 1 starting date, but for some insects a later starting date is used. For example, a degree-day system developed for bluegrass billbugs predicts that adults will emerge from overwintering sites and begin laying eggs when 280–350 degree-days (base 50°F) have accumulated from a March 1 starting date. Degree-day accumulations coinciding with occurrence of vulnerable life stages have been worked out for various turfgrass insects. When available, these are given in the sections on particular pests.

Annual degree-day accumulations are compiled by most Agricultural Experiment Stations and are available free of charge from your Cooperative Extension office. When you observe an important phenological event (e.g., first appearance of cutworms on putting greens), call your county agent and request the accumulated degree-days to that date. Keep records of these correlations over several years and you will have a system for forecasting insect activity. By checking the current degree-days once or twice a week in the spring, you can predict when the vulnerable life stages of insect pests will appear.

DECIDING IF TREATMENT IS JUSTIFIED

Manage the Causes, Not Just the Symptoms

Outbreaks of turf pests, whether they be weeds, insects, or disease, are usually indicative of an underlying problem. The *reactive* turf manager tends to treat the symptoms without taking into account the underlying factors that encouraged the problem to develop in the first place. The *responsive* turf manager, by comparison, will draw upon experience, past records, phenology charts, soil tests, or consultation with experts to try to determine and remedy the underlying reason *why* the pest outbreak has occurred.

Simply identifying the symptom (such as chinch bug damage to a home lawn) and applying an insecticide is merely reactive, and will not lessen the possibility of the problem reoccurring. Determining *why* the outbreak occurred, and making the necessary agronomic and cultural adjustments in your management programs, is the mark of the most skillful turf managers. With chinch bugs, for example, the long-term solution may be reducing the thatch layer, overseeding with endophytic grasses, and cutting back on insecticides to allow natural enemies to do their job. Sound agronomic growing principles should be the foundation of any IPM program.

Tolerance Levels and Action Thresholds

In order to evaluate the damage potential of pest populations and to make decisions on control actions, turf managers must develop a "feel" for what level of pest activity is intolerable in a particular situation. Despite the public's perception that lawns and golf courses should be absolutely pest-free, in reality, healthy turf areas will always have some insects, weeds, and other pests. Finding a few insects in a lawn, fairway, or even a putting green doesn't necessarily mean that control action is warranted. The decision whether or not to treat is best guided by tolerance levels or action thresholds.

The **tolerance level** is simply the amount of damage that can be reasonably tolerated in a particular situation. Below the tolerance level, most people would probably not even notice that turf quality is reduced. Above the tolerance level, the damage would be considered unaccept-

Table 3.1. Calculating Degree-Day Accumulations.

1. **Determine the average temperature for each day:**

   Daily maximum temperature + Daily minimum temperature ÷ 2 = Daily average temperature

2. **Determine the degree days:**

   Daily average temperature – 50 = Daily degree-days

3. **Total the daily degree-days for each day**, beginning January 1 and continuing until the pest has reached its vulnerable stage.

Sample Degree-Day Accumulations

Date	Maximum Temperature	Minimum Temperature	Total	Average	After Subtracting 50	Accumulation Over Time
3/14	66	42	108	54	4	4
3/15	70	46	116	58	8	12
3/16	75	49	124	62	12	24

able by most people. Obviously, tolerance levels for pest damage are very low on golf putting greens, somewhat higher on lawns and fairways, and higher still in the roughs. The **action threshold** is the density of pests that will cause injury exceeding the tolerance level if nothing is done. In other words, control actions are warranted when pest densities approach or exceed the action threshold. Below the action threshold, natural factors will suppress the pest population and the turf will outgrow the damage on its own. Remember — the goal is to reduce unnecessary insecticide applications without jeopardizing the quality of the turf.

A number of factors must be considered when establishing tolerance levels, or when deciding whether or not to treat. These include the *location* of the turf, and *how it is used*. Is it a high traffic area? For residential and commercial lawns, certain locations (e.g., main entrance areas) have higher perceived value than the backyard or rear parking lot areas. Consider, too, the *aesthetics and replacement value*. The more valuable the turf in terms of cost of renovation or replacement, the lower the acceptable level of damage from the turf manager's perspective. Having to renovate a putting green is very expensive when one considers not only the turf replacement and labor costs, but also the lost playing time and revenues, and the damage to the superintendent's reputation. Pests whose damage reduces the *playability or safety* of athletic turf may increase the risk of injury to athletes. Action thresholds will be lower on such sites than in out-of-play areas.

Agronomic and cultural factors also must be considered in the decision-making process. The first step is *correct identification* of the pest that is causing the problem. This helps you to assess the pest's damage potential, understand the life cycle, and select the proper method and timing for control. Identifying the *type of turf* helps in evaluating pest pressure and the need for control. Some turfgrasses are especially susceptible to certain pests, such as ground pearls in centipedegrass, or southern chinch bug in St. Augustinegrass lawns. In the transition zone, turf-type tall fescues are usually more tolerant of insect injury than are Kentucky bluegrasses. Overseeding endophyte-enhanced ryegrasses and fescues into existing stands may reduce the need for insecticides. Planting better-adapted species or cultivars will yield long-term benefits for IPM. The *time of year* also determines the damage potential of a pest infestation, and whether or not treatment is warranted. For example, treating for white grubs in late spring or late fall may be ill-advised because most of the population has stopped feeding and is moving deeper in the soil for pupation or overwintering.

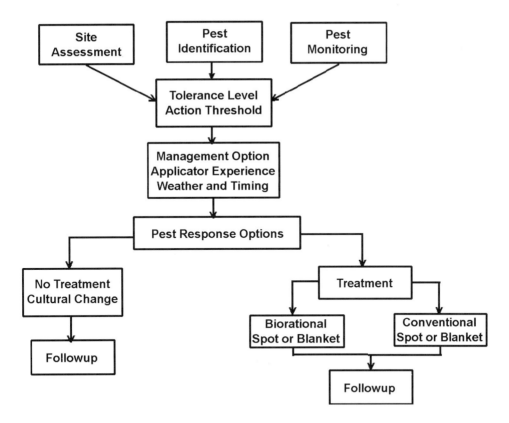

Figure 3.10. *General decision-making processes involved in integrated pest management (redrawn from Catron, 1994).*

Cultural practices, including fertility, mowing, and watering, also affect action thresholds for insect pests. In general, the healthier the turf, the better it will be able to tolerate or outgrow insect damage. Damage from insects can often be minimized or avoided by manipulating cultural practices. This can be a balancing act, however. Altering cultural practices too much can shift the pressure from one pest to another, or otherwise compromise turf quality. For example, light fertilization and irrigation in late summer may mask the injury from white grubs while promoting regrowth of roots. But excessive fertilization in spring encourages shallow rooting and thatch buildup, with increased susceptibility to grubs, chinch bugs, and greenbugs. When a professional begins evaluating pest pressure so that threshold levels can be determined, he or she quickly realizes that this requires both experience and common sense. *Regardless of the insect pest, no single action threshold will apply to all situations.*

By taking into account the pest's biology, as well as the general agronomic and cultural factors just discussed, you can follow a logical process in deciding whether or not a control action is warranted (Figure 3.10). Note how the various factors interact with one another and where there are built-in safeguards to reduce the unnecessary use of pesticides.

SELECTED REFERENCES

Catron, P. 1994. A lawn care alternative service, pp. 603–610. *In* Leslie, A. (Ed.). *Handbook of integrated pest management for turf and ornamentals,* Lewis Publishers, Boca Raton, FL.

Hellman, L. 1994. Insect detection and sampling techniques, pp. 331–336. *In* Leslie, A. (Ed.). *Handbook of integrated pest management for turf and ornamentals,* Lewis Publishers, Boca Raton, FL.

McCarty, L.B. and M.L. Elliott. 1994. Pest management strategies for golf courses, pp. 193–202. *In* Leslie, A. (Ed.). *Handbook of integrated pest management for turf and ornamentals,* Lewis Publishers, Boca Raton, FL.

Orton, D. 1996. Using plants to time pest control. *Grounds Maintenance* 31(4):14–19.

Shetlar, D. 1995. Insect and mite control on woody ornamentals and herbaceous perennials. Ohio State Univ. Coop. Ext. Serv. Bull. 504, Columbus, OH.

4

INSECTICIDES — TYPES AND MODES OF ACTION

Despite growing interest in so-called "biorational" alternatives, conventional insecticides will continue to play a key role in turfgrass management. Indeed, applying an insecticide may be the only practical way to prevent severe damage when sudden or unexpected outbreaks of pest insects occur. Insecticides provide a safety net we can fall back on when the more benign tactics of IPM are not enough.

Unfortunately, turfgrass insecticides were so overused in the past that the public now casts a wary eye whenever they are applied. In fact, the average citizen is more fearful of pesticides than of such activities as driving in a car, playing youth football, or eating fat-rich fast foods, all of which pose much higher levels of risk than do pesticides used in landscape maintenance. Tempting as it may be to downplay these fears, they must be treated as real — probably not justified, but real. Professional turf managers should consider insecticides tools to be conserved and used sparingly, and only as needed. Because of the high costs involved, many chemical companies are no longer developing insecticides for the turfgrass market.

Public perceptions aside, irresponsible use of insecticides *can* cause problems. Some insecticides can contaminate surface water or groundwater sources, or have adverse effects on birds or other wildlife if improperly used. Blanket applications can destroy populations of beneficial insects that help to keep harmful insects in check. Certain insecticides will destroy earthworm populations, leading to soil compaction and thatch accumulation. Excessive use can promote resistance in target pests, rendering future treatments ineffective. Pesticide sprays can drift into adjacent yards where they may contaminate gardens or endanger children or pets. In extreme cases, careless use of insecticides can poison the applicator or pose hazards to bystanders or people who use the turf following the application. Fortunately, despite these potential hazards, the overwhelming majority of scientific evidence indicates that turfgrass insecticides do not pose a significant risk if they are used sensibly and in accordance with label directions.

The technology and laws governing pesticide use are constantly changing. Professionals who use these tools in the public view must understand how they work, and how to use them in a safe and legal manner. *The label on the pesticide container is the best source of information on how to use that product safely.* Turf managers who purchase and apply pesticides have a responsibility to maintain their competence through ongoing education and training.

Insecticides are usually thought of as synthetic chemicals used to kill insects. However, not all insecticides are chemicals in the usual sense. Microbial insecticides such as *Bacillus thuringiensis* and entomopathogenic nematodes are living agents. Soaps and insect growth regulators kill insects by disrupting their cell membranes or upsetting their molting process. These products are essentially nontoxic to vertebrates. Botanical insecticides are derived from plants.

Pesticide usage in the United States is regulated by federal, state, and local laws. You should therefore understand the accepted legal definition of a **pesticide**, which is: "*...any substance or mixture of substances intended for preventing, destroying, repelling, or mitigating any pests, as well as any substance or mixture of substances intended for use as a plant growth regulator, defoliant, or desiccant.*" Besides **insecticides**, other kinds of pesticides include **miticides**, used to control mites; **herbicides**, used to control weeds; **fungicides**, which control fungal pathogens; and **nematicides**, which control plant-parasitic nematodes.

This chapter provides an overview of the kinds of insecticides used in landscape pest management, and how they work. The next two chapters concern safe handling and use of insecticides, and getting the most out of your insecticide applications.

TRADE NAMES, COMMON NAMES, AND CHEMICAL NAMES

Most turfgrass managers know the insecticides they use by their **trade names**. Trade names (brand names) are given by manufacturers or formulators; the names are registered with the U.S. patent office to prevent others from using them for their products. Because the patent rights may be held by more than one manufacturer, it is fairly common for an insecticide to have several trade names for the various formulations. To avoid confusion, each compound is also assigned an approved **common name**. Finally, every insecticide has a **chemical name** that describes its chemical structure. The following is an example of the names for a widely used turf insecticide:

trade name(s): Dylox®; Proxol®
common name: trichlorfon
chemical name: dimethyl (2,2,2-trichloro-1-hydroxyethyl) phosphonate

It is important to understand the equivalence of these names, because pesticide recommendations may be given as either common names or trade names. Common and trade names of some widely used turfgrass insecticides are listed in Table 4.1.

INSECTICIDE TOXICITY

Routes of Entry

Most insecticides must enter the insect's body in order to control the pest. **Stomach poisons** enter the body through the gut wall and must be eaten to have a lethal effect. Some insecticides are taken up and translocated within treated plants. These so-called **systemic insecticides** act as stomach poisons, especially for sap-feeding insects such as aphids and leafhoppers. Most modern insecticides act as **contact poisons**. They are absorbed through the body wall when the insect is hit by the spray, when it walks on the treated foliage, or as it moves through the thatch and soil. Contact poisons also enter through the digestive tract when the insect feeds on treated plant tissues. Thus, most turfgrass insecticides have multiple entry sites into the target pests. Traces of pesticides remaining on or in the treated turf are called **residues**; an insecticide that has a continued lethal effect over a period of time is said to be **residual**. The residual effectiveness of turfgrass insecticides varies from several months to a few hours or less.

Table 4.1. Common and Trade Names, Formulation, Manufacturer, and Chemical Class of Some Commonly Used Turfgrass Insecticides. (Signal Words Correspond to Toxicity Ratings Given in Table 4.2.)

Common Name	Trade Name	Formulation	Manufacturer	Class[a]	Signal Word[b]
Acephate	Orthene®	75 SP	Valent	OP	Caution
Azadirachtin	Turplex®	3% EC	O.M. Scott	Botanical	Caution
Bendiocarb	Turcam®	2.5 G	AgrEvo	Carbamate	Caution*
Bendiocarb	Turcam®	76 W		Carbamate	Warning*
Bifenthrin	Talstar®	10 WP	FMC	Pyrethroid	Warning
Bifenthrin	Talstar®	0.2 G		Pyrethroid	Caution
Carbaryl	Sevin®	4 F	LESCO	Carbamate	Caution
Carbaryl	Sevin®	6.3 G		Carbamate	Caution
Chlorpyrifos	Dursban®	4 E	DowElanco	OP	Warning
Chlorpyrifos	Dursban®	50 W		OP	Warning
Cyfluthrin	Tempo®	2 EC	Bayer	Pyrethroid	Warning
Cyfluthrin	Tempo®	20 WP		Pyrethroid	Caution
Diazinon	Diazinon®	5 G	LESCO	OP	Caution
Diazinon	Diazinon®	4 EC		OP	Warning
Dicofol	Kelthane®	4 EC	Rohm & Haas	Chlorinated Hydrocarbon	Caution
Ethoprop	Mocap®	10 G	Rhone-Poulenc	OP	Warning
Fipronil	Choice®	0.1 G	Rhone-Poulenc	Phenyl pyrazole	Warning
Fluvalinate	Mavrik®	2 F	Sandoz	Pyrethroid	Caution
Fonofos	Crusade®	5 G	Zeneca	OP	Warning
Fonofos	Mainstay®	2 G	LESCO	OP	Caution
Halofenozide	MACH 2®	2 G	RohMid	MAC	Caution
Imidacloprid	Merit®	75 WSP	Bayer	Chloronicotinyl	Caution
Imidacloprid	Merit®	0.5 G		Chloronicotinyl	Caution
Isazofos	Triumph®	4 E	Novartis	OP	Warning*
Isofenphos	Oftanol®	5 G	Bayer	OP	Caution
Isofenphos	Oftanol®	2 F		OP	Warning
Lambda-cyhalothrin	Scimitar®	10 WP	Zeneca	Pyrethroid	Warning
Permethrin	Astro®	3.2 EC	FMC	Pyrethroid	Caution
Trichlorfon	Proxol®	80 SP	AgrEvo	OP	Warning
Trichlorfon	Dylox®	6.2 G	Bayer	OP	Caution

[a] OP = organophosphate; MAC = molt accelerating compound.
[b] Asterisk (*) denotes Restricted Use Pesticide.

Modes of Action

Mode of action refers to the manner in which the insecticide acts upon an insect to kill it. Most turfgrass insecticides act as nerve poisons. As with humans, the insect nervous system is composed of a network of elongated nerve cells, called **neurons**. Three types of neurons are classified by function: sensory neurons, motor neurons, and interneurons (Figure 4.1). **Sensory neurons** carry sensory information from the mouthparts, antennae, and other sense organs to the central nervous system. **Motor neurons** carry impulses away from the central nervous system to stimulate muscles and glands. **Interneurons** connect sensory and motor neurons within the central nervous system. Each neuron consists of one or more receptor fibrils, a cell body, and an elongated extension of the cell body called an **axon**. The axon is the part of the neuron that transmits the nerve impulses to other cells. The ends of adjacent neurons do not quite touch

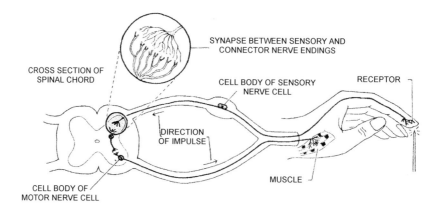

Figure 4.1. *Diagram of nerve communication in a human (from Whitford et al., 1992).*

one another. Rather, there is a short gap, called a **synapse**, at the juncture between two neurons and between neurons and cells of muscles or glands.

Nervous impulses are transmitted along the neurons in the form of electrical energy. When an impulse moving along the axon reaches a synapse, it dies out. As this happens, a chemical called **acetylcholine** is secreted. This chemical transmitter crosses the synapse and induces an impulse in the adjacent neuron, or stimulates a muscle or gland. Once the impulse has been transmitted, an enzyme called **cholinesterase** breaks down the acetylcholine, returning the synapse to its resting state. The cholinesterase clears the system before another nerve transmission occurs.

Some insecticides, notably pyrethroids and organochlorines, act by disrupting transmission of electrical impulses along the axons. These insecticides act as **axonic poisons**. Organophosphates and carbamates kill in a different manner. These insecticides inhibit or tie up cholinesterase, causing a buildup of acetylcholine in the synapses and a malfunction of the transmitting system. Exposure to these **synaptic poisons** results in rapid nerve firing, tremors and convulsions, paralysis, and death.

Some insecticides have other modes of action. **Physical poisons** block a metabolic process by physical rather than biochemical means. Oils, for example, kill mainly by clogging the insects' respiratory system and suffocating them. Insecticidal soaps remove the protective waxes on the insects' cuticle and disrupt cell membranes. Insect growth regulators (IGRs) kill insects by disrupting the molting process.

Measuring Pesticide Toxicity

Used carelessly, insecticides can be hazardous to humans. Professional applicators should understand the principles of toxicity and the distinction between toxicity and hazard (see Chapter 5). **Toxicity** is the inherent poisonous potency of a substance under controlled conditions. The manufacturer must provide an estimate of a pesticide's inherent toxicity to humans before it can be registered and sold. These tests obviously cannot be performed on people, so test animals such as mice, white rats, or rabbits are used. Groups of test animals are exposed to a series of increasing dosages and mortality is determined. Toxicity is based on feeding (**oral**), skin application (**dermal**) and respiratory (**inhalation**) tests. The amount of the technical pesticide that will kill 50% of the test animals is referred to as the "**LD$_{50}$**" (Lethal Dose 50). The LD$_{50}$ is given as the number of milligrams of toxicant per kilogram of body weight. This is abbreviated as "mg/kg." Note that *the lower the LD$_{50}$, the more toxic the compound* (that is, a smaller dose was required to cause 50% mortality). The dermal LD$_{50}$ can indicate the relative degree of hazard which could result from skin contact during application. Oral and dermal LD$_{50}$

values will be listed on the product's **Material Safety Data Sheet** (**MSDS**). Again, these toxicity ratings usually correspond to the concentrated, formulated material, rather than the diluted spray solution.

In environmental studies where effects of pesticides on aquatic organisms are a concern, toxicity is often expressed as an **LC_{50}**, the concentration of pesticide in water that kills 50% of the fish or other test animals. LC_{50} values are usually expressed in parts per million (ppm) or parts per billion (ppb).

Keep in mind that the LD_{50} is a reference figure used to rank pesticide formulations according to their relative toxicity. Dose, dilution, length of exposure, and route of entry into a person's body are other important factors in estimating a pesticide's toxicity to humans.

Toxicity and Labeling

Pesticide law in the United States requires that all pesticide labels contain **signal words** in bold print that give the user an indication of the product's toxicity, and thus a measure of its potential hazard. Insecticides (and other pesticides) are grouped into four toxicity categories, each with its own signal word (Table 4.2). In addition to the signal words DANGER–POISON, highly toxic pesticides must have a skull and crossbones symbol. All categories also must bear the words "Keep Out of Reach of Children" on the label.

TYPES OF SYNTHETIC INSECTICIDES USED ON TURF

Organophosphates

Many of the insecticides currently registered for turf and landscape use belong to this category. Such familiar insecticides as diazinon, chlorpyrifos (Dursban®), trichlorfon (Dylox®, Proxol®) and acephate (Orthene®) are organophosphates (also called "OPs"). Some OPs (e.g., malathion) have relatively low mammalian toxicity, but as a group they are generally the most toxic of all turfgrass pesticides to humans and other vertebrates. Organophosphates are chemically unstable or nonpersistent, meaning that the residues break down into nontoxic compounds within a few hours, days, or weeks. Thus, proper timing is important when controlling insects with OPs.

Organophosphates are effective against a wide range of plant-feeding insects. A few also have some activity against mites. Some OPs (e.g., acephate) are translocated systemically within plants, a feature that is useful against sap-sucking insects such as aphids and leafhoppers. Organophosphates kill by both ingestion and contact. Unfortunately, they are generally at least as toxic to beneficial insects such as predators and honeybees as they are to pests. Some OPs are highly toxic to birds and earthworms (see Chapter 7), whereas others are less toxic to these groups.

Organophosphates are nerve poisons. They kill by interfering with cholinesterase, the enzyme that helps to regulate the transmission of nervous impulses. By tying up cholinesterase, OP insecticides cause the insect's nerves to be stimulated in an uncontrolled manner. The result is tremors, convulsions, paralysis, and death. Organophosphates should be used with caution because they affect our own nervous system in a similar manner. Repeated exposures can have cumulative effects over time. Some OPs used in agriculture are highly toxic to humans, but most of the ones used on turf are somewhat less toxic.

Carbamates

Carbamate insecticides used on turf include carbaryl (Sevin®) and bendiocarb (Turcam®, Ficam®). Another one, methiocarb (Mesurol®), is used for control of slugs and snails in gar-

Table 4.2. Signal Words Used in Pesticide Labeling. (Signal Words Reflect the Single Most Serious *Type* of Toxic Effect Achieved During Laboratory Testing of the *Formulated* Product; the Signal Word on a Given Label is Assigned on the Basis of Oral *or* Dermal *or* Respiratory Effects, but Generally Not All Three. Signal Words May Also be Based on Eye Irritation.)

Signal Word	Toxicity Class	Oral Toxicity		Dermal Toxicity	
		LD_{50} [a]	Amount Which Might Kill	LD_{50}	Skin Effects
DANGER	Highly toxic	Up to and including 50 mg/kg	A taste to a teaspoonful (≤5 mL)	Up to and including 200 mg/kg	Corrosive
WARNING	Moderately toxic	From 50 to 500 mg/kg	A teaspoonful to an ounce (5–30 mL)	From 200 to 2000 mg/kg	Severe irritation at 72 hours
CAUTION	Slightly toxic	500 to 5,000 mg/kg	An ounce to a pint (30–470 mL)	2000 to 20,000 mg/kg	Mild to moderate
CAUTION	Practically nontoxic	Greater than 5000 mg/kg	More than 1 pint (>470 mL)	Greater than 20,000 mg/kg	None to mild

[a] LD_{50} values are stated in mg of pesticide per kg of body weight. One mg/kg = one part per million (ppm); and 1 ppm can be thought of as 1 in. in 16 miles, or 1 drop in 50 gal, or 1 sec. in 12 days, etc.

Note: All pesticide labels must include the statement, *KEEP OUT OF REACH OF CHILDREN.*

dens. Carbamates have a similar mode of action to the organophosphates; however, cholinesterase inhibition is shorter and reversible, so that cumulative effects are less of a hazard. Like organophosphates, carbamates are fast-acting, with fairly short residual activity. They are effective against a wide range of insects. Because of its low mammalian toxicity, carbaryl is a commonly used home and garden insecticide. On the downside, carbamates are ineffective against spider mites and may even aggravate mite problems. They are highly toxic to earthworms, honeybees, and beneficial parasitic wasps. Bendiocarb is highly toxic to birds.

Pyrethroids

Pyrethroids are the fastest-growing group of turfgrass insecticides. These synthetic compounds mimic the chemical structure and activity of pyrethrum, a natural botanical insecticide. However, pyrethroids have certain advantages over natural pyrethrum. Like pyrethrum, they are fast-acting, with quick "knockdown" activity that rapidly incapacitates the target insects. However, poisoned insects are less likely to recover than with natural pyrethrum. Pyrethroids are active against a wide range of insect pests. Some, such as bifenthrin (Talstar®), lambda-cyhalothrin (Scimitar®), and fluvalinate (Mavrik®), also have activity against spider mites. Pyrethroids have longer residual than natural pyrethrum; most are effective on plant foliage for a week or more. Finally, while natural pyrethrum is too expensive to be used in commercial landscape management, synthetic pyrethroids can be used at about the same cost as organophosphates and carbamates. This is because they are used at very low rates, typically 0.05 to 0.2 lb of active ingredient per acre (56–224 g a.i./ha). Remember this when purchasing pyrethroids, because the cost per gallon seems quite high until you consider the low application rates. Most pyrethroids have relatively low toxicity to mammals and birds, but exposure to the spray mist may cause skin irritation in humans. Pyrethroids are highly toxic to fish. They are relatively insoluble in water and are not prone to leaching. They are nonsystemic (i.e., not translocated) within plants. Other pyrethroids used on turf include cyfluthrin (Tempo®) and permethrin (Astro®).

Phenyl Pyrazoles

Phenyl pyrazoles are a new class of insecticides with a unique mode of action — they block the passage of chloride ions through the gamma-aminobutyric acid (GABA) regulated chloride channel, thereby disrupting the insect's nervous system. The class is currently represented by fipronil (Chipco Choice®). Fipronil has both contact and ingestion activity. It is systemic when applied as a soil treatment, with long residual control. Fipronil is presently labeled for use against mole crickets and fire ants in turf.

Chloronicotinyls

Chloronicotinyls are a recently developed class of synthetic insecticides whose mode of action resembles that of the natural botanical product nicotine. The class is currently represented by a single compound, **imidacloprid**. Imidacloprid (Merit®) is a broad-spectrum, long-residual insecticide that is effective at low rates. It is used to control soil- and crown-inhabiting pests of turf, including white grubs, billbugs, and annual bluegrass weevil. It kills by both contact and ingestion. Imidacloprid is highly systemic, so soil applications are taken up by the roots and translocated within the plant. This makes it effective against a variety of sucking insects on ornamentals. Its primary mode of action is post-synaptic blockage of the nicotinic acetylcholine receptor sites of the insect nerve. This disrupts operation of the nervous system, resulting in death. Because of its novel mode of action, imidacloprid is effective against insects that have become resistant to other classes of insecticides. Imidacloprid has relatively low mammalian toxicity and generally good environmental characteristics.

Organochlorines

Organochlorines were the main insecticides used during the 1950s and 1960s. Chlordane, DDT, and dieldrin were widely used in landscape settings until environmental and human safety concerns forced their cancellation. These compounds had extremely long persistence in the environment as well as high fat solubility — a combination that resulted in accumulation of residues in animal tissues, including body fat and milk. Some were also found to be mildly carcinogenic. A few organochlorines are still used for controlling landscape pests. These include dicofol (Kelthane®), used against mites, and lindane for borer control in woody plants. The chemical structure of the latter two compounds is such that they are not prone to the aforementioned problems. Organochlorines function as nerve poisons, acting on the nerve axon, as do pyrethroids. Despite their long history of use, the exact mode of action is still not completely understood.

BIORATIONAL INSECTICIDES

The term "**biorational insecticide**" has come into favor in this era of environmental awareness and concerns about potential side-effects of pesticides. The term is derived from two words, biological and rational, suggesting pesticides of natural origin that have few or no adverse effects on nontarget organisms or the environment. In reality, there is no legally clear, absolute definition of biorational. The EPA regards biorational pesticides as having different modes of action than conventional pesticides, with greater selectivity and lower risks to humans, wildlife, and the environment. As restrictions on conventional insecticides mount, biorationals will undoubtedly play a bigger role in turfgrass management.

These products do not kill insects in the same manner as conventional, broad-spectrum insecticides. Some biorationals are much more effective against some pests than others. Thus, accurate identification of the target pest may be more important with biorationals than with conventional insecticides. Turf managers should understand the strengths and limitations of these products, and what special conditions must be met in order to use them successfully.

Botanicals

Botanical insecticides are extracted from plants. The active ingredients are substances that the plants themselves use in their defense against insects. Despite the perception that these "natural" products must be safer than synthetic pesticides, some botanical insecticides (e.g., nicotine) are actually quite toxic to humans. Others (e.g., pyrethrins) can cause severe allergic reactions in some people. Nevertheless, two botanical insecticides see occasional use against certain turfgrass insect pests.

Azadirachtin (Neem). Azadirachtin is extracted from seeds of the neem tree, which originated in India and Burma. When azadirachtin enters the insect, either through contact or ingestion, it acts as a growth regulator by interfering with the activity of ecdysone, the key molting hormone. Affected insects are unable to complete the molting process and usually die a few days after exposure. Azadirachtin is also a feeding deterrent for some insects. Because its mode of action is specific for insects, azadirachtin has low toxicity to humans, pets, or wildlife. At present, several products containing azadirachtin (BioNeem®, Turplex®, Azatin®) are available for use against insects on turf or ornamentals. Azadirachtin will give some control of turf-infesting caterpillars such as sod webworms, cutworms, and armyworms. The key to successful use is to monitor the pest and apply the material when the larvae are young and actively growing.

Pyrethrum. Pyrethrum is a natural insecticide extracted from flower petals of certain tropical *Chrysanthemum* species. It is used in household aerosol insect sprays because it has rapid "knockdown" capability against flying or crawling insects. However, unless it is formulated with a synergist such as piperonyl butoxide, many of the stunned insects soon recover to full activity. Pyrethrum breaks down quickly in the presence of sunlight, which is a desirable feature when treating home-grown vegetables or fruits close to harvest. However, because of its short residual and high cost, pyrethrum is not very useful against turf insects. Some people are quite allergic to pyrethrum.

Microbial Insecticides

Bacillus thuringiensis **(Bt)**. *Bacillus thuringiensis* is the most widely used microbial insecticide on urban landscape plants. Because of its low toxicity, Bt is well-suited for the home and garden market. Bt is a soil bacterium, common in nature, and several strains have been found that are toxic to insects. Each strain has specific activity against a limited range of pests. Bt can be readily grown on artificial media, making it fairly inexpensive to produce. Several companies sell products containing the *kurstaki* strain (*B. thuringiensis* var. *kurstaki*) under different trade names, such as Dipel®, Caterpillar Attack®, Thuricide®, and Javelin®. These products are specific for caterpillars (larvae of butterflies and moths). Products containing another strain, *B. thuringiensis* var. *tenebrionis,* are effective against elm leaf beetles and certain other leaf beetles on shade trees. Yet another recently discovered strain, *B. thuringiensis japonensis* strain Buibui, is active against root-feeding white grubs.

How Bt kills insects is fairly well understood. The bacteria contain insecticidal proteins, called delta-endotoxins, which form crystals within the sporulating cells. When the bacteria are eaten by a susceptible insect, the crystals dissolve and the toxins bind to specific receptor sites in the gut lining, causing rapid paralysis of the gut. The insect stops feeding as the gut wall deteriorates. Death of insects that have ingested Bt products often takes several days, usually by starvation. Older larvae are generally much less susceptible than are young larvae. Some species of caterpillars are resistant to Bt because their gut pH is too high to allow the toxic protein crystals to dissolve. The limited range of activity shown by each strain of Bt is related to an inability of its toxic proteins to bind to the gut of nonsusceptible insects.

Conventional Bt products are designed to be mixed with water and sprayed on foliage for short-term control of caterpillars. They are applied with conventional equipment. *Bacillus thuringiensis* has no direct adverse side effects on wildlife or pets, and it is considered essentially nontoxic to humans. This is useful for landscape applications where spray drift might occur. Bt is effective for control of young bagworms, tent caterpillars, and other leaf-feeding caterpillars on trees and shrubs. The keys to success are to treat when the larvae are still small, and to get good coverage on the underside of leaves.

Although they are labeled for use against sod webworms, cutworms, and other turf-infesting caterpillars, Bt products are not widely used on turf. One reason for this is their short residual. Bt is degraded by direct sunlight, so that activity may be lost in a day or two. Other limitations include slow action, lack of contact activity, and inability to kill larger larvae. Success with Bt requires close monitoring and application when the larvae are small. Multiple treatments will be needed if egg hatch is extended. If you use Bt against webworms or cutworms, try to treat late in the day. That way, these night-active pests will feed on the material before any degradation by sunlight occurs. Several companies are developing Bt insecticides in which the protein toxins are encapsulated to protect them against rapid degradation in the field. These new, more persistent Bt products should be on the market soon. Ongoing research seeks to incorporate genes encoding for delta-endotoxins into plants, so that the plants themselves will produce Bt toxins and gain extended protection from insects.

The newest Bt strain to be developed is Bt *japonensis* strain Buibui. This strain provides good control of Japanese beetle, northern and southern masked chafers, and green June beetle grubs. Grubs of May beetles (*Phyllophaga* spp.) and black turfgrass ataenius seem to be somewhat less sensitive. The material is applied as a drench or spray and watered in, as with conventional soil insecticides. Bt Buibui appears to be nontoxic to humans, pets, wildlife, and other nontarget species. Microbial insecticides containing Bt Buibui are presently being developed.

Milky disease bacteria. Dust formulations containing spores of *Bacillus popilliae* Dutky, the causal agent of milky disease, have been marketed for many years for control of Japanese beetle grubs. Use and limitations of these products are discussed in Chapter 8 (see Japanese Beetle — Management).

Fungus-based insecticides. *Beauveria bassiana* (Balsamo) is a naturally occurring fungus that infects chinch bugs and several other turfgrass insects. This fungus has been associated with natural collapse of chinch bug populations under certain conditions, namely hot, humid weather and high moisture levels. Spores of *Beauveria* adhere to the insect cuticle. Upon germination, the fungus penetrates through the body wall, killing the victim. Infected insects become covered with a mass of white, cottony fungus that later sporulates on the surface of the carcass. A commercial product containing *Beauveria* fungus, called Naturalis®-T (Troy Biosciences, Inc., Phoenix, Arizona) has been marketed for control of chinch bugs, white grubs, mole crickets, and certain other pests. At present, fungus-based insecticides have not been adequately tested to say what level of control they may provide, and under what conditions.

Entomopathogenic nematodes. Entomopathogenic nematodes are microscopic roundworms that attack and kill insect larvae, reproducing within the dead hosts (Figure 4.2). These beneficial nematodes occur naturally in almost all soils. They are harmless to plants, humans, pets, and wildlife, and will not contaminate surrounding streams, lakes, or groundwater sources. No worker protection measures are necessary and the turf can be used immediately after treatment. Several nematode-based products have been developed for turf insect control. These products contain millions of nematodes suspended in a polymer gel (Figure 4.3). The nematodes are alive, but in suspended animation. They become mobilized once water is added. Entomopathogenic nematodes are seemingly well-suited for turf insect control. They attack a broad range of pests, can be mass-produced at fairly low cost, and can be applied with standard spray equipment. Because they are classified as predators rather than microbial insecticides, nematodes are exempt from EPA registration. This makes it much less expensive for companies to bring new nematode-based products to the market.

Under suitable application conditions, the infective-stage nematodes seek out insect larvae and pupae in the soil. They penetrate the victim and release a type of bacteria that are carried within the nematodes' bodies. The bacteria kill the infected insect, usually within a day or two. The nematodes then reproduce within the pest cadaver, releasing thousands of offspring which enter the soil to search out new insect victims (Figure 4.4).

Different species and strains of nematodes vary in their activity against different insect pests. *Steinernema carpocapsae* is the species most often used in commercial formulations because it has proved easiest to mass produce on artificial media. It will kill insects that inhabit the upper soil or thatch, such as billbugs, sod webworms, cutworms, and armyworms. However, it has limited mobility, making it an erratic performer against white grubs, which live deeper in the soil. Two other nematodes, *Heterorhabditis bacteriophora* and *Steinernema glaseri*, work better against grubs because they are more active and move down in the soil profile to seek out victims. Unfortunately, these relatively more grub-active species have proven harder to mass produce. Another species, *Steinernema riobravis*, is active against mole crickets (see Mole Crickets — Management, Chapter 8).

Nematode-based products will give poor results unless certain environmental conditions are met. Nematodes move over soil particles on thin films of water. They cannot survive in dry soils. They are also extremely sensitive to heat and sunlight, and will perish in a matter of minutes when exposed to full sun. Turf should be irrigated before treatment to thoroughly wet the upper soil, and irrigated again with at least 1/2 in. (1.3 cm) of water immediately after application to move the nematodes into the thatch and soil. Apply the nematodes in early morn-

Figure 4.2. *Entomopathogenic nematodes completely filling the body cavity of a recently killed white grub. Soon, the nematodes will emerge to seek out and destroy additional hosts (courtesy M. Klein, USDA).*

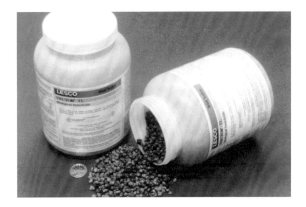

Figure 4.3. *Water-dispersible granules containing dehydrated entomopathogenic nematodes. Each pellet contains about 40,000 nematodes (courtesy Biosys, Inc.).*

ing or late in the day to prevent exposure to strong sunlight. It is important to follow the directions regarding storage and application rates. Nematode products containing *S. carpocapsae* can be effective against webworms and cutworms, but performance against grubs and other root-feeders has been erratic. Ongoing research may yield nematode products with better activity against white grubs.

Abamectin (Avermectin®) is a powerful insecticidal toxin derived from fermentation of *Streptomyces* bacteria. Products containing abamectin are currently registered for control of mites and leafminers on woody ornamentals (Avid®), and as a fire ant bait (Affirm®).

Spinosad is representative of a new class of insecticides called Naturalytes. It contains two fermentation-derived substances produced by the bacterium *Saccharopolyspora spinosa*, a naturally occurring microorganism. Spinosad acts as both a contact and a stomach poison, but is more effective if eaten by the target insect. Like pyrethroids, it has fairly short residual, and is active at very low use rates. Spinosad affects the insect nervous system in a unique manner, causing tremors, rapid paralysis, and death. It has low toxicity to humans and wildlife. Watch for spinosad-based insecticides being developed for the turf and landscape market. Registration of one such product, Conserve® SC, was granted in 1997. It has shown good activity against armyworms, fall armyworms, sod webworms, and cutworms.

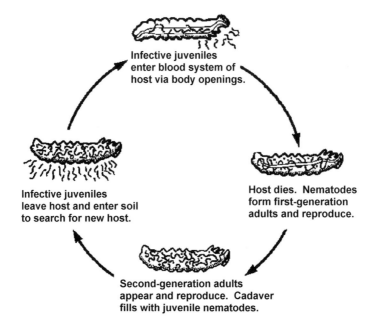

Figure 4.4. *Life cycle of entomopathogenic nematodes (courtesy Biosys, Inc.).*

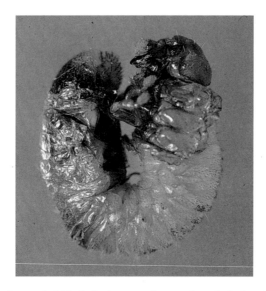

Figure 4.5. *Masked chafer grub killed during an abnormal molt induced by exposure to a molt accelerating compound (photo by W. Mesner).*

Other Biorationals

Molt Accelerating Compounds. Molt accelerating compounds (MACs) are a novel class of insecticides that kill by disrupting the normal molting process of target pests. One such compound, halofenozide (MACH 2®), mimics the action of ecdysone, the insect molting hormone. Ingestion of even a minute amount of halofenozide causes grubs and caterpillars to attempt a premature, lethal molt (Figure 4.5). Halofenozide has provided excellent control of Japanese beetle and masked chafer grubs, with 6 weeks or longer residual in the soil. European chafer and oriental beetle grubs may be somewhat less susceptible than other grub species. Halofenozide has also shown good activity against cutworms, sod webworms, and armyworms. MACs typically must be eaten by the pests to be effective. They are essentially nontoxic to humans, pets, and wildlife. Other MAC products are being developed for control of turfgrass insects.

Soaps. Commercial insecticidal soaps such as Safer® soap are derived from plant fats and oils. They kill insects by disrupting the exoskeleton and breaking down cell membranes. Soaps generally work best against small, soft-bodied insects such as aphids, scale crawlers, mealybugs, and young caterpillars, as well as spider mites. Soap sprays will not work unless the liquid contacts the target pests; they have little or no residual activity. These weaknesses limit their usefulness against most turf insects. Insecticidal soaps are no more toxic to humans than other soaps or detergents. Some soap formulations contain added components such as pyrethrins or citrus oils, which changes their toxicity level.

Oils. Highly-refined petroleum oils (**dormant oils** or **horticultural oils**) are used for control of small insects and mites on trees and shrubs. Oil sprays kill insects by suffocation and through cell membrane disruption. Petroleum oils are not used on turfgrass because of phytotoxicity problems, and because they have no residual activity.

INSECTICIDE FORMULATIONS

Insecticides are rarely used or applied in their pure or technical grade form. During manufacture, the active ingredient is mixed or formulated with inert ingredients to make the final product more convenient to handle, and safer and easier to apply. The mixture of active and inert ingredients is called an **insecticide formulation**. Some formulations, such as granules, are ready for use out of the package. Others, such as wettable powders and emulsifiable concentrates, must be diluted with water. Insecticides come in many different formulations; only the ones used by landscape managers are discussed here.

Dry Formulations

Several types of dry formulations are used for insect control in outdoor landscapes. On packaging for dry formulations, the number and abbreviation listed after the product name denote the *concentration* (% active ingredient) and *type* of formulation, respectively. For example, Tempo 75 WP contains 75% active ingredient in a wettable powder, while Mocap 5 G contains 5% active ingredient formulated on granules. Here are some strengths and weaknesses of these dry formulations:

Dusts (D). Dusts are dry mixtures of insecticide with some type of inert powder such as talc, organic flour, or pulverized clay. The percentage active ingredient in dusts usually ranges from 1% to 10%, and they are applied in the form purchased. Dusts are not used for treating turf because they leave an unsightly deposit, and because of problems with windborne drift and poor adherence to foliage. For these reasons they are also a poor choice for treating trees and shrubs. Dusts are often used for controlling wasps, ants, and other nest-dwelling pests because they can be puffed into cracks or the nest opening with an applicator.

Wettable Powders (WP *or* W). Wettable powders look like dusts but are designed to be mixed with water and applied as a spray. They are more concentrated than dusts, containing 15–95% active ingredient. A surfactant or wetting agent is included in the formulation so that the particles can be wetted and suspended in water. Spray mixes made with wettable powders should be frequently agitated to prevent the particles from settling out in the tank. There is less chance of injuring plants with WPs than with emulsifiable concentrates or oil sprays. To make them easier to handle and mix, WPs are sometimes sold in pre-measured packets that dissolve when tossed in water (Figure 4.6).

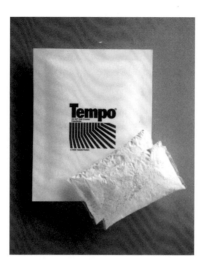

Figure 4.6. *Pre-measured packets that dissolve in the spray tank simplify handling and mixing of insecticides (courtesy Bayer, Inc.).*

Soluble Powders (SP). Unlike wettable powders, soluble powders dissolve in water, forming a true solution. Once they are dissolved, no further agitation is needed to keep them in solution. Most SPs are formulated in strengths of 50% or more active ingredient.

Granules (G). Granular formulations are made by incorporating the active ingredient onto coarse particles of a porous material like ground corncobs, vermiculite, clay, or even fertilizer pellets. The concentration of active ingredient typically ranges from 0.5% to 20%. Granules are applied by scattering or spreading them on the target site. Because granules are heavy, there is minimal airborne drift, but care must be taken not to scatter them on sidewalks and driveways bordering treated turf areas. After application, it is usually necessary to wet the granules by irrigation (or rainfall) to release the active ingredient. Granules are used mainly for soil treatment against such pests as white grubs.

Baits (B). Pesticides formulated as baits are used in outdoor landscapes for control of fire ants, mole crickets, slugs, and certain nuisance vertebrates such as voles and pocket gophers. Baits contain a food substance attractive to the pest, together with a stomach poison. The concentration of active ingredient is usually 5% or less.

Liquid Formulations

Many insecticides and miticides are formulated as liquids that are mixed with water and applied as sprays. Liquid formulations are usually sold in bottles, cans, gallon-sized jugs, or larger pails and drums. Emulsifiable concentrates and flowable formulations are the types most commonly used on turf and ornamentals. The trade name for liquid formulations is usually followed by a number and letter. The number indicates the concentration in *pounds of active ingredient per gallon;* the letter denotes the type of formulation. For example, a 1 gal jug of Dursban 4 E contains 4 lb of active ingredient formulated as an emulsifiable concentrate. Sevin 2 F contains 2 lb active ingredient per gal in a flowable formulation.

Emulsifiable Concentrates (EC *or* E). Emulsifiable concentrates are concentrated insecticides dissolved in oil or other solvents. They contain an emulsifier, or detergent-like substance, that allows the solvent and insecticide to be mixed in water within the spray tank. The emulsifier also reduces the surface tension of the spray, allowing it to spread and wet the treated surfaces. Most ECs form a white emulsion when mixed in the tank. Some ECs will remain mixed in water for a long time; with others the oil-insecticide droplets will settle out fairly quickly. It is therefore a good practice to give hand-held sprayers a brief shaking periodically during use. Remember that ECs contain a certain amount of oil solvent which, even though mixed with water, may damage plant foliage if applied when the temperature is above 85°F (30°C). Wettable powder formulations are less likely to cause plant injury under these conditions.

Flowables (F *or* L). Flowables are finely ground pesticide particles wet-milled with a clay diluent and water. This leaves the technical material with a thick, milkshake-like consistency. The formulation can then be mixed with water for spraying. Flowables have the same characteristics as wettable powders (e.g., settling out in the spray tank if not agitated), but are easier to handle during mixing.

SELECTED REFERENCES

Bennett, G.E., J.M. Owens, and R.M. Corrigan. 1988. Pesticides, pp. 55–100. In: *Truman's scientific guide to pest control operations.* Edgell Communications, Duluth, MN.

Marer, O.J., M.L. Flint, and M.W. Stimmann. 1988. *The safe and effective use of pesticides.* Univ. Calif. Div. Agric. Nat. Res. Publ. 3324.

Ware, G.W. 1994. *The pesticide book* (4th ed.). Thompson Publ., Fresno, CA.

Whitford, F., C.R. Edwards, J.J. Neal, A.G. Martin, and A. Blessing. 1992. Pesticides and personal safety. Purdue Univ. Coop. Ext. Serv. Bull. E-62.

5

USING INSECTICIDES SAFELY

THE TANGLED WEB OF COMPLIANCE

Pesticide use on lawns, golf courses, and sports fields is governed by an increasingly complex web of federal, state, and local regulations. Public scrutiny of pesticide usage is greater than ever before. Professional turf managers have an obligation to follow all label directions, and to use pesticides in a manner that safeguards public health and the environment. As an applicator, you have responsibility and legal liability for safety in treated areas during and after an application. Failure to abide by the law is not only wrong, but it can have serious financial consequences as well. You are also responsible for safe storage, transportation, and disposal of pesticides and their containers, as well as safety of your employees who handle pesticides.

The following is a brief overview of the major laws and regulations governing pesticide use on turf. This chapter cannot possibly cover all of the compliance issues — there are too many state and local variations. Turf managers who apply pesticides, or who supervise others who do so, must become familiar with their own local codes and laws. Ignorance of pesticide laws can put you in a situation that will result in heavy fines, imprisonment, or both.

Application Restrictions

On the federal level, use of pesticides on lawns, golf courses, and sports fields comes under the umbrella of the **Federal Insecticide, Fungicide, and Rodenticide Act (FIFRA)**, which regulates a multitude of issues ranging from manufacture to final disposal. FIFRA has been amended several times to expand the protection of pesticide applicators, the public, and the environment. Its major provisions include:

1. All pesticides must bear a label which lists the manufacturer's name and address, name, brand, and trademark of the product, an ingredient statement and net contents, an appropriate warning statement, and directions for safe use.
2. The federal Environmental Protection Agency (EPA) must register all pesticides and pesticide uses. The manufacturer must provide scientific evidence for the product's safety and effectiveness before it may be registered.

3. All pesticides must be used only as directed on the labeling. Applicators who use pesticides in a way that is "inconsistent with the labeling" are subject to penalties.
4. All pesticides registered with the EPA will be designated as either unclassified, or as restricted-use. Anyone who applies restricted-use pesticides must be certified in the state in which he or she works.
5. States may register pesticides on a limited basis when intended for special local needs.
6. States may establish stricter standards governing pesticides, but not more lenient ones.

If you violate FIFRA, you are subject to civil penalties which can be as high as $5,000 for each offense. Before the EPA can fine you, you are entitled to a local hearing. Some violations of the law may also subject you to criminal penalties of as much as $25,000 or one year in prison, or both. States may establish higher penalties.

Pesticides designated by the EPA as **unclassified** (formerly called **general-use pesticides**) are ones that can be sold without a permit and can be used by anyone. The EPA may classify a product as a **restricted-use pesticide** if it could cause harm to humans or the environment unless it is applied by a certified applicator who has the knowledge to use these pesticides safely. Only a **certified applicator** may use or supervise the use of restricted-use pesticides. To become certified, you must pass a test as evidence of your competency to handle and use these pesticides safely. Individual states usually handle certification. In most states, there is a special subdivision for commercial applicators who perform pest control on turf and ornamentals. Your state Cooperative Extension Service provides training programs and has study materials to prepare you for certification. Many states require that lawn applicators pass a test regardless of which categories of pesticides they apply.

The **Occupational Safety and Health Administration (OSHA)** also regulates pesticide usage because of the potential hazards to applicators. These laws require employers to have a written hazard communication plan, and to keep a material safety data sheet (MSDS) for each pesticide handled by employees. The manufacturer provides the MSDS sheet describing the chemical, its hazards, and what to do in the event of an emergency, but the *employer* must ensure that employees are made aware of and follow the guidelines for application, including the use of protective clothing. Failure to comply with these laws could make a golf course or business legally liable for poisoning or other adverse health effects that workers may have incurred on the job.

The EPA strengthened its regulations to protect agricultural workers and pesticide handlers by issuing the **Worker Protection Standard** (WPS) in 1992. This law includes provisions for posting notices about applications, specifies minimum waiting periods for reentering treated areas, and strengthens requirements for training workers in pesticide safety. The WPS does *not* cover pesticides applied on plants in ornamental gardens, parks, golf courses, and public or private lawns and grounds that are intended only for decorative or environmental benefit. The WPS *does* cover pesticide applications on commercial sod farms.

The purpose of the **Endangered Species Act** is to prevent pesticides from harming endangered or threatened plants or animals, or their habitats. The EPA consults with the U.S. Fish and Wildlife Service to determine which pesticides could potentially endanger these species. New provisions of this law require that labels of specified pesticides list the counties where endangered species occur. Individual county map bulletins contain a map showing the area within a county where pesticide use is restricted to safeguard a protected species. Users of targeted pesticides must comply with these restrictions in all listed counties in which they operate.

Many states and communities have even stricter pesticide regulations than those of the EPA. Many communities require posting of signs or public notices on lawns or golf courses where pesticides have been applied. Some require *prior* notification of patrons and even neighbors.

Transport and Disposal of Pesticides

Methods for transporting or disposing of pesticides and their containers are also regulated by law. The **Transportation Safety Act** (1974) regulates shipping or hauling of hazardous materials, which under this law includes some pesticides. Warning placards or signs and a manifest of materials may be required on vehicles transporting such substances.

Federal regulations for disposing of a pesticide are usually listed on the product label. These rules are listed in the EPA's Code of Federal Regulations (CFR 40: 165.8). Open dumping or burning of pesticides is prohibited by FIFRA, and disposal of pesticides or other pollutants into sewers or surface waters such as lakes, rivers, or oceans violates the **Clean Water Act**. Many pesticides must be treated as hazardous wastes under EPA regulations. You must comply with state and local laws governing pesticide disposal. Most states have specially designated incinerators or landfills for this purpose. Procedures for dealing with pesticide spills are usually covered under state or local regulations.

HOW (AND WHY) TO READ A PESTICIDE LABEL

The statement "ALWAYS READ AND FOLLOW ALL LABEL DIRECTIONS" is the most important message in this chapter. This cannot be overstated. These words should serve as the professional's guide before he or she applies any type of pesticide.

Pesticide labels and labeling give you instructions on how to use the product safely and correctly. The information printed on or attached to the pesticide container is the **label**. **Labeling** includes the label itself, plus any brochures, leaflets, or other information provided by the manufacturer that accompanies the product when you buy it. *Remember, the pesticide user is bound by law to follow all directions in the labeling!*

Make it a habit to read the label:

1. *Before purchasing the pesticide.* Make sure that it is registered for your intended use, and that there are no restrictions that pose problems for use at your application sites. For example, some insecticides are registered for home lawns but may not be used on golf course fairways. Find out what protective equipment and special application equipment is needed.
2. *Before mixing and applying the pesticide.* The label tells you the correct rate, and how to mix and apply the product safely.
3. *When storing the pesticide.* The label tells how best to store the pesticide to prevent breakdown, contamination, or fire hazards.
4. *Before disposing of unused pesticide and empty containers.* The label tells how to dispose of excess pesticide, spray mixture, rinsate, or the container so you will be in compliance with state and federal laws.

An example of the format for a restricted-use pesticide label is shown in Figure 5.1. The example is keyed as follows:

1. **Product Name** (also called Brand or Trade Name). This is the name by which the pesticide is advertised.
2. **Active Ingredients**. Listed by either chemical name or common name. Must be stated as a percentage by weight or pounds per gallon of concentrate.
3. **Inert Ingredients**. Need not be named, but the label must show what percentage of the total weight they comprise.
   (4–6) *Precautionary Statements, including:*
4. **Hazards to Humans and Domestic Animals**. Warns you of possible hazards to humans, and pets or other domestic animals. Special precautions, including necessary protective equipment, appear here.

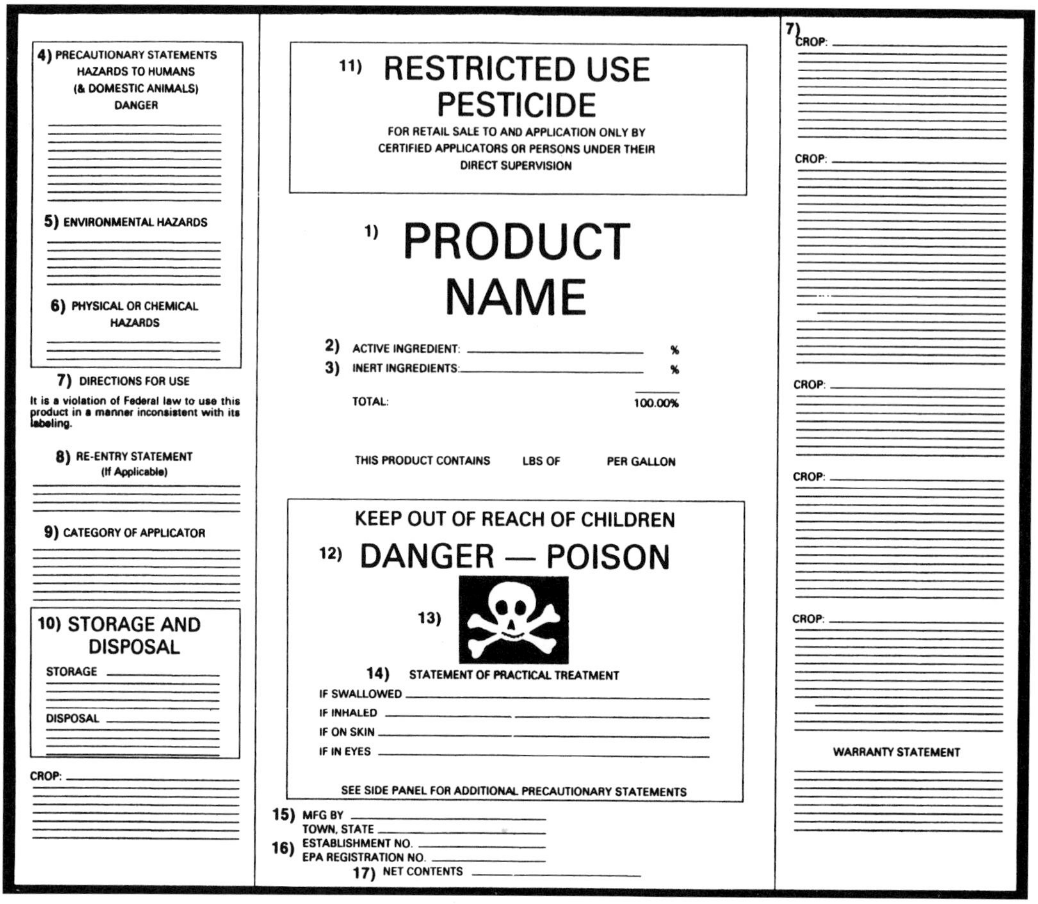

Figure 5.1. Components of a restricted-use pesticide label as required by law. See text for explanation of numbers (from U.S. EPA).

5. **Environmental Hazards**. Watch for special warning statements about hazards to birds, fish, wildlife, honeybees, endangered species, and surface or groundwater. Some products are classified as restricted-use because of environmental hazards alone.
6. **Physical and Chemical Hazards**. Warns of any special potential hazards such as fire, explosion, or chemical corrosion.
7. **Directions for Use**. These directions tell the proper way to use the product. Tells what pests the product is registered to control, where it can be used, when and how much to use, and in what form the product should be applied. This section also says whether the product is for general or restricted use.

   Misuse Statement. You are warned here that if you fail to follow label directions exactly, you are violating federal law.

   Worker Protection Standard (WPS). This part of the label will usually be called "Agricultural Use Requirements" and states that you must comply with WPS requirements if you are affected by WPS (e.g., on sod farms).
8. **Reentry Statement**. Tells how long you must wait before people can reenter a treated area without appropriate protective clothing. It is illegal to ignore reentry intervals. Some states set reentry intervals that are not specified on the label — you are responsible to determine whether one has been set.
9. **Category of Applicator**. If required for this product, this section will limit use to certain categories of commercial applicators.

10. **Storage and Disposal Directions**. All pesticide labeling contains some instructions for storing and disposing of the pesticide and its container. State and local laws vary, however, so the labeling usually does not give exact disposal instructions.

11. **Classification Statement and "Restricted-Use Pesticide" Block**. Labels for all restricted-use pesticides will state "Restricted Use Pesticide" in a box at the top of the front panel. Below this heading there is usually a statement describing the reason for the restricted-use classification, and the category of certified applicator who can purchase and use the product. For example, the label for isazofos (Triumph® 4 E) states:

    "RESTRICTED USE PESTICIDE For retail sale to and use only by certified applicators or persons under their direct supervision, and only for those uses covered by the certified applicator's certification. Restricted due to avian, fish, and aquatic organism toxicity."

    Unclassified pesticides have no such designation on the product label.

12. **Signal Words.** A signal word — DANGER, WARNING, or CAUTION — must appear in large letters on the front of the pesticide label. Signal words indicate how acutely toxic the undiluted product is to humans.

    DANGER — This word signals you that the pesticide is highly toxic. A taste to a teaspoon of the undiluted product, if swallowed, could kill you. Any product that is highly toxic orally, dermally, or through inhalation, or that causes severe eye damage or skin burning will be labeled DANGER. Pesticides in this group usually are restricted. Most of these pesticides have the word POISON printed in red and the skull and crossbones symbol on the label. Products that carry the DANGER signal word solely because of skin and eye irritation potential will not carry the word POISON or the skull and crossbones symbol.

    WARNING — This word signifies that the product is moderately likely to cause acute illness from oral, dermal, or inhalation exposure, or that it causes moderate skin or eye irritation. Swallowing as little as a teaspoon to a tablespoon of the undiluted product might kill you.

    CAUTION — This word signals you that the product is slightly toxic or relatively nontoxic. The pesticide has only slight potential to cause acute illness from oral, dermal, or inhalation exposure. The skin or eye irritation it would cause, if any, is likely to be slight.

13. **Skull and crossbones** symbol that alerts you to highly toxic pesticides.

14. **Statement of Practical Treatment**. This section outlines emergency first aid measures in case of exposure or poisoning. Typical statements include: "In case of contact with skin, wash immediately with soap and water," or "If swallowed, induce vomiting." You are told what types of exposure require medical attention. All DANGER labels and some WARNING and CAUTION labels have a statement for doctors describing appropriate medical procedures for poisoning emergencies. They may also list an antidote. *In cases of possible poisoning, always take the pesticide label to the attending physician.*

15. **Name and Address of Manufacturer**. Manufacturers often, but not always, also list an emergency contact telephone number.

16. **Registration and Establishment Numbers**. The registration number appears on the label and shows that the pesticide has been granted registration by the EPA. The establishment number identifies the factory where the product was manufactured. It may be on either the pesticide label or container.

17. **Net Contents**. Tells how much formulated product is in the container.

USING PESTICIDES SAFELY

Most insecticides kill insects by acting as nerve poisons. Our nervous system is similar in many respects to that of insects, so many insecticides also have the potential to be harmful or toxic to humans. Other insecticides are less likely to cause internal poisoning, but can nevertheless be harmful by irritating the eyes or skin. Fortunately, we can avoid these harmful effects from insecticides by reducing or eliminating exposure.

Toxicity versus Hazard

Toxicity is the capacity of a substance to cause harm to a living organism. Some pesticides are inherently more toxic than others. Toxicity is always dose-related: that is, the more toxic the pesticide, the smaller the dose required to cause harm. Conversely, even such relatively non-toxic substances as coffee or table salt can be harmful or fatal if consumed in very high doses. Whenever possible, choose pesticides that are least toxic to humans (i.e., ones that have high LD_{50} values).

It is important to understand the difference between toxicity and hazard. **Hazard** refers to the risk or danger of harmful effects when a pesticide is used or applied. Hazard varies according to **exposure**. The greater the exposure, the more danger there is in using a given pesticide. Therefore, the hazard or risk associated with using a pesticide depends on both the toxicity of the product *and* the probability of exposure. An experienced professional can use moderately toxic products with little hazard, whereas an untrained homeowner might use an over-the-counter product in a hazardous way. The hazards associated with pesticides can be reduced by using products with relatively low toxicity, and by taking precautions to minimize exposure. The degree of hazard associated with a pesticide application depends on:

- Toxicity of the active ingredient
- Concentration of the active ingredient
- Type of formulation
- Rate and frequency of application
- Method of application
- Persistence in the environment
- Type of protective clothing worn
- Care and judgement of the applicator

Dilution is one way that we reduce toxicity. For example, many pyrethroids bear the CAUTION signal word, indicating that the formulated product is only slightly toxic. They are diluted 2000- to 4000-fold with water before being applied on turf, so toxicity and hazard are further reduced. Formulation also affects the degree of hazard. Granular formulations, as compared with dusts or liquids, usually result in less exposure for the applicator. Exposure to turf users can be reduced by post-treatment irrigation, treating on days when a golf course is closed to play, and restricting access to treated areas until the spray residues are dry. Information regarding the toxicity and hazard of pesticides can be found on the pesticide labels and material safety data sheets (MSDS). Remember, there are two factors in the hazard equation: toxicity *and* exposure.

$$\text{HAZARD (RISK)} = \text{TOXICITY} \times \text{EXPOSURE}$$

HARMFUL EFFECTS AND EMERGENCY RESPONSE

Routes of Exposure

Pesticides can enter a person's body in several different ways (Figure 5.2). The usual routes are **dermal** (absorption through the skin), **respiratory** (inhalation through the lungs), **oral** (ingestion by mouth), and **ocular** (through the eyes). Once inside, the pesticide may be picked up by the blood and transported to sites of action, including the nervous system, kidneys, liver, or lungs.

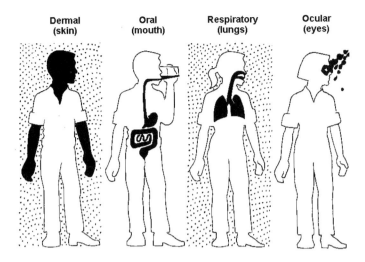

Figure 5.2. The four most common ways for pesticide exposure to occur (from Marer, 1988; with permission).

Dermal exposure is the most frequent route of exposure for pesticide applicators. The greatest risk occurs during handling and mixing of the concentrated product. Dermal exposures also result from wearing pesticide-contaminated clothing or protective gear, handling leaky hoses or spray guns, spraying in the wind, and by contact with sprayed surfaces before the residues have dried. Oil-based formulations (e.g., emulsifiable concentrates) tend to be absorbed the fastest, while wettable powders, dusts, baits, and granules are slow to penetrate skin. Pesticides will absorb through skin on certain regions of the body faster than others (Figure 5.3). The groin area and armpits allow particularly rapid absorption. Hot, sweaty skin absorbs more pesticide than dry, cool skin. To prevent dermal exposure, wear protective clothing when mixing or applying pesticides, launder the clothing often, keep your safety equipment clean, and wash promptly and thoroughly if you accidentally get pesticide on your skin.

The lungs provide a rapid point of entry of pesticides into the bloodstream. Landscape managers may have **respiratory exposure** when they inhale spray mist or drift. This may occur on windy days, or when spraying tree canopies overhead. Dusts or vapors may also be inhaled when you pour or mix concentrated pesticides. Respiratory exposure can be prevented by wearing a respirator in such situations.

Oral exposures may occur when a person or animal accidentally drinks a pesticide, eats or drinks contaminated foods or beverages, or accidentally splashes a pesticide into their mouth. This may also occur if one blows out clogged nozzles, starts siphonage of liquid concentrates by mouth (don't do this), or eats or smokes with pesticide-contaminated hands. Using a face shield during mixing guards against concentrated pesticide getting into your mouth or eyes. Don't store food in areas where pesticides are mixed or applied. Keep pesticides in their original, labeled containers. *Never transfer them into beverage bottles or food containers of any kind!* Mark the utensils that you use for mixing and measuring pesticides, and never use them for food preparation, serving, or eating.

Serious injury can result if pesticides enter your eyes. **Eye exposures** can be caused by splashing pesticides in your face during mixing, accidents with spray equipment, spraying on windy days without eye protection, or rubbing your eyes with contaminated gloves or hands. You can protect your eyes by wearing a face shield or goggles in situations where exposures might occur.

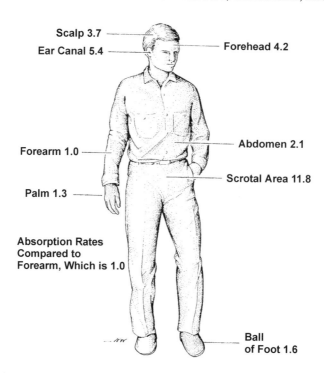

Figure 5.3. Rates of absorption of pesticides through the skin on different body regions, with forearm given a rating of 1.0 (from Hathaway, 1987; with permission).

Harmful Effects

Insecticides are designed to disrupt essential metabolic processes of insect pests. The degree to which a product is toxic to humans is determined, in large part, by whether its mode of action affects us in the same manner as it does the target pests. Products that affect insect-specific target sites (e.g., growth regulators that disrupt molting) generally have low toxicity to humans. Organophosphates and carbamates pose a greater hazard because they inhibit our nervous system in essentially the same manner that they affect insects. Insecticides can cause several types of harmful effects in humans: acute effects, delayed effects, chronic effects, and allergic effects.

Acute toxic effects are pesticide-related illnesses that appear soon (usually within 24 hours) after exposure. Many insecticides can cause acute poisoning if enough is swallowed, poured on the skin, or inhaled. Symptoms of acute insecticide poisoning are discussed later in this section. **Delayed effects** are illnesses that do not appear until some time after exposure to pesticides. Delayed effects may occur when a person has **repeated exposure** to insecticides over a period of days, weeks, or months. Recall that organophosphate and carbamate insecticides inhibit cholinesterase, an enzyme that is necessary for proper functioning of the nervous system in both insects and humans. A small exposure may cause no apparent problems. Cholinesterase is inhibited, but not enough to cause illness. But repeated exposures over several days or weeks may cause a cumulative reduction in cholinesterase levels. At that point, even a small additional exposure could trigger severe illness.

Repeated exposure to some pesticides is also suspected to cause **chronic effects**, that is, delayed or long-term health effects. Chronic effects may include deterioration of organs (especially the liver) and the nervous system, injury to the reproductive system, increased incidence of miscarriage, birth defects, or cancer. Fortunately, the registration process required by the EPA for all pesticides requires extensive testing with laboratory animals for both acute and chronic problems. Pesticides that are found to cause unacceptable risks from chronic exposure are not granted registration, or are removed from use. Numerous studies have shown that modern insecticides pose a very low long-term cancer risk — far less than hundreds of other frequently contacted substances and foods. Nevertheless, it is impossible to say for every pesticide what the possible chronic effects of too much exposure may be. As with acute toxicity, chronic toxicity is dose-related. Any chronic effects would show up first in persons with the greatest exposure (e.g., professional applicators). This is another good reason to use protective equipment, to read and follow label directions, and to treat all pesticides with respect. *Minimizing exposure is the key to pesticide safety.*

Some people can become sensitized to certain pesticides. After being exposed once or a few times without harmful effect, they develop a severe allergy-like response upon further exposure. These **allergic effects** may involve skin irritation, such as a rash or blisters, eye and nose irritation, or systemic effects, such as asthma. Some people seem to be more chemically sensitive than others. They develop allergies to many types of chemicals in their environment, including pesticides. Persons who develop such allergies may have to stop using those products. Reducing exposure through protective clothing and safety gear often alleviates the problem.

Symptoms of Poisoning by Organophosphate Insecticides

Organophosphate insecticides are generally the most toxic pesticides used by turfgrass managers. These products act as neurotoxins, interfering with proper signaling between nerve cells and between nerves and the muscles they activate (see Chapter 4 — Mode of Action). Normal functioning of muscles requires a nerve signal to activate a muscle contraction. When the nerve receives a signal from the central nervous system, the end of the nerve releases a chemical called **acetylcholine** at its site of contact with a muscle (the **neuromuscular junction**). The acetylcholine signals the muscle to contract. Acetylcholine is also used to transmit nervous impulses across **synapses**, the short gaps between one nerve and another. Normally, the acetylcholine is then removed by an enzyme, **cholinesterase**, and the muscle can then relax. If acetylcholine is not removed, the muscles remain contracted. Organophosphates are **cholinesterase inhibitors**; that is, they "tie up" cholinesterase and prevent it from clearing the acetylcholine from neuromuscular junctions. If the muscles that move the diaphragm are paralyzed, the victim cannot breathe. If the synapses are not cleared, control of the nervous system is lost. Organophosphates can inhibit cholinesterase irreversibly, leading to chronic loss. This makes them generally more dangerous than carbamates, for which the effects are more quickly reversed.

Two kinds of clues are indicators of pesticide poisoning. Some are sensations of which only the victim will be aware, such as blurred vision or nausea. These are **symptoms**. Other clues, like muscle twitches, pinpoint pupils, drooling, or passing out, may be evident to someone else. These are called **signs**. If you or your employees work with insecticides, you should know what your own symptoms might mean, and what signs of poisoning to look for in others. Some symptoms of pesticide poisoning, such as headache, fatigue, or stomach cramps, are similar to maladies you might experience from other causes. If you develop some of these symptoms, it does not necessarily mean you've been poisoned — it may be heat exhaustion, or the chili and beans you had for lunch. It is the *pattern* of symptoms and signs that distinguishes pesticide poisoning from other kinds of illness.

If a person has been poisoned by organophosphates, the symptoms and signs go through stages:

- Mild Poisoning
  - Fatigue
  - Headache
  - Dizziness

  - Blurred vision
  - Excessive sweating and drooling
  - Stomach cramps or diarrhea
- Moderate Poisoning
  - Unable to walk
  - Weakness
  - Tightness in the chest
  - Muscle twitches
  - Constriction of pupils in the eye
  - Earlier symptoms become more severe
- Severe Poisoning
  - Unconsciousness
  - Severe constriction of eyes ("pinpoint pupils") even in darkness
  - Muscle tremors or convulsions
  - Secretions from the nose and mouth
  - Breathing difficulty
  - Death (if not treated)

Symptoms of Poisoning by Carbamate Insecticides

Most of the carbamates used on turf have fairly low toxicity to humans. Nevertheless, carbamates are cholinesterase inhibitors and overexposure can be harmful. Carbamate poisoning produces the same signs and symptoms as with organophosphates. However, carbamate poisoning is usually easier for the physician to treat because the toxic effects are reversible. For this reason, most carbamates are somewhat safer to work with than organophosphates.

Medical Tests for Applicators

Because of irreversible inhibition, repeated exposure to organophosphates during the spray season can deplete an applicator's cholinesterase to dangerously low levels, making the person vulnerable to poisoning from any further exposure to either organophosphates *or* carbamates. Some companies require a program of cholinesterase tests for employees who apply insecticides on a daily basis. This consists of an initial blood test at the beginning of the spray season to determine a person's baseline level of cholinesterase. This will vary among individuals; everyone has their own normal level. Then, periodically during the spray season, the applicator is retested. If their cholinesterase drops below a critical level, the consulting physician may advise them not to work with insecticides until their level returns to normal. The body continually makes new cholinesterase, so levels should return to normal within a few weeks.

Toxicity of Pyrethroid Insecticides

Pyrethroid insecticides are neurotoxins, but they are not cholinesterase inhibitors. Rather, they disrupt the electrical signal as it travels within the insect's nerve. Pyrethroids are quite toxic to insects and fish, but most have relatively low acute toxicity to humans and other mammals. Thus, cases of pyrethroid poisoning are rare among turf and landscape applicators. Pyrethroids can irritate the skin, especially on the face, neck, and hands, for several hours after exposure to spray mist. The itching sensation usually disappears within a day. Pyrethroids can also irritate the eyes. These problems can be avoided by wearing protective clothing, including long sleeves, gloves, and boots for routine applications. Wear goggles or a full face shield when handling concentrates or when spraying overhead or in light wind. Some persons experience allergic-type reactions to pyrethroids, including respiratory reactions similar to asthma or intense hay fever.

WHAT TO DO IN CASE OF PESTICIDE POISONING

Regardless of the size of your operation, you should have a plan of action in case of an accidental pesticide poisoning. Identify a doctor or hospital that can be contacted in emergency situations, and post emergency telephone numbers and addresses. Also post the number of your state poison control center. Learn to recognize the pattern of symptoms that occurs with poisoning, and train your employees in emergency procedures.

Seek medical help promptly if you or a coworker experience illness or unusual symptoms while or after working with pesticides. Don't wait to become dangerously sick before getting to a doctor or clinic. Don't allow a person who may have been poisoned to drive — he or she may become dizzy, disoriented, or unconscious. If emergency medical help can't get to the victim, then have someone drive the victim to the hospital. *Bring along the pesticide label or container* — it contains instructions for the doctor regarding appropriate medical treatment.

Emergency First Aid for Pesticide Poisoning

Medical antidotes for pesticide poisoning should be given only by a doctor. Your job is to help stabilize the victim before medical help is available. The pesticide labeling will list specific first aid instructions for you to follow.

If you are alone with the victim, (1) *make sure the victim is breathing;* (2) *stop the source of pesticide exposure as soon as possible;* then (3) *call for emergency medical personnel.* If others are present, send someone to call for medical help.

First — Give mouth-to-mouth respiration or cardiopulmonary resuscitation (CPR) if breathing has stopped. Most deaths in pesticide poisoning cases are caused by respiratory failure. Victims will usually recover if the supply of oxygen to the body can be maintained. Then, take steps to prevent further exposure to the pesticide:

Pesticides on the Skin. Wash the pesticide off the victim as quickly as possible. Get the contaminated clothing off — this is no time for modesty!

- Remove contaminated clothing and drench the skin with clean water. Use a hose, faucet, shower, or immerse the victim in a creek or pond.
- Wash skin and hair thoroughly with soap and water. A whole-body shower is best, if available.
- Dry the victim and wrap in a blanket or any clean clothing at hand. Don't allow the person to become overheated or chilled. Get the victim to a doctor.
- If the pesticide has burned the skin, cover immediately with a loose, clean, dry, soft cloth or bandage.
- Do *not* apply ointments, greases, or powders to skin injured by chemical burns.
- Keep victim flat, warm, and comfortable until medical help arrives.

Pesticide in Mouth or Swallowed. If a person splashes pesticide into their mouth, rinse with plenty of water. If a pesticide is swallowed, consult the pesticide label to determine whether or not to induce vomiting. *Do not induce vomiting unless the label says to do so.* There are some corrosive pesticides for which vomiting will cause additional harm. Do not induce vomiting if the victim has swallowed an emulsifiable concentrate or oil solution. These pesticides may cause death if inhaled during vomiting. Never induce vomiting in victims who are unconscious or convulsive.

If the label says to induce vomiting, fast action can mean the difference between life and death:

- Position the victim face down or kneeling forward. Don't allow the victim to lie on his back, because vomit could be inhaled and cause more damage.
- Put your finger or the blunt end of a spoon at back of victim's throat, or give Syrup of Ipecac (2 tablespoons [30 mL] followed by 1–2 glasses of water) to induce vomiting.

Regardless of whether or not vomiting is induced, get the victim to medical help immediately.
Pesticide in the Eye. Wash out the affected eye as quickly, but as gently, as possible. Use an eyewash dispenser, if available. If not, hold eyelids open and rinse with lots of clean, running water. Continue rinsing for at least 15 minutes. Do not use chemicals or medicines in the rinse water.
Inhaled Pesticides.

- Get victim to fresh air right away.
- Loosen tight clothing that would constrict breathing.
- Apply artificial respiration if breathing has stopped.
- If victim is convulsing, make sure he does not fall and strike his head. Pull the chin forward so that the tongue does not block the air passage. Watch the victim's breathing.
- Keep the victim quiet and warm until emergency medical help arrives.

Poison Control Centers and Sources for Emergency Information

Poison control centers have been established in each state and in many communities. These centers provide information regarding treatment of poisoning emergencies, including pesticides. This free service is available 24 hours a day, every day. Contact your local health department to find out the telephone number and location of the nearest poison control center. Post this phone number near the telephone, in service vehicles, and keep a copy in your wallet and first-aid kit. It could be a life-saver.

In case of a pesticide poisoning, tell the attending physician what pesticide was involved, or better yet, bring the labeling. Provide the telephone number of the poison control center in case the doctor does not have it at hand. Usually, these centers provide specific treatment information only to doctors. Thus, you should call the doctor or emergency medical team first, and call the poison control center only if you cannot reach a physician.

Most pesticide labels now list a 24-hour "hot line" telephone number to dispense information regarding emergency first-aid for poisoning. This is usually a toll-free number. Pesticide manufacturers in the United States have also established a 24-hour, toll-free "hot line" for emergency information for pesticide users and medical personnel. This is called the **CHEMTREC number**. This important service provides information on what to do in case of accidents with pesticides, including poisonings and spills. **The CHEMTREC emergency hot line can be reached by dialing (800) 424-9300.** It's a good idea to post this number in your pesticide storage and mixing area, and carry it in your service vehicles.

Another service is the National Pesticide Telecommunication Network (NPTN) from which you can get information about health effects of particular pesticides, as well as symptoms and treatment for pesticide poisonings. The NPTN number is (800) 858-7378. Finally, you can get specific information about pesticide poisoning from: National Clearinghouse for Poison Control Centers; U.S. Department of Health, Education and Welfare; Food and Drug Administration; Bureau of Drugs; 5401 Westbard Ave.; Bethesda, Maryland 20016.

PERSONAL PROTECTIVE EQUIPMENT

Personal protective equipment (PPE) is clothing and other gear that protects an applicator from being exposed to pesticides. It may include coveralls, chemical-resistant gloves, boots, hats, and aprons, protective eyewear, and respirators. *Employers are required by law to provide employees with all the PPE listed on the pesticide label for the job that they will be performing.* The applicator is legally required to follow all PPE instructions that appear on the label or labeling.

PPE protects you only if the pesticide remains on the outside of the material. Once an insecticide gets inside your clothing, coveralls, gloves, or boots, the PPE can make matters worse by holding the chemical against your skin. When this occurs, the insecticide is more likely to cause irritation or chemical burns, and more will go through your skin and into your bloodstream. Choose gloves, boots, aprons, and coveralls made from **chemical-resistant materials**. Chemical resistance means that pesticides will not pass through the material. Chemical-resistant gloves and boots are made from neoprene, butyl, nitrile, or natural rubber. Many different types and styles of lightweight, comfortable PPE are available through safety supply stores and catalogs, pesticide dealers, and garden and nursery supply houses (see Appendix 3).

To be of real value, PPE must be comfortable enough that it will be worn by applicators. Common sense, safety precautions specified on the labeling, and the task at hand will determine the degree of hazard, and the amount and type of PPE that is appropriate for the job. Showing up at someone's doorstep dressed like Darth Vader doesn't do much for reassuring the homeowner that the products that you are applying to their lawn will not harm their family. On the other hand, people who apply pesticides day in and day out have far greater risk of exposure than the public — a fact worth explaining to concerned bystanders.

Body covering. Any time you handle or apply pesticides, wear at least a long-sleeved shirt and long-legged pants (Figure 5.4). Normal apparel (that is, cotton or cotton/polyester blends) provides adequate protection for most turf applications. For an added degree of protection, water/soil-repellent finishes such as ScotchGuard® or Zepel® can be applied to normal work apparel. A moderately heavy application of these repellents has been shown to offer the same level of protection as olefin coveralls. The soil-repellent finishes need to be reapplied after each laundering.

Some pesticide labels require coveralls to be worn over your shirt and pants. Coveralls have the advantage of being easily removed if they become contaminated or when you finish the job. Cotton coveralls are comfortable, but they are hard to decontaminate. Also, they tend to wick and hold liquid pesticides against your skin. Disposable coveralls made from nonwoven, bonded fiber materials are better because they are both lightweight and chemical-resistant. This type of coverall is cheap enough to be thrown away when contaminated, eliminating the need for laundering. Reusable protective clothing made from neoprene, polyvinyl chloride, latex rubber, or similar materials is advisable when you are mixing and loading concentrated pesticides (Figure 5.5). Avoid the kind with a woven fabric lining — such linings absorb pesticides and are hard to decontaminate.

Gloves and Boots. For turf and landscape applicators, the greatest exposure to pesticides is usually on the hands and forearms, and lower body and feet. Unlined, chemical-resistant gloves and boots should be worn whenever you are mixing or applying insecticides. Avoid leather, fabric, or fabric-lined gloves (or ones with cuffs made from these materials) — they absorb insecticide and cannot be decontaminated. Similarly, leather or canvas shoes should never be worn alone — use unlined, pull-on boots made from rubber, latex, butyl, nitrile, or neoprene. These are easy to wash off when they are contaminated. Gloves should extend at least half-way to your elbows, and boots should be calf-high.

Always start out with clean gloves and footwear. Don't just grab whatever pair is lying around — it may already be contaminated. If you get pesticides inside your gloves or boots, take them off right away, wash your skin, and put on a clean pair. Keep an extra set or two with you and change whenever you think the insides have become contaminated. Sleeves should usually be outside of gloves to keep pesticides from running down the sleeves and into the gloves. For the same reason, many experts suggest that pants legs be worn outside of boots. If spray is being directed upward into a tree canopy by a spraygun, then gloves should be outside of your sleeves.

Headgear. Wear something to protect your head. A wide-brimmed, waterproof hat will protect your neck, eyes, mouth, and face from spray drift. Avoid hats with a leather or cloth

Figure 5.4. Minimum personal protective equipment needed by turfgrass applicators, including chemical-resistant boots, gloves, and long pants or disposable coveralls.

Figure 5.5. Personal protective equipment appropriate for mixing and loading many pesticide concentrates, including chemical-resistant gloves, boots and apron, eye protection, and respirator.

sweatband, as they are very hard to decontaminate. Plastic hardhats with a plastic sweatband are good for when you are spraying — they are waterproof and cool in hot weather. Always wear a hat when spraying overhead.

Chemical-Resistant Apron. Use a chemical-resistant apron or raincoat during mixing and loading of concentrated pesticides to keep splashes and spills from soaking the front of your coverall. Remember, the groin area is the site of most rapid dermal absorption of pesticides.

Eyewear. Wear goggles with indirect vents or a face shield when there is any chance of getting pesticides or spray mist in your eyes. Face shields attach to the visor of a plastic helmet or have a separate headband. Eye protection should always be worn during mixing and loading, and when working with pressurized systems. Be careful when opening tightly sealed containers that have been stored in a warm area. Pressure may have built up that could cause the material to spray in your face. Try to find eyewear with straps made of neoprene; elastic fabric straps absorb pesticides and are hard to decontaminate.

Respiratory Protection. Your lungs are much more absorbent than your skin. A **respirator** is a rubber mask that fits over your nose and mouth to protect you from breathing pesticide-contaminated air (Figure 5.5). Get the type that has replaceable cartridges and filters to remove dusts, particles, mists, and vapors. The product label will say whether you must use a respirator and, if so, what filters or cartridges to use. You *must* wear an approved respiratory device if the label directs you to do so. Supervisors are required by law to provide applicators with respiratory protection as specified on the pesticide label, and to train them in its proper use. Landscape applicators may need to use a respirator when mixing and loading insecticides (especially wettable powders and granules that produce dust), when exposed to spray drift, or when spraying trees. Keep the respirator clean, and change the cartridges at the specified intervals. Store the respirator in a zip-lock storage bag to keep it clean. Make sure that your respirator is ready to protect you, and is not a hazard itself.

Mixing Pesticides

Mixing is the process of diluting a pesticide concentrate to a much less concentrated form for use. Be extra careful when carrying, opening, and pouring concentrated pesticides. Any accident with the concentrate increases the hazard from exposure. Whenever handling concentrated pesticides, you should wear chemical-resistant PPE, including safety gloves, boots, goggles or a full face shield, and adequate protective clothing including an apron and/or coveralls (Figure 5.5). A respirator may be required to prevent inhalation of billowing dust or vapors. When adding concentrates to a spray tank, put one-third to one-half of the needed water into the tank before adding the pesticide. You should then triple-rinse the empty pesticide container or measuring device and add the rinsate to the tank before agitating and adding the final volume of water. Carry extra water on service vehicles for rinsing containers and measuring cups. It's also a good idea to mix all concentrates outside of the customer's premises or other sensitive areas to reduce possible liability in case of spills. Make sure that your application equipment is calibrated, and that you mix and apply the amount recommended on the label. Remember, it is illegal and unnecessary to apply insecticides at rates higher than those specified on the label.

Cleaning and Laundering Pesticide-Contaminated Clothing

Rinse off your rubber boots and gloves under running water before taking them off. Boots, gloves, helmets, goggles, respirators, and other bulky items can be hand washed in warm soapy water. Turn your boots and gloves inside out for drying, and then store them in plastic bags to keep them clean. Contaminated garments should not be reworn until they have been washed. Launder them often, preferably after each workday. The longer the contaminated clothing remains unwashed, the more difficult it is to remove the pesticides.

Don't allow your contaminated work clothes to be washed with the family laundry. It will cause other items to be contaminated. Keep your clothing in a plastic garbage bag or separate hamper or pail, and wash it separately. It is best to presoak contaminated clothing in hot water containing a heavy-duty liquid detergent. Let the presoak water drain, then refill with fresh water for the regular wash cycle. Limit the number of garments per load to maximize water volume, agitation, and dilution. Use a phosphate detergent or heavy duty liquid detergent, and hot wash water. Water temperature for the rinse cycle is less critical. Depending on the extent of contamination, two or three washings may be necessary. After washing heavily contaminated clothing, swab down the inside of the washer tub and run the washer through a cycle before using it for the family wash. Line drying is preferable to machine drying. Many insecticides break down in sunlight, and you won't have the potential for contaminating the dryer.

Persons handling and laundering the contaminated garments also need to protect themselves from exposure to pesticides on the clothing. Get rid of work clothes or leather boots that become heavily contaminated with moderately or highly toxic pesticides, especially concentrates. Studies have shown that such garments remain a hazard even after repeated washings. A good general rule is: "If in doubt...throw it out."

STORING, TRANSPORTING, AND DISPOSING OF PESTICIDES

Pesticide Storage

Pesticides should be stored in a locked and posted place, preferably a room or storage building set aside for this purpose. Children and unauthorized persons should not be able to reach them. The storage facility should have warning signs on doors and windows; posting of approved fire code signs may also be required by state or local laws. The facility should keep the pesticides dry, cool, and out of direct sunlight, and be well enough insulated to keep the chemicals from overheating or freezing. The storage place should preferably be of fire-resistant construction, with a floor of cement or some other material that will not absorb spilled liquids. It should have good lighting and an exhaust fan for ventilation, but should never be vented to other inside areas. Each storage site must have an immediate supply of clean water. A fire extinguisher should be available nearby, as well as materials to deal with any pesticide spills. Store all pesticides in their original containers. Don't allow the labels to be removed or to become unreadable. It's best to store liquid formulations away from dusts, granules, or baits.

Check all containers periodically for leaks or breaks. If one is damaged, you can (1) use the contents immediately at a rate and site allowed by the label; or (2) transfer the contents to a container that has held exactly the same pesticide; or (3) transfer the contents (with or without the damaged container) to another container that can be tightly closed. If possible, remove the label from the original container and attach it to the new one, or else mark the new container with the name and EPA registration number of the product, and get a copy of the label from the pesticide dealer or manufacturer (whose telephone number is usually on the label) as soon as possible. *Never transfer a pesticide to a container that might cause people to mistake it for food or drink.* Try to buy only as much product as you need for one spray season so you won't have a lot left over to store. Mark each container with the date of purchase before it is stored, and use older materials first. Keep a notebook with copies of the labeling and MSDS sheets, and an up-to-date inventory of the pesticides you have in storage. Finally, check your state and local laws regarding pesticide storage. You may be required to notify state and local officials or the local fire department about the location and amount of pesticides on hand.

Transporting Pesticides

The safest way to transport pesticides is in the back of a truck. Containers should be fastened down so there is no chance of breakage or spillage. Keep paper and cardboard packages dry, and keep all containers away from food and passengers. If pesticide is spilled in or from the vehicle, clean it up immediately. Never carry pesticides in the passenger section of your vehicle. They may give off hazardous vapors than can make you sick or affect your ability to drive. Leaks or spills may poison you or your passengers, and the residues are almost impossible to remove from the seat fabric. Whenever possible, transport pesticides in a locked compartment. Never leave unlocked pesticides unattended. You are responsible and liable if accidents occur.

Disposing of Pesticides

Because pesticides are poisons, they must be disposed of in specific ways that are outlined on the label. Disposal of pesticide containers and excess pesticide is regulated under the federal Resource Conservation and Recovery Act. Check with your EPA regional headquarters and state enforcement agencies concerning disposal rules and regulations in your state. Disposal generally must be done in specially designated landfills or special incinerators at a federally regulated toxic chemical disposal site. Most sanitary landfills are not suitable. The best way to dispose of excess diluted pesticides is to use them up as directed on the label. Container rinsates should be disposed of by adding them to the tank during the mixing process. *Do not flush pesticides down toilets, or pour them down drains or storm sewers!*

The best strategy to deal with excess pesticides is to plan ahead so as to avoid having them. Buy only as much product as is needed for one spray season. Mix only as much diluted pesticide as is needed for a job. If you have leftover pesticides in their original containers, you may be able to find another licensed applicator who can use them. Sometimes, the distributor will take back unopened containers. Otherwise, store them until they can be used. There are licensed pesticide disposal facilities in many states, but their services are usually expensive. Plan ahead to avoid costly and difficult disposal problems.

Disposal of pesticide containers also is regulated under law. Try to avoid the need to dispose of pesticide containers as wastes. Where possible, use soluble packaging (see Figure 4.6), use containers that are designed to be refilled by the pesticide dealer, or arrange to have empty containers recycled or reconditioned. Instructions for disposing of the container are generally given on the label. Containers for liquid concentrates should be **triple-rinsed** (or pressure-rinsed) to remove pesticide residues before disposal. To triple-rinse a container, first drain the contents into the spray tank for at least 30 seconds. Then, fill the empty container about one-quarter full with water, close it tightly, and shake or rotate it so the water rinses the inside completely. Pour the rinse water from the container into the mixing tank and repeat the rinse and drain sequence two more times. Alternatively, use a pressure rinse nozzle to rinse the inside of the container. Plastic or metal containers should be punctured after rinsing to prevent their reuse. They can then be crushed, if possible, to reduce disposal volume. Triple-rinsed containers are not classified as hazardous waste under federal law. They can be disposed of as regular trash in a sanitary landfill, but be sure to check state regulations. Bags or cartons that contained powders or granules should be completely emptied. You can then dispose of them as regular trash.

How to Deal with Spills

Pesticide spills range from minor leaks to major accidents involving dumping drums of hazardous material on public roadways, near waterways, or at other sensitive sites. All spills should be treated as emergencies and dealt with immediately. If anyone has been injured or contaminated, administer first aid and send for medical help before tackling the spill. Put on gloves, boots, and other PPE before contacting the spill or breathing its fumes. Keep a spill cleanup kit (Table 5.1) in your storage and mixing area, and in your service vehicles. *You can get advice on managing spills and other chemical emergencies by calling the Chemtrec number (1-800-424-9300).*

Your first objective should be to contain the spill as quickly as possible. Try to stop it at the source. If a small container is leaking, put it in a larger container such as a plastic drum or bag. If a spray tank is overflowing, turn off the inflow and try to cap the tank. Ruptured paper bags or cardboard packages with dry formulations can be patched with duct tape. Next, move quickly to confine the spill. For small spills of 1–2 gal (4–8 L) or less, you should have enough cat litter or dry absorbent (e.g., the type made for oil and gas spills on garage floors) to be thrown onto the spill. This will stop it from spreading, and soak up the liquid for later disposal. If you don't have absorbent products, shovel soil, mulch, sand, sawdust, bath towels, paper, or any other absorbent material onto the spill. If it continues to spread, dike it up with additional absorbent. Try to redirect the spill away from streams or other bodies of water. *Do not rinse it down a drain or storm sewer.* Once the spill is contained, shovel or sweep the contaminated absorbent into large plastic garbage bags or another leakproof container for disposal. Dispose of it as you would excess pesticides. Call your state pesticide regulatory agency for specific instructions. Dusts, wettable powders, or granules can be swept up with a broom and dustpan. Keep a supply of plastic trash bags on hand for such situations.

Table 5.1. Suggested List of Safety-Related Equipment Which Should be Carried in Vehicles of Commercial Lawn and Landscape Applicators. (Refer to the Text for the Use and Importance of Each Item [adapted from Bennett et al., 1988].)

Clean Water (2–3 gal.) and soap to wash contaminated skin

Safety and Emergency Response Guide Book

Fire Extinguisher (Type ABC)

Protective Clothing (all enclosed in separate, clean, sealed plastic bags), including:
  boots (waterproof and chemical-resistant)
  gloves (chemical-resistant)
  extra clothing (coveralls)
  respirators
  spare respirator cartridges
  goggles
  hard hat

Medical First Aid Kit, including:
  Band-Aids, compresses, adhesive tape
  1 oz. bottle of Syrup of Ipecac (to induce vomiting)
  small bottle of soap solution
  shaped plastic airway for artificial respiration
  teaspoon
  tongue depressors
  blanket (in sealed plastic pouch)
  drinking cup

Pesticide Spill Control Kit, including:
  absorbent (kitty litter, etc.)
  large plastic bags
  brooms and dustpan
  towels
  rags
  shovel
  detergent (for cleanup)

Index Card containing telephone numbers of local poison control center, emergency
  room or clinic, and Chemtrec

Spare Change for emergency telephone calls

Once you've collected as much of the spilled material as possible, take steps to decontaminate the spill site. Nonporous surfaces such as sealed concrete or tile can be washed with water and strong detergent. Commercial decontamination solutions are sold for this purpose. Soak up the wash solution with fresh absorbent, then sweep up the absorbent and dispose of it as excess pesticide. Do not hose down the area or allow the wash solution to run off the spill site. Porous surfaces such as soil, unsealed wood, or carpet may have to be removed and discarded as excess pesticide. Clean your PPE, wash yourself thoroughly, and launder clothing after finishing with the spill. Most state or local pesticide regulatory agencies require that you notify them of any substantial pesticide spill.

Special spill-control products are sold that form a gel as they absorb a pesticide. Once collected, this gel can be added to a spray tank, diluted with water, and used in a spray application, eliminating the problem of disposal.

If a spill is too large to handle, try first to contain the pesticide with soil, absorbent, or whatever means possible. Keep people away from the area and call, or send someone to call, the police and fire departments. Tell them the circumstances of the spill and what products are involved. Pesticide fires are especially dangerous because of the toxic smoke and fumes generated by burning chemicals. Carry a fire extinguisher (Type ABC) on service vehicles and keep one in the pesticide storage facility. Do not endanger your health by trying to fight a large pesticide fire. Evacuate upwind to a safe distance and call the fire department for help. However, don't allow them to hose down the spill unless an authorized person directs them to do so. If you spill pesticides on a state highway, call the state police or highway department immediately. If the spill occurs on a county or city road, call the sheriff, police, or fire department. Don't leave until responsible help arrives. If water is contaminated, notify state health officials and water quality authorities. By acting responsibly in the event of an accident, you are much less likely to face stiff fines or other penalties.

Less Is Better

When dealing with pesticides, a good rule of thumb is *"less is better."* The less pesticide purchased, stored, transported, mixed, applied, and disposed of, the better off you are from the standpoint of safety, liability, and compliance issues. Should a spill or other mishap occur, the ensuing problems will be less if smaller amounts of pesticide are involved.

Safety Training and Liability

Safety consciousness is important in every aspect of professional turf management. This requires a commitment to thinking, planning, and acting in a safe manner (Table 5.1). Hold regular meetings with your agronomic staff to discuss safety and emergency issues. Your employees should be training and retraining constantly in order to reduce the chances of pesticide-related accidents. If you or your organization is sued for a pesticide-related mishap, a key part of the legal defense is being able to document your commitment to safety. Thus, it is important to have clear policy guidelines, to conform to OSHA guidelines for providing a safe work environment for employees, and to keep written records documenting your safety training program.

ARE INSECTICIDES SAFE?

Public perception about the hazards of pesticides is often negative, and professional turf managers will encounter people who will question the safety of insecticides used on lawns and golf courses. You may wonder about this, too, reading about some of the potential hazards in this chapter. Are the benefits of insecticides worth the risks posed by these chemicals? Professional turf managers must be able to discuss this issue with clients and legislators, and to allay their concerns through logic and available scientific information.

First, we must understand that there is a small but vocal segment of society for whom the use of pesticides will never be acceptable. These people have decided that all pesticides are bad. Other people are **chemophobic**, having irrational fears of pesticides and other chemicals. Trying to convince these groups that insecticides have a role in turf management is a no-win situation. Fortunately, most people are open-minded about this issue and are willing to discuss their concerns. They can be reassured if you respond to their questions openly and professionally.

First, stress your commitment to responsible pesticide use. Assure them that you share their concern for safeguarding public health and the environment. Explain that pesticides will be used only as necessary, in the manner specified on the product's label. Explain that a pesticide can be labeled only after years of testing has shown that proper use will not pose an unreasonable risk. Do not claim that your spray program is "completely safe." From a legal standpoint, nothing is ever completely safe. Don't say that the pesticides you are using are "EPA-approved," as this implies that the government guarantees their safety. The Environmental Protection Agency does not approve or recommend pesticides; it evaluates, registers, and regulates them, establishing legal restrictions on their use. EPA registration does not mean that a pesticide poses no hazard — the professional applicator is responsible for safe use!

Some people are suspicious of pesticides because they are chemicals. Yet many useful, commonly encountered chemicals have the potential to be toxic if handled carelessly or abused. Ordinary table salt, caffeine, aspirin, cosmetics, paint, cleaning substances, and a host of other substances can be toxic or fatal if misused or consumed at a high enough dose. We are not exposed during ordinary use to enough of these chemicals to cause unacceptable risks or hazards. Even such highly toxic substances as gasoline and oven cleaners are safe to use if exposure is minimized. Whether or not a potentially toxic substance is harmful depends not only on how much one is exposed to, but also how often. Our body is capable of detoxifying small amounts of toxic substances at one time. For example, most people can drink three or four cups of coffee a day with no adverse health effects. But if you were to drink a month's worth of coffee at one time, that dose of caffeine might kill you.

What are the actual risks of using pesticides? Analyses of health and safety records show that pesticides account for relatively few fatal poisonings in the United States (on average, about 10–20 deaths per year). This includes all types of pesticides, including rodenticides. Most of the deaths are suicides. Others, unfortunately, involve young children who accidentally drink pesticides that were stored improperly within the home. Compare this with more than 50,000 deaths from traffic accidents, 3000 for swimming accidents, and an average of about 20–25 per year for scholastic football. Fatalities from pesticide poisonings occur about as often as deaths from dog attacks. The risk of dying from a bee sting or from hitting a deer with your car is much greater than by pesticide exposure. Anti-pesticide extremists lead the public to believe that droves of Americans are dying of pesticide exposure each year (Figure 5.6). This is simply not true.

What about potential chronic effects of pesticides, such as cancer? Scientific studies indicate that turfgrass insecticides present a very low long-term cancer risk, far less than hundreds of other frequently contacted substances and foods. The vast majority of cancer-causing agents (carcinogens) are not acute carcinogens, causing cancer from a single exposure. Rather, one must be exposed repeatedly before damage occurs, usually at a high enough level that the body does not have time to detoxify the residues or repair the damage. A good example is tobacco smoking. If you smoke a single cigarette, your body readily detoxifies the small dose of nicotine and tar, and there is little or no harm. Constant smoking, however, does not allow your body to recover, and cancer risks go up accordingly.

What causes human cancer? The Congressional Office of Technology Assessment commissioned one of the most extensive studies on this topic (Doll and Peto, 1981). They found that the leading causes of cancer, by far, are use of tobacco and poor diet (i.e., high fat; low fiber), followed by reproductive and sexual behaviors. Although lawn pesticides were not specifically examined, the authors concluded that "the occurrence of pesticides as dietary pollutants seems unimportant," and that cancer hazards from environmental pollutants (including pesticides) were negligible compared to other preventable causes. Although there is no scientific evidence that modern turf insecticides pose a significant cancer hazard, it is still good practice to minimize exposure whenever pesticides are used.

Are people at risk if they use a turf area shortly after an insecticide application? Bystander exposure may occur via (1) spray drift; (2) inhalation of pesticide that volatilizes from recently treated turf; or (3) contact of skin with residues on the grass, or on clothing that has contacted the grass (so-called **dislodgeable residues**). Several careful studies (e.g., Sears et al., 1987; Hurto and Yeary, 1993; Cooper et al., 1995) have addressed this concern. The results indicate that the greatest potential for exposure is during the first hour or two after application. Once a spray has thoroughly dried, volatilization and dislodgeable residues drop dramatically. These studies indicate that if reasonable reentry precautions are taken, exposure of turf users to pesticides is unlikely to even approach, let alone exceed, established acceptable levels.

Several common-sense practices will further reduce potential exposure to bystanders and turf users. Where possible, use products with low acute toxicity to humans. When it is neces-

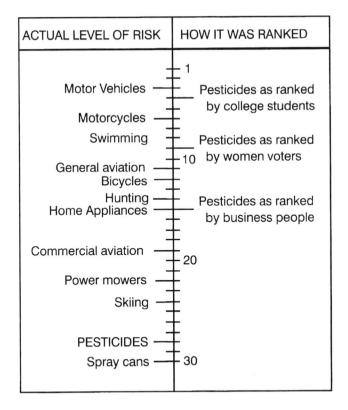

Figure 5.6. *Actual pesticide risk, and risk as perceived by the public (redrawn from Gold, 1990).*

sary to treat, do so on days when the golf course is closed to play, or in the evening. Post signs to discourage turf use until the application is thoroughly dry, whether or not required by law. Apply pesticides at higher spray volumes and use nozzles that emit coarser spray droplets to reduce airborne drift of mist. Use granular formulations to reduce pesticide contact with the turf canopy. Sweep granules off sidewalks and driveways. Avoid applying granules when the grass foliage is wet. When applying soil insecticides, immediate watering-in will reduce surface residues. Mow the turf before application to reduce pesticide residues in the upper foliage.

Occasional dental X-rays pose little hazard for the patient, but the X-ray technician always leaves the room to avoid constant exposure. For the same reasons, professional applicators should minimize personal exposure to pesticides. Wear protective apparel and use safe handling practices. You needn't be afraid of working with insecticides, but you should respect them.

SELECTED REFERENCES

Anonymous. 1991. *Applying pesticides correctly. A guide for private and commercial applicators.* U.S. Environmental Protection Agency, Washington, D.C.

Bennett, G.E., J.M. Owens, and R.M. Corrigan. 1988. Pesticides, pp. 55–100. In: *Truman's scientific guide to pest control operations.* Edgell Communications, Duluth, MN.

Cooper, R.J., J.M. Clark, and K.C. Murphy. 1995. Volatilization and dislodgeable residues are important avenues of pesticide fate. *U.S. Golf Assoc. Green Section Record* 33:19–22.

Doll, R. and R. Peto. 1981. The causes of cancer: quantitative estimates of available risks of cancer in the United States. *J. Nat. Cancer Inst.* 66:1192–1265.

Gold, R. 1990. Pesticide safety, pp. 1075–1093. *In* A. Mallis (Ed.). *Handbook of Pest Control.* Franzak & Foster Co., Cleveland, OH.

Hathaway, L.R. 1987. *Agricultural safety*. Deere & Co., Moline, IL.

Hurto, K.A. and R.A. Yeary. 1993. Exposure to pesticides following application to turfgrass sites. *Internat. Turfgrass Soc. J.* 7:127–133.

Marer, P.J., M.L. Flint, and M.W. Stimmann. 1988. *The safe and effective use of pesticides*. Univ. California Statewide Integrated Pest Management Program. Div. Agric. & Nat. Res. Pub. 3324.

Sears, M.K., C. Bowley, H. Braun, and G.R. Stephenson. 1987. Dislodgeable residues and persistence of diazinon, chlorpyrifos, and isofenphos following their application to turfgrass. *Pest. Sci.* 15:353–360.

Shetlar, D. 1993. The plain facts. *Lawn and Landscape Maintenance*; Nov. 1993, pp. 37–44.

Ware, G.W. 1994. *The pesticide book* (4th ed.). Thompson Publ., Fresno, CA.

6

USING INSECTICIDES EFFECTIVELY

The arsenal of insecticides available to turf managers changes as new products are developed and others are phased out, but the principles for controlling insect pests remain the same. Regardless of the insecticide, good control depends on identifying the pest, knowing its life cycle and habits, and then placing the insecticide in the appropriate target zone at the correct time. While this seems simple enough, many factors in the turf environment can cause insecticides to perform poorly. Even when the product, rate, and timing are correct, insecticides can still be deactivated in the spray tank, degraded by heat and sunlight at the turf surface, trapped in the thatch, or broken down by soil microbes before they reach their target. Treatments also may fail because the pests have become resistant, or because they've moved out of the target zone.

TARGET PRINCIPLE — BASIS FOR CONTROL WITH INSECTICIDES

Turfgrass is made up of leaves, stems, and roots of grass plants, together with the underlying thatch and soil. This perennial plant cover consists of distinct zones which are attacked by different groups of insect pests (Figure 6.1). Some pests (e.g., greenbug, bermudagrass mite) live on the stems and leaves. Pests that live and feed within this upper **foliar/stem zone** tend to be fairly easy to control because of their exposure. Other pests, such as sod webworms and cutworms, hide in the **stem/thatch zone**, coming out at night to chew the foliage. Billbugs lay eggs in grass stems, within which their larvae then feed. These stem/thatch-inhabiting pests may evade detection until their damage appears. Root-feeding white grubs, mole crickets, and other insects that inhabit the **thatch/soil zone** are often the hardest to manage. These subterranean pests often go undetected until significant injury has occurred. Controlling them is confounded by the difficulty of getting insecticide residues through the thatch and into the root zone.

For an insecticide to be effective, the turf manager must deliver it to the specific target zone in which the pest feeds or hides. This is the **"Target Principle."** In the case of grubs, the target pest feeds in the upper soil, under a mat of thatch. For greenbugs, the target zone is the grass foliage. Which insecticide formulation you choose (liquid, granules, etc.), the manner and timing of the application, and whether or not the treatment is watered in will depend on the particular target zone in which the pest is found.

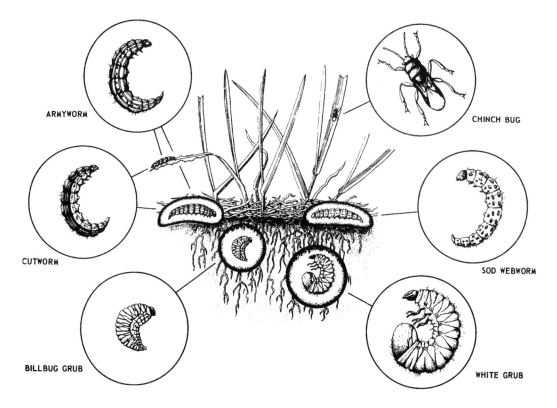

Figure 6.1. *The Target Principle dictates that insecticide residues be placed in the specific target zone in which the pest occurs (adapted from O.M. Scott & Sons Co.).*

Soil-Inhabiting Insects

Soil-inhabiting pests such as white grubs and mole crickets can be controlled with either granular or liquid applications. Regardless of the mode of application, the insecticide must be **watered in** to move the residues through the thatch to the target zone. Watering in can be by **post-treatment irrigation** or timely rainfall, although the latter strategy is risky if the weather forecast is wrong and the anticipated downpour does not occur. Watering in is necessary to activate granular insecticides, and to move liquid insecticides off the grass blades and through the thatch. Post-treatment irrigation also causes the insects to move closer to the soil surface where they will have greater contact with the residues. If the soil is not already moist from rainfall or irrigation, it is also a good idea to irrigate with 1/2–1 in. (1.25–2.5 cm) of water a day *before* the treatment is scheduled, to bring the insects up close to the surface. However, do not apply soil insecticides to saturated soils.

Do not apply liquid insecticides to dry thatch — the spray is likely to evaporate before penetrating. Irrigate the day before to moisten the thatch. Wetting the thatch and soil organic matter also reduces the amount of insecticide that gets tied up there. Use coarse sprays, because fine sprays tend to volatilize more quickly and are more prone to drift. Many turf managers use a volume of 1-1/2–2 gal per 1000 ft^2 (6.1–8.2 L per 100 m^2) for cool-season grasses. Higher spray volume may be needed to penetrate the deep thatch of warm-season turfgrasses. An additional 1/2–1 in. of water should be applied immediately after treatment. The objective is to wash the insecticide off the foliage before the residues have dried, and to leach the material through the thatch to the target zone.

When applying granular insecticides, the grass should be dry so the particles bounce off the foliage and sift down into the thatch. This helps to protect the insecticide from UV light, reduces exposure to birds and bystanders, and brings the concentrated particle closer to the target zone. Granular formulations are a bit more "forgiving" than liquids if post-treatment irrigation is unavoidably delayed. Nevertheless, granular insecticides, like liquids, should be watered in with 1/2–1 in. of water as soon as possible after application. When controlling root-feeding pests, remember: *If there's no watering in or rainfall, there's no grub control.* This holds, regardless of the formulation and mode of application.

Leaf-, Stem-, and Thatch-Dwelling Pests

Leaf-, stem-, and thatch-inhabiting insects tend to be easier to control than the root-feeders. The approach for these pests is opposite that for root-feeding pests. In this case, the objective is to leave insecticide residues on the foliage, stems, and upper thatch. Liquid applications are generally best for this purpose. Control with liquid applications occurs either by (1) hitting the insect with the spray; or (2) future contact as the pest crawls over residues on the foliage or thatch, or consumes the treated grass, or both. Most control occurs within the first day or two after application.

Spray volume must be enough for complete and uniform coverage; usually 1-1/2–2 gal per 1000 ft^2 (6.1–8.2 L per 100 m^2) is sufficient for cool-season grasses. Coarse sprays are best to minimize drift. Applications should be timed to coincide with the pests' feeding activity and presence of vulnerable life stages. Sprays for night-active caterpillars, such as sod webworms or cutworms, may work best if applied late in the day. This ensures that the larvae will contact fresh residues as they crawl on the thatch surface and consume the freshly treated foliage. When controlling leaf- and stem-feeders with liquid sprays, delay irrigation and mowing for at least 1 to 2 days after application to allow time for contact activity and consumption of treated foliage. Note that some insecticides have labels that require post-treatment irrigation. These may not be good choices for surface feeders.

When spraying short-residual insecticides for chinch bugs and adult billbugs, control can sometimes be enhanced by applying a light post-treatment irrigation (about 1/8 in. [4–5 mm] of water) before the spray dries. This washes the insecticide into the stem/thatch target zone where these pests reside. If spray volume is higher than 2 gal per 1000 ft^2 (8.2 L per 100 m^2) then post-treatment irrigation is usually unnecessary when controlling these pests.

Cutworms, sod webworms, adult billbugs, and other pests that feed near the surface can also be controlled with granular applications. If granules are used, a light (1/8 in.) post-treatment irrigation is required to activate the insecticide. The objective is to leave the residues in the stem/upper thatch target zone. This contrasts with the strategy for grubs, where heavier irrigation is applied to leach the insecticide *through* the thatch, down into the soil.

Liquid and granular applications have their respective advantages and disadvantages against leaf- and stem-feeders. Sprays give greater mortality from initial contact, and they leave residues in the upper thatch that provide some residual control. Granules, in contrast, have little initial contact activity. Because they bounce off the foliage, granules are not effective against foliage-dwelling pests such as mites, greenbugs, or two-lined spittlebugs unless the insecticide is systemic. Once in the upper thatch, however, granules may provide somewhat longer residual control of thatch-dwelling pests. This is because the insecticide is less prone to breakdown in sunlight than it would be as a residue on the leaf blades. Also, it is leached from the granules over a longer period of time. Some of the newer soil insecticides (e.g. imidacloprid, halofenozide) are systemic, providing good control of some leaf- and stem-feeders.

WHY INSECTICIDE TREATMENTS SOMETIMES FAIL

Every year, I get calls from turf managers concerning treatment "failures." While "bad insecticide" is often blamed, much more often the poor control is caused by something other than the product itself. By being aware of the factors that cause insecticides to perform below expectations, you may be able to avoid some treatment failures.

Insecticide Selection

Not all insecticides are the same. Products vary in their range of activity; some are labeled for control of many pests, some for relatively few. Certain products, especially biorationals such as *Bacillus thuringiensis* or azadirachtin (neem), work best against young, actively growing larvae but perform poorly against older larvae, pupae, or adults. For reasons that are not clear, even closely related insects, such as different species of white grubs, can differ markedly in their sensitivity to particular products. When choosing an insecticide, find out as much as you can about its range of activity and residual properties. Imidacloprid (Merit®) and trichlorfon (Dylox®, Proxol®), for example, are both labeled for grub control, but they have different characteristics that make one or the other better suited for a given situation. Imidacloprid has long residual, a plus for preventive control. Trichlorfon is shorter-lived but works better against large larvae, making it the more effective product for curative control. Performance of insecticides is affected by soil type, thatch, and other site-specific characteristics. Read the label to confirm that the product is registered for the target pest. Experiment with different products, or consult your Cooperative Extension office about recommendations for your state. Experience will tell you which insecticides work best at your sites.

Incorrect Identification

Identification is the first step in understanding a pest's life cycle, which is the key to effective control. If you misidentify a mature grub of the black turfgrass ataenius as a young Japanese beetle grub, the timing of your treatment may be way off. An insecticide that controls chinch bugs may be ineffective against clover mites. The color plates in this book will help you to identify common turfgrass insects. Consult a local "bug" expert (Appendix 1) if you are unsure of the pest's ID.

Wrong Formulation

Choice of formulation, and whether or not pre- or post-treatment irrigation is applied, can affect treatment performance. Mode of application should be based on the Target Principle (see Figure 6.1).

Bad Timing

Most pests have a "window of vulnerability," that is, a period in their life cycle when they are easiest to control. In general, young nymphs and larvae are easier to kill than larger, nearly mature ones. If you fail to monitor the turf, an infestation can get a head start and you'll have to deal with a more mature pest population. Nonfeeding stages, including eggs and pupae, are usually not vulnerable to insecticides. A golf superintendent who treats for cutworms a week after damage appears on the putting greens may miss the mark because most of the population will already have pupated. Billbugs can be controlled by targeting the adult females with a short-residual insecticide in the spring, but once they've laid eggs in the grass stems, a different approach must be used. The time of day that an application is made can also be important. Entomopathogenic nematodes, for example, are best applied in early morning or late in the day to avoid deactivation by heat and sunlight.

Poor Calibration

Proper calibration of application equipment is a must for accurate and uniform coverage. You may get only partial control, or none at all, if your application rate is only half what the label calls for. Calibrate your equipment, and recheck it periodically.

Deactivation in the Spray Tank

Alkaline Hydrolysis. Some insecticides are sensitive to alkaline (basic) conditions and will be rapidly broken down (hydrolyzed) in the spray tank if mixed with alkaline water (pH > 7). Trichlorfon (Dylox®, Proxol®) is especially sensitive to deactivation by alkaline hydrolysis. Most insecticides that are pH-sensitive have buffers added to the formulation to help keep the pH near neutral (pH = 7). Nevertheless, it is wise to know your water pH, and to test it periodically. Tank mixes generally should be kept near neutral or slightly acidic (pH < 7). Water pH can be checked with an inexpensive pen-like pH meter, or with indicator papers that change color according to pH. If you are using alkaline water, mix in the insecticide, agitate for a few minutes, and then take a reading. If the pH of the tank mix remains above 7, a commercial buffering agent can be added to adjust the pH downward to the 6 to 6.5 range. Low (acidic) water pH is usually not a problem. Most pesticides that are affected by pH will state so on the label. Agitation and warming can cause the pH of tank mixes to change during the day, especially if fertilizers or other chemicals were added. If the whole tank mix is not applied immediately after mixing, take periodic readings during the day to see if the pH needs to be adjusted.

Tank mixing. Turf managers may wish to combine two or more pesticides, or a pesticide and a fertilizer, so they can be applied at the same time. Occasionally, the chemicals are incompatible, causing deactivation of the insecticide or undesirable gelling, clumping, or severe separation in the spray tank. Such incompatible mixtures will clog nozzle screens and spray tips, inhibit even distribution of the active ingredients in the spray tank, and prevent effective coverage. Chemical interaction among pesticides can also cause loss of activity. Incompatibility may be due to the chemical nature of the materials, the order in which they are mixed in the tank, or the types of formulations being mixed. Read the pesticide label for any information about incompatibility in tank mixes. Pesticide formulations of the same type are usually compatible because they contain the same types of solvents and inert ingredients. When combining chemicals in the spray tank, always add the formulations in the following order: (1) wettable powders; (2) flowables; (3) water-soluble concentrates; then (4) emulsifiable concentrates. For example, when combining a wettable powder with a water-soluble concentrate, add the wettable powder to the spray tank first.

A "jar test" will enable you to evaluate new pesticide mixtures for compatibility before mixing a full tank. This quick test can save you the expense and major hassle of disposing of a large quantity of incompatible mix:

Jar Test for Testing Compatibility of Pesticide Mixtures (modified from Marer et al., 1988):

1. Measure 1 pint (473 mL) of the intended spray water into a clear quart (946 mL) glass jar.
2. Adjust pH if necessary.
3. Add intended ingredients in the following order, stirring well each time:
   a. any surfactants or compatibility agents: add 1 teaspoon (5 mL) for each pint/100 gal (473 mL/378.5 L) of planned final spray mixture.
   b. wettable powders and dry flowable formulations: add 1 tablespoon (15 mL) for each lb/100 gal (453.6 g/378.5 L) of planned final spray mixture.
   c. water-soluble concentrates or solutions: add 1 teaspoon (5 mL) for each pint/100 gal (473 mL/378.5 L) of planned final spray mixture.
   d. emulsifiable concentrates and flowable formulations: add same amount as (c).

    e. soluble powder formulations: add same amount as (c).
    f. remaining adjuvants: add same as (c).
4. After mixing, let the solution stand for 15 minutes. Stir well, and observe for evidence of incompatibility:
    a. *Compatible:* Smooth uniform mixture, combines well after stirring. OK to use chemicals together in the spray tank.
    b. *Incompatible:* Separation, clumping, curdling, formation of precipitate, crystals, or woolly-looking mass; material settles out quickly after stirring and/or is difficult to suspend.
5. Pesticides used in the jar test should be poured into the spray tank. Triple-rinse the jar and all measuring utensils and pour the rinsate into the tank. Do not allow jars or utensils that have contacted pesticides to be used for any other purpose.
    If the jar test suggests incompatibility, do not mix that combination in the spray tank. Unfortunately, the jar test cannot tell you whether any chemical deactivation has occurred.

There are several possible remedies if pesticide incompatibility develops in the spray tank. First, try increasing the agitation and using a water stream to break up the clumps and get the mixture recirculating. If the pesticides still clump or separate, try adding a commercial compatibility extender (available from pesticide dealers) while continuing agitation. You may have to change nozzle screens to a larger size and clean them frequently. If clumping persists, dilute the tank mix with additional water and filter off large aggregates. If the tank mix cannot be sprayed on a legal application site, it must be emptied into appropriate containers and disposed of in the same manner as any other unused pesticide.

Breakdown on the Surface

Volatilization. Volatilization is the loss of pesticide from the grass and/or soil surface by evaporation into the atmosphere. Volatilization of insecticides is a concern both from the standpoint of human exposure, and because it reduces the effectiveness of the application. When sprays are applied to turfgrass, much of the active ingredient can be lost through volatility even before the residues are dry. Loss to volatilization depends on a pesticide's vapor pressure (tendency to evaporate) and on weather conditions on the day of application. Volatility losses are generally greater for emulsifiable concentrates than for wettable powders, flowables, or granules. Windy conditions increase volatilization of pesticides, as do high air temperatures. Making applications on cool, cloudy days or late in the day when winds are calm and the turf canopy has cooled can reduce initial losses to volatilization (Figure 6.2). Volatility losses are also greatly reduced if the turf is irrigated soon after the application (Figure 6.3). Of course, irrigation must be compatible with the intent of the application. For foliage-feeders such as sod webworms or cutworms, the residues should not be watered in. To reduce volatility losses, applications for these pests should be made late in the day.

Photodecomposition. When an insecticide is exposed to direct sunlight, it can absorb energy from ultraviolet (UV) radiation, and that energy can break chemical bonds, causing deactivation. Photodecomposition can greatly reduce the activity of certain pesticides. Microbial insecticides (e.g., *Bacillus thuringiensis*) and botanicals tend to be susceptible to this problem. Some insecticides have UV blockers added to the formulation. Nevertheless, UV-sensitive products are best applied toward evening to reduce exposure to sunlight. If grubs or other root-feeders are the target, immediate watering-in reduces loss from photodegradation.

Irrigation, Soil Moisture, and Temperature

When controlling soil-inhabiting pests, the importance of post-treatment irrigation cannot be overstated (see Target Principle, this chapter). Failure to adequately water-in the insecticide is

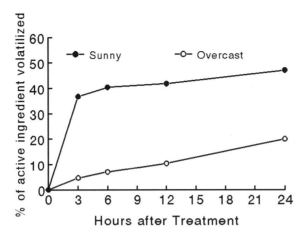

Figure 6.2. Comparison of losses of chlorpyrifos (Dursban®) from volatility when sprays are applied under sunny versus overcast conditions (data from Price, 1983).

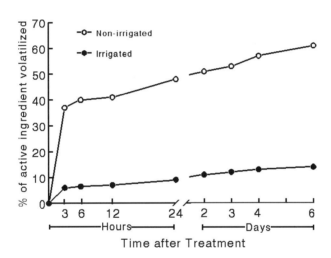

Figure 6.3. Comparison of losses of chlorpyrifos (Dursban®) from volatility when sprays are applied with or without post-treatment irrigation (data from Price, 1983).

probably the most common reason for poor grub control, especially with liquid applications on home lawns. By the time the homeowner irrigates, the residues have long since dried on the surface and become bound to the grass and thatch. Significant losses from volatility and photo-decomposition may also have occurred. Often the "irrigation" consists of waving a garden hose over the lawn a few times. Granular soil insecticides are usually more forgiving than liquids if post-treatment irrigation is delayed.

Soil insects such as white grubs and mole crickets move up or down in the soil profile in response to moisture and temperature. Most species of grubs "go deep" in mid to late fall to escape freezing; they do not return to the root zone until the soil warms in the spring. When summer heat and drought cause the upper soil to dry out, both grubs and mole crickets move down to cooler, moister soil. The deeper the pests, the harder they are to control. Even with watering-in, soil insecticides rarely penetrate deeper than 1 in. (2.5 cm) into the soil, or less if thatch is present. If environmental conditions have caused the pests to move below the critical 1 in. depth, many will escape contact with the insecticide. Thus, pre-treatment irrigation can boost your success by causing the insects to move up close to the soil surface. This should be done a day or two beforehand to allow time for the pests to respond, and to avoid having a saturated soil during treatment. During severe summer droughts, mole crickets may be too deep to be brought to the surface by irrigation. In such cases, it is best to wait for rainfall to thoroughly wet the soil and bring the crickets up. Experience is the best guide in such situations.

Because insects are cold-blooded animals, their activity is directly related to the temperature of their surroundings. Insects become sluggish and their feeding is reduced in the late fall and early spring. Their metabolism also slows down during cool periods (60°F [16°C] or less) during the growing season. Cold, sluggish insects consume less insecticide and are less active, so they contact and absorb less of the toxin through their exoskeleton. Thus, insects may be harder to control in cool soils. Grub treatments applied too late in the fall, or too early in the spring, may be wasted if the larvae have moved out of the root zone.

Failure to Penetrate Thatch

Thatch is a tightly intermingled layer of living and dead roots, rhizomes, stolons, plant crowns, stems, and organic debris that accumulates on the soil surface beneath the grass canopy (Figure 6.4). A small amount of thatch (<1/2 in. or 12 mm) is beneficial in that it provides resilience and helps to retain moisture at the soil surface. However, thatch represents a second canopy layer through which an insecticide must penetrate to reach the soil. Even with post-treatment irrigation, most of the insecticide may become trapped in the thatch and never reach the target zone. Pesticides bound up in the thatch are subject to chemical or microbial breakdown. Thus, a moderate to heavy thatch layer will greatly reduce the effectiveness of insecticides applied for grubs and other soil-inhabiting pests.

One way to compare the sensitivity of insecticides to this problem is to measure the amount of thatch required to bind 50% of the insecticide applied (Figure 6.5). Of the common turf insecticides, chlorpyrifos (Dursban®) is the most tightly bound up by thatch and other organic matter. Consequently, it provides poor grub control in most soils. Trichlorfon (Dylox®, Proxol®), is much less sensitive to binding in thatch and would be a better choice for controlling grubs in thatchy turf.

Water, either natural rainfall or irrigation, is the most effective medium for leaching an insecticide through the thatch. Insecticides vary in their water solubility (Figure 6.6). In general, insecticides that are relatively water soluble (e.g., trichlorfon) penetrate thatch most easily, whereas compounds with low solubility (e.g., chlorpyrifos) are more likely to be trapped. Bendiocarb (Turcam®) is an exception to this pattern: it is relatively insoluble, yet is less sensitive to thatch than are some other, more soluble materials.

Deactivation in the Soil

Chemical degradation. Once an insecticide reaches the soil, other factors can reduce its longevity and effectiveness. Soils are a chemically active environment that can rapidly degrade some pesticides. As occurs with alkaline hydrolysis in tank mixes (see above), some insecticides are sensitive to soils with high (basic or alkaline) pH. Trichlorfon (Dylox®, Proxol®), for example, will persist for several weeks in acidic soils, and for several days in a neutral soil, but breaks down in a few hours in highly alkaline soils. Most other insecticides are less sensitive to soil pH. High amounts of organic matter and high clay content are other factors that may cause insecticides to perform poorly in some soils.

Microbial degradation. Because most pesticides are organic compounds composed mainly of carbon, hydrogen, and oxygen, they can be used as a food source by certain bacteria and fungi. Microbial breakdown is the main way that most pesticides degrade in the soil. Each spadeful of soil contains millions of microbes that can degrade an insecticide, rendering it nontoxic. This is beneficial from an environmental perspective, but it can cause treatment fail-

Figure 6.4. *Excessive thatch poses a barrier to penetration of soil insecticides.*

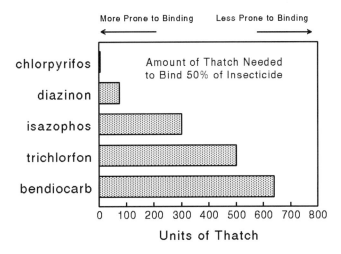

Figure 6.5. *Comparative amount of thatch required to bind 50% of some turfgrass insecticides (data from Niemczyk and Krueger, 1982).*

ures when an insecticide is degraded before the pests are controlled. Soils with high populations of these microorganisms are said to be "aggressive" due to their capacity to rapidly deactivate pesticides. Microbe populations are greatest in soils with high organic matter; such soils are more likely to be aggressive.

Many soil microbes are somewhat specific in the types of pesticides they will degrade. When an insecticide is applied repeatedly on the same site, the microorganisms that "feed" on that compound may increase to unusually high levels. If this occurs, the pesticide will be degraded very rapidly the next time it is applied. This phenomenon, called **accelerated microbial degradation** (or **enhanced biodegradation**) has been implicated in treatment failures on golf courses and home lawns. While accelerated degradation has been a problem with only a few turf insecticides so far, it *could* occur with many other soil insecticides. The best way to safeguard against creating an aggressive soil is to use insecticides only when necessary. Avoid preventive or calendar-type treatments, and do not use the same insecticide repeatedly on the same site. If multiple treatments are necessary within a growing season, try to alternate among different classes of insecticides. If you experience a treatment failure, try a different product — don't just reapply at a higher rate. In short, reduce overall use of insecticides, and don't overdo it with any one product.

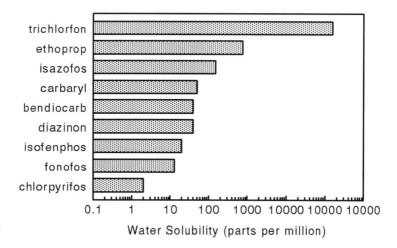

Figure 6.6. *Comparative water solubility of some turfgrass insecticides. Higher numbers correspond to relatively more soluble products (data from product labels and Material Safety Data Sheets).*

Pest Resistance

Repeated exposure to insecticides can sometimes lead to development of resistance within a pest population. An insecticide that initially gives good control of a turfgrass pest can be rendered ineffective within a few years because of selection for a resistant strain. Even low levels of resistance are a problem, because it becomes necessary to treat more often and at higher rates to achieve the same level of control. The mechanism of resistance involves the process of natural selection. Genetic variation in any pest population means that some individuals are likely to possess genes controlling traits rendering them resistant. These mutant individuals may have less sensitive target sites, or more active detoxification enzymes. Repeated insecticide applications exert a strong selective force favoring survival of those individuals having genes for resistance, and these genes are then transmitted to offspring. Before long, the susceptible strains have been killed off, and most of the population consists of resistant individuals. The speed with which resistance develops is a function of (1) the proportion of the population that is exposed; (2) the frequency of insecticide application; (3) the persistence of the insecticide; and (4) the reproductive rate of the population.

Resistance to organophosphate insecticides has occurred with several major insect pests, most notably southern chinch bugs in south Florida and greenbugs in the Midwest. These species have rapid development and produce many generations per year, and each was targeted for repeated sprays by the lawn care industry. With this combination of factors, it is not surprising that they've become immune to certain insecticides. Several practices can be used to reduce the likelihood of such pests becoming resistant. These include (1) reducing treatment frequency by spot treating instead of using cover sprays; (2) using short-residual insecticides; (3) alternating between different insecticide classes; and (4) using resistant grasses and other nonchemical methods.

Resistance to insecticides is less likely to occur in white grubs and other pests with annual life cycles. Genetic change is slower in such species, the adults are mobile and constantly outcrossing, and only a small portion of the interbreeding population is exposed to a particular insecticide in a given year. If treatments fail against white grubs, it is probably due to causes other than pest resistance. Resistance of white grubs *was* a problem in the 1960s when widespread use of persistent insecticides such as chlordane was the norm. The incidence of resistance in grubs may increase if the turf industry reverts to excessive use of long-residual insecticides.

Not All Insects or Insecticides Are the Same

Even closely related insects, such as different species of white grubs, may differ in their inherent susceptibility to particular insecticides. European chafer grubs, for example, seem to be harder to control than Japanese beetle grubs with some products. This target-specificity seems to be especially marked for some biorational products, such as insect growth regulators and entomopathogenic nematodes. The nematodes *Steinernema glaseri* and *Heterorhabditis bacteriophora*, for example, are more effective against white grubs than is the more commonly marketed *S. carpocapsae*. Conversely, *S. carpocapsae* is effective against billbugs, sod webworms, and cutworms. Knowing what species of insects you are dealing with, and keeping records of which products work best against particular pests, will help you to avoid treatment failures.

Standard insecticides, too, vary with regard to persistence, speed of kill, activity against particular pest species and instars, and movement through thatch and soil. Every insecticide has a characteristic lag period between the time it is applied and the point when maximal mortality of the pest population occurs. Pyrethroids take out surface-feeding caterpillars quickly, whereas *Bacillus thuringiensis* may require several days. A fast-acting soil insecticide like trichlorfon (Dylox®, Proxol®) may kill grubs in less than a week, whereas a slower-acting product like bendiocarb (Turcam®) may not give its full level of control for several weeks. These differences in lag time should be taken into account when choosing an insecticide. For grubs, a fast-acting, short-residual product might be best for spot treating heavily infested turf in the fall. Conversely, a slower-acting, longer-residual product might be better for mid to late summer treatments, when damage from newly hatched grubs will be minor, and some of the eggs have yet to hatch. Again, site-specific experience will be your best guide.

ADDITIONAL CONSIDERATIONS

Which Formulation Is Best?

Many insecticides come in both liquid and granular formulations. Research has shown there is usually little difference in performance between liquids and granules *so long as the insecticide is delivered to the target zone at the proper time*. Liquid applications are required when the objective is to leave a residue on the grass blades. Liquids sometimes provide better control of pests occupying the stem/thatch target zone (e.g., sod webworms) because the insects eat the treated foliage as well as encountering the residues in the thatch. For soil-inhabiting pests, it is often assumed that granular formulations work better than liquids. In reality, there is usually little difference so long as the treatments are timed correctly and promptly watered-in. Indeed, several of the most effective grub insecticides are available only as spray formulations.

There are some situations in which one type of formulation might be better suited than another. For soil insects, granular products are the better choice if post-treatment irrigation must be delayed. In such cases, liquids would lose more activity from volatilization and photodegradation, and be difficult to move off the grass blades once the spray had dried. From an environmental standpoint, granular formulations may be more attractive to birds. This should not be a problem if the application is watered-in, but if irrigation is delayed it could be a concern. In contrast, granular materials are less prone to drift and may be safer to handle than spray formulations. When comparing the relative cost of different formulations, consider the time that will be required to make the application (including mixing, loading, and container disposal), the type of equipment available, and the accuracy of your employees in applying sprays or granules. Choose the type of formulation that your operation uses most effectively.

Using Spray Adjuvants

Adjuvants are substances added to a pesticide formulation or tank mix to improve its performance, ease of application, or safety. Some of the most common adjuvants are **surfactants**, substances that alter the dispersing, spreading, and wetting properties of spray droplets. **Spreaders** are adjuvants that allow the pesticide to form a uniform coating over the treated surfaces, while **stickers** improve adhesion and help the pesticide to stay on the foliage. Other adjuvants may be added to the pesticide to reduce foaming of mixtures that require agitation, or to reduce drift. **Buffers** allow pesticides to be mixed with water or other pesticides of different acidity or alkalinity, whereas **compatibility agents** aid in combining and mixing different pesticides effectively. A turf manager might add a spreader/sticker to the tank mix to improve coverage and adhesion to grass blades, or a surfactant or wetting agent to help the insecticide to move more readily through the thatch.

Distributors of spray adjuvants sometimes claim that these products will dramatically increase performance of pesticides. However, the limited testing that has been done on them suggests that any advantage is likely to be subtle. Adjuvants are not a substitute for skillful turf culture, nor will they revolutionize your management program. Advertisements for some products claim that insecticide rates can be reduced by using high rates of the adjuvant. The cost of the adjuvant, however, may outweigh any savings in pesticide costs. As with all products, be wary of claims that seem to good to be true. Experiment with them on your own, and seek advice regarding their attributes from reliable sources.

Subsurface Application

Subsurface application is a fairly new application technology for controlling soil-inhabiting pests such as white grubs or mole crickets. The basic idea is to place the insecticide directly into the soil where the pest resides. This concept has several potential advantages. First, by delivering the insecticide to the target zone, less is tied up in the thatch. Losses from volatilization or photodecomposition are reduced. Less surface residues mean reduced hazard to turf users or wildlife. Spray drift and odor are also reduced. If treatments prove more effective when applied subsurface, then insecticides could be used at lower rates while still retaining good control. Research on subsurface application is underway at several universities. Some subsurface equipment is already in use by custom applicators, and as part of the fleet on some golf courses. So far, there are mixed reviews regarding the advantages and disadvantages of this technique.

Several kinds of machinery have been developed for subsurface placement of insecticides. One type is a high-pressure injector for liquid applications. This system has a series of nozzles with tiny openings that ride just above the turf surface. The system generates very high pressure, which forces the insecticide down into the soil. The nozzles are typically 3–4 in. (7.6–10.1 cm) apart, producing a series of bands of pesticide that penetrate to depths of 1 in. (2.54 cm) or more in sandy soils. A drawback of this system is its relatively slow speed of application. Also, it is somewhat prone to the nozzles clogging, and maintenance time may be relatively high. Another type of subsurface liquid applicator cuts slits in the turf, and then injects a low-pressure stream of insecticide into the furrows. A third type of system is designed for subsurface placement of granular formulations. This applicator is basically a modified slit seeder or overseeder device. It cuts a series of parallel slits in the turf and drops the granules down into them. This type of equipment has good speed of application, and some units can be used for other purposes, such as dethatching.

Are the benefits of subsurface application worth the expense? Some comparative trials have shown better control of mole crickets or white grubs using subsurface placement. However, the advantage is often small, and other tests have shown little or no advantage. Tests to determine the feasibility of using reduced rates have shown the same mixed results. The effectiveness of subsurface application will improve as the equipment is refined. While this new technology is probably not a "silver bullet" that will revolutionize insect control, it may have some benefits for those who constantly deal with mole crickets or white grubs. The best advice is to learn as much as possible about the subject before investing in subsurface equipment or contracting for such services.

CALCULATIONS TO SAVE YOU MONEY

When you purchase pesticides or fertilizers, consider the cost per unit area, not the cost per pound or gallon. Be wary of sales promotions that tell you what a great deal a particular product is because it costs only so much a pound. Ask how many square feet or how many acres it will treat, or do the calculations yourself. It can save you money. Consider the following examples:

Example 1. Insecticide A costs $65 for a 2.5 gal (= 20 pints) jug, whereas Insecticide B costs $65 for a 1 pint bottle. Both will do a good job controlling cutworms. Insecticide A, which gives you 20 times as much material for the same price, appears to be the better buy. But is it?

The cost that matters is the cost per 1000 ft^2. Assume Insecticide A is a carbamate applied at a rate of 6 oz per 1000 ft^2, whereas Insecticide B is a pyrethroid used at only 1/5 oz per 1000 ft^2. Thus, Insecticide B is used at only 1/30th the rate of Insecticide A. The cost works out to about $1.22 per 1000 ft^2 ($53 per acre) for Insecticide A, but only $0.81 per 1000 ft^2 ($35 per acre) for Insecticide B. Thus, Insecticide B turns out to be the better buy.

Example 2. Zappem, a granular insecticide, is available in both 5 G and 10 G formulations. A 40 lb bag of Zappem 5 G costs $50; the same amount of Zappem 10 G costs $65. The label rate is 4 lb of active ingredient per acre. Which is the better deal?

For granular insecticides, the number before the "G" represents the *percentage of active ingredient in the formulation.* Zappem 5 G contains 5% active ingredient; there is 0.05 × 40, or 2 lb of active ingredient per bag. You will need two bags to treat an acre of fairway, at a total cost of $100. Zappem 10 G contains 10% active ingredient; each bag contains 0.1 × 40, or 4 lb of active ingredient, so you will need only one bag to do the job. Buying the 10 G formulation, which costs more per pound, saves you $35 per acre.

Example 3. Wipeout, a liquid insecticide, comes in both a 2 E and a 4 E formulation. A gallon of Wipeout 2 E costs $40; a gallon of Wipeout 4 E costs $60. The label rate is 2 lb active ingredient per acre. You are planning to treat 5 acres of turf. Which formulation is the better deal?

For emulsifiable concentrates, the number before the "E" or "EC" denotes the *pounds of active ingredient per gallon* (not the % active ingredient!). Thus, a gallon of Wipeout 2 E contains 2 lb of active ingredient, whereas a gallon of the 4 E product contains twice that amount. You need 5 gal of the 2 E formulation to treat 5 acres (cost = 5 × $40, or $200), but only half as much of the 4 E product to treat the same area (cost = 2.5 × $60, or $150). Wipeout 2 E is cheaper per gallon, but costs more to use on a per-acre basis.

In general, more concentrated formulations are cheaper to use because you pay about the same for inert ingredients, packaging, shipping, and handling regardless of the formulation's strength. Granular materials are often somewhat more expensive to use than liquids. Of course, choice of formulation also depends on the target pest, what type of equipment is available, and other factors.

INTERPRETING INSECTICIDE RESEARCH

Every year, turfgrass entomologists conduct dozens of independent trials to evaluate the performance of new insecticides against grubs, mole crickets, cutworms, and other pests. Registered products are usually included in these tests as standards. The manufacturer must submit **efficacy data** — that is, proof that the new insecticide is effective — as part of the registration process. The manufacturer usually pays a testing fee, called a grant-in-aid, to the university. Part or all of these funds can be used by the researcher to pay student assistants, purchase equipment, or otherwise support their research or extension program.

It is often confusing for nonscientists to interpret the data reported by researchers and pesticide companies. Practically every issue of the trade journals contains advertisements showing that Product A outperformed Product B in several university trials. The differences are often minor (e.g., 90% versus 85% control), yet they are touted as being "significant." Should we be convinced that Product A really is the better performer? Not necessarily. For each trial in which A beats B, there may be just as many others in which B beats A. Those are likely to be the ones that the manufacturer of Product B will feature in *their* advertisements! This is not to say that university tests are unreliable, only that performance of insecticides varies from trial to trial, and under different conditions. What works best in sandy soils of North Carolina may not perform as well in heavy clay soils of Kentucky. Differences in "% control" on the order of 5–10% are usually meaningless. Subtle differences that may be "significant" by a statistical analysis of the research data may be insignificant in real practice. Remember, too, that 100% control is unrealistic and unnecessary. Experience, and the advice of your local independent turf expert, are the best guidelines for deciding which products are most effective in your region.

Also, be aware that some nonconventional products are exempt from EPA registration and require no supporting data in order to be sold. Beware of products that sound too good to be true. Before using a new product in a situation that could cost you your job, ask to see the performance data. Try it on a small area first to see how it works under your conditions. Experiment, and reach your own conclusions.

SELECTED REFERENCES

Cooper, R.J. 1993. Volatilization as an avenue for pesticide dissipation. *Internat. Turfgrass Res. J.* 7:116–126.

Hull, R.J. 1995. The fate of pesticides used on turf. *Turfgrass Trends* 4:2–11.

Kenna, M.P. 1995. What happens to pesticides applied to golf courses? *U.S. Golf Assoc. Green Section Record.*

Marer, P.J. 1988. *The safe and effective use of pesticides.* Univ. California Statewide Integrated Pest Management Program. Div. Agric. & Nat. Res. Pub. 3324.

Niemczyk, H.D. and H.R. Krueger. 1982. Binding of insecticides on turfgrass thatch, pp. 61–63. *In:* H.D. Niemczyk and B.G. Joyner (Eds.). *Advances in turfgrass entomology.* ChemLawn Corp., Columbus, OH.

Niemczyk, H.D. 1981. *Destructive turf insects.* Gray Printing Co., Fostoria, OH.

Niemczyk, H.D. 1993. Accelerated degradation of turfgrass pesticides: a review. *Internat. Turfgrass Soc. Res. J.* 7:148–151.

Price, D.B. 1983. *Dissipation of pesticides applied to turf with emphasis on volatilization.* M.S. Thesis, Univ. of Kentucky.

Villani, M.G. 1995. Relationships among soil insects, soil insecticides, and soil physical properties. *Turfgrass Trends* 4:11–17.

SAFEGUARDING THE ENVIRONMENT

One of the most important issues related to use of insecticides on lawns and golf courses concerns the potential for harm to desirable **nontarget species** such as birds, fish, and other wildlife. Because many insecticides act on the nervous system or on other metabolic pathways common to all animals, they have the potential to kill birds or fish if used carelessly. Such accidents draw intense scrutiny and public outcry. Federal wildlife protection laws have led to more stringent review and regulation of turfgrass pesticides. Furthermore, the trend toward preserving and integrating wildlife habitat on golf courses, and the growing popularity of fish ponds and gardening to attract wildlife to home landscapes, mean that birds and fish are more likely to come in contact with areas where pesticides are used.

Insecticides can also harm earthworms and other beneficial invertebrates that inhabit the turf. Eliminating earthworms can aggravate soil compaction and lead to excessive accumulation of thatch. Destruction of insect predators and parasites can allow pest populations to build to outbreak levels. Preserving these beneficial species is important for maintaining a healthy, stable turf.

Used as directed on the label, turfgrass insecticides should have little or no opportunity to harm wildlife. Nevertheless, the potential for adverse side effects is greater for some products than for others. Awareness of these differences will help you to minimize risk of harm to nontarget species. Proper timing, control of spray drift or surface runoff, and treating only when and where necessary also help to reduce risks of adverse side effects from pesticides.

REDUCING HAZARDS OF INSECTICIDES TO BIRDS

Some insecticides carry explicit warnings on the label concerning toxicity to birds or fish. However, potential hazards of pesticides to wildlife are not always clearly communicated in the directions, or else the reader may overlook them among the other warnings and information on the label.

For birds, the greatest hazard is to herbivorous waterfowl, including geese and some ducks which often feed, nest, or rest in turf environments such as golf courses (Figure 7.1). There have been a number of waterfowl kills resulting from use of organophosphate insecticides on turf; one of the worst involved several hundred Canada geese on a golf course. Turf managers must be very cautious when using insecticides in areas that might be frequented by waterfowl. Granular insecticides are a particular concern because they may be picked up as the birds for-

Figure 7.1. *Geese and ducks are especially sensitive to certain insecticides used on turf. Use special care on sites such as this one.*

age along the edge of lakes, ponds or streams. Liquid insecticides that are allowed to remain in the turf foliage are also a potential hazard. Turf-foraging birds such as the American robin (*Turdus migratorius*), common grackle (*Quiscalus quiscala*) and the European starling (*Sturnus vulgaris*) that probe the thatch layer and upper soil for earthworms and insects are also at risk from lawn insecticides, both from direct contact and ingestion of contaminated prey. Irrigation to move insecticide residues into the soil will help to reduce exposure of birds.

The relative toxicity of pesticides to birds is expressed in terms of an oral LD_{50} value, the dose of the active ingredient that, when ingested in a single meal, is needed to kill 50% of the test animals (see Chapter 4). This value is adjusted for the weight of the animal and is expressed in terms of milligrams (mg) of pesticide required per kilogram (kg) of body weight. The lower the LD_{50}, the greater the toxicity.

The turfgrass insecticides most toxic to birds are mostly organophosphates, including diazinon, ethoprop, isazofos, and chlorpyrifos (Table 7.1). Bendiocarb, a carbamate, is also highly toxic. These insecticides are considerably more toxic to birds than they are to mammals. Diazinon, for example, is 100 times more toxic to birds (LD_{50} value = 3.5 mg/kg) than to rats (LD_{50} = about 350 mg/kg). Diazinon typically carries the signal word "Warning," indicating moderate toxicity, but it would be in the highest toxicity category (signal word "Danger-Poison") if risk to birds were the criterion upon which label warnings were based. Consuming only a few granules of diazinon is lethal for many birds. That is one reason why diazinon is now banned for use on golf courses and sod farms. Choosing products with low toxicity to birds should be a priority on sites where exposures might occur.

REDUCING HAZARDS OF INSECTICIDES TO FISH

Toxicity of pesticides to fish and other aquatic animals is expressed as an LC_{50} value, the concentration that kills 50% of the test animals when the pesticide is added to water. LC_{50} values are expressed in parts per million (ppm) or parts per billion (ppb), with lower values corresponding to more toxic chemicals. Studies on fish are usually conducted over a 4-day exposure period.

Table 7.1. Acute Avian (Bird) Toxicity of Insecticides and Miticides Used in Tree and Turf Care. (LD$_{50}$ Values for Single Feed Acute Toxicity of Mallard Ducks are Given Unless Otherwise Indicated.)

Pesticide (Trade Name)	LD$_{50}$ Value	Pesticide Class
Highly toxic to birds (*equivalent to Category I—Danger/Poison label—pesticides for human exposure, oral LD$_{50}$ 0–50*)		
Bendiocarb (Turcam®, Ficam®)	3.1 mg/kg	Carbamate
Diazinon (Diazinon®)	3.5 mg/kg	Organophosphate
Ethoprop (Mocap®)	4.2–61 mg/kg	Organophosphate
Moderately toxic to birds (*equivalent to Category II—Warning label—pesticides for human exposure, oral LD$_{50}$ 51–500*)		
Isazofos (Triumph®)	61 mg/kg	Organophosphate
Chlorpyrifos (Dursban®)	76.6 mg/kg	Organophosphate
Fonofos (Crusade®)	128 mg/kg	Organophosphate
Imidacloprid (Merit®)	152 mg/kg	Chloronicotinyl
Isofenphos (Oftanol®)	145 mg/kg[a]	Organophosphate
Acephate (Orthene®)	350 mg/kg	Organophosphate
Lower toxicity to birds (*equivalent to Category III—Caution label—pesticides for human exposure, oral LD$_{50}$ 501+*)		
Malathion (Malathion®)	1485 mg/kg	Organophosphate
Bifenthrin (Talstar®)	> 2150 mg/kg	Pyrethroid
Carbaryl (Sevin®, Sevimol®)	> 2179 mg/kg	Carbamate
Cyfluthrin (Tempo®)	> 5000 mg/kg	Pyrethroid
Fluvalinate (Mavrik®)	> 2510 mg/kg	Pyrethroid

[a] Data for bobwhite quail.
Source: Manufacturer's Material Safety Data Sheets and EXTOXNET Extension Toxicology Network.

Some insecticides, especially pyrethroids (e.g., bifenthrin, fluvalinate, cyfluthrin), are extremely toxic to fish (Table 7.2). For example, the active ingredient in bifenthrin (Talstar®) has an LC$_{50}$ value of only 0.15 part per billion, equivalent to 1 teaspoon (5 mL) per 8,680,560 gal (>32 million L) of water! Although binding of pyrethroids to organic matter in natural ponds somewhat reduces this hazard, these compounds are nevertheless extremely toxic to fish. Avoid using them around streams, ponds, and lakes, especially where endangered aquatic species occur. Some pyrethroids are classified as "restricted use" because of their toxicity to fish. A number of miticides (hexakis, dienochlor, and dicofol) are quite toxic to fish, whereas they are much less hazardous as a group to birds and mammals. Most of the organophosphate turfgrass insecticides are also quite toxic to fish. Off-site contamination by many commonly used turf insecticides can cause fish kills or other environmental problems.

Under certain conditions, pesticides may enter streams, ponds, and lakes as runoff from treated areas. This may occur when pesticides are applied to water-saturated soils, followed by additional irrigation or rainfall that causes ponding and runoff of contaminated surface water. Before applying materials that require watering-in, be sure that underlying soils can absorb the irrigation water. If soils are saturated or heavy rain is forecast, it is best to postpone the application until the soil has drained. Various studies have shown that once the residues have dried on turf foliage or become bound in the thatch, the amount of pesticides dislodged by irrigation or rainfall and transported in runoff is very low. It is wise, nevertheless, to avoid use of insecticides around waterways. Leave an untreated buffer zone should treatment be necessary.

Turfgrass insecticides should never be applied directly to water, to areas where surface water is present, or when weather conditions will result in aerial drift into waterways. Never drain rinse water from spray equipment into ditches, streams, or other water sources. Use an anti-backflow device when drawing spray mix water directly from a pond or lake.

Table 7.2. Acute Toxicity of Insecticides and Miticides Used in Turf Care to Rainbow Trout. (LC_{50} [Lethal Concentration in Water] Values for 96-Hour Exposure to Active Ingredient. Insecticides are Listed in Order from Most to Least Toxic.)

Insecticide (Trade Name)	LC_{50} Value[a]	Pesticide Class
Bifenthrin (Talstar®)	0.15 ppb	Pyrethroid
Cyfluthrin (Tempo®)	0.68 ppb	Pyrethroid
Fluvalinate (Mavrik®)	2.9 ppb	Pyrethroid
Isazofos (Triumph®)	6.3 ppb	Organophosphate
Fonofos (Crusade®)	50 ppb	Organophosphate
Dicofol (Kelthane®)	53–86 ppb	Chlorinated hydrocarbon
Diazinon (Diazinon®)	635 ppb	Organophosphate
Ethoprop (Mocap®)	1.02–1.85 ppm	Organophosphate
Bendiocarb (Turcam®, Ficam®)	1.55 ppm	Carbamate
Isofenphos (Oftanol®)	1.8 ppm	Organophosphate
Carbaryl (Sevin®, Sevimol®)	1.95 ppm	Carbamate
Malathion (Malathion®)	2.00 ppm	Organophosphate
Chlorpyrifos (Dursban®)	3.0 ppm	Organophosphate
Trichlorfon (Dylox®, Proxol®)	3.2 ppm	Organophosphate
Acephate (Orthene®)	> 1000 ppm	Organophosphate

[a] ppb = parts per billion; ppm = parts per million. One ppm = about 3/4 teaspoon per 1000 gal (1 mL per 1000 L) of water; one ppb = about 3/4 teaspoon per 1 million gal.

PROTECTING HONEYBEES

Many insecticides, especially carbamates and pyrethroids, are highly toxic to bees. Honeybees may be poisoned by exposure to the spray itself, or to residues on blooming flowers or weeds. Don't allow spray drift to contaminate border areas where bees are actively foraging on blooming plants. Recently, honeybee populations in the United States have been decimated by a disease called American foulbrood, and from infection by tiny, parasitic mites. Some environmental groups have wrongly blamed lawn insecticides for these declines. Regardless of the true mortality factors, the impact of insecticides on honeybees is a sensitive environmental issue.

PRESERVING EARTHWORM POPULATIONS

Earthworms are sometimes viewed as pests because their habit of depositing soil on the surface as "castings" can disrupt the smoothness and uniformity of putting greens and other fine turf. This nuisance is generally more than offset by the benefits that earthworms provide by enhancing soil aeration, water infiltration, and breakdown of thatch (see Chapter 14). Preservation of earthworms is important where thatch is a concern.

Carbamate insecticides, including carbaryl (Sevin®) and bendiocarb (Turcam®, Ficam®), and certain organophosphates, such as ethoprop (Mocap®) and fonofos (Crusade®), are highly toxic to earthworms (Figure 7.2). A single application of these products can suppress worm populations for a whole growing season. Two fungicides, benomyl and thiophanate-methyl, also are highly toxic to worms. Treatment with the aforementioned products in spring (April–May) or fall (September–October) will have the greatest impact because earthworms are near the surface during those periods. Other insecticides, including pyrethroids, isofenphos, imidacloprid, halofenozide, and entomopathogenic nematodes, are compatible with earthworms. Similarly, herbicides, plant growth regulators, and most fungicides have little or no adverse effects on earthworms.

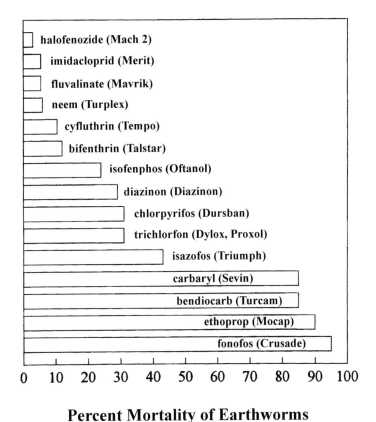

Percent Mortality of Earthworms

Figure 7.2. Relative toxicity of some turfgrass insecticides to earthworms (data from Potter, 1994).

Some fertilizers (e.g., ammonium nitrate), when applied at high rates, cause the soil to become more acidic. This may inhibit microbial activity. Earthworms are also intolerant of low soil pH and tend to be sparse in acidic soils. Excessive fertilization can therefore encourage thatch accumulation, both by increasing production of organic matter and by inhibiting decomposition processes.

Because earthworms are a preferred food for moles, pesticides are sometimes applied in the hope of reducing the food supply and causing the moles to go elsewhere. There is, however, no scientific evidence that eliminating earthworms will alleviate problems with moles, nor are there any pesticides registered for use against earthworms in turf. Effective ways to manage problem moles are covered in Chapter 15. Where soil compaction and thatch are of concern, turf managers would be well advised to choose pesticides that are relatively less toxic to earthworms.

PRESERVING BENEFICIAL INSECTS AND SPIDERS

Healthy turfgrass is inhabited by a multitude of insects, mites, spiders, and other small invertebrates which feed on plant debris, fungi, or other insects. Many of these creatures are predators or parasitoids. Along with various diseases, they are important in suppressing pest populations (see Chapter 14). Practically every turfgrass pest has one or more **natural enemies** associated with it. The fact that pest outbreaks are uncommon in low-maintenance turf suggests that most pests are normally held in check by these natural controls.

Conventional insecticides generally are at least as toxic to beneficial insects as to pests. Consequently, overuse of insecticides can lead to increased pest problems by destroying the pests' natural enemies. In Florida, for example, outbreaks of southern chinch bugs were documented on heavily treated lawns, but not on neighboring untreated lawns where predators and parasitoids were abundant. Repeated spraying of home lawns in New Jersey was followed by outbreaks of winter grain mite and hairy chinch bug, evidently because the insecticide killed the predators that normally keep these pests in check. Outbreaks of greenbugs also are more common on high-maintenance lawns than on untreated turf. Turf managers can reduce the potential for such problems by cutting back on insecticides, except where they are needed. Some of the newer insecticides, including insect growth regulators and entomopathogenic nematodes, appear to have low impact on beneficial insects.

PROTECTING GROUNDWATER

Half the people in the United States, and about 90% of rural residents, depend upon **groundwater** as a source of drinking water. Groundwater forms when water moves below the earth's surface and accumulates in empty spaces in and around rocks and porous materials. If enough gathers in one area, it becomes a source of fresh water, supplying wells and springs. Concern about the quality and potential contamination of this essential natural resource has made groundwater protection a national priority.

Pesticides are most likely to enter groundwater from runoff and downward leaching from treated areas. Transport by these mechanisms is a function of product chemistry, soil type, rainfall or irrigation, topography, geology, and the manner of application.

Turfgrass, with its underlying thatch and organic matter, is a very effective barrier to downward movement of pesticides. Only rarely does the combination of conditions occur which would allow pesticides applied to the turf surface to reach groundwater sources. By being aware of these conditions, you can use pesticides in a manner that will greatly reduce any chance for groundwater contamination.

Pesticides vary in their potential for leaching to groundwater. Such movement is influenced by three major characteristics: **solubility**, **soil adsorption**, and **persistence**. Insecticides vary greatly in water solubility (Figure 6.6). Highly soluble compounds tend to pose higher risk for movement into groundwater. Regarding soil adsorption, some insecticides become tightly bound (adsorbed) to soil particles and organic matter and do not move in soil. Others are less strongly adsorbed, and are more likely to move. In general, the higher the water solubility of a pesticide, the less likely it is to become adsorbed by soil and thatch. Finally, some pesticides are more persistent than others; i.e., they take a long time to break down. Other things being equal, more persistent insecticides are more likely to reach groundwater over a period of time.

Soil characteristics also affect rates of leaching of insecticides in soil. Soil permeability is a measure of how fast water will percolate downward in a particular soil. Chemicals are more likely to reach groundwater through more permeable soils. Coarse, sandy soils allow more rapid downward movement of water and dissolved chemicals. Fine-textured soils generally restrict downward water movement, and they contain more silt and organic matter upon which chemicals are adsorbed. Soils with a high percentage of clay or organic matter adsorb the most pesticides. Organic matter increases the water-holding capacity as well as the amount of pesticide that is adsorbed.

Many golf greens are constructed for maximum infiltration and percolation of water through rooting media. The root zone mixture generally includes at least 85% by volume (97% by mass) sand. This, together with low cation exchange capacity, allows for rapid downward leaching of pesticides through the root zone profile. Movement of pesticides is a potential source of contamination of the effluent water from the greens into surface water drainage channels. Fortunately, several studies have shown that the tight thatch overlying the rooting media of putting greens is very effective in trapping and degrading pesticides. Thus, in most cases only minute amounts of pesticides will leach below the thatch zone.

The permeability of the geological layers between the soil and the groundwater, and the distance of groundwater from the surface, will also affect the movement of surface-applied pesticides to groundwater. Be especially careful when mixing or applying pesticides near wells or areas where sinkholes are present because they may allow runoff or spills to move directly into groundwater. Avoid treatments to saturated soils because excess surface water due to rain or over-irrigation increases the chance of runoff into waterways and downward movement of pesticides to groundwater. Never mix or dispose of pesticides in drainage areas near sinkholes or waterways.

If you must apply pesticides on sandy soil with low organic matter content, or to areas where groundwater is near the soil surface, remember that products with higher water solubility, longer persistence, and low soil adsorption have a greater risk of reaching groundwater. Your local Soil Conservation Service or Cooperative Extension office can provide information on soils, location of groundwater, and any special concerns in your area.

SELECTED REFERENCES

Anonymous. 1990. *Protecting our groundwater. A grower's guide.* Produced cooperatively by the Amer. Farm Bur. Fed., Nat. Agric. Aviation Assoc., Nat. Agric. Chem. Assoc. and U.S. Dept. Agric.

Brewer, L.W., R.A. Hummel, and R.J. Kendall. 1993. Avian response to organophosphorus pesticides applied to turf, pp. 320–330. *In*: Racke, K.D. and A.R. Leslie (Eds). *Pesticides in urban environments.* ACS Symp. Series 522, Am. Chem. Soc., Washington, DC.

Gold, A.J. and P.M. Groffman. 1993. Leaching of agrichemicals from suburban areas, pp. 182–190. *In*: Racke, K.D. and A.R. Leslie (Eds). *Pesticides in urban environments.* ACS Symp. Series 522, Am. Chem. Soc., Washington, DC.

Potter, D.A. 1994. Effects of pesticides on beneficial invertebrates in turf, pp. 59–70. *In*: A.R. Leslie (Ed.). *Integrated pest management for turfgrass and ornamentals.* Lewis Publishers, Boca Raton, FL.

Smith, A.E. and W.R. Tillotson. 1993. Potential leaching of herbicides applied to golf course greens, pp. 168–181. *In*: Racke, K.D. and A.R. Leslie (Eds). *Pesticides in urban environments.* ACS Symp. Series 522, Am. Chem. Soc., Washington, DC.

Seyler, L.A., J.W. Allan, D.A. Rutz, and M.A. Kamrin (Eds.). 1994. *EXTOXNET. Extension Toxicology Network.* Coop. Ext. Serv.; Cornell Univ., Michigan State Univ., Oregon State Univ., and Univ. Calif., Davis.

8

ROOT-INFESTING INSECT PESTS

Insects that live in the soil and feed upon roots and rhizomes are among the most devastating pests of turf. Turfgrasses can usually outgrow the loss of foliage from surface-feeding insects so long as the crown is unharmed. Substantial loss of roots, however, will severely weaken or kill the grass by preventing uptake of water and nutrients. Various species of white grubs are major subterranean pests of cool-season grasses. These pests can chew off most of the root system so the damaged turf can be lifted from the soil like a loose carpet. Mole crickets are highly destructive to warm-season turfgrasses such as bermudagrass, especially on southern golf courses. Mole crickets feed on grass roots as well as aboveground tissues, and their tunneling activity uproots the plants, causing them to die from desiccation. Control of these soil-dwelling pests is difficult because surface-applied insecticides have to penetrate through the turf canopy and thatch layer in order to reach the target zone.

In addition to the aforementioned major pests, several other root-feeding insects cause sporadic damage in some geographic areas. These include Australian sod flies, dichondra flea beetles, European crane flies, ground pearls, and March flies. Relatively little is known about the biology or management of these infrequent, root-feeding pests.

AUSTRALIAN SOD FLY
Inopus rubriceps (Macquart)
(Plate 1)

Importance and Nature of Injury. This pest causes occasional injury to turfgrasses in California. The larvae feed by extracting sap from the roots, weakening or killing the plants. Infestations of 90 or more larvae per ft^2 (100 per 0.1 m^2) have been reported. Affected plants show withering of foliage and pitted roots where the larvae have fed. The lawn turf thins out by late summer, the grass eventually being replaced by broad-leaved weeds. Large numbers of adult flies emerging in the fall can be a nuisance on lawns.

Plants Attacked. All turfgrasses grown in California are susceptible.

Origin and Distribution. This pest is native to eastern Australia, where it infests such crops as sugar cane, corn, and pastures. It was first reported in California in 1948, where serious damage to lawns was observed. It seems to be most common in the San Francisco Bay area, south to San Mateo County. Little is known about its present range in the United States, but damage to turf has evidently not been reported except in California.

Distinguishing Characteristics. The adults are dark-colored flies that may be seen on the grass in the fall. They fold their wings flat over the abdomen when at rest. Males are about 1/4 in. (6–7 mm) long, black with yellowish legs. Females are slightly larger (8–9 mm long), black, with reddish legs and a red head. Eggs are oblong, about 1/32 in. (0.8 mm) in length, and opaque white at first, becoming light amber when close to hatching. Eggs are deposited in crevices in the soil. Mature larvae are about 3/8 in. (7–11 mm) long, tan, with a dark head and dark, stiff bristles on the body.

Life History and Habits. The life history of this pest is poorly known. Adults emerge in the fall from late September to early November; peak adult activity usually occurs in October. In some years, smaller numbers of adults may also emerge in May. The flies live only a week or so, mating and laying eggs in the soil. Each female may deposit 200 or more eggs. Eggs hatch in about 12 days, and the larvae begin feeding upon grass roots. Larvae may feed for nearly 2 years before pupating in the soil. The pupal stage lasts about a month.

Management. Little specific management information is available.

DICHONDRA FLEA BEETLE
Chaetocnema repens McCrea
(Plate 14)

Importance and Nature of Injury. The dichondra flea beetle is a destructive pest of dichondra lawns in southern and central California. The beetles feed on upper leaf surfaces, causing distinct, crescent-shaped scars. When enough of the tissue is eaten away, the leaf turns brown. More severe damage is caused by the larvae, which occur within the upper 1–2 in. (2.5–5 cm) of soil. Larvae feed on the fine roots and outer surfaces of larger roots, working their way to the crown. Small larvae may burrow into the roots. Loss of roots causes the plants to wilt and die, often in large patches. When the damage is localized or spotty it may be mistaken for drought stress or fertilizer burn. The damage often begins next to sidewalks. When infestations are severe, the whole lawn can be destroyed within a month after the first symptoms appear.

Plants Attacked. This pest attacks only broad-leaved dichondra lawns. It does not damage turfgrasses or other economic crops.

Distribution. Dichondra flea beetles are a problem in California wherever dichondra lawns are grown (Figure 8.1).

Distinguishing Characteristics. The adult beetles are about 1/16 in. (1.5–1.7 mm) long, broadly oval, and dark reddish-black to reddish-brown with a bronze sheen. The femur of the hind legs is conspicuously enlarged, and the adults tend to jump when disturbed. The wing covers have longitudinal grooves with fine punctures. The front and middle pairs of legs and the antennae are yellowish-red. The tiny (0.5 mm), whitish eggs are laid on leaves and stems. Larvae, elongate and whitish with a light brown head, are found in the soil around the plant roots. Mature larvae are just under 1/4 in. (5–6 mm) long.

Life History and Habits. The adults overwinter in the upper soil or under plant debris near dichondra lawns. In May, the beetles become active, mating and laying eggs on leaves and stems near the soil surface. Eggs hatch in about 3 days; larval development is then completed in

Figure 8.1. *Distribution of the dichondra flea beetle in the continental United States.*

about 23–25 days. Pupation occurs in the soil; the new adults emerge about 5 days later. A complete generation takes about a month. There is continuous activity from May to October, with 4–6 generations per year. The adult beetles seek overwintering sites in November.

Management. Appearance of crescent-shaped feeding scars on the foliage is usually the first sign of this pest. Inspect closely for small, dark-colored beetles on the upper surface of leaves. Passing your open palm slowly just over the dichondra lawn causes the beetles to jump, and some will land on the back of your hand or arm, where they are easily spotted. Adults can also be sampled with a sweep net. Insecticide labels rarely include dichondra as a target site or list dichondra flea beetle as a target pest. Broad-spectrum insecticides will control the adult, which is the most accessible life stage.

EUROPEAN CRANE FLY OR LEATHERJACKET
Tipula paludosa (Meigan)
(Plate 2)

(*Note:* Other species of crane flies are sporadic pests of cool-season turf across the United States and southern Canada. They can be managed like the European crane fly.)

Importance and Nature of Injury. Larvae of crane flies are called "leatherjackets" because they are very tough-skinned. Leatherjackets use their rasping mouthparts to feed on roots, rhizomes, crowns, and leaf blades. They remain underground on bright days, but come to the surface to feed on damp, warm nights. Feeding aboveground may also occur on dark, cloudy days. Their nightly tunneling to the surface disrupts the soil and uproots young seedlings. Heavily infested turf may harbor 100 or more larvae per ft^2 (108 per 0.1 m^2). Most of the damage occurs in spring, when the larvae feed vigorously before pupation. Damaged turf appears sparse, with missing foliage and bare patches. Close inspection reveals large numbers of larvae in the thatch and upper soil. The adult flies emerge in late summer and may gather on the sides of homes and other structures. The adults are harmless, but their resemblance to giant mosquitoes may cause concern.

Plants Attacked. Leatherjackets attack all cool-season turfgrasses, as well as grasses in pastures and hayfields. They prefer moist, thatchy turf and wet soils that are high in organic matter.

Distribution. The European crane fly is an introduced pest that occurs in northwestern Oregon, western Washington state, southern British Columbia, and Nova Scotia. It is a major problem in England and continental Europe. Other, less damaging species of crane flies occur throughout the cool-season turfgrass zones.

Distinguishing Characteristics. Adult crane flies look like giant mosquitoes. The body is brownish-tan and slender, about 3/4 to 1 in. (19–25 mm) long, with one pair of narrow, smoky-brown wings and very long, slender legs. Eggs are shiny black, elongate-oval, and about 3/64 in. (1.1 mm) long. Eggs are laid in the soil. The worm-like, cylindrical larvae range in color from olive-gray to greenish-brown. Full-grown ones are about 1 in. (2.5 cm) long. The larva withdraws its small, black-pointed head into the front part of the body when disturbed. The tail end bears two spiracles (breathing holes) on a plate-like structure that is surrounded by six fleshy, finger-like lobes. The pupa is translucent, greenish-brown, with the developing legs, wing pads, and antennae glued to the sides. The last five segments of the pupa have backward-pointing spines that enable it to wriggle to the soil surface when the adult is ready to emerge.

Life History and Habits. European crane flies have one generation per year. Adults emerge soon after sunset in August and September. Mating occurs on the foliage, and the female lays most of her 200–300 eggs on the night that she emerges. Eggs are laid just under the soil surface. They are sensitive to drying out and will perish unless the soil is moist. The eggs hatch in 11–15 days, and the small, brownish larvae begin feeding on fine roots, rhizomes, and foliage. By late fall, they have molted twice and reached the third instar. Larvae feed sparingly during the winter until molting to the fourth instar in early spring. Growth is rapid in April and May, the period of greatest damage. Larvae usually stop feeding by late May and begin moving downward as deep as 3 in. (7.5 cm) below the soil surface. There, the full-grown larvae remain relatively inactive until pupating in late July or mid-August. The pupa remains underground for 11–12 days before working its way to the surface. The empty pupal case is often left protruding from the ground where the adult has emerged.

Management. With its mild winters, cool summers, and abundant rainfall, the Pacific Northwest is well-suited for the European crane fly. A wet September followed by a mild winter seems to encourage outbreaks the following spring. Withholding irrigation in late August and September may reduce the survival of eggs and larvae. Ryegrasses may be less preferred than other grasses. Larvae can be sampled by taking cores with a golf hole cutter and breaking apart the soil by hand. A damage threshold of 15–20 leatherjackets per ft^2 (16–22 per m^2) has been suggested. Products containing the nematode *Steinernema carpocapsae* have given good control of leatherjackets. Conventional insecticides are also effective if applied when the larvae are active.

GROUND PEARLS
Margarodes species
(Plate 2)

Importance and Nature of Injury. Ground pearls are unusual, soil-dwelling insects that infest roots of warm-season turfgrasses. They are named for the pearl-like appearance of the cysts that enclose the immature stages. Ground pearls cause sporadic, occasionally severe damage on lawns, golf courses, sod farms, and sports fields. Females and nymphs suck juices from the roots, resulting in scattered, irregular patches of sparse or dying grass. The injury appears in summer, especially during periods of drought. The symptoms may be mistaken for injury from southern chinch bugs, but with ground pearls, no insects will be found at the base of the plants or in the thatch. Presence of females or cysts can be confirmed by digging up the soil in suspected areas and examining the roots to 5 in. (12.5 cm) or greater depth. The pearl-like cysts will usually be most abundant near the boundary between damaged and apparently healthy turf.

The density of ground pearls often varies considerably from spot to spot, even within a small infested area. Ground pearls are believed to produce a toxic saliva that hastens the death of plants. Once the grass has died out it rarely grows back; only weeds will grow in these damaged areas.

Plants Attacked. Hybrid bermudagrasses and centipedegrass are most susceptible, but St. Augustinegrass and zoysiagrass also are attacked.

Distribution. Ground pearls attack warm-season turfgrasses from North Carolina to Florida, and across to Southern California (Figure 8.2). *Margarodes meridionalis* Morrill is the most common species in turf.

Distinguishing Characteristics. Most of the life cycle occurs underground. Adult females are soft-bodied, pink-colored, pear-shaped insects, about 1/16 in. (1.6 mm) long. The front legs are robust, with stout claws; the middle and hind pairs of legs are shorter. Eggs are laid in clusters enclosed in a white, waxy sac. Newly hatched nymphs, called crawlers, are <1/100 in. (0.2 mm) long. Crawlers disperse in the soil, inserting their sucking mouthparts into grass roots. The crawler then molts, losing its legs and antennae, and secretes a waxy material that hardens into a globular shell, or cyst. The nymph develops inside the cyst, its mouthparts extending through the wall and into a grass root. The cyst, resembling a miniature pearl, is enlarged as the insect grows. Cysts range from about the size of a grain of sand to just over 1/16 in. across (0.5–2 mm). Their color varies from pearly white to yellowish or purple. Adult males are tiny, pinkish to white gnat-like insects with delicate wings. Males are short-lived and rarely seen. They lack functional mouthparts and do not damage turf.

Life History and Habits. Little is known about the habits of ground pearls. Winter is passed in the nymphal stage, inside the pearl or cyst. Adults emerge from the cysts in late spring and crawl to the surface, where mating occurs. The pink females may be seen slowly moving about on the soil surface during late May and June. Mated females burrow down in the soil about 2–3 in. (5–7.5 cm) and secrete a whitish, waxy material that covers the body and forms a sac in which the eggs are laid. Egg-laying begins in June and continues into July. Eggs are laid in clusters among the grass roots, each female depositing about 100 eggs over a 1–2 week period. Within a cluster, the eggs begin hatching 9–15 days after the first ones are laid. Most of the eggs hatch by early August. The young crawlers disperse, attach to roots, and begin forming the distinctive cysts. There is normally one generation per year, but if conditions are unfavorable some individuals may take 2 or even 3 years to complete their life cycle.

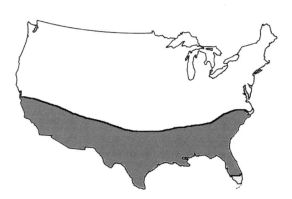

Figure 8.2. Distribution of ground pearls in the continental United States.

Management. No insecticides are presently labeled for ground pearls. Attempts at chemical control have failed because the pearls may be as deep as 10 in. (25 cm), and because the nymphs are protected by the waxy cyst throughout most of their life. Relative susceptibility of the various life stages to insecticides is unknown, so the optimal timing for treatments has not been determined. Targeting the emerging females, or use of systemic insecticides in spring against the developing stages, are tactics being investigated. Killing the turf with herbicides and then reseeding, resodding, or sprigging will not get rid of ground pearls because the encysted nymphs can survive for long periods under drought, or without food. Turf that is reestablished in damaged areas is likely to be attacked and killed. At present, the only effective control is to reduce other stresses, and to fertilize and irrigate to enhance turf vigor. These practices may help to slow the spread of damage, but they will not eliminate the problem.

MARCH FLIES
Bibio and *Dilophus* species
(Plate 1)

Importance and Nature of Injury. March flies are medium-sized, dark flies that are occasionally seen swarming over turf. They favor moist lawns with excessive thatch or decaying plant material. The larvae feed mainly on organic matter but occasionally damage roots of turfgrasses. March flies tend to infest turf that has already been damaged by other soil insects or diseases such as snow mold. Larvae are sometimes found under patches of dead turf that appear in the spring after snowmelt. The damaged turf easily pulls up to reveal numerous light-brown, worm-like maggots. Although March fly larvae are usually not the primary cause of turf loss, their feeding may contribute to the damage.

Plants Attacked. March fly larvae are occasional, minor pests of cool-season turfgrasses, especially moist lawns with dense thatch and soils with high organic matter.

Distribution. Various species occur through much of the world. Infestation of turf has been reported in North America, Europe, and Asia.

Distinguishing Characteristics. The adults are about as long as a housefly, with a stout, humpbacked thorax and narrow abdomen. They are usually black, with brown or yellow legs. The wings are held flat over the abdomen, and each wing has a dark spot midway down the front margin. Some species have dark-colored wings. Males have huge eyes that practically cover the head; eyes of females are smaller. Clusters of several hundred eggs are laid in areas of moist, decaying organic matter. Individual eggs are elongate and about 1/32 in. (0.8 mm) long. They are cream-colored at first, darkening to light reddish-brown before hatching. Larvae are fleshy and worm-like, dirty white to tan in color, with a nearly black head. Mature larvae range from 5/16 to 3/4 in. (8–19 mm) long, depending on the species. Pupae are found in the soil. They are a bit smaller than the full-sized larvae, yellowish-white, with visible wing pads, legs, and antennae.

Life History and Habits. March flies are so named because some species emerge in early spring. Those associated with turfgrass tend to be most abundant in April and May, depending on species, location, and weather. Swarms of adults may occur on moist, thatchy lawns. Adults are active on warm sunny days, flying short distances close to the ground. The flies themselves are harmless; they feed by sipping nectar from flowering plants. Adults live for only about a week. After mating, the females seek out moist, organic soil in which to lay eggs. The female fly burrows into the thatch and soil and forms a small egg chamber about an inch or so (2–4 cm) below the surface. Within this chamber, she deposits a mass of 100–400 eggs. Eggs hatch in about 3–5 weeks, depending on soil temperatures. Newly hatched larvae are legless; the tapered body has long bristles that help them to move through the soil. Larvae feed mainly on decaying plant material, but will sometimes gnaw roots that have been damaged by other soil insects. They may occur under piles of grass clippings, leaf litter, or manure. As the larva molts and grows, the body bristles are shed and a row of short fleshy projections develops on each segment. Larvae may become dormant during dry periods in summer, resuming feeding and growth in the fall. They are active under snow cover and may aggregate under patches of snow mold or grub-damaged turf. By late winter, the larvae are nearly mature. They then burrow 3/8 to 3/4 in. (1–2 cm) into the soil to pupate. A few weeks later, the adult flies dig to the surface to start a new annual cycle.

Management. March flies are rarely found in healthy turf. Controlling white grubs, billbugs, or fungal diseases should reduce the chances of March fly infestation. Cultural practices that reduce thatch buildup will discourage infestations. Avoid applying manure during periods when adult flies are active. No insecticides are currently registered for control of March fly larvae.

MOLE CRICKETS
Tawny mole cricket: *Scapteriscus vicinus* Scudder
Southern mole cricket: *Scapteriscus borellii* Giglio-Tos (= *S. acletus* Rehn & Hebard)
Short-winged mole cricket: *Scapteriscus abbreviatus* Scudder
Northern mole cricket: *Neocurtilla hexadactyla* (Perty)
(Plates 3,4)

Mole crickets are the most destructive insect pests of golf courses, lawns, and sod farms in the southeastern United States. These pests account for hundreds of millions of dollars in damage and control costs every year. Infestations may go undetected until the turf begins to die out in late summer and fall. By then, the nymphs are large and difficult to control. Effective management of mole crickets requires understanding of their life cycle and a year-round program that includes scouting, mapping, sampling, and timely use of insecticides.

Species, Origin, and Distribution. The tawny mole cricket (previously misidentified as the Changa or Puerto Rican mole cricket) and the southern mole cricket are the most destructive mole crickets found in the United States. Both species were inadvertently introduced into the southeastern United States from South America around 1900, and have spread north and west. They now are common throughout the Coastal Plain region south of a line running from the middle of North Carolina through mid-Louisiana to southeastern Texas (Figure 8.3). Colder temperatures will probably limit spread of the tawny and southern mole crickets to the north. Arid conditions may hinder their western expansion; however, a localized infestation of southern mole crickets is established around Yuma, Arizona. In South America, tawny and southern mole crickets are widespread in Argentina, Uruguay, and Brazil.

Two other species of mole crickets infest turfgrasses in the United States. The short-winged mole cricket, like the other *Scapteriscus* species, arrived in Florida and Georgia from South America about 1900. The adults have short wings and are incapable of dispersing by flight. This is probably why they are concentrated in coastal areas around ports of entry. Short-winged mole crickets occur mainly in southeastern Florida, and in the areas around Tampa and Sarasota–Fort Myers. Where they occur, they can be as damaging as tawny mole crickets. Localized populations occur elsewhere in Florida, as well as in Georgia, Haiti, Nassau, Puerto Rico, Cuba, and the Virgin Islands. The northern mole cricket, *Neocurtilla hexadactyla* (Perry) is a native species found in the eastern half of the United States from Nebraska to Texas, and from southern Canada to Florida. It prefers moist, low-lying areas and is seldom, if ever, a pest in turf.

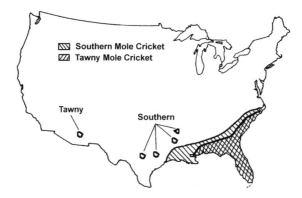

Figure 8.3. Distribution of tawny and southern mole crickets in the continental United States.

Distinguishing Characteristics. Adult mole crickets are well adapted for burrowing. They have large, beady eyes, broad, spade-like front legs to dig tunnels, and an enlarged, hardened prothorax used to shape and pack the soil. The body is cylindrical, about 1 to 1-1/4 in. (30–34 mm) long by about 3/8 in. (8–10 mm) wide, and covered with a dense coat of fine hairs. The forewings overlap and are shorter than the abdomen. The membranous hindwings are folded fan-like under the forewings and extend past the tip of the abdomen, except in the short-winged mole cricket.

Tawny and southern mole crickets are fairly easy to tell apart. Tawny crickets are slightly larger and more robust, and have a broader prothorax. The coloration of the two species is usually distinct. The tawny is tan to golden-brown with a mottled pattern on the pronotum (the top of the thorax behind the head). The southern mole cricket is grayish to reddish-brown and occurs in two color forms, having either a dark pronotum with four distinct, pale-colored spots, or a mottled pronotum. The most reliable way to separate the two species is to examine the tibial dactyls (digging claws) on the front legs. In tawny crickets, the dactyls are separated by a space narrower than their width and the space is V-shaped. In the southern mole cricket, the space is almost as great as the width of one dactyl and is U-shaped (Figure 8.4). The southern mole cricket is the more active species. When captured, it will often "play dead" and then suddenly begin moving rapidly. The tawny mole cricket is slower moving and typically does not play dead when handled.

The other mole crickets are also fairly easy to recognize. The northern mole cricket is distinguished by having four tibial dactyls (Figure 8.4). Short-winged mole crickets, like the southern mole cricket, have a distinct gap between the tibial dactyls, but the dactyls are slightly divergent. The hindwings extend no more than one-third the length of the abdomen, and the hind legs are distinctly mottled. Only in the short-winged mole cricket are the adult wings shorter than the pronotum. Large juveniles (nymphs) of other mole crickets also have short wings, but the right and left ones do not overlap.

Mole crickets have three developmental stages: eggs, nymphs, and adults. Eggs are round, translucent, and whitish; clutches of 25–60 eggs are laid in chambers excavated 4–12 in. (10–30 cm) below the soil surface. Newly hatched nymphs are small, <1/4 in. (6 mm) long, but grow larger as they develop through six to eight molts. Young nymphs are wingless, but otherwise resemble small adults. Older nymphs have visible wing pads which enlarge with each molt. You can tell the nymphs apart by examining the digging claws, as described for the adults. Adult males differ from females in having their forewings modified for sound production. Males have a harp-shaped resonating cell at the base of the wings.

Feeding Habits. Tawny and short-winged mole crickets are mainly vegetarians, feeding on grasses and other plants (Figure 8.5). They may leave their burrows at night to bite off stems

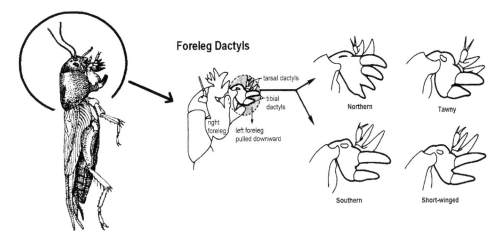

Figure 8.4. Leg characteristics for distinguishing among species of mole crickets (adapted from Walker et al., 1984). Turn the cricket on its left side, pull down the left foreleg, and examine the digging claws (dactyls). See text for explanation of differences.

and leaves, which are dragged into the burrow and consumed. Roots may be eaten at any time. In contrast, southern mole crickets are mostly carnivorous, preying on a variety of soil-inhabiting insects and earthworms. They may also feed sparingly on plant material. Food preferences are the same for nymphs and adults.

Nature of Injury. Because of its root-feeding habits, the tawny mole cricket is the species most damaging to turfgrasses. Heavily infested turf has almost no root system and is easily damaged by foot traffic, golf carts, or recreational play. Tawny, southern, and short-winged mole crickets also cause extensive damage by tunneling just below the soil surface. This activity uproots the plants, causing the roots to dry out and killing the grass. Tunneling is especially destructive to newly sprigged or seeded areas. Sod infested with mole crickets is hard to transplant. On golf putting greens, the burrows push up the soil, affecting ball roll. Individual tunnels may exceed 20 ft (6 m) in length. Within turf sites or pastures, tawny mole crickets tend to burrow in grassy areas, whereas southern mole crickets prefer the more bare, sandy areas. When mole crickets are abundant, their tunneling is so extensive that the ground feels spongy underfoot. During mating and overwintering the adults often throw up mounds of soil around their burrows. The worst damage occurs from August through early October when the large nymphs are actively feeding and the turf is under environmental stress. Damage from tunneling also occurs when the overwintered crickets become active in late winter and spring. Injury is usually minimal or absent during June and July, but increases thereafter as the nymphs feed and grow.

Mole cricket damage is affected by differences in the growth habit of particular turfgrasses, and by cultural practices. Damage is accentuated in bahiagrass because its open growth habit allows greater drying out of the root system once the soil is disturbed. When bermudagrass is mowed close, such as on golf fairways, rooting depth is reduced. This makes the turf more susceptible to uprooting and desiccation from tunneling by mole crickets. St. Augustinegrass does not seem to show as severe a response, probably because of its more canopy-like growth habit and coarser root system. Zoysiagrass is rarely damaged by mole crickets. Among cultivars of St. Augustinegrass, bahiagrass, and bermudagrass, those with the finest texture are most heavily damaged.

Plants Attacked. Dactylon and hybrid bermudagrasses, bahiagrass, and St. Augustinegrass are most susceptible, followed by centipedegrass. Pasture grasses and seedlings of ornamentals, vegetables, and tobacco may also be damaged.

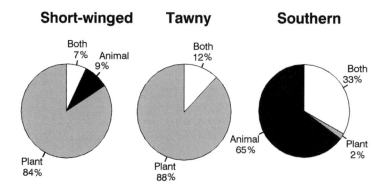

Figure 8.5. Feeding habits of pest mole crickets, as determined by examination of gut contents. Note that tawny and short-winged mole crickets are mainly herbivorous, whereas southern mole crickets are mainly carnivorous (adapted from Walker et al., 1984 and USDA).

Life History and Habits. In central Florida and northward, both the tawny and southern mole crickets have one generation each year. Their life cycles are similar, except that most of the tawny cricket population overwinters as adults, whereas most southern mole crickets overwinter as large nymphs (Figure 8.6). The seasonal cycle may be a month earlier in central Florida than in cooler, more northern parts of the range. Knowledge of the timing of local population cycles is important for effective management.

Mole crickets spend most of their lives underground. They overwinter in deep burrows but may become active during warm periods in winter, producing short tunnels near the surface. When the soil warms in March and April and night temperatures approach 60°F (15°C), their tunneling and feeding increase. Crickets that overwintered as nymphs will develop into adults in the spring.

Presence of mole crickets is most obvious during the springtime flights, when large numbers may be attracted to outdoor lights. Mole crickets fly to locate mates and new egg-laying sites, and for long-range dispersal. In northern Florida, the tawny cricket flies from mid-February to May, whereas the southern mole cricket begins and ends its flights a few weeks later, from April to July (Figure 8.7). Enormous numbers of both species may fly on the same night. Flights typically are heaviest on warm, clear nights following a rain. Individual crickets can fly several miles, and may fly more than once. The practical consequence of dispersal flights is that sites that have been treated for mole crickets are rapidly reinfested. Both species also have a minor flight period in October–November, but the crickets apparently do not mate at this time. In southern Florida, the southern mole cricket has two distinct summer flights, the latter apparently representing a second generation of adults (Figure 8.7).

Flights of both species begin soon after dusk and last about 60–90 minutes. The male first locates a suitable site to call for a mate. This is typically a grassy area on moist, light sandy soil. After digging a small chamber that opens to the surface, he produces a calling song to attract females. The chamber acts as a megaphone to amplify the mating call. The call of each species is distinctive, differing in tone and pulse rate. Tawny mole crickets produce a buzz-like trill, with intermittent silent periods of less than 1 second. Southern mole cricket songs are more musical and continuous. The calls can be heard coming from the ground for a hour or so, just after dusk.

The female may lay eggs near where she mated, or she may disperse by flying. After finding a suitable site, she feeds and tunnels for about 2 weeks before egg-laying begins. She then digs a small chamber, about the size of a golf ball, in which a clutch of 25–60 gray or brownish eggs is laid. Egg chambers are formed 4–12 in. (10–30 cm) below the surface. If she survives long enough, a female may construct several such chambers and lay as many as 150 eggs. Most of

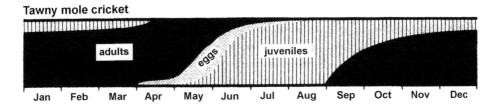

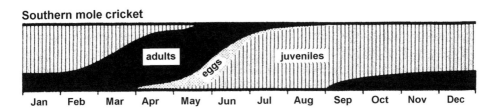

Figure 8.6. *Seasonal occurrence of life stages of tawny and southern mole crickets in northern and central Florida. Note the difference between the two species in the proportion of overwintering crickets that are juveniles (from Walker et al., 1984).*

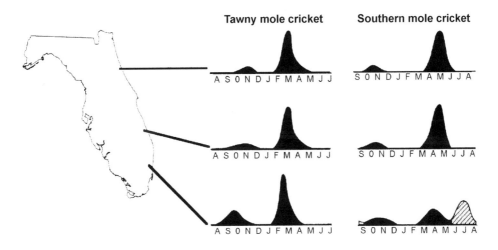

Figure 8.7. *Flight periods of tawny and southern mole crickets in northern, central, and southern Florida. Small fall flights precede larger spring flights of a single generation (see Figure 8.6). In southern Florida, summer flights of southern mole crickets (hatched area) represent a second generation of adults (from Walker et al., 1984).*

the parental adults die off soon after mating and egg-laying. In northern Florida, tawny mole crickets begin egg-laying in late March, continuing through mid-June. Eggs take about 3 weeks to develop into nymphs in warm soil. Most eggs hatch during May and June, and nearly all of the young nymphs will have hatched out by early July. In contrast, southern mole crickets may lay eggs later into the summer, and it is not uncommon to find young hatchlings in August and September. Again, some latitudinal variation will occur.

After hatching, the nymphs tunnel to the surface and feed in the upper soil and litter. Feeding and growth continue through the summer and fall, so that by December about 85% of tawny mole cricket nymphs will have reached adulthood. The rest will overwinter as large nymphs, maturing by the following spring. In contrast, only about 25% of the southern mole crickets reach adulthood by winter, with most of the population overwintering as nymphs (Figure 8.6). Although some adults of both species are present in the fall, there is little mating and no eggs are laid until the following spring. Both species have a minor flight of adults in the fall, consisting mainly of dispersing females.

Mole crickets burrow and feed mainly at night. Most activity is just below the soil surface, especially on warm nights following rains or irrigation. The crickets may also come to the surface to forage at such times. They return to their permanent burrows during the day and may remain there for long periods when conditions are dry.

The life cycle of the short-winged mole cricket is not as well known. This species cannot fly; rather, it disperses by tunneling or crawling. It may also be inadvertently transported in sod or soil. All life stages seem to be present at all seasons of the year, but there is a peak of egg-laying in late spring or summer, and a lesser peak in winter. Short-winged mole crickets feed on roots, stems, and leaves in a manner similar to tawny mole crickets. Where they are abundant, short-winged mole crickets cause considerable damage.

Managing Mole Crickets

Mole crickets are among the most difficult of the turfgrass insects to control. Managing these pests is not a one-time, single-treatment operation. Unlike most other destructive insects that can be eliminated after infestations develop, mole crickets require a systematic, annual plan. Proper timing of applications is at least as important as the choice of insecticide. It is important to know *where* the damaging infestations are likely to occur, *when* the eggs hatch, and *how* hatching progresses to determine when the vulnerable young nymphs are present. Most experienced turf managers follow a systematic approach that includes (1) site assessment and mapping; (2) properly timed insecticide applications; and (3) evaluation and revision of control strategies.

Site Assessment and Mapping. As temperatures warm in early spring, overwintered mole crickets become active. Spring is the best time to scout for tunneling and mound-making activity by the large nymphs and adults. This will reveal areas where mole crickets are abundant and eggs are being laid. By recording and mapping locations of infested areas, you can target high-risk sites for treatment later in the season, after the more vulnerable new-generation nymphs have hatched.

Maps indicating infested areas can be kept on photocopied blueprints, aerial photos, golf score cards, or on the computer (Figure 3.1). Noting landmarks such as large trees, yardage markers, and bunkers will help you to relocate specific infestation sites. A frame made from PVC pipe subdivided by strings into nine smaller squares is useful for rating the damage. The grid is thrown over an infested site and the number of sections with tunnels or damage is counted, providing a numerical rating that can be recorded on the map. Two people can map a golf course in about 6–8 hours. Annual re-mapping requires less time because infestations tend to recur in the same spots unless management practices vary significantly and turf quality changes. Few golf courses will require wall-to-wall treatments. Once you develop a good mole cricket map, it's quicker and more cost-effective to target infested areas than to treat the entire site. By helping you to pinpoint mole cricket "hot-spots," mapping saves labor and reduces pesticide usage and costs.

Timing of Controls. Controlling mole crickets in spring before they lay eggs is rarely effective in the long run. In spring, the crickets are large and not very susceptible to insecticides. They tend to retreat underground in response to cold or dry weather. During egg-laying, females burrow deep into the soil, out of reach of insecticides. As spring progresses, more and more eggs will have been deposited that are not affected by treatments. Finally, the adults are constantly on the move in search of mates and egg-laying sites. A treatment applied one week may not protect against new migrants that reinfest the turf a couple of weeks later. Thus, the benefits from spring treatment will be short-lived at best. Spring applications may be justified to reduce tunneling damage in highly-maintained turf areas or sod fields, but they will not usually eliminate the need for treatment later in the season. The best approach is to spot-treat as necessary to protect high-priority areas, and to map the locations of adult activity for treatment later, after the eggs have hatched.

The best time to control mole crickets with conventional, short-residual insecticides is mid-summer, after most eggs have hatched but when the crickets are still small. This usually falls around mid to late June in north and central Florida, earlier in south Florida, and as much as 2–3 weeks later in North Carolina. Treatments in June or July against the young nymphs will be more effective than later applications against larger mole crickets. If tunneling activity was noted during the spring, there is a good chance that the area will be reinfested with new-generation nymphs.

Effective control of mole crickets requires monitoring the seasonal cycle to determine when the eggs have hatched. Some golf superintendents track the flights with electronic callers that mimic the songs of male crickets. These traps are not useful for direct control because only a small fraction of the population is caught. Noting numbers of crickets attracted to outdoor lights can also give an estimate of the flight period. However, most turf managers use soap flushes to monitor seasonal development of the mole cricket population.

Sampling with a disclosing solution (Chapter 3) is useful for verifying that eggs have hatched, and for estimating the density of nymphs. Mow the grass beforehand so the crickets will be easier to spot. Mix two tablespoons (30 mL) of lemon-scented liquid dishwashing detergent in 2 gal (8 L) of water and pour, or apply with a sprinkling can, over about a square yard (0.8 m^2) of turf. If crickets are present, most will come to the surface within a few minutes. Watch the soaked area for movement. The smallest nymphs are hard to see, and they may stop moving when they surface. Water the sampled area after flushing to reduce any chance of sun scalding. Soap flush sampling is most effective in summer, during periods when the soil is warm and moist, and the nymphs are burrowing and feeding close to the surface. It works best when applied a day or so after rains or deep irrigation. During cooler periods in spring and fall, or during extended dry spells, most of the population may be too deep in the soil to be reached by the drench. In very dry soils, pre-sampling irrigation and a second drench of water may be needed to flush the crickets.

What density of mole crickets justifies a treatment? That depends on the location (i.e., green, tee, or fairway) and condition of the turf. Experience is your best guide. Effective mapping and selective treatment of greens, tees, and fairways will result in savings that can be applied to infested areas in roughs, which can serve as reservoirs for reinfestation of high-profile areas. Most lawns will tolerate low densities of mole crickets.

Soap flushes of early season tawny crickets can provide information about egg development, egg-laying, and hatch. Tawny crickets deposit most of their eggs in a single clutch that hatches in about 3 weeks. One trick is to soap-flush the females, tear off the head and skin, and examine the mass of eggs. Females containing eggs that feel like firm "beads" between the fingers would probably have deposited those eggs within a week or so. If most females examined have eggs of this type, you can expect peak egg hatch in about a month unless there are late frosts or spring drought occurs.

By starting soap flushes in early June and comparing the abundance and size of the nymphs each week, you can gauge the development of the current year's brood. Remember — mole crickets are easiest to control when they are small. The ideal timing with short-residual insecticides is after most of the eggs have hatched, but before the earliest hatching crickets have reached 1/2 in. (1.25 cm) in length. That way, you'll control most of the annual brood, and enough insecticide residue will remain to kill many of the late-hatching stragglers. This treatment period is sometimes overlooked because symptoms of the crickets' spring feeding and tunnelling are no longer obvious. If you wait until damage from the new brood shows up in the late summer, however, the crickets will be large and much harder to kill.

Improving Effectiveness of Treatments. Mole crickets are most active near the surface on warm nights, especially after rainfall or irrigation. Treatments applied during very dry conditions are often wasted because the crickets are deep in the soil. Make sure the soil is moist when applying a treatment. Wait until after a rain or irrigate several hours beforehand. Treat late in the day to reduce breakdown of the insecticide by sunlight and to increase contact with the night-feeding crickets. Don't treat unless the overnight temperature is expected to be above 60°F (15.5°C).

Various short-residual insecticides are labeled for mole cricket control. As discussed above, these usually work best against the young nymphs. Most products — except baits — specify that they should be watered in with 1/4 to 1/2 in. (6–12 mm) of irrigation. Imidacloprid (Merit®), which has a longer residual than other products, works best if applied just before or at the beginning of egg hatch. Timing of application, differences in soil texture and soil organic matter, and pH of the tank mix can alter the performance of particular insecticides. Read the label and product information sheets, and consult your Cooperative Extension office for information about which products work best in your area.

Some insecticides for mole crickets are formulated as baits. Insecticidal baits should not be watered in or applied if rain is expected within 24 hours. The bait will be ruined if it becomes water-soaked. Irrigate 3–4 hours *before* treatment to bring the crickets to the surface, where they will feed on the bait. Apply the bait late in the day. Bait applications following rainfall are useful for treating roughs or other areas where no irrigation is available to water in other products. Baits seem to be most effective when applied from mid-July through September. Baits may also be somewhat effective against adults in fall and spring.

Subsurface application, in which specialized equipment is used to place liquid or granular insecticides below the turf surface, is being evaluated for control of mole crickets. Subsurface equipment is more expensive and generally slower than conventional methods of application, but offers the potential advantages of reduced surface residues (less hazard) and control at lower rates of application (see Chapter 6). So far, the verdict is mixed regarding benefits of subsurface placement for mole cricket control. Subsurface application technology is changing rapidly as the equipment is evaluated and improved. You should learn as much as possible about the subject before investing in subsurface application equipment or contracting for such services.

Another concept in mole cricket control involves subsurface application of fipronil (Chipco® Choice®) using a slit applicator that uses disc coulters which cut narrow slits into the soil to allow for placement of the granules at the turf-soil interface. This tactic reportedly provides several months of residual control, allowing a broader application window than most other products.

Nonchemical Options. Biological insecticides containing the beneficial nematodes *Steinernema riobravis* and *Steinernema scapterisci* have been marketed for several years. These microscopic worms infect and kill only mole crickets. They do not harm beneficial insects, wildlife, or groundwater, nor do they feed on grass plants. These nematodes are effective mainly against the adult crickets, not the nymphs. The nematodes release bacteria that kill the cricket, and then use the carcass as a nursery to produce tens of thousands of infective juveniles that are released into the soil. The nematodes are mixed with water and applied with conventional spray equipment. As with chemical insecticides, they should be applied late in the day to warm, moist (pre-watered) soil. Post-treatment irrigation is essential when applying nematodes. Mole cricket infection must occur or the nematodes will soon die.

Plate 1. Fly pests of turf: A. March fly (left to right): mature larva, prepupa, pupa,
B. Australian sod fly larvae, **C.** Adult frit fly, **D.** Frit fly larva, **E.** Typical symptoms of frit
fly, showing yellowing of central leaf, **F.** Frit fly damage to bentgrass putting green.

Plate 2. European crane fly: A. Adult female, **B.** Larvae, called "leatherjackets," **C.** Larvae in lawn, **D**. Severe cranefly damage.

Ground pearls: **E.** Nymphal cysts, **F.** Mature female, **G.** Close-up of females, **H.** Damage to centipedegrass.

Plate 3. Mole crickets: A. Southern mole cricket, **B.** Tawny mole cricket, **C.** Short-winged mole cricket, **D.** Northern mole cricket, **E.** Dactyls (digging claws) of tawny (above) with narrow, V-shaped gap and southern (below) with wider, U-shaped gap, **F.** Southern (left) and tawny (right) mole crickets, showing typical coloration, **G.** Life stages (left to right), egg, small to large nymphs, adult.

Plate 4. Mole crickets: A. Sampling frame and supplies for soap flushing, **B.** Aftermath of soap flush (tawny mole cricket), **C.** Tawny mole cricket mounds, **D, E, F, G.** Tawny mole cricket damage to bermudagrass, **H.** Burrowing mounds and ridges of southern mole cricket.

Plate 5. White grubs: A. Typical damage (masked chafers), **B.** Turf rolled back to reveal grubs, **C.** Severe damage to fairway (masked chafers), **D.** Masked chafer grub, **E.** Newly laid and swollen eggs, and newly hatched grubs (masked chafer), **F.** (counterclockwise, from lower right): egg, 1st-, 2nd-, and 3rd-instar grubs (Japanese beetle), **G.** Raccoon digging, **H.** Damage by animal seeking white grubs.

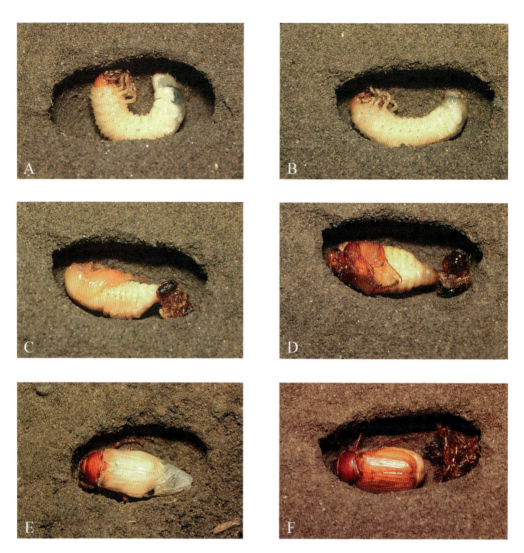

Plate 6. Transformation of white grub to an adult, illustrated by European chafer:
A. Larva in earthen cell, **B.** Prepupa, **C.** Young pupa, **D.** Mature pupa, **E.** Newly formed adult with transparent wing covers and unfolded hindwings, **F.** Mature beetle ready to emerge from soil.

Plate 7. Asiatic garden beetle: A. Adult beetle, **B.** Adults mating at night,
C. 3rd-instar grub, showing characteristic bulbous stipes (arrow), **D.** Raster of 3rd instar.

Oriental beetle: E. Adults, showing color variations, **F.** Most common color form,
G. Raster of 3rd instar grub.

Plate 8. Black turfgrass ataenius: A. Life stages (left to right): larva, pupa, callow adult, mature adult, **B.** Adults on postage stamp, **C.** 3rd-instar grubs in soil, **D.** Turf rolled back to reveal grubs, **E.** Damage to fairway.

Plate 9. European chafer: A. Adult male, **B.** Beetle mating flight to locust tree, **C.** Mating in tree, **D.** 3rd-instar grub actively feeding (left), and mature grub ready to pupate (right), **E.** Raster of 3rd-instar grub, **F.** Grub damage to lawn, with skunk digging.

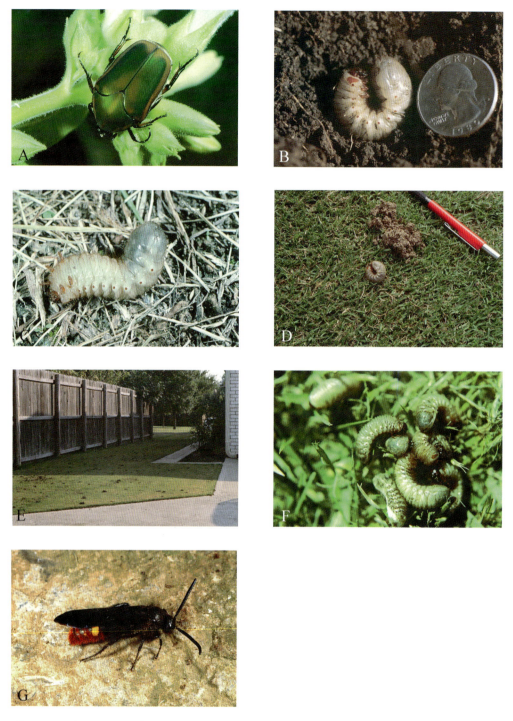

Plate 10. Green June beetle: A. Adult beetle, **B.** 3rd-instar grub, **C.** Mature grub crawling on its back, **D.** Young 3rd-instar, with burrow and mound, **E.** Damage (mounds) in bermudagrass, **F.** Dead grubs on surface following insecticide application, **G.** *Scolia dubia* wasp, a parasitoid of green June beetle grubs.

Plate 11. Japanese beetle: A. Adult beetles, **B.** Males attracted to virgin female emerging from turf, **C.** Aggregation of beetles, **D.** Typical top-down damage to tree, **E.** Milky-diseased grub (left) and normal grub; note color of blood droplet at clipped legs, **F.** Raster of 3rd-instar grub, **G.** Grub damage with skunk digging, **H.** Probe holes from birds feeding on grubs.

Plate 12. May beetles (*Phyllophaga* species): A, B. Adults of two different species, **C.** Newly hatched grubs, **D.** Typical 3rd-instar grub, **E, F.** Modifications of raster, showing zipper-like pattern of hairs, **G.** Mature grub of *Phyllophaga crinita* from Texas, **H.** Damage from *P. crinita* grubs, from armadillo digging.

Plate 13. Masked chafers: A. Males of southern (left) and northern (right) masked chafer, **B.** Southern male taking flight at dusk, **C.** Male southerns clustering around virgin female, **D.** 3rd-instar grubs of masked chafer (left) and Japanese beetle (right), showing relative size, **E.** Grub in soil, **F.** Raster of southern masked chafer, **G.** Severe damage to lawn, **H.** Damage to tee. (See also Plate 5).

Plate 14. Pests of dichondra lawns: A. Dichondra flea beetle, **B.** Crescent-shaped adult feeding scars on leaf, **C.** Flea beetle injury on dichondra, **D.** Flea beetle larva, **E, F.** Flea beetle damage to dichondra lawn. **G.** Vegetable weevil adults, **H.** Vegetable weevil larvae from dichondra.

Plate 15. Annual bluegrass weevil: A. Adult weevil, **B.** Larva in stem, **C.** Mature larva feeding at crown, **D.** Mature larva, **E.** Early summer damage mainly at edge of fairways, **F.** Severe damage to annual bluegrass, **G.** Damage to annual bluegrass on predominantly bentgrass putting green.

Plate 16. Bluegrass billbug: A. Adult bluegrass billbug, **B.** Mature larva, **C.** Larva in stem, **D.** Larval frass in root zone, **E.** "Tug-test" for billbug damage; stems will break off at crown, **F.** Frass visible at broken ends of stems, **G.** Damage to Kentucky bluegrass lawn.

Plate 17. Turf-infesting billbugs: A. Bluegrass billbug, **B.** Hunting billbug, **C.** Denver billbug, **D.** Phoenix billbug, **E.** Typical small and large billbug larvae, **F.** Severe billbug damage.

Plate 18. Hairy chinch bug: A. Long-winged and short-winged adult forms,
B. Nymphs and adult, relative to size of a pinhead, **C.** Size of newly hatched nymph,
D. Typical damage to Kentucky bluegrass lawn in full sun, **E.** Severe damage to lawn,
F. Big-eyed bug, a predator.

Southern chinch bug: G. Adult on St. Augustinegrass, **H.** Severe damage to lawn.

Plate 19. Greenbugs: A. Adults and nymphs feeding on Kentucky bluegrass, **B.** Close-up on grass blade, **C.** Typical damage under dripline of tree, **D.** Damage alongside house; note characteristic burnt-orange hue, **E.** Sweep net sample from infested lawn, **F.** Overwintering eggs on dead grass blade.

Plate 20. Sucking pests of warm-season grasses: A. Rhodesgrass mealybug adult female, **B.** Rhodegrass mealybug nymph, **C.** Bermudagrass scales, **D.** Bermudagrass scale damage, **E.** Two-lined spittlebug adult, **F.** Two-lined spittlebug nymphal spittle mass, **G.** Two-lined spittlebug feeding damage, **H.** Leafhopper on bermudagrass.

Plate 21. Mite pests of cool-season grasses: A. Clover mite on tall fescue, **B.** Clover mites, **C.** Clover mites—note elongate front legs, **D.** Winter grain mites, **E.** Winter grain mite feeding damage, **F.** Banks grass mite, **G.** Banks grass mite damage, **H.** Brown wheat mite.

Plate 22. Eriophyid mite pests of warm-season grasses: A. Bermudagrass mite; nomal (left) and mite-damaged (right) bermudagrass showing "witches' broom" effect, **B.** Bermudagrass mite damage, **C.** Bermudagrass mites under leaf sheath, **D.** Tufted growth caused by buffalograss mite, **E.** Buffalograss mites on internode, **F.** "Buggy-whip" injury caused by zoysiagrass mite.

Plate 23. Armyworms: A. Amyworm larva, **B.** Armyworm moth, **C.** Damage to turf caused by armyworms moving from adjacent wheat, **D.** Armyworms hiding in damaged Kentucky bluegrass, **E.** Armyworm damage to lawn, **F.** Fall armyworm showing inverted Y-marking on head, **G.** Fall armyworm adult, **H.** Lawn armyworms, partially grown.

Plate 24. Cutworms: A. Black cutworm moth, **B.** Black cutworm eggs laid on tips of creeping bentgrass, **C.** Full-sized black cutworm, **D.** Black cutworm and feeding damage on putting green, **E.** Black cutworm damage around aerification hole. **F.** Bronzed cutworm, **G.** Bronzed cutworm damage to lawn, **H.** Variegated cutworm.

Plate 25. Temperate-region sod webworms: A. Bluegrass webworm adult moth in typical resting posture, **B.** Striped sod webworm moth, **C.** *Crambus agitatellus* moth, **D.** Eggs of bluegrass webworm, **E.** Sod webworm with green frass and chewed grass blades, **F.** Sod webworm, **G.** Damage to Kentucky bluegrass, with bird peck holes, **H.** Severe sod webworm damage, with mainly clover and weeds remaining.

Plate 26. Other turf-infesting caterpillars: A. Cranberry girdler moth, **B.** Cranberry girdler larvae in soil, **C.** Moth of burrowing sod webworm, **D.** Burrowing sod webworm, **E.** Burrowing sod webworm in tunnel, **F.** Silken burrow linings of burrowing sod webworm, resembling cigarette papers, left on turf surface.

Plate 27. Caterpillars attacking warm-season grasses: A. Tropical sod webworm moth, **B.** Tropical sod webworm, **C.** Fiery skipper adult, **D.** Fiery skipper larva, **E.** Striped grass looper moth, **F.** Striped grass looper, **G.** Grass webworm, mature larva, **H.** Grass webworm damage to bermudagrass.

Plate 28. Ant pests in turf: A. Red imported fire ant workers, **B.** Winged fire ant queen,
C. Fire ant mound, **D.** Fire ant mound disturbed, **E.** Harvester ants eating snail,
F. Harvester ant mound, with cleared vegetation, **G.** Nuisance ant damage in St.
Augustinegrass, **H.** Ant mounds on putting green.

Plate 29. Stinging or biting pests: A. Yellowjacket wasp, **B.** Paper wasps on nest,
C. Baldfaced hornet nest, **D.** Cicada killer wasp with burrow and mound, **E.** Adult female
Lyme disease tick (top), showing small size compared to females of lone star tick (left)
and American dog tick (right), **F.** Flea.

Dangerous spiders *not* normally found in turf: G. Black widow, **H.** Brown recluse.

Plate 30. Nuisance pests in turf:
A. Millipede, **B.** Centipede, **C.** Earwigs,
D. Sowbug, **E.** Slug, **F.** Crayfish burrow,
G. Shed nymphal skin of cicada,
H. Short-tailed cricket, **I.** Earthworm
castings on golf fairway.

Plate 31. Beneficial natural enemies in turf: A. Predatory ground beetles, **B.** Ladybird beetle larva, a predator of greenbugs, **C.** Green lacewing, **D.** Wolf spider, E. *Tiphia* wasp, a parasitoid of white grubs, **F.** *Tiphia* larva feeding on grub, **G.** Mature *Tiphia* larva (left) with remains of grub (right), **H.** Cocoon of *Tiphia* wasp.

Plate 32. Vertebrate animal damage to turf: A. Typical ridges of eastern mole,
B. Typical mounds of star-nosed mole, **C.** Meadow vole damage after snow melt,
D. Pocket gopher mounds on bermudagrass golf fairway, **E.** Birds feeding on turf
caterpillars, **F.** Crow damage, **G.** Skunk digging for white grubs, **H.** Close-up of skunk
damage, showing characteristic golf ball–sized pits. See also Plates 5,9,11,12, and 25.

Like most biological controls, nematodes may not be as reliable as chemical insecticides. Incidence of treatment failures tends to be higher than with conventional products. Most often, the pests are suppressed rather than eliminated. As with short-residual insecticides, use of nematodes in spring or fall reduces immediate turf damage done by the adults but usually does not replace the need for treating heavily infested areas in mid-summer. Nematodes may be an alternative for treating near waterways or other environmentally sensitive sites.

A biological insecticide containing the fungus *Beauveria bassiana* (Naturalis®-T) has recently been marketed for control of mole crickets and certain other turf insects. There is presently little information on the level of suppression that this product may provide.

Efforts have been directed at area-wide biological control of mole crickets using introduced natural enemies. A red-eyed, parasitic fly, *Ormia depleta* (Wiedemann), originally from Brazil, has been established throughout most of Florida and released in North and South Carolina and Georgia. *Larra bicolor* F., a sphecid wasp that parasitizes adult and nymphal mole crickets, was also imported into south Florida. These beneficial agents, unfortunately, do not seem to have had a major impact on mole cricket populations. Neither parasite is commercially available for release.

Evaluation and Revision of Control Strategies. Weather, soil moisture, and other factors affect mole cricket behavior and control with insecticides. How well a particular product works can vary widely from site to site, and in different years. No one treatment is 100% effective. Turf managers should follow up after treatment to verify if a control measure was successful. Wait a week or so after application, apply a soap flush, and see what's still present in the soil. High-priority sites should be scouted for damage beginning in early August, with retreatment as necessary. Careful mapping in spring will simplify the fall followup because you'll already know where to look. However, be alert for "hot spots" that may previously have been missed. Mole crickets are quite mobile and reinfestations are common. Remember, when it comes to mole crickets, every turf situation is unique. These general guidelines provide a starting point, but you'll need to develop a customized plan that includes site knowledge, timely control, and evaluation.

WHITE GRUBS — INTRODUCTION
(Plates 5-13)

White grubs (sometimes called grubworms, or simply grubs) are the most widespread and destructive insect pests of turfgrasses in the cool-season and transition zones (Plate 5). White grubs damage turfgrasses by chewing off the roots near the soil surface. When this is accompanied by hot weather and drought, the loss of turf can be swift and severe. Vertebrate predators, including birds, skunks, raccoons, armadillos, foxes, wild pigs, and moles, may dig up infested turf to feed on the grubs. These varmints often cause more damage than the grubs themselves. Because they feed underground, grubs may not be detected until considerable loss of roots has occurred. Grubs are difficult to control because soil insecticides must penetrate the turf canopy and thatch layer in order to reach the upper soil. Turf managers must rely on gravity and irrigation to leach the insecticide into the target zone.

White grubs are the larvae of stout-bodied beetles called **scarabs** or scarabaeids. At least 10 species of white grubs are pests of turfgrasses in North America. Among native grub species, the most important and widespread are the northern and southern masked chafers, *Cyclocephala borealis* and *C. lurida*, black turfgrass ataenius, *Ataenius spretulus*, May beetles (*Phyllophaga* species), and the green June beetle, *Cotinis nitida*. Other native species include the southwestern masked chafer, *Cyclocephala pasadenae*, and the western masked chafer, *C. hirta*. Several other species of turf-infesting scarabs were accidentally introduced into the United States from the Orient or Europe between 1916 and 1940. Of these, the Japanese beetle, *Popillia japonica*, has become a severe pest through most of the eastern United States. Three other introduced species — the European chafer, *Rhizotrogus majalis*, the oriental beetle, *Anomala orientalis*, and the Asiatic garden beetle, *Maladera castanea* — are of regional importance, mainly in the Northeast. Grubs of another introduced species, *Aphodius granarius*, are minor pests, mainly in the Great Lakes region and northern Great Plains.

The various species of white grubs are generally similar in appearance, habits, and the damage they cause. The following overview provides a basis for understanding the biology and management of the group as a whole. Important species are then discussed in more detail in individual sections.

Signs of Infestation

White grubs chew off the roots close to the soil surface or just below the thatch. Early turf symptoms include gradual thinning, yellowing, wilting in spite of adequate soil moisture, and appearance of scattered, irregular dead patches. As damage continues the dead patches join together and increase in size. Infested turf feels spongy underfoot because of the grubs having churned up the underlying soil. Turf that is grub-damaged is not well-anchored to the soil; it can be pulled up or rolled back like a carpet, exposing the white, C-shaped larvae (Plate 5). Often, the grubs that you see are only part of the infestation; others are feeding just under the soil surface. If the damaged turf does not pull up easily, the brown patches are usually from other causes — dog urine, chemical spills, fertilizer burn, drought, localized dry spot, or disease. Presence of moles, flocks of foraging birds, or digging by skunks, raccoons, armadillos, or other predators often indicates that grubs are present.

Grubs of the green June beetle differ somewhat in feeding habits from other grub species. They feed more on decaying organic matter than on living roots, but damage the turf by burrowing and pushing up mounds of soil, much like miniature moles.

Description of Life Stages

White grubs undergo complete metamorphosis; the life stages consist of eggs, larvae, pupae and adults (Figure 8.8). The adults are stout, oval beetles that range in length from <3/16 in. (5 mm) for black turfgrass ataenius, to about 1 in. (25 mm) for green June beetle and larger *Phyllophaga* species. Depending upon species, their color ranges from green to various shades of tan, brown, or black. The front wings are hardened into shell-like wing covers, called **elytra**, that meet in a line down the middle of the back. The membranous hindwings are folded under the elytra, except when the beetle flies. The tibiae of the front legs have stout teeth on their outer margins that help the beetle to burrow in soil. The last three segments of the antennae are flattened and held together to form a distinct club. Males of most species can be distinguished from females by their larger antennal club.

Female scarabs deposit their eggs in moist soil, typically 1–4 in. (2.5–10 cm) deep in the root zone of turf or pasture grasses. Eggs of the various species are similar in appearance, except for size. Eggs are shiny, milky white, and oval when first laid, becoming swollen and more spherical after they have absorbed water from surrounding soil. The eggshell is elastic and stretches to accommodate the growing embryo. The dark mandibles of the tiny grub are visible within eggs that are close to hatching.

Grubs of the different species also resemble one another except for size (Figure 8.9). The length of mature grubs ranges from about 3/8 in. (10 mm) for the black turfgrass ataenius to nearly 2 in. (50 mm) for the green June beetle. Mature grubs of medium-sized species such as Japanese beetles and masked chafers are about 3/4 to 1 in. (19–25 mm) long. The body consists of a distinct brown head with chewing mandibles, a thorax with three pairs of short, jointed legs, and a 10-segmented abdomen (Figure 8.8). The thorax and abdomen are gray-white, whit-

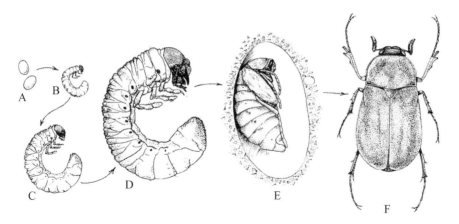

Figure 8.8. Life stages of a May beetle, a typical scarab. From eggs (A), three larval instars develop (B,C, and D), pupation occurs in a cell in the soil (E), and finally the adult beetle (F) emerges (from Pfadt, 1978, with permission).

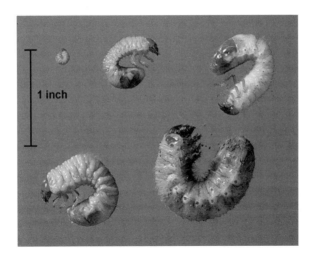

Figure 8.9. Variation in size of species of turf-infesting white grubs collected from one Kentucky golf course in September. Clockwise from upper left: black turfgrass ataenius, Japanese beetle, masked chafer, green June beetle, May beetle (photo by W. Mesner).

ish, or cream colored, but the hind part of the abdomen often appears dark colored because of ingested soil and plant material in the gut. The skin is transversely wrinkled and covered with scattered, short brown hairs. White grubs assume a characteristic C-shaped posture when feeding or at rest. All species have three larval instars, increasing in size with each molt. The head of a newly molted grub is wider than the thorax and abdomen. As the larva grows, its thorax and abdomen fill out until they are wider than the hardened head capsule, which remains the same size until the next molt.

When the grub is nearly mature it forms an earthen cell in which to pupate (Plate 6). It first transforms to a **prepupa**, a brief, nonfeeding stage. The prepupa somewhat resembles the larva, but is more wrinkled and tender. It eliminates most of the soil and fecal matter from the gut, so the abdomen becomes uniformly light colored. The **pupa** is whitish at first, darkening with age and taking on the adult coloration just before the beetle emerges. The developing wings and legs are folded close to the body, but are clearly visible (Figure 8.8). In some species (e.g.,

European chafer), the **exuviae** (cast skin) of the larva is sloughed off and remains attached to the hind end of the pupa. Other species (e.g., Japanese beetles) pupate within the thin, mesh-like exuviae, which surrounds the pupa like a shroud. The exuviae splits lengthwise as the pupa matures and the adult nears emergence.

Identification of Grub Species

Most adult scarabs are easily distinguished from one another on the basis of size, coloration, and habits, i.e., whether active by day or night, or if they are observed feeding on plants. However, adults of some of the May beetles (*Phyllophaga* species) are so similar in general appearance that an expert is needed for species identification.

Turf managers more often are concerned with identifying the larvae. This is especially important when "fine-tuning" management programs because some insecticides seem to work better against some grub species than others. It's good to know what species of grub you are dealing with. White grubs can be identified by examining the **raster** — an area of spines, hairs, and bare spaces on the underside of the last abdominal segment, just in front of the anus (Figure 8.10). The rastral pattern is like a fingerprint; each species has a different arrangement of spines and hairs. A 10- to 15-power hand lens is adequate for viewing these features. The rastral pattern stays the same for all larval instars. The shape of the anal slit is also useful for species identification. This slit may be transverse (crosswise), as in Japanese beetle grubs, longitudinal, as in the Asiatic garden beetle, or Y-shaped, with the stem of the Y shorter than the arms, as in May beetle grubs (Figure 8.10). Mature grubs of the black turfgrass ataenius are quite small, whereas those of the green June beetle are larger than other turf-infesting species. Size alone can be misleading, however, because first or second instars of large species are about the same size as mature grubs of small to medium-sized species. Live green June beetle grubs can be easily identified by their unique habit of crawling on their back.

Life Cycles and Seasonal Occurrence of Damage

Japanese beetles, masked chafers, European chafers, Asiatic garden beetles, oriental beetles, and green June beetles have annual (1-year) life cycles (Figure 8.11). These species mate and lay their eggs in mid-summer, mainly from late June to mid-August. The eggs hatch in 2–3 weeks and the hatchlings, about the size of a bluegrass seed, begin feeding on fine roots and organic matter. The grubs grow quickly, molting twice and becoming nearly full-sized by fall. Vigorous feeding continues until about the time of first frost (early October to November, depending on latitude), when declining soil temperatures cause the grubs to move deeper into the soil for overwintering. In early spring (March or April) when the soil begins to warm, the grubs move back up to the root zone and resume feeding. When the grubs are mature (typically mid-May to mid-June, depending upon species and latitude), they stop feeding, move deeper into the soil and transform into pupae. The new adults emerge several weeks later to complete the 1-year cycle.

Damage from grubs with annual life cycles usually shows up in late summer and early fall, after the larvae have become second and third instars. Symptoms are compounded when the turf is stressed by heat and drought. Injury is usually less apparent during the shorter, spring feeding period because temperatures are moderate, soil moisture is adequate, and the turf tolerates and outgrows the loss of roots.

Grub species with annual life cycles do not damage turf in June and July because, at that time, the population consists of life stages (pupae, adults, and eggs) that do not eat roots. In contrast, most May beetle species take 2 or 3 years to complete their life cycle, with continuous feeding throughout the second summer (see May Beetles). Another grub pest, the black turfgrass ataenius, has *two* generations per year except in northern parts of its range. If grub damage appears in June or July, either black turfgrass ataenius or May beetles are likely to be involved.

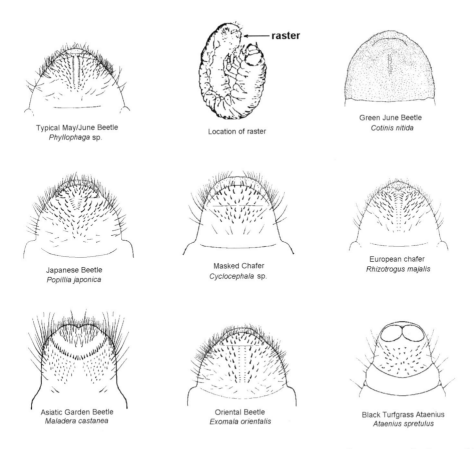

Figure 8.10. *Turf-infesting white grubs can be identified by examining the pattern of spines and hairs on the raster. A 10- or 15-power hand lens is adequate for this purpose. Species are not drawn to scale (adapted from Ohio State University Cooperative Extension Service).*

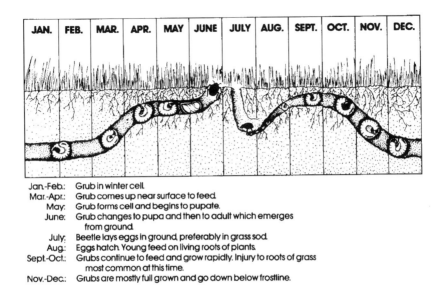

Figure 8.11. *Seasonal cycle of white grubs with an annual life cycle, such as masked chafers (adapted from Shurtleff et al., 1987; with permission).*

Most turf-infesting scarabs overwinter as larvae. Exceptions are the black turfgrass ataenius, which overwinters as adults, and May beetles, which overwinter as adults during the final year of the multi-year life cycle.

Activity and Feeding Habits of Adults

Adults of some white grubs (e.g., Japanese beetles, green June beetle, May beetles, Asiatic garden beetles) feed on leaves, flowers, and fruits. Japanese beetles, in particular, are major pests of woody and herbaceous ornamentals. Green June beetles feed on over-ripe fruit, sap oozing from bark wounds, and other sugary substances, whereas May beetles feed on leaves of oaks and other hardwood trees. Black turfgrass ataenius adults eat decaying organic matter or dung. Other scarabs (e.g., European chafers, Oriental beetles, and masked chafers) feed very little or not at all as adults. Because they are active by day, adult Japanese beetles and green June beetles are usually obvious as they fly about or feed on plants. Adults of most other species hide in the soil by day, becoming active at dusk or after dark. These scarabs may not be noticed except when they are attracted to outdoor lights.

MANAGING WHITE GRUBS IN TURF

Early Detection, Sampling, and Monitoring

Being alert to the signs and symptoms of white grubs can help you to avoid unexpected loss of turf and the need for costly reseeding or resodding of damaged areas. Sites with heavy beetle activity in June and July are more likely to have grubs in late summer. Swarms of masked chafer beetles skimming over the grass at dusk, green June beetles buzz-bombing the turf by day, or large numbers of tiny black turfgrass ataenius adults crawling on putting greens or flying in late afternoon are early warning signs. Dark colored, parasitic wasps hovering over the turf in late summer usually indicate presence of grubs. Be suspicious if moles, skunks, or flocks of birds find the turf attractive. Sample to confirm if grubs are present, however, because these predators may be after earthworms or other soil insects. Keep a close watch on areas that have been infested in past years, because the same sites often are reinfested.

Monitoring and sampling are keys to early diagnosis of grub problems. Most conventional insecticides, as well as entomopathogenic nematodes and insect growth regulators, work best against young insects — the younger the better. Early detection and proper timing are especially important when applying curative treatments. It takes an observant turf manager to detect the small grubs before the brown patches begin to show up and the damage gets out of hand. If a long-residual insecticide (e.g., imidacloprid, halofenozide) is used for preventive treatment, targeting those sites where heavy beetle activity is observed is less wasteful and more environmentally sound than going "wall-to-wall" with the insecticide.

When using short-residual insecticides for curative control, sample the turf first to determine if grubs are abundant enough to warrant the treatment. Concentrate on probable "hot-spots" — open, sunny locations, south-facing slopes, sites that were irrigated during beetle flights, tee and green banks on golf courses, and areas with a past history of grub problems. Japanese beetles lay eggs in moist, well-maintained turf near favored food plants. Adults of most night-flying species are attracted to outdoor lights and may deposit eggs in nearby turf. Black turfgrass ataenius and green June beetles prefer sites with a high amount of organic matter, decaying thatch, or where manure-based fertilizer was applied.

One method of sampling for grubs is to cut three sides of a square turf area, up to 1 ft² (0.1 m²) in size, with a flat-blade spade. Peel back the flap and examine the roots and soil to about 3 in. (7.5 cm) depth. After examining the sod, tamp it down and keep it watered to encourage regrowth. A standard golf cup cutter, 4-1/4 in. (11 cm) in diameter, is handy for sampling grubs.

Inspecting core samples in a grid pattern across the turf area can help you to determine the extent of an infestation. Multiply the number of grubs per core by 10 to estimate the average density per square foot. Golf fairways can be mapped by examining four plugs across the fairway at about 30 yard (27 m) intervals. With experience, a sampling crew of four or five persons can map an 18-hole golf course in about a day.

Examine multiple samples. Don't assume that the infestation will be uniform throughout an area. Grub infestations are usually patchy, probably because gradients in soil moisture and texture affect where the eggs are laid. It's rarely necessary to treat an entire lawn or fairway. Finding a few grubs does not necessarily justify control. Well managed, vigorous turf will outgrow considerable loss of roots without showing damage. Effects of light to moderate grub infestations can often be masked by irrigation to alleviate stress, together with a light fertilization to enhance recovery. The threshold density needed to cause visible damage will vary depending on grub and grass species, and with the overall vigor and use of the turf. Many turf managers begin to get "nervous" at about 6 to 10 grubs per square foot (0.1 m^2).

Knowledge of grub life cycles will help you to get the most out of your sampling, and to be more efficient with curative controls. Begin sampling several weeks before you expect grubs in order to monitor when eggs have hatched. Concentrate on suspected infestation sites. For species with annual life cycles (e.g., Japanese beetle, masked chafers), implement the full sampling plan for when most of the grubs have hatched out. This will typically be late July to early August in the transition zone, and about two weeks later in the Northeast. Mapping and record-keeping are helpful in tracking high-risk sites.

Another approach is to monitor the flight period of adult beetles using light traps for night-flying scarabs, or scent traps for Japanese beetles. Record the numbers of beetles captured each week or plot them on graph paper. The counts can be estimated by volume using a cup or other measure — there's no need to count every beetle. If the captures decline for 2 weeks in a row, the peak egg-laying period has probably passed. Eggs of most species hatch within 2–3 weeks. Therefore, an insecticide applied 3–4 weeks after peak beetle activity would allow time for most of the grubs to have hatched out. First emergence and peak flight of beetles can also be predicted from degree-day accumulations (see Chapter 4). Information on local timing for grub treatments is available from your county Extension office or state Agricultural Experiment Station (Appendix 1).

Cultural Control

Rainfall and soil moisture can affect the severity of grub damage during a given growing season, as well as densities of beetles and grubs the following year. In areas where summers are normally hot and dry, rainfall or irrigation during July and early August tends to favor survival of the eggs and young larvae. Eggs, in particular, must absorb water from the surrounding soil in order to develop and hatch. Watering during peak beetle activity in mid-summer tends to attract egg-laying females, particularly when soil in surrounding areas is dry. Thus, irrigated lawns and fairways will often have higher densities of grubs in late summer and fall.

Once the eggs have hatched, however, soil moisture begins to work in your favor. Now, rainfall or irrigation will mask the feeding damage and encourage regrowth of roots. Irrigated turf often will tolerate 15 or more grubs per ft^2 (16 per 0.1 m^2) before showing signs of injury. You can expect the number of grubs to be inversely related to the amount of rainfall in late summer. Moderate fertilization of cool-season grasses in the fall also helps to promote recovery of grub-damaged turf. In contrast, heavy nitrogen fertilization in spring tends to encourage excessive shoot growth at the expense of roots. This may weaken the turf stand and accentuate effects of grub damage and other stresses in the fall.

Environmental effects on white grub populations seem to vary somewhat from region to region, and among different grub species. In the Northeast, for example, densities of European chafer grubs seem to be highest in years when the spring was warm and relatively dry. Entomologists still know little about why grubs may be more, or less, abundant at particular sites, or in particular years.

Adult beetles of some species of white grubs are strongly attracted to favored food plants, increasing the likelihood that they will lay eggs in nearby, moist turf. Japanese beetles, for example, feed heavily on linden, Norway maple, purple-leaf plum, and sassafras, whereas many May beetles are especially fond of oaks. Avoiding use of such plants alongside golf course fairways or in home or commercial landscapes will reduce the reservoir of egg-laying adults. Certain wild plants may also draw large numbers of beetles; eliminating these plants may reduce grub populations in adjacent golf fairways. Specific recommendations are given in the sections on particular grub species. Green June beetle adults are attracted to sites with high organic matter, especially heavily manured areas. Removing composted yard waste and avoiding manure-based fertilizers encourages them to go elsewhere for egg-laying.

Host Plant Resistance

All species of cool-season turfgrasses, and many warm-season grasses, are susceptible to attack by white grubs. Resistant cultivars have not been found. Among cool-season grasses, tall fescue is generally more tolerant of grub damage than Kentucky bluegrass, creeping bentgrass, or perennial ryegrass. Once damaged, however, turfgrasses that produce rhizomes or stolons and have creeping, spreading growth habits (e.g., creeping bentgrass, Kentucky bluegrass) tend to fill in dead patches and recover more quickly than species with bunch-type growth. Endophytes of perennial ryegrass, tall fescue, and fine-leaf fescues don't seem to provide much resistance against grubs, evidently because the associated toxins do not occur at high enough levels in the roots. However, endophytes may possibly enhance stress tolerance and recovery of turf from grub damage.

Biological Control

Natural Enemies. Naturally occurring predators, parasites, and diseases are important in suppressing white grub populations. Ground beetles, ants, and other beneficial insects feed on the eggs and young grubs, and certain wasps and flies parasitize the older grubs (Chapter 14). Unfortunately, none of these beneficial agents is commercially available for use in biological control. Natural enemies, nonetheless, are important buffers against grub outbreaks and they should be conserved whenever possible. This is best accomplished by spot-treating rather than going "wall-to-wall" with insecticides, and using broad-spectrum insecticides only when necessary.

Entomopathogenic Nematodes. Insect-parasitic nematodes have been marketed for control of grubs and other pests (see Chapter 4). Most nematode-based products have contained *Steinernema carpocapsae,* a species that seems to be relatively ineffective against grubs. Other nematodes, notably *Steinernema glaseri* and *Heterorhabditis bacteriophora,* are more active against white grubs, but there have been technical problems in formulating these species into stable commercial products. Ongoing research is likely to provide other, more effective nematode-based products for control of white grubs.

Milky Disease. Milky disease is a fatal disease of white grubs caused by a spore-forming bacterium called *Bacillus popilliae.* Several strains of milky disease bacteria infect various species of white grubs; each strain tends to be specific for that type of grub. These bacteria do not infect beneficial insects, or pests other than scarab grubs. They are harmless to earthworms, wildlife, and humans. Milky disease bacteria occur naturally in the soil, where the spores may remain viable for many years. Feeding grubs may ingest some bacterial spores along with roots, organic matter, and soil. If enough spores are ingested, they lodge in the lining of the midgut, germinate, and begin to multiply. As the disease proceeds, the bacteria invade the body cavity and proliferate as vegetative cells and spores. The blood of infected grubs, which is normally clear or translucent, becomes so laden with spores that it turns a milky-white color. Fully-diseased grubs may contain as many as 2–5 billion spores. When the grub dies and decays, its carcass releases large numbers of infective spores into the soil. These may eventually infect other, nearby grubs, perpetuating and spreading the disease within the grub population. Although milky disease is inevitably fatal, it often takes a month or more for the diseased grubs to die.

Dusts containing spores of *B. popilliae* have been marketed for many years under the trade names Doom® and Japidemic® (Fairfax Biological Laboratory, Inc., Clinton Corners, New York), or Milky Spore (St. Gabriel Laboratories, Gainesville, Virginia). These products are made by grinding up diseased Japanese beetle grubs with talc and standardizing the concentration at an estimated 100 million spores per gram of dust. According to the manufacturer, the spore dust should be applied by placing teaspoon-sized (about 2 gram) amounts every 4 ft (1.3 m) in a grid pattern over the infested area. Over time, the spores become incorporated into the soil, where they may provide some long-term suppression of Japanese beetle grubs.

Although milky disease is one of many factors that can contribute to population suppression, it is uncertain whether application of spore dust will provide much benefit on golf courses or home lawns. Milky disease is very slow-acting. Even under ideal conditions, it takes several years for the pathogen to build up in a grub population. The idea that this process can be accelerated by a surface application of spore dust was based on research conducted during the 1940s and 1950s at sites with very high grub populations (>30 grubs per ft^2) that could not be tolerated today. Even in these older trials, the pattern of performance was quite variable. Milky disease products have performed poorly in recent trials on golf courses. Furthermore, because the commercial dust is made from Japanese beetle grubs, it is not effective against other grub species. Milky disease products have been in short supply in recent years. They are expensive because the spore dust must be made from living, diseased grubs. So far, efforts to mass-produce the spores on artificial media have not been successful. If this hurdle can be overcome, it may allow development of milky disease products with better virulence and effectiveness.

Fungus-Based Insecticides. A bioinsecticide containing the fungus *Beauveria bassiana* (Naturalis®-T) has recently been marketed for control of white grubs and certain other turf insects. There is presently little information on the level of suppression, if any, that this product may provide.

Chemical Control

When grubs are abundant, applying a soil insecticide may be the only practical way to avoid severe damage and loss of turf. There are two schools of thought concerning grub control: the curative or corrective approach, and preventive control. With **curative control**, the treatment is applied in late summer, after the eggs have hatched and grubs are present. Curative control can be *selective*, wherein sites are treated only if monitoring and sampling indicate that high grub populations are present, or it can be *nonselective*, such as when a lawn service company treats all clients' lawns in late summer, regardless of whether or not they are infested. With selective curative control, the decision to treat is based on site inspection and sampling, or past history of infestation.

With **preventive control**, an insecticide is applied as insurance, before a possible grub problem develops. This approach is attractive because it is easy to implement and requires that less time be spent in monitoring, sampling, and decision-making. Potential damage is avoided or minimized, which can result in fewer callbacks for lawn service companies and better peace of mind for golf superintendents. Preventive control requires use of an insecticide with relatively long residual activity (e.g., imidacloprid, halofenozide). *The main drawback of preventive control is that the decision to treat must be made before one knows the full extent of the grub infestation. Since white grub outbreaks tend to be localized and sporadic, preventive control often results in areas being treated unnecessarily.* For example, studies have shown that in most areas, only a small fraction of lawns will require grub control in a given year. *Nonselective curative control is equally inefficient from this standpoint.* The current climate regarding pesticides demands that turfgrass managers make every effort to reduce the nonessential use of insecticides. This means that the industry must shift toward more selective applications. Nevertheless, preventive treatment *can* fit into an IPM program if it is limited to high-risk sites (i.e., where heavy beetle activity was noted, or where perennial infestations have occurred).

Selective Curative Approach

Most soil insecticides have fairly short residual toxicity (usually 2–3 weeks or less). Proper timing of applications is therefore important. For grubs with annual life cycles, the preferred period for curative control is after the eggs have hatched, but before the grubs are large enough to cause visible damage. Smaller grubs are much easier to control. For grub species with annual life cycles, curative controls work best if applied from late July to mid-August in the transition zone, or 2–3 weeks later (i.e., mid to late August) in the Northeast. The optimum timing can vary by several weeks, however, depending on grub species, geographical location, and soil temperatures in a given year. Monitoring and sampling will help to pinpoint when the eggs have hatched and first and second instars are present. Sampling also helps you to target areas with high grub populations.

Grub infestations may go undetected until the brown patches appear in September or early October. Lawn care firms face this situation when responding to grub-related service calls. By the time that severe damage shows up, grubs with 1-year life cycles are usually third instars, weighing about 80 times as much as newly hatched grubs. These large grubs are much harder to control. In such situations, mow the turf and collect clippings to increase penetration of the insecticide, and irrigate beforehand to bring the grubs close to the surface. Use a fast-acting, short-residual insecticide, and be sure to water it in. Treatments will be ineffective once the grubs have begun to dig down in response to cooler soil temperatures.

Curative treatments are sometimes applied in April or May, after the grubs have returned to the root zone. There are several reasons why spring is generally *not* the best time for *curative* control. Post-overwintering grubs are large and hard to kill, and the target period for treatments is brief. Weather conditions are moderate, the turf is vigorous, and the plants will usually outgrow whatever damage the grubs may do before transforming to pupae. Also, use of a short-residual insecticide in April or May affords no protection against reinfestation by egg-laying beetles flying in later in the season. Spring treatment is seldom justified unless skunks or raccoons are digging, the turf is unduly stressed, or grubs are so abundant that damage is inevitable. Before applying a curative spring treatment, check to make sure the grubs are still active and have not already begun to go deep to pupate. Also — note that areas that did not have a damaging infestation, or that were successfully treated, in the previous fall should not need to be treated the following spring. No "new" grubs will materialize over the winter.

Preventive Approach

Turfgrass managers who use imidacloprid (Merit®) for grub control must rethink the traditional guidelines for treatment timing. This product behaves differently from most other soil insecticides. Imidacloprid has sufficient persistence to control the fall brood of white grubs if applied any time between spring (as early as April or May) until just before egg hatch. Like other soil insecticides, it must be watered in to be effective. However, the granular formulation is relatively forgiving if irrigation must be delayed for a few days. These characteristics are useful on sites without irrigation systems because the treatment can be made just before a good spring rain is forecast. In general, however, the optimum period for using imidacloprid is in June or July, during the month or so preceding egg hatch until the time when grubs are beginning to hatch out. *Be aware that while imidacloprid is highly effective against young, newly-hatched grubs, it does not work as well against older, 2nd- or 3rd-instar grubs.* Other insecticides generally work better for curative treatments.

Halofenozide (MACH 2®) is another product with sufficient persistence in soil to provide preventive control of grubs. Halofenozide is the first molt accelerating compound to be labeled for use on turf. It provides at least 6 weeks of residual effectiveness, so applications made during late June or July will control young grubs that hatch from eggs in late July or early August. As with imidacloprid, preventive applications of halofenozide are best applied during the month preceding egg hatch until the time when young grubs are present. Unlike imidacloprid, halofenozide is also effective against larger, 2nd- and 3rd-instar grubs. However, some grub species (e.g., European chafer grubs) seem to be less sensitive to halofenozide than others. Both imidacloprid and halofenozide have low mammalian toxicity and a relatively favorable environmental profile.

Isofenphos (Oftanol®) also has relatively long residual, though not as long as imidacloprid. Most other soil insecticides are too short-lived to provide preventive control.

Optimizing Effectiveness of Grub Treatments

For best results with any soil insecticide, mow the turf and rake out the dead grass and thatch before treatment. This enhances the penetration of the spray or granules by reducing the amount of insecticide bound up by surface debris. Irrigate with 1/2 to 1 in. (1.25–2.5 cm) of water immediately after treatment to leach the insecticide into the root zone where the grubs are feeding. Irrigation can be measured by placing rain gauges or disposable pie pans in the treated area. Try to wet the soil to about 1 in. (2.5 cm) depth. Irrigation also draws the grubs closer to the soil surface, increasing their contact with the insecticide residues. If irrigation is not available, try to time the application for just before a good rain. Liquid and granular applications are usually equally effective if immediately watered in. However, granular formulations may be more forgiving in situations where post-treatment irrigation is delayed. Imidacloprid and halofenozide, with their long residual, provide more leeway if irrigation or rainfall are delayed. Note that *immediate* post-treatment irrigation or rainfall is required by the label of some soil insecticides.

Control may be enhanced by returning grass clippings to the turf for one or two mowings after a grub treatment. Don't expect overnight kill. Affected grubs usually turn yellow or brown within a week after treatment. Don't wait more than 3 weeks to recheck the grub infestation, especially if the original population was high. If the density has not been substantially reduced, it may be necessary to re-treat. Do not exceed labeled rates; instead, try a different insecticide. Remember, the smaller the grubs, the easier they are to control. Encourage recovery of grub-damaged turf by watering to alleviate stress. Fertilizing cool-season grasses in the fall will help to promote regrowth of roots. Overseed thinned, damaged areas in the fall to prevent weed encroachment the following spring.

White grubs are especially hard to control in thatchy turf because most of the insecticide becomes tied up in the organic matter and fails to reach the root zone. Pre- or post-treatment irrigation does not change this binding. Trichlorfon is relatively good at penetrating thatch. If the thatch layer is more than 1/2 in. (1.25 cm) thick, consider removing it with a dethatching machine before applying a grub treatment.

No insecticide is 100% effective all of the time; rather, a successful treatment will usually kill 75–90% of the grubs present. Different products perform better or worse in different soil types, and against different species or sizes of grubs. Experiment, and keep records of product performance, or check with your Cooperative Extension office or turf expert about which products are working best against grubs in your area.

Some grub control failures may be caused by enhanced microbial degradation, whereby soil microbes break down the insecticide residues more rapidly than usual (see Chapter 6). This is more likely to occur in soils that have been conditioned by repeated insecticide use — a good reason to avoid unnecessary applications, and to alternate insecticides when treatments are needed.

APHODIUS GRUBS
Aphodius granarius (L.) and *Aphodius paradalis* Le Conte

Importance and Nature of Injury. Small grubs of two species belonging to the genus *Aphodius* are occasional pests of turf, especially golf course fairways. Grubs of *Aphodius* are often found alongside those of the black turfgrass ataenius, with which they are often confused. *Aphodius* seems to be less frequently associated with turf than is the black turfgrass ataenius, but it is nevertheless capable of inflicting serious damage.

Plants Attacked. Adults and grubs of *Aphodius* feed mainly on decaying organic matter, particularly animal manure. The grubs occasionally infest cool-season turfgrasses, feeding on the same species as the black turfgrass ataenius and causing similar damage.

Origin and Distribution. *Aphodius granarius* is an introduced European species that has become widely distributed in the United States and southern Canada. Most of the reported damage to turfgrasses has occurred in the Great Lakes region, including Ohio, Michigan, and Ontario, Canada, and in the northern Great Plains. *Aphodius pardalis* is a West Coast species that infests turfs on golf courses, lawns, and bowling greens.

Distinguishing Characteristics. Adults and grubs of *Aphodius* are similar in size and appearance to those of the black turfgrass ataenius. *Aphodius* adults are usually black with a reddish tinge, with reddish-brown legs and paler antennae. *Aphodius* adults have two triangular projections on the outer edge of the tibia of the hind leg, whereas *Ataenius* lacks these projections. Eggs and larvae of *Aphodius* resemble those of the black turfgrass ataenius. The grubs of the two species are physically similar in size, but can be separated by slight differences in the raster. The raster of *Aphodius* grubs has two rows of short spines forming a definite V-shaped pattern, whereas that of *Ataenius* grubs has a random arrangement of spines. A good-quality 10x or 15x hand lens is needed to see these features.

Life History and Habits. The seasonal life history of *Aphodius* is poorly known. In Ohio, adults were collected from mid-April to early June, and again in the fall. The beetles become active during the first warm days of spring; egg-laying apparently begins 2–3 weeks earlier than in black turfgrass ataenius. Adults migrating from nonturf areas are sometimes seen on the surface of turf and may be confused with *Ataenius* adults. In Ontario, adults reportedly were present in May, and again in late summer and fall. There, larvae were present in June, peaked in early July, and declined by the end of July. In New Jersey, *A. granarius* reportedly has one generation per year, overwintering as adults. Observations from Ohio, Michigan, and Ontario also suggest that there is one generation per year, although two annual generations may possibly occur in more southern parts of the species' range. Even less is known about *A. pardalis*, the western species.

Management. Little specific information is available regarding control of *Aphodius*. The grubs should be susceptible to soil insecticides applied as described for black turfgrass ataenius. Egg-laying adults may be attracted to lawns or other sites that are amended with composted manure or other organic matter.

ASIATIC GARDEN BEETLE
Maladera castanea (Arrow)
(Plate 7)

Importance and Nature of Injury. The Asiatic garden beetle (AGB) is usually a fairly minor pest of turf and ornamentals. Nevertheless, it can be locally abundant and damaging, especially in the Northeast. AGB grubs feed on roots of turfgrasses, causing typical white grub injury — wilting, thinning, and irregular dead patches. Well-kept, irrigated turf that is near weedy lots containing the beetles' favored food plants is more likely to be infested. AGB grubs are usually less destructive than an equal number of Japanese beetle or Oriental beetle grubs. This is probably because they feed deeper, typically 2–3 in. (5–7.5 cm) below the surface, leaving more of the root system intact. With heavy infestations, however, there may be 100 or more grubs per square foot, resulting in severe damage. Adult AGB feed on more than 100 plant species, chewing the leaves and causing a ragged appearance. Feeding begins at the leaf margin and may continue until only the midvein is left. AGB do not skeletonize the foliage in the manner of Japanese beetles. Where AGB are abundant, favored plants may be nearly stripped of foliage or flowers.

Plants Attacked. AGB adults are especially fond of box elder, butterfly bush, cherry, Devil's walkingstick, Japanese barberry, oriental cherry, peach, rose, strawberry, sumac, and viburnum. The favored flowers are those of aster, chrysanthemum, dahlia, delphinium, gaillardia, goldenrod, hemp, sunflower, and strawflower. The grubs feed on roots of all cool-season turfgrasses, as well as weeds and vegetables.

Origin and Distribution. The AGB is native to Japan and China, where it is not an important pest. It was first found in New Jersey in 1921, and within 20 years it had spread along the Atlantic seaboard from Massachusetts to South Carolina, and west to Pennsylvania and Ohio. It is now abundant in suburban areas around New York City and Philadelphia, and in western Long Island, northeastern New Jersey, and southeastern Connecticut (Figure 8.12). Populations are scattered and localized outside of these areas of continuous infestation.

Distinguishing Characteristics. The adult beetle is dull chestnut brown, with a velvety appearance and a slight iridescent sheen. The wing covers don't quite reach the tip of the abdomen, leaving the last two segments mostly exposed. The thorax, viewed from beneath, is partly covered with yellow hairs, and each visible segment of the abdomen has a row of backward-pointing yellow hairs that extends across its width. The upper surface of the wing covers is bald except for a row of fine hairs on the outer margins. Another distinctive feature is the presence of scattered, small erect hairs on the top of the head. The hind legs are distinctly larger and broader than the other legs. The beetles range from 5/16 to 7/16 in. (8–11 mm) long, and 3/16 to 1/4 in. (5–6.4 mm) wide.

Eggs are pearly-white, oval, and about 1 mm in diameter. They are laid in clusters, each with 3–19 eggs that are loosely held together by a gelatinous secretion. After absorbing soil moisture the eggs become almost spherical.

Larvae range in length from about 1/18 in. (1.4 mm) when newly hatched, to about 3/4 in. (19 mm) when fully mature. They are typical white grubs, having a C-shaped body, brown head, and six jointed legs. The body color always remains somewhat lighter than in other white

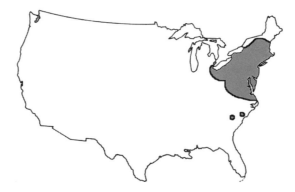

Figure 8.12. Distribution of the Asiatic garden beetle in the continental United States.

grub species. The key identifying feature is a *single, transverse curved row of spines on the raster, together with a Y-shaped anal opening* (Figure 8.10). The hind legs have tufts of hairs, and very small claws relative to those on the other legs. Another distinctive feature of the grub is a whitish, enlarged, bulbous structure (the stipes) on each maxilla, beside the jaws. The mouthparts are usually moving, so that at first glance the grub appears to be chewing on a bit of whitish plant material.

Pupation occurs within an earthen cell, as is typical for turf-infesting scarabs. The pupa is about 3/8 in. (7–10 mm) long, white at first, turning tan as it matures. The pupa is initially enclosed in the last larval skin, but this soon splits and is pushed back over the tip of the abdomen, so the pupa lies exposed in its earthen cell. This pupal characteristic is shared by the European chafer and May beetles.

Life History and Habits. The AGB completes its life cycle in one year. The seasonal pattern of development is similar to that of the Japanese beetle (Figure 8.21). At the latitude of New York City, the beetles begin emerging in late June. They are most abundant from mid-July to mid-August, but a few can be found as late as October. Females burrow into the soil to lay eggs, mostly at 1–2 in. (2.5–5 cm) depth. Individual females live about a month, depositing about 60 eggs. Eggs may be present from early July until October. The eggs hatch in about 10 days; the grubs then feed on tender roots and decaying organic matter until fall. Most grubs will attain the final (3rd) instar by first frost, but about 25% will overwinter as second instars. About mid-October the grubs burrow deeper in the soil, spending the winter 8–17 in. (20–43 cm) below the surface in a semi-dormant state. About mid-April, the grubs move back up to the root zone, where they feed until mid-June. During this time, grubs that overwintered as second instars will complete their development. The mature grub forms an earthen cell, 1-1/2 to 4 in. (4–10 cm) below the surface, in which to pupate. Pupae occur mainly from mid-June until mid-July. The pupal stage is short, lasting only about 10 days. New adults remain in the pupal cell for a few days until they've become fully hardened and their color changes from whitish to chestnut brown. They then burrow upward and emerge from the soil.

Adult AGB are active only at night. By day, they hide in moist soil around favored food plants, or in nearby turf or grassland. The beetles are sluggish and will not fly on cool nights when temperatures remain below 70°F (21°C). On such nights they will crawl up and feed sparingly upon low-growing vegetation. In contrast, the beetles are very active on warm nights in July and August and often swarm about in great numbers, feeding heavily on favored food plants. They can be a nuisance when they are attracted to outdoor lights. Thousands of beetles may accumulate on window screens or well-lit storefronts, or swarm around open-air restaurants, swimming pools, golf driving ranges, and similar well-lit sites.

The beetles are attracted to overgrown, weedy areas containing favored food plants such as goldenrod, ragweed, white clover, wild aster, and wild carrots. Such plants also provide a shaded environment, with cool, moist soil where the adults hide during the day. Certain nonfood plants, especially orange hawkweed, *Hieracium aurantiacum* (Compositae), and nonfavored hosts such as sorrel, may also shelter large numbers of beetles. Grubs of AGB are often abundant in irrigated turf near such weedy sites.

Management. AGB grubs can be managed in the same manner as other root-feeding white grubs with an annual life cycle (see White Grubs — Introduction). Eliminating adjacent weedy habitat containing preferred food plants or orange hawkweed may help to reduce beetle populations. Summer drought reduces the survival of eggs and young grubs in nonirrigated sites. Withholding irrigation during peak beetle flights may encourage females to lay their eggs elsewhere. Healthy turf may tolerate 15 or more grubs per square foot before showing damage, but this will depend upon mowing height, soil moisture, and overall vigor of the stand. Remedial irrigation and fertilization in fall encourage recovery of grub-damaged turf. Adult feeding damage on ornamentals can be reduced with the same insecticides that are effective against Japanese beetles. The AGB has few specific natural enemies, at least in the United States. The grubs are apparently not susceptible to milky disease. A *Tiphia* wasp parasitizes the grubs in Japan, but efforts to establish it in the United States were unsuccessful.

BLACK TURFGRASS ATAENIUS
Ataenius spretulus Haldeman
(Plate 8)

Importance and Nature of Injury. This small white grub causes sporadic, severe damage to golf courses in the cool-season turfgrass zones. Fairways, approaches, tees, and greens may be infested. Occurrence of black turfgrass ataenius (BTA) tends to be spotty, so that only certain golf courses in a locality will be affected. Damage to home lawns is uncommon.

The seasonal life cycle of the BTA differs from that of other root-feeding scarabs in that there are two generations per year throughout most of its range. In the latitude of southern Ohio and West Virginia, the injury appears about mid-June and mid-August, coinciding with the first and second annual broods of grubs. In more northern regions, where there is only one generation per year, the damage shows up in July and August. The first symptoms are patches of thin or wilted turf resembling drought stress, except that the grass does not recover with irrigation. Wilting is most visible when one views the turf toward the sun. As root loss continues, the turf dies in irregular patches that coalesce into larger dead areas. Heavily infested turf feels spongy underfoot and can be pulled up like a loose carpet. Large numbers of small grubs, pupae, and/or reddish or black adults will be found in the soil under the dead patches. Grubs of BTA seem to thrive in short-cut turf with a moist, compacted layer of thatch. Irrigated fairways with a high percentage of annual bluegrass are especially susceptible. BTA are small, but they often occur at higher densities than other grub species. Populations of 200–300 grubs per ft^2 (215–325 per 0.1 m^2) are not uncommon. Birds, skunks, and moles tear up the turf to eat the grubs. Birds may also pull up tufts of grass on putting greens while foraging for the adult beetles. Golf superintendents may mistake this damage as a sign of cutworm activity.

Plants Attacked. The grubs commonly damage bentgrasses, annual bluegrass, and Kentucky bluegrass on golf courses. They eat decaying organic matter as well as living plant roots. The adults feed on manure and decaying organic matter.

Distribution. The BTA is native to North America, where it occurs in all states east of the Rocky Mountains, as well as in California (Figure 8.13). Damage to golf courses has occurred

Figure 8.13. Distribution of the black turfgrass ataenius in the continental United States.

mainly in the northern half of the United States, from New England and the mid-Atlantic states west to Colorado, and from Kentucky and Missouri north to the Great Lakes and southern Ontario, Canada.

Distinguishing Characteristics. Adult BTA are small, shiny black beetles, 3/16 in. to just under 1/4 in. (3.6–5.5 mm) long and about half as wide, with distinct longitudinal grooves on the wing covers. Newly emerged adults are reddish brown, but darken in a few days. Eggs are pearly white and tiny, less than 1/32 in. (0.7 mm × 0.5 mm) after absorbing water from the soil. *Larvae are typical white grubs, but much smaller than other common, turf-infesting species.* Newly hatched grubs are only about 1/10 in. (2.4 mm) long and hard to see. Second instars measure 3/16 in. (5 mm), and mature third instars are only 3/8 in. (7–0 mm) long, or about the size of Lincoln's hair on a U.S. penny. Mature BTA grubs may be mistaken for young grubs of other species, such as Japanese beetle, masked chafers, and European chafer. BTA grubs have two distinctive, pad-like structures at the tip of the abdomen just in front of the anal slit, and a scattered pattern of spines on the raster (Figure 8.10). These features are fairly easy to make out with a 10x hand lens. When BTA grubs are viewed from the top, the dorsal blood vessel and rear portion of the gut appear almost black in contrast to the gray-white body. When mature, the grubs go down 1/2 to 3 in. (1–8 cm) into the soil and excavate a cavity in which to pupate. The pupa is small, about 3/16 in. (4.2–5.7 mm) long, with the wings and legs folded close to the body. It is cream colored at first, becoming reddish-brown before the beetle emerges.

Life History and Habits. As mentioned above, the BTA has two generations per growing season in Ohio and further south (Figure 8.14). There is only one generation in the Great Lakes states, upstate New York, northern New England, Ontario, and other northern parts of the species' range. Adults spend the winter along the edges of wooded roughs or in woodlots along the perimeter of the golf course. The overwintering beetles take shelter under leaves, pine needles, piles of grass clippings or other debris, or in the upper 1–2 in. (2.5–5 cm) of soil. Most of the overwintering females will have already mated. Adults usually begin emerging after several warm days in late March. In the latitude of southern Ohio, the beetles begin returning to fair-ways and greens about when crocus (*Crocus vernus*) and eastern redbud (*Cercis canadensis*) are blooming. Movement of adults continues through April and early May. Swarms of the small, black beetles may be seen on putting greens, flying over fairways on warm afternoons, or around lights at night. Adults are sometimes collected in mowing baskets along with the clip-pings. The beetles land on the turf and quickly burrow down. Egg-laying begins in early May and continues until mid-June. Clusters of 11–12 eggs are laid within cavities formed by the female near the soil-thatch interface. Eggs hatch in about a week, and the grubs feed on fine

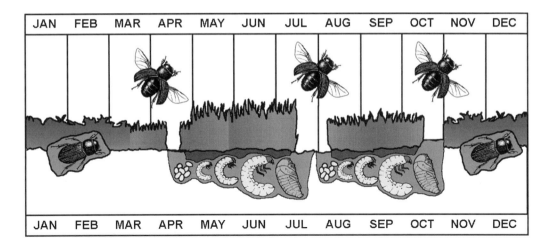

Figure 8.14. Seasonal life cycle of the black turfgrass ataenius, showing two generations per year (from University of Nebraska Cooperative Extension Service, drawn by J. Kalisch).

roots and organic matter. This first generation of grubs is present from late May until early July (Figure 8.14), with damage typically showing up in June. Individual grubs take about 4 weeks to mature. They then burrow down, pupate, and emerge as adults from late June to early July. These beetles mate and lay eggs during July and early August, producing a second generation of grubs which damages the turf in August and early September, especially if rainfall is scarce. These grubs mature and pupate in late August or September, producing new adults that mate and fly back to overwintering sites in the fall. Because each pulse of beetles lays eggs over a period of several weeks, the generations overlap and more than one life stage is usually present at a given time (Figure 8.14). In northern regions where only one generation occurs, most damage from BTA occurs in July and August when the grubs are nearly mature.

Management. See White Grubs — Introduction. Golf superintendents who normally expect to see grub damage in late summer may be caught off guard to find numerous small grubs attacking the turf in June. BTA should be suspected in this situation because grubs with annual life cycles (e.g., Japanese beetles, masked chafers, European chafers) will be mostly pupae or adults at that time. Damage from the second brood of BTA grubs shows up in August, about when other grub species are just getting started. Thus, full-sized BTA grubs are often mistaken for first instars of the larger, annual grub species. Look for the characteristic pad-like structures on the underside of the last abdominal segment to confirm that you're dealing with BTA.

When sampling suspected areas for BTA, examine both the thatch and soil for grubs and other life stages. Vigorous turf will usually tolerate 30–50 BTA grubs per ft^2 (32–54 per 0.1 m^2) unless the grass is further stressed by drought, soil compaction, or disease. Higher densities may be cause for concern. Infestations on golf courses are often localized within a few fairways. These can usually be spot-treated. Less often, whole fairways will require treatment.

The occurrence of various life stages of BTA during the growing season is closely correlated with flowering dates of certain indicator plants, at least in the Midwest. In early spring, females returning from overwintering sites begin laying eggs about when Vanhoutte spirea (*Spiraea vanhouttei*), and horse chestnut (*Aesculus hippocastanum*) come into full bloom, and black locust (*Robinia pseudoacacia*) is showing first bloom. In most years, this occurs during the first half of May in southern Ohio and in early June in western New York. First generation grubs begin hatching when multiflora rose (*Rosa multiflora*) is in full bloom. The summer generation of adults begins emerging when summer phlox (*Phlox paniculata*) is in full bloom, and second generation eggs are laid when rose of Sharon (*Hibiscus syriacus*) is in full bloom. Tracking the seasonal development of these plants helps in timing of treatments. Flight activity of adult BTA can also be monitored with light traps to bracket periods of egg-laying in April and May, and again in mid-summer.

BTA can be controlled by the curative approach, targeting the young grubs with a short-residual insecticide soon after the eggs have hatched. Insecticides that work well against Japanese beetle grubs are generally also effective against BTA. Irrigate the site immediately after treatment to move the insecticide through the thatch, and to keep the grubs close to the surface. As always, the younger the grubs, the easier they are to control.

Preventive control may be warranted on golf courses having recurring problems with BTA. One option is to apply a long-residual insecticide (e.g., imidacloprid) during the egg-laying period in spring. Post-treatment irrigation or rainfall must occur to move the residues to the target zone. This treatment will control the first generation of grubs, and provide residual control of second-generation grubs that hatch later in the season. Another approach is to apply a short-residual insecticide when the overwintering beetles are migrating back to turf in early spring. The idea is to deposit a residue in the upper thatch so the females are killed as they burrow in to lay eggs. Timing is tricky — too early, and the residues will disappear before egg-laying begins; too late, and many females will have already deposited their eggs. Irrigate lightly to wash the insecticide off the grass blades and into the upper thatch, where the beetles seek shelter. Keeping a close watch on BTA activity in April and early May can help golf superintendents to be more selective with treatments. Watch for swarms of adults flying over the turf or crawling on putting greens. Such areas, and sites with history of BTA infestation, are at greatest risk.

Nematode-based products containing *Steinernema carpocapsae* have not given consistent control. BTA grubs are susceptible to their own strain of naturally occurring milky disease. However, they are not susceptible to commercial milky disease products.

EUROPEAN CHAFER
Rhizotrogus majalis (Razoumowsky) (called *Amphimallon majalis* before 1978)
(Plate 9)

Importance and Nature of Injury. The European chafer is a pest of regional importance mainly in the northeastern United States. It is often the most damaging grub species in those areas where it occurs. The grubs cause wilting, thinning, and irregular dead patches of turf that can be easily pulled from the soil. Densities of 20–30 grubs per ft^2 (18–28 per m^2) are common in lawn and golf course turf. European chafer grubs are larger and therefore more destructive than equal numbers of Japanese beetle grubs. Also, they feed later into the fall and resume feeding earlier in the spring. Damage usually shows up in September, especially when the turf is stressed by heat and drought. Injury may go unnoticed in the fall if conditions are cool, with abundant soil moisture. Severe damage may then appear in spring when the grubs resume feeding on the previously weakened turf. The adult beetles nibble the margins of tree leaves, but they do no real damage.

Plants Attacked. European chafer grubs feed on roots of all cool-season grasses, whether in turf or pastures. They also damage roots of many weed grasses, broad-leaved weeds, and field, forage, and nursery crops.

Origin and Distribution. This species is native to Europe, where it is a serious turf pest in France, Spain, Belgium, southern Germany, and Switzerland. It does not occur in England. The European chafer was first found in the United States in 1940, near Newark, New York. It has since spread to Connecticut, Rhode Island, Massachusetts, most of upstate New York, parts of

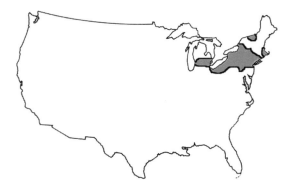

Figure 8.15. *Distribution of the European chafer in the continental United States.*

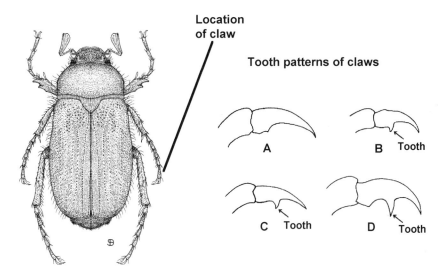

Figure 8.16. *Differences in the tarsal claws between adults of the European chafer and native May beetles, with which they are sometimes confused. (A) European chafer, (B)* Phyllophaga tristis, *(C)* P. gracilis, *(D)* P. hirticula *(adult, courtesy of D. Shetlar; others adapted from Tashiro et al., 1969).*

Pennsylvania, northern Ohio, and southern Michigan, along the Niagara frontier into southern Ontario, and along the eastern seaboard to Maryland (Figure 8.15).

Distinguishing Characteristics. The adults are medium-sized, light reddish-brown beetles, about 9/16 in. (13–15 mm) long, with a slightly darker head and pronotum (Figure 8.16). The trailing edge of the pronotum bears a narrow band of light yellow hairs, and the underside of the thorax is covered with pale yellow hairs. The tip of the abdomen protrudes beyond the wing covers. The wing covers have distinct longitudinal grooves and minute punctations. Adult European chafers look much like light-colored May beetles (*Phyllophaga* species), but are slightly smaller. They lack a tooth on the tarsal claws of the middle legs, whereas claws of *Phyllophaga* beetles have a distinct tooth (Figure 8.16). Also, European chafers have more distinct grooves on the wing covers. Another distinction is that *Phyllophaga* adults chew holes in leaves, whereas feeding by European chafer adults is inconspicuous.

Newly-laid eggs are shiny, oval, and milky white, becoming dull gray after a few days. The eggs become more spherical after absorbing soil moisture, swelling to about 3/32 × 7/64 in. (2.3 × 2.7 mm) just before hatching.

The larvae are typical C-shaped white grubs with a yellow-brown head and six distinct, jointed legs. The raster has two distinct, nearly parallel rows of small spines that *diverge outward at the tip of the abdomen*, like a slightly open zipper (Figure 8.10). This pattern, together with a Y-shaped anal slit, distinguishes European chafer grubs from other turf-infesting species in North America. The newly hatched grubs are translucent white, but the end of the abdomen becomes darker after they have fed. Fully grown third instars are just under 1 in. (23 mm) long.

The prepupa and pupa resemble those of other turf-infesting scarabs. The pupae are about 5/8 in. (16 mm) long, smaller than *Phyllophaga* but larger than Japanese beetle pupae. Unlike Japanese beetle or oriental beetle pupae, which lie within the shed larval skin, the European chafer pupa sloughs off the larval skin to the posterior end.

Life History and Habits. The European chafer has a 1-year life cycle resembling those of other annual white grubs (Figure 8.11). In upstate New York and Michigan, the adults begin emerging in mid-June and are most abundant from late June until mid-July. Adult flights are practically over by late July. These events may occur about 2 weeks earlier in Ohio, Pennsylvania, and New Jersey. The beetles are most active on warm, clear nights when the temperature is above 66°F (19°C). On each favorable night, large numbers emerge from the soil at sundown (about 8:30 p.m.), and crawl up grass blades to take flight. They fly to nearby trees or other objects silhouetted against the sky, swarming about the branches by the thousands. Their buzzing sound and appearance resemble a swarm of bees. After about 30 minutes, when the sky becomes dark, the swarming stops and the beetles settle on the foliage, often in such numbers that the limbs bend over. Fortunately, they don't feed much — the tree is just a place to have a mating orgy. Beginning about 10 p.m., mating pairs begin to fall to the ground, and thousands can be dislodged by shaking the tree. Flights back to the ground continue through the night, with all beetles returning to the soil before daybreak. Individual beetles may return to trees several times to re-mate during their 1–2 week lifespan. Late in the flight period their carcasses may litter the ground beneath trees used for swarming.

A female will lay 20–40 eggs in her lifetime. Eggs are laid singly, 2–4 in. (5–10 cm) deep in moist soil, and hatch in about 2 weeks. Most will have hatched by late July. The grub population consists mainly of first instars in early to mid-August, second instars by mid-August to early September, and third instars by mid-September to early October. The grubs continue to feed into November, a full month later than Japanese beetle grubs, before going deeper in the soil. They overwinter just under the frost line. The grubs return to the upper 1–2 in. (2.5–5 cm) in March as the ground thaws. Vigorous feeding continues until mid to late May. By early June, the grubs begin to move deeper, 2–10 in. (5–25 cm) into the soil, and form earthen cells in which they pupate. The prepupal and pupal stages last 2–4 days and about 2 weeks, respectively. The first beetles of the new generation begin emerging in mid-June.

European chafer grubs show considerable vertical movement in response to soil moisture and temperature. Most remain in the upper 2 in. (5 cm) of soil whenever moisture is adequate. They may burrow down 8 in. (20 cm) or more during periods of drought, migrating back close to the surface within a day or so after a good rain or deep irrigation. Where there is thick sod or heavy snow cover, the grubs may remain in the root zone, feeding even in winter.

The grubs are susceptible to their own strain of milky disease bacteria, but incidence of infection is usually low. Several parasitic insects attack the grubs in Europe, but efforts to establish them in the United States were unsuccessful. General predators such as ants and ground beetles, as well as birds, skunks, and moles, feed on immature stages.

Management. Management tactics are the same as for other root-feeding grubs with annual life cycles (see White Grubs — Introduction). Densities of 5–10 grubs per ft² (0.1 m²) may warrant treatment. In western New York, Connecticut, and Rhode Island, the best time for curative control with short-residual insecticides is August 15 to September 1 in most years. Most eggs have hatched by then, but the grubs are still small. Some eggs may not hatch until mid-September, so continue to monitor. Control is more difficult later in the fall as the grubs grow larger. An alternative approach is to apply a long-residual insecticide (e.g., imidacloprid, halofenozide) before, or about the time of egg hatch. The best timing for such preventive control is during the first few weeks of adult flight. Beetle activity can be timed by observing indicator plants, at least in upstate New York. Pupation coincides with full bloom of Vanhoutte spirea (*Spiraea vanhouttei*), beetles begin to fly at first bloom of hybrid tea and floribunda roses, and peak flight generally occurs at full bloom of common catalpa (*Catalpa bignonioides*). Adult activity can also be monitored with light traps. Commercial milky disease products are not effective against European chafer grubs. Nematode products containing *S. carpocapsae* have not given consistent control. A survey of home lawns in western New York showed that European chafer grubs are most often associated with front lawns, lawns less than 20 years old, lawns with a high percentage (60% or more) of Kentucky bluegrass, and lawns in open, nonshady areas.

GREEN JUNE BEETLE
Cotinis nitida L.
(Plate 10)

Importance and Nature of Injury. Green June beetle (GJB) adults and grubs always attract attention in areas where they are abundant. The large grubs feed mainly on decomposing organic matter, including compost, thatch and grass clippings. They don't eat living roots to the same extent as other turf-infesting scarabs, but they nevertheless cause considerable damage by their burrowing and tunneling. This disturbs the root system, dislodges the grass, and loosens the surface soil, causing it to dry out. This upheaval may cause the turf to wilt or die, especially during hot, dry periods in late summer. The resultant thinning allows weed encroachment. GJB grubs make distinct, open vertical burrows with a surface hole about the diameter of a man's thumb. Loose soil is thrown out at the mouth of the burrow at night, forming small mounds about 2–3 in. (50–75 mm) across. GJB mounds resemble ant hills except that the soil particles are coarser, but not as coarse as those in earthworm castings. They are large enough to deflect golf balls or dull the blades of reel mowers. When GJB mounds on greens and approaches are packed down by foot traffic or machinery, the underlying grass is smothered. Heavily infested athletic fields feel spongy or uneven underfoot. Predators such as birds, moles, and skunks damage the turf as they dig for the grubs. Controlling this pest with insecticides can result in an unsightly mess, because the grubs tend to die on the turf surface.

Adult GJB feed on ripening fruits, oozing tree sap, and other sugary substances. They may also damage tree leaves. Like the grubs, adults throw up little piles of soil as they burrow in and out of the turf for egg-laying and resting. On greens, small mounds resembling miniature mole burrows mark the beetles' presence beneath the surface. Golfers and homeowners panic when they see swarms of beetles "buzz-bombing" over the turf in mid-summer. The flying beetles are sometimes mistaken for wasps.

Origin and Distribution. The GJB is native to the eastern United States. It is widely distributed east of the Mississippi river as far north as St. Louis and Columbus, Ohio in the Midwest, farther north to New York City along the Atlantic coast, and west to Texas, Oklahoma, and Kansas (Figure 8.17). It is especially common in the transition zone from Kentucky and Tennessee east to the Carolinas.

Plants Attacked. GJB beetle grubs prefer moist soils with plenty of decaying organic matter. High soil organic matter is more important than the species of turfgrass present. The grubs also infest pastures and gardens, especially where manure fertilizer or compost has been applied.

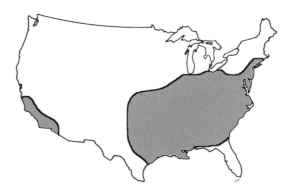

Figure 8.17. Distribution of the green June beetle in the continental United States.

Figure 8.18. Green June beetle grub crawling on its back (from USDA).

Distinguishing Characteristics. Adult GJB are larger than Japanese beetles or common May beetles, measuring 3/4 to 1 in. (19–25 mm) long and about 1/2 in. (12.5 mm) wide. The color of the upper body and wing covers varies from dull brown with lengthwise stripes of green, to uniform, velvety forest green. The outer margins of the wing covers range from tan to orange-yellow. The underside is shiny, metallic green or gold. GJB grubs are larger, more robust, and more parallel-sided than other grub species. They have stubby legs and short mouthparts in relation to overall body size. GJB grubs can be easily recognized by their unique mode of locomotion — they "shimmy" along on their backs, like a lumbering, upside-down caterpillar (Figure 8.18). No other turf-infesting white grub in the United States moves in this manner.

Newly laid eggs are dull white and about 1/16 in. (1.5 mm) in diameter. Eggs become larger (1/8 in. or 3 mm) and more spherical after they've absorbed moisture from the soil. Newly hatched grubs are about 1/4 in. (6–7 mm) long, second instars are 5/8 to 3/4 in. (15–17 mm) long, and third instars range from just over 1 in. (28 mm) to nearly 2 in. (45–48 mm) long when mature. Stiff bristles on the back of the abdomen provide traction when the grub crawls on its back. When nearly mature, the grub forms a cocoon-like cell, suggestive of a bird's egg, composed of soil particles held together by a sticky secretion. Pupation occurs within this cell. The pupa is large, about 1 in. (25 mm) long and 1/2 in. (12.5 mm) wide. It is whitish at first, gradually darkening and taking on tints of the adult coloration before the beetle emerges.

Life History and Habits. GJB beetles have a 1-year life cycle (Figure 8.19). Adults begin to emerge in late June. Adult activity is usually concentrated in a 2–3 week period in mid-July in Kentucky, Virginia, and Maryland; peak flight may be 2–3 weeks earlier to the south, and 1–2 weeks later in more northern regions. The beetles are active by day. At night, they rest on vegetation or just under the thatch. In the morning, swarms of male beetles take flight, dive-bombing back and forth about 6–18 in. (15–45 cm) over the turf in search of females in the grass. The buzzing sounds produced by the beetles may cause unfounded fear of being attacked or stung. Females attract the males with an airborne sex pheromone. The beetles may form jostling clusters in the grass as several males try to mate with a single female.

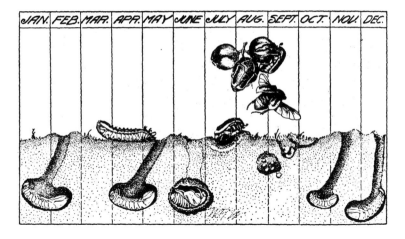

Figure 8.19. *Seasonal life cycle of the green June beetle (from Chittenden, 1922).*

Egg-laying females are attracted to piles of rotting mulch or vegetation, decomposing animal manure, or moist soils containing abundant organic matter. They also favor turfgrass sites treated with manure-based fertilizers. The female burrows down 2–5 in. (5–13 cm), excavates a small cavity, and deposits a cluster of 10–30 eggs. Each egg cluster is enclosed in a walnut-sized ball of soil held together by a sticky secretion. Each female makes several such egg chambers, depositing as many as 60–75 eggs over a 2-week span. The eggs hatch in about 2 weeks, and by early August, the young grubs are feeding at the soil/thatch interface. By mid-fall they will have molted twice, reaching about three-quarters of their full size. GJB grubs may burrow down 18 in. (46 cm), or even deeper in sandy soils. The grub rests at the bottom of the burrow by day, but may come to the surface at night to graze on thatch, decomposing grass clippings, or other organic matter. They are especially active on the surface following rains or heavy dew. The burrows and mounds may not be apparent until fall. Burrowing and surface feeding also occur in the spring, following overwintering. As the large grubs creep about on the turf surface, they may wind up in swimming pools, garages, or basements.

Natural Enemies. Where GJB is abundant, golfers and homeowners may be alarmed to see swarms of rather large, dark-colored wasps hovering over the turf in August or September. This beneficial wasp, *Scolia dubia,* is a parasitoid of GJB grubs (see Scoliid Wasps, Chapter 14). The wasps are about 3/4 in. (19 mm) long, with a wingspan of about 1-1/4 in. (32 mm). The wings are purplish-black, and the abdomen has reddish-brown markings and two conspicuous yellow spots. The female wasp enters the burrow, paralyzes the grub by stinging it, and attaches an egg to its underside. Upon hatching, the wasp larva slowly consumes the helpless victim. The wasp passes the winter in a cocoon at the bottom of the burrow, pupating in the spring. A new generation of wasps emerges about the middle of August. Fortunately, the wasps are not aggressive and will not sting unless picked up or stepped on with bare feet.

Management. Population levels of GJB tend to fluctuate in cycles of several years, possibly reflecting delayed impact of parasitic wasps (see above) or other natural controls. Damage is most likely to occur where grubs were previously abundant, or where heavy mating flights of beetles were observed. Composted yard waste, or use of manure-based fertilizers in spring or early summer, may attract the egg-laying females. For light infestations, soil mounds can be swept or raked down around tees and putting greens. Cultural practices to enhance turf vigor will help to mask the damage and encourage recovery. Overseed thinned, damaged areas in the fall to prevent weed encroachment the following spring.

GJB grubs are fairly easy to control with soil insecticides. Granular materials must be watered to activate the insecticide, but deep, post-treatment irrigation seems to be less critical than with other grub species. Treatments made late in the day are most effective because the grubs feed on or near the surface at night. *However, be forewarned! Unlike other species, GJB grubs often will die on the turf surface.* You are likely to find thousands of rotting grubs littering the turf on the morning after an application. This can be an unsightly, smelly mess on golf fairways, putting greens, and athletic fields. The insecticide-contaminated grubs may possibly pose a hazard to foraging birds. If GJB requires treatment, try to do so before the grubs have reached their full size. Use of long-residual products (e.g., imidacloprid, halofenozide) for preventive control of other grub species will eliminate young green June beetle grubs at the same time.

JAPANESE BEETLE
Popillia japonica Newman
(Plate 11)

Importance and Nature of Injury. The Japanese beetle is among the worst pests of turfgrasses and woody landscape plants in the eastern United States. Hundreds of millions of dollars are expended for controlling the beetles and grubs, and for renovating or replacing damaged turf and ornamentals. Japanese beetle grubs cause typical root-feeding injury (see White Grubs — Introduction). The most severe damage usually appears from late August to early October, after the grubs have attained the third instar. Turf may also be damaged in the spring, after the grubs have returned to the root zone following hibernation. Injury is usually less evident in the spring because the turf is vigorous and under less environmental stress. Moles, skunks, raccoons, birds, and other varmints may damage the turf to feed on the grubs.

The adult beetles attack a wide range of ornamental plants. They usually feed from the upper leaf surface, leaving only a lace-like skeleton of veins. Damaged leaves turn brown, die, and drop off. Preferred hosts such as lindens, purple-leaf plum, and Norway maple may be completely defoliated. The beetles are especially fond of flowers and fruit; they may wreak havoc with blooming plants such as roses and hibiscus.

Plants Attacked. Japanese beetle grubs feed on roots of all cool-season turfgrasses, as well as roots of many lawn weeds and other plants. The adults feed on nearly 300 plant species ranging from roses to poison ivy. Many popular shade trees and ornamentals are among their preferred food plants (Table 8.1).

Origin and Distribution. The Japanese beetle is native to the main islands of Japan, where it is not a major pest. It was accidentally introduced into New Jersey about 1916. The eastern United States provided a favorable climate, plenty of grassland for developing grubs, diverse food plants for the adults, and no effective natural enemies. The species thrived under these conditions and steadily expanded its geographic range. Japanese beetles are now established in most states east of the Mississippi River, except for Florida, Mississippi, and Minnesota (Figure 8.20). They have also spread northward into parts of southern Ontario. Rainfall and soil temperature are the factors that will most likely determine the species' ability to spread beyond its present range. It is unlikely to survive in the semiarid plains or desert regions west of the 100th meridian (central Nebraska, western Kansas), except possibly in well-irrigated sites. Isolated infestations have been found in California and Oregon; these probably originated from beetles transported in commerce. Eradication and quarantine efforts have so far prevented establishment in those states.

Distinguishing Characteristics. The adult beetle is an attractive, broadly oval insect, 5/16 to 7/16 in. (8–11 mm) long, and about 1/4 in. (5–7 mm) wide. The head and body are shiny,

Table 8.1. Landscape Plants Likely to Be Attacked by Adult Japanese Beetles.

Scientific Name	Common Name
Acer palmatum	Japanese maple
Acer platanoides	Norway maple
Aesculus hippocastanum	Horsechestnut
Althaea rosea	Hollyhock
Betula populifolia	Gray birch
Castanea dentata	American chestnut
Hibiscus syriacus	Rose of Sharon, Shrub Althea
Juglans nigra	Black walnut
Malus species	Flowering crabapple,[a] apple
Platanus acerifolia	London planetree
Populus nigra italica	Lombardy poplar
Prunus species	Cherry, black cherry, plum, peach, etc.
Rosa species	Roses
Sassafras albidum	Sassafras
Sorbus americana	American mountain ash
Tilia americana	American linden
Ulmus americana	American elm
Ulmus procera	English elm
Vitis species	Grape

[a] Some cultivars (e.g., *Baccata* v. *jackii*, Jewelberry, Harvest Gold, David, Louisa) are relatively resistant.

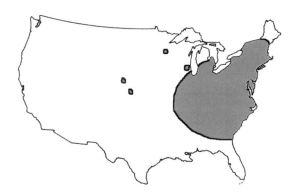

Figure 8.20. Distribution of the Japanese beetle in the continental United States.

metallic green, with darker green legs. The hard, coppery-brown wing covers do not quite reach the tip of the abdomen. Each side of the abdomen has five patches of white hairs, and there is another pair of white tufts on the upper surface of the last abdominal segment, just behind the wing covers. These tufts distinguish this species from all other beetles that resemble it. Females are usually slightly larger than males.

Newly laid eggs are about 1/16 in. (1.5 mm) long, pearly white, and oblong. Eggs absorb moisture from the soil, becoming spherical and doubling in size within a few days. The developing embryo can be seen within eggs that are close to hatching. The larvae are typical white grubs with three pairs of distinct, jointed legs, and a yellowish-brown head capsule. They usually assume a C-shaped position in the soil. Japanese beetle grubs can be recognized by their distinctive rastral pattern which includes *two rows of short spines that are arranged in the shape of a truncated V* (Figure 8.10). Newly hatched grubs are about 1/16 in. (1.5 mm) long and

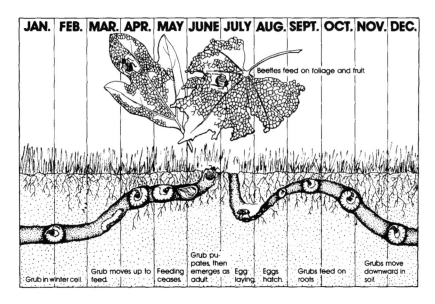

JAN.	FEB.	MAR.	APR.	MAY	JUNE	JULY	AUG.	SEPT.	OCT.	NOV.	DEC.

Beetles feed on foliage and fruit.

Grub in winter cell — Grub moves up to feed — Feeding ceases — Grub pupates, then emerges as adult. — Egg laying. — Eggs hatch. — Grubs feed on roots — Grubs move downward in soil.

Figure 8.21. Seasonal life cycle of the Japanese beetle (from Shurtleff et al., 1987; with permission).

translucent white; the abdominal area becomes grayish once they have fed. As with all white grubs, there are three larval instars. Full-sized, third-instar grubs are about 1 to 1-1/8 in. (25–30 mm) long. They are smaller than masked chafers, European chafers, or May beetles, but much larger than black turfgrass ataenius. When ready to pupate, the grub stops feeding, voids its gut, and becomes a pale and somewhat shrunken prepupa. It then transforms to a pupa within the mesh-like, cast skin of the mature grub. The pupa is the typical scarab type, measuring about 1/2 in. (14 mm) long and 1/4 in. (7 mm) wide. It is cream colored at first, gradually becoming tan or light reddish-brown. The pupa takes on the metallic-green markings just before the adult emerges.

Life History and Habits. The JB has a 1-year life cycle throughout most of its range in the United States (Figure 8.21). Emergence of adults from the soil, and the subsequent timing of egg-laying and larval hatch, vary with latitude and with spring temperatures in a given year. In Kentucky, the beetles usually begin to emerge in early to mid-June, and adult beetle activity peaks in early July. These events may occur about 2 weeks earlier in the Carolinas, and 2–3 weeks later in more northern states.

Mating and egg-laying begin soon after emergence. Virgin females produce a potent airborne sex pheromone. Early in the seasonal flight period, males fly over the turf in search of emerging females. Jostling clusters of 20–100 or more males may accumulate on the ground around a single female. Females also re-mate on food plants before each bout of egg-laying. The beetles usually feed in groups, typically starting at the top of a tree or shrub and working downward. They seem to prefer plants in direct sunlight, and tend to aggregate on foliage that has been damaged by other Japanese beetles. Females may leave the host plant in late afternoon and fly to a suitable site in which to lay eggs. Areas with moist, loamy soil covered with well-maintained turf or pasture grasses are preferred, especially when such sites are near favored food plants. Females will seek out lush golf fairways or irrigated home lawns rather than lay their eggs in dry, compacted soil. Eggs are deposited in small clutches (1–4 eggs) in the upper 3 in. (7.5 cm) of soil. The cycle of feeding and egg-laying is repeated every few days. The normal lifespan of a female is 30–45 days, during which she may deposit 40–60 eggs.

Eggs hatch in about 2 weeks, and the young grubs, about the size of a bluegrass seed, begin feeding on fine roots and organic matter. In late summer, most grubs will be in the upper 2 in. (5 cm) of soil. They may go deeper during periods of drought. The grubs molt and become second instars after 2–3 weeks, and third instars after 3–4 weeks more. They continue to feed and grow until late fall, or about the time of first frost. The grubs begin to go deeper when soil temperatures cool to about 60°F (15°C). Most grubs overwinter 2–8 in. below the soil surface. They begin to move back up into the root zone when soil temperatures warm to 50°F (10°C), usually in March. They feed vigorously for another 4–6 weeks, then go slightly deeper and form an earthen cell in which they pupate. At the latitude of Kentucky, Virginia, and Maryland, the population consists of mainly adults and eggs in July, first- and second-instar grubs by mid-August, second and third instars by early September, third instars from late September to May, and prepupae and pupae in May and early June. This sequence will be 2–3 weeks later in more northern parts of the beetle's range, and somewhat earlier in the south.

Management of Adults

Note that adults and grubs of this species cause different types of damage. Moreover, since the beetles can fly considerable distances from other areas, controlling one life stage will not necessarily preclude problems with the other.

Plant Selection. Use of resistant species when replacing plant material or planning a landscape is a key to managing the adults. Some plants (e.g., lindens or purple leaf plums) are so attractive that they will almost always sustain heavy damage (Table 8.1). On golf courses, such trees serve as a perpetual reservoir of egg-laying beetles. Certain wild plants, such as bracken, elder, grape, Indian mallow, multiflora rose, sassafras, smartweed, and Virginia creeper, will also draw numerous beetles, and eliminating these plants may reduce egg-laying in adjacent golf fairways. When planning landscapes or replacing damaged plant material, consider species that are relatively resistant to Japanese beetles (Table 8.2). Although plant selection is important, other tactics must be used to protect turf and susceptible plants that are already present in landscapes.

Physical Removal and Exclusion of Beetles. Removing beetles by hand may provide adequate control for small plantings, especially when numbers are low. Beetles on plants are sluggish in the morning and can be killed by shaking them into a bucket of soapy water. High-value plants such as roses can be protected by covering them with fine netting or Reemay® fabric during the peak of beetle activity. Obviously, these tactics are only practical on a small scale.

Trapping. Commercial Japanese beetle traps usually employ two types of baits: a sweet-smelling food-type lure, and a synthetic sex pheromone that mimics the scent of virgin females. These traps may attract many thousands of beetles per day (Figure 8.22). Studies have shown that small-scale use of traps will not protect landscape plantings from damage. Indeed, traps attract many more beetles than are actually caught, so that susceptible plants along the flight path or vicinity of the trap are likely to sustain much *more* damage than if no traps were used. Mass trapping with hundreds of traps has been suggested as a means of reducing Japanese beetle populations on golf courses or in suburban neighborhoods, but it's doubtful that this tactic would provide any lasting benefit where the beetle is established. Small-scale use of traps also is unlikely to reduce grub infestations. If you experiment with traps, place them well away from gardens and landscape plants.

Chemical Control. Various insecticides are labeled for use against adult Japanese beetles. Carbaryl (Sevin®) has been the homeowner and industry standard for many years. Professionals can also use pyrethroids. Where beetles are abundant, weekly applications may be necessary to

Table 8.2. Landscape Plants Seldom Damaged by Adult Japanese Beetles.

Scientific Name	Common Name
Acer negundo	Boxelder*
Acer rubrum	Red maple
Acer saccharinum	Silver maple
Buxus sempervirens	Boxwood
Carya ovata	Shagbark hickory*
Cornus florida	Flowering dogwood
Diospyros virginiana	Persimmon*
Euonymus species	Euonymus (all species)
Fraxinus americana	White ash
Fraxinus pennsylvanica	Green ash
Ilex species	Holly (all species)
Juglans cinerea	Butternut*
Liriodendron tulipifera	Tuliptree
Liquidamar styraciflua	American sweetgum*
Magnolia species	Magnolia (all species)
Morus rubra	Red Mulberry
Populus alba	White poplar
Pyrus species	Ornamental pears
Quercus alba	White oak*
Quercus coccinea	Scarlet oak*
Quercus rubra	Red oak*
Quercus velutina	Black oak*
Sambucus canadensis	American elder*
Syringa vulgaris	Common lilac

Most evergreen ornamentals, including *Abies* (fir), *Juniperus*, *Taxus*, *Thuja* (arborvitae), *Rhododendron*, *Picea* (spruce), *Pinus* (pine) and *Tsuga* (hemlock) are not attacked.

* Species marked with an asterisk may suffer occasional light feeding.

protect highly favored host plants. Insecticidal soaps will kill beetles that are hit by the spray, but give no residual protection. Products containing neem or pyrethrum are not very effective. Sprays made from ground-up beetles or similar home-made concoctions are worthless.

Management of Grubs

Cultural Control. Eggs and young grubs cannot survive in very dry soils. Female beetles seek out moist or irrigated sites for egg-laying, especially during drought. Withholding irrigation during peak beetle flight may help to reduce subsequent grub populations. In contrast, rainfall or irrigation in late August and September will help the turf to tolerate and recover from grub damage. Japanese beetle grubs feed on all cool-season turfgrasses, including endophytic cultivars. Tall fescue will generally tolerate more grubs than Kentucky bluegrass or perennial ryegrass.

Biological Control. Milky disease spore dust has been marketed for many years for control of Japanese beetle grubs (see White Grubs — Introduction). Even in a best-case scenario, milky disease is very slow-acting, requiring several years before any suppression of the population may occur. Milky disease products have performed poorly in recent tests, and the spore dust has been in short supply. Similarly, performance of nematode-based products containing *Steinernema*

Figure 8.22. *Japanese beetle traps attract large numbers of beetles, but their value in plant protection is dubious.*

carpocapsae has been quite inconsistent. Ongoing research may provide nematode strains that are more effective against white grubs.

Two species of *Tiphia* wasps attack Japanese beetle grubs, and a parasitic fly, *Hyperecteina aldrichi*, attacks the adults (see Chapter 13). These parasitoids provide some suppression, but their occurrence is sporadic and they cannot be relied upon for control. Naturally occurring predators, especially ants and ground beetles, also help to suppress Japanese beetle populations by feeding on the eggs and grubs. None of these natural enemies is commercially available for mass release. Nevertheless, wise turf managers will strive to conserve these natural buffers by cutting back on nonessential use of broad-spectrum insecticides. Several species of naturally occurring fungal pathogens (e.g., *Beauveria*, *Metarrhizium*) occasionally infect the grubs. A biological insecticide containing the *Beauveria* fungus (Naturalis®-T) has recently been marketed, but its performance against white grubs has not been established.

Chemical Control. (See White Grubs — Introduction). Soil insecticides usually provide good control of Japanese beetle grubs if the timing is right, the treatment is watered in, and there is not too much thatch. The traditional approach is to apply a short-residual insecticide after the eggs have hatched, but before the grubs have caused visible damage. The ideal treatment "window" for curative control is early to mid-August in most areas. Curative treatments can also be made after the damage appears, but the larger the grubs, the harder they are to control. Insecticides are ineffective once the grubs have begun to move deeper for overwintering. Spring treatments are usually unnecessary unless the infestation is severe.

Another option is preventive treatment with a long-residual insecticide (e.g., imidacloprid, halofenozide). Application of imidacloprid during May, June, or July will control the young grubs as they hatch out in late July or early August. Halofenozide can be applied preventively as early as mid-June, or used in late summer for curative control. Because infestations tend to be localized and sporadic, wall-to-wall preventive treatments may be unnecessary and wasteful. Preventive control may be warranted, however, on high-risk sites with recurring grub problems. *See "White Grubs — Introduction" for more about preventive vs. curative control.*

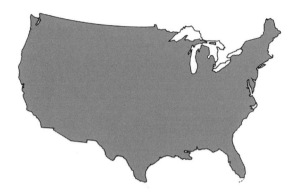

Figure 8.23. Distribution of various May beetle species in the continental United States.

MAY BEETLES
Various species of *Phyllophaga*
(Plate 12)

Importance and Nature of Injury. Larvae of various species of May beetles feed on the roots of turfgrasses, causing typical white grub injury (see White Grubs — Introduction). May beetle grubs can be quite destructive due to their large size, and because they sever the roots close to the surface. Fortunately, they tend to occur at lower densities than grubs of other turf-infesting species, such as Japanese beetles or masked chafers. *Phyllophaga crinita* is an exception — it is a major turf pest in Texas, especially in the lower Rio Grande valley. May beetle grubs also damage roots of young nursery stock and field crops such as corn and soybeans. The adults feed on tree leaves, chewing out the tissue between the veins. Whole trees are sometimes defoliated in the spring.

Plants Attacked. The grubs attack roots of all common turfgrasses. Favored food plants of the adult beetles include oak, hickory, walnut, persimmon, birch, elm, and poplar.

Origin and Distribution. About 25 species of May beetles may infest turfgrasses in North America (Figure 8.23). A few, such as *Phyllophaga anxia* and *P. fervida*, are found throughout the United States. Most of the other important species, including *P. fusca, hirticola, implicata, inversa* and *rugosa,* occur in the eastern half, from the Great Plains to the Atlantic coast. *Phyllophaga crinita* is abundant in Texas and Oklahoma, east to Alabama and Georgia. Another species, *P. latifrons,* damages St. Augustinegrass in Florida. *Phyllophaga* grubs are less common in the southwestern states or California. Despite their name, adults of some species are active in April, whereas others may fly as late as August. Don't confuse this group with the green June beetle (*Cotinis nitida*), an unrelated species with very different habits.

Distinguishing Characteristics. The adults are medium- to large-sized, heavy-bodied, brownish beetles. Most species are 5/8 to 1 in. (11–23.5 cm) long, with coloration ranging from light brown, to reddish brown, to almost black. Body pubescence also varies; some species are nearly hairless, whereas others are quite fuzzy. Often, it takes an expert to distinguish among the various species. Eggs are laid singly in small earthen cells. They are pearly white and oval when newly laid, becoming more spherical once they've absorbed water from the soil. Mature eggs are just under 1/8 in. (2.5–3 mm) across. May beetle grubs have a V- or Y-shaped anal slit with the stem of the Y shorter than the arms. However, their key distinguishing feature is presence of two parallel rows of short spines on the raster, a pattern that resembles a zipper (Figure 8.10). Fully grown, 3rd-instar grubs are about 1 to 1-1/2 in. (25–38 mm) long in average-sized spe-

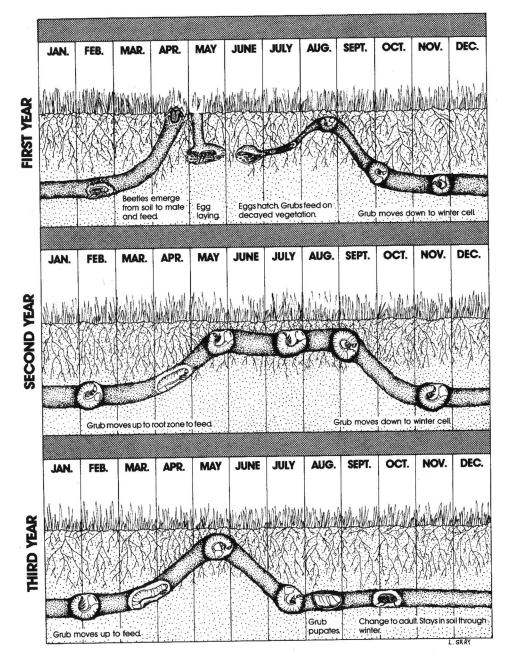

Figure 8.24. *Three-year life cycle typical of many species of May beetles (from Shurtleff et al., 1987; with permission).*

cies. Pupation occurs in an earthen cell. The shed skin of the larva is sloughed off the end of the pupa, as also occurs with European chafer and Asiatic garden beetle pupae.

Life History and Habits. May beetles have life cycles that last for 1–4 years, depending on the species. Most of the ones that occur in the northern half of the United States have a 3-year life cycle (Figure 8.24), whereas 2-year life cycles are common in the transition zone and farther south. A few species, notably *P. crinita* and *P. latifrons*, have 1-year cycles. Adults of most species are active from April to June, depending on latitude. The beetles emerge just after sundown and fly to the tops of trees to feed and mate, returning to the soil before dawn. Heavy populations can severely defoliate oaks, maples, and other favored trees. Emergence and flight activity are heaviest for several nights after a good rain. The beetles are clumsy fliers, buzzing around porch lights and against lighted window screens. After mating, females fly to turf or pasture and burrow down 2–6 in. (5–15 cm) to lay eggs in moist soil. Each female lays 20–50 eggs in her lifetime. Eggs hatch in 3–4 weeks and the young grubs begin to feed on fine roots and organic matter.

In Texas, adults of *P. crinita* deposit their eggs from June to early August. The grubs develop quickly, becoming nearly full-sized and causing the most damage in late summer and fall. Feeding continues into the winter so long as soil temperatures do not get too cold. The grubs pupate in February and March but the beetles remain underground in earthen cells, emerging in June to complete the 1-year cycle.

Most May beetle species with 2-year life cycles develop only as far as the 2nd instar by the end of the first growing season. After hibernation, the grubs resume feeding in early spring, molting to 3rd instars in April or May. These reach full size and pupate by the end of the second summer. Most species transform to adults by late fall, but the beetles remain in their earthen cells and don't emerge until the following spring. This usually occurs in May or June, depending on species and locality. Grubs of species with 3-year cycles (Figure 8.24) feed throughout the first two summers, hibernating twice. They don't pupate until midway through the third summer. The adults are usually fully formed by early fall, but the beetles do not emerge from the soil until the following spring. Because of overlapping generations and presence of more than one species, it is common to find several sizes of May beetle grubs together at a given site.

Regardless of whether the species has a 2-year or 3-year cycle, the greatest damage occurs during the second year. With 3-year May beetles, this is because the 3rd instars feed throughout the summer and fall, as compared to only spring and early summer in the final year. In either case, the injury usually shows up in late summer or fall, especially when the turf is further stressed by drought.

May beetle grubs are susceptible to their own naturally occurring strains of milky disease bacteria, but these usually have minor impact on populations. Several kinds of parasitic flies and wasps attack the beetles or grubs. None of these natural controls is commercially available. Skunks, moles, raccoons, birds, and other predators feed on the larvae, often causing more turf damage than the grubs themselves.

Management. In the northern United States, May beetle grubs are usually not abundant enough to cause extensive damage to turf. They often co-occur with smaller species, such as masked chafers or Japanese beetles. Failure to eliminate the large May beetle grubs along with the more abundant target species may be misinterpreted as a failed treatment. As with all grubs, May beetles are easiest to control when the larvae are small. Southern species with 1-year life cycles (*P. crinita*; *P. latifrons*) can be managed like annual white grubs (see White Grubs — Introduction), except that spring treatments are not effective because the population consists of mostly pupae and adults.

NORTHERN AND SOUTHERN MASKED CHAFERS
Cyclocephala borealis Arrow and *Cyclocephala lurida* (Bland) (Former scientific names include *Ochrosidia villosa* Burmeister for northern masked chafer and *Cyclocephala immaculata* Olivier for southern masked chafer)
(Plates 5, 13)

Importance and Nature of Injury. Masked chafer grubs are among the most destructive pests of lawns and golf courses in the Midwest and north central United States, as well as the transition zone. The larvae cause typical root-feeding damage (see White Grubs — Introduc-

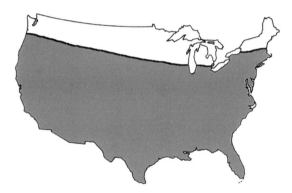

Figure 8.25. Distribution of masked chafers in the continental United States.

tion). Densities of 25–50 or more grubs per ft² (0.1 m²) are common. The damage typically shows up from mid-August through October, especially when the turf is stressed by heat and drought. Areas in full sun, south-facing slopes, and lawns, fairways, tees, and green banks having well-drained, moist soil with high organic matter are especially hard hit. Injury is usually less evident during the spring feeding period because there is less environmental stress. Predators such as birds, skunks, and moles may dig up the turf while foraging on the grubs. Adult masked chafers do not feed or cause any direct damage to turf or other plants.

Plants Attacked. Masked chafer grubs seem to thrive in moist, loamy, well-drained soils that are rich in humus. They eat the roots of all cool-season turfgrasses, including endophytic ryegrasses and fescues. The grubs are fond of decaying organic matter and are often abundant under mulched plant beds, compost heaps, cooled manure piles, and similar sites.

Origin and Distribution. Both the northern masked chafer (NMC) and southern masked chafer (SMC) are native to North America and are widely distributed east of the Rocky Mountains (Figure 8.25). NMC occurs from southern New York, west to the Rockies and south to Kansas, Missouri, Tennessee, and North Carolina. SMC is especially abundant in the transition zone of Kentucky and Tennessee, west to the Rockies and south to Texas. Distributions of the two species overlap throughout much of the Midwest. A related species, *Cyclocephala hirta* LeConte, is common in central California, and another, *C. pasadenae* Casey, is common in parts of Texas west to California. The latter two species can be managed in a similar manner to NMC and SMC.

Distinguishing Characteristics. The larvae are typical white grubs with a C-shaped body form and six jointed legs. Grubs of the NMC and SMC are virtually indistinguishable. Newly hatched grubs are about 3/16 in. (4–5 mm) and translucent white, becoming grayish after they have fed. Mature, third-instar grubs are 7/8 to 1 in. (23–25 mm) long. They are larger and more robust than Japanese beetle grubs, and have a reddish-brown head capsule, as compared to a more yellow-brown head in Japanese beetles. The raster bears about 25–30 stout, *evenly spaced bristles in no distinct pattern* (Figure 8.10). Pupae are about 11/16 in. (17 mm) long and are formed underground within an earthen cell. They are creamy white at first, becoming reddish-brown as they mature. NMC adults are dull yellow-brown beetles, 7/16 in. to just under 1/2 in. (11–12 mm) long and about 1/4 in. (6–7 mm) wide. Adult SMC are similar in size to NMC, but more shiny, and reddish-brown. Females are slightly smaller than males. Males and females of both species have a band of darker, chocolate-brown color across the head and eyes. This "mask" distinguishes them from other scarab species of similar size and coloration. NMC beetles have dense hair on the underside of the thorax, and the males have scattered, erect hairs on the wing covers. Adults of the SMC lack these hairs. The claws on the front legs and the antennal club are longer in males than in females. Newly laid eggs of both species are pearly white, oval, and about 1/16 in. (1.7 × 1.3 mm) long. The eggs become larger and spherical after absorbing water from surrounding soil.

Life Cycle and Habits. Masked chafers have a 1-year life cycle (Figure 8.11). Adults of both the NMC and SMC are active in June and July. At the latitude of Kentucky, flight and mating activity usually peak in late June and early July. The beetles rest in the soil under turfgrass during the day. SMC adults emerge around dusk and are active until about 11 p.m. The males take flight, cruising back and forth over the turf in search of mates. Swarms of small brown beetles may be noticed as they skim over lawns and golf fairways at dusk. Flights are greatest on warm, humid evenings, especially on the first night or two following a heavy rain. Virgin females remain on the ground or climb grass blades. They produce an airborne sex pheromone to attract males. Small "orgies" of beetles occur on the turf surface, with several males jostling to mate with the same female. As soon as she mates, the female burrows down into the turf, often with the male in tow. NMC have similar mating behavior, except that it occurs mostly after midnight. Unlike Japanese beetles or May beetles, masked chafers do not feed as adults. The beetles are strongly attracted to lights. They will bang against well-lit windows and screen doors and find their way into homes. They are a nuisance, but cannot bite or cause any real harm indoors.

Eggs of both species are laid singly or in small clusters in the upper 1–2 in. (2.5–5 cm) of soil. The eggs hatch in 14–18 days at 70–75°F (21–24°C). Most eggs have hatched by early August. The grubs grow quickly when there is adequate soil moisture, molting to second instars in about 3 weeks at 80°F (27°C). Many have attained the third instar by early September. The grubs continue to feed and gain weight until about mid to late October when declining soil temperatures force them to go deeper for overwintering. They hibernate in an earthen cell below the frost line, mostly at depths of 4–10 in. (10–25 cm), but sometimes deeper in more northern areas. They move back up to the root zone in early spring (late March to early April in Kentucky) and resume feeding. The grubs are fully mature by mid to late May. They then go slightly deeper (3–6 in. or 7.5–10 cm) and form an earthen cell in which to pupate. A prepupal stage (4–6 days) precedes the pupal stage, which lasts for 14–20 days (average, 16 days). The first adults begin emerging in early June, completing the 1-year cycle.

Natural enemies of masked chafers include predators such as ants and ground beetles, parasitic wasps and flies, and several kinds of pathogenic soil fungi. *Tiphia* wasps (see Chapter 14) may parasitize a high percentage of masked chafer grubs, but their occurrence is spotty and unpredictable. None of the aforementioned agents is commercially available for release. Masked chafer grubs are susceptible to their own strain of milky disease, but the causal bacteria have not been formulated in commercial products.

Management. (See White Grubs — Introduction). Unlike Japanese beetles, masked chafers do not feed as adults. Mated females often burrow down to lay eggs at the same site from which they emerged. Consequently, the same areas tend to be reinfested year after year. Females will disperse, however, if the soil becomes flooded or too dry. Be alert for swarms of small brown beetles skimming over the turf at sunset in late June and July. This is an indicator of impending "hot-spots" for southern masked chafer grubs. Northern masked chafers are active after midnight, so they won't ordinarily be seen. Mole, skunk, or bird activity can be an indicator of grub problems, although these varmints may be after earthworms, turf caterpillars, or other prey. Masked chafer beetles can be monitored with black light traps; this can help to fine-tune treatment timing. In general, most eggs will have hatched by about 3 weeks after peak flight. Light traps can't be used to locate specific infestation sites because the trapped beetles may have come from some distance away.

Masked chafer eggs must absorb soil moisture in order to survive. They shrivel and die in dry soils (less than 10% moisture). During dry periods in June and July, the females will be attracted to irrigated lawns, tee banks, fairways, and similar moist sites for egg-laying. Thus, irrigation (or rainfall) in midsummer tends to favor survival of eggs, resulting in higher overall grub populations. Rainfall or irrigation in late summer, however, tends to mask the injury and promote recovery of the turf. The worst damage tends to occur in years in which there is abundant rainfall in July, followed by heat and drought in late summer and fall.

Cultural practices that enhance vigor (irrigation, fall fertilization, higher mowing height) will help turf to tolerate and outgrow the damage from white grubs. Vigorous turf will often tolerate 15 or more grubs per ft^2 (16 per 0.1 m^2) without visible symptoms, but stressed turf may show damage with half that number. Tall fescue is generally more tolerant of grubs than are other cool-season grasses.

At the latitude of Kentucky and Maryland, the best period for curative control of masked chafers is from early to mid-August, after the eggs have hatched but when the grubs are still small. This treatment window may be 1–2 weeks earlier or later in more southern or northern locales. Grubs can be controlled curatively after damage has appeared, but as they grow larger the grubs are progressively harder to kill. Imidacloprid or halofenozide can be used for preventive control (see White Grubs — Introduction). Entomopathogenic nematodes have given inconsistent control of masked chafer grubs. Masked chafers are not susceptible to commercial milky disease products.

ORIENTAL BEETLE
Exomala orientalis (Waterhouse) (This species was formerly called *Anomala orientalis* Waterhouse)
(Plate 7)

Importance and Nature of Injury. The Oriental beetle is a pest of regional importance in the northeastern United States. The larvae cause typical grub damage (see White Grubs — Introduction). Oriental beetle grubs seem to prefer well-kept, open, sunny lawns with rich sandy loam and plenty of moisture. Densities of 40–60 grubs per ft^2 (0.1 m^2) are fairly common and can cause severe damage. Fortunately, the adults feed very little compared to Japanese beetles.

Plants Attacked. Oriental beetle grubs eat the roots of all cool-season turfgrasses. They also infest strawberry beds and nursery stock, as well as roots of potted plants that are grown outdoors. Adults nibble the petals of various flowers, but their damage is minor.

Origin and Distribution. The Oriental beetle is common in New York, Pennsylvania, Connecticut, Rhode Island, Massachusetts, and New Jersey; it occurs west to Ohio and south to the Carolinas (Figure 8.26). It is native to the Philippines but was accidentally introduced to Japan, and from there to Hawaii and Connecticut sometime before 1920. This species was called the "Asiatic beetle" when it was first discovered in the United States; this name was later replaced by Oriental beetle.

Distinguishing Characteristics. The adults are spiny-legged, broadly rounded beetles, about 3/8 in. (9–10 mm) long. They are mostly straw-colored, with variable black markings on the thorax and wing covers. The coloration ranges from mostly straw-colored to almost entirely brownish-black. The head is usually solid dark brown. The wing covers have distinct longitudinal grooves.

Newly laid eggs are milky-white, oblong, and just under 1/16 in. (1.5 mm) long, becoming slightly larger and more spherical after a few days in moist soil. The grubs resemble those of Japanese beetles. Both species have a transverse anal slit, but they can be easily separated by

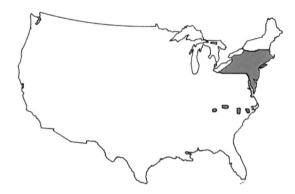

Figure 8.26. *Distribution of the Oriental beetle in the continental United States.*

examining the pattern of hairs on the raster (Figure 8.10). Oriental beetle grubs have two *parallel* rows of 10–16 (usually 11–14) short, stout inward-pointing spines, whereas Japanese beetles have two rows of 6–7 spines forming a *distinct V*. They might also be confused with young May beetle grubs, but the latter have a Y-shaped anal opening. Mature Oriental beetle grubs are just under 1 in. (20–25 cm) long. The prepupa is wrinkled and flaccid, resembling that of Japanese beetles. The pupa, about 3/8 in. (10 mm) long, is cream colored at first, becoming light brown. It has a thick fringe of hairs at the tip of the abdomen. Pupation occurs in an earthen cell. The pupa lies enshrouded in the old larval skin, which splits open as the pupa matures.

Life History and Habits. Oriental beetles have a 1-year life cycle similar to that of Japanese beetles and Asiatic garden beetles (Figure 8.21). Adults begin emerging in late June and are most abundant in mid-July. A few may still be around into late August. The beetles are weak flyers, but they may fly short distances during the day. They are sometimes found on flowers, or seen at night crawling on the ground under lights, but they don't swarm around lights in the manner of Asiatic garden beetles. Females deposit their eggs singly, 1–9 in. (2.5–23 cm) deep in moist soil. Females lay about 25 eggs apiece, mainly in July and early August. Eggs hatch in about 3 weeks at normal summer temperatures. The grub population consists mainly of first instars in August, second instars by early September, and third instars by early October. The grubs feed by severing plant roots close to the soil surface. The damage usually appears by early September. The grubs go deeper in late fall when soil temperature drops to about 50°F (10°C). They hibernate in an earthen cell, 8–16 in. (20–40 cm) underground. They return to the root zone in April and May. Feeding continues until early June, when the grubs again burrow down 3–9 in. (8–23 cm) to pupate. The prepupal and pupal periods last about 1 and 2 weeks, respectively. Most of the grubs pupate by mid to late June. The beetles begin emerging in late June, completing the annual cycle.

Management. See White Grubs — Introduction. In areas where the species occurs, Oriental beetle grubs often occur in mixed populations with Japanese beetle grubs. Timing for curative or preventive applications are the same for both species. Oriental beetle grubs are vulnerable to a specific, naturally occurring strain of milky disease, but they are not susceptible to commercial milky disease products. The adults are less conspicuous than Japanese beetles, so turf managers may not be forewarned that a grub infestation is developing. Digging by skunks, moles, or other varmints may reveal their presence. Damage thresholds will vary with the value and condition of the turf. Irrigation and fall fertilization will encourage recovery of grub-damaged turf. The female sex pheromone was recently identified and may find use in monitoring for this pest.

SELECTED REFERENCES

General References

Brandenburg, R.L. and M.G. Villani (Eds.). 1995. *Handbook of turfgrass insect pests*. Entomol. Soc. Am., Lanham, MD.

Ritcher, P.O. 1966. *White grubs and their allies: A study of North American scarabaeid larvae*. Oregon. Univ. Press, Corvallis, OR.

Shurtleff, M., R. Randell, and T. Fermanian. 1987. *Controlling turfgrass pests*. Prentice-Hall, Inc., New York, NY.

Tashiro, H. 1987. *Turfgrass insects of the United States and Canada*. Cornell Univ. Press, Ithaca, NY.

Watschke, T.L., P.H. Dernoeden, and D.J. Shetlar. 1995. *Managing turfgrass pests*. Lewis Publishers, Boca Raton, FL.

Aphodius Grubs

Sears, M.K. 1979. Damage to golf course fairways by *Aphodius granarius* (L.) (Coleoptera: Scarabaeidae). *Proc. Entomol. Soc. Ontario* 109:48.

Asiatic Garden Beetle

Hallock, H.C. and I.M. Hawley. 1936. Life history and control of the Asiatic garden beetle. *U.S. Dept. Agric. Circ.* 246.

Hallock, H.C. 1936. Notes on the biology and control of the Asiatic garden beetle. *J. Econ. Entomol.* 29:348–356.

Australian Sod Fly

Campbell, R.L. and C.S. Koehler. 1971. Biological observations on *Inopus rubriceps* (Diptera: Stratiomyiidae). *Ann. Entomol. Soc. Am.* 64:1–11.

Black Turfgrass Ataenius

Niemczyk, H.D. and G.S. Wegner. 1982. Life history and control of the black turfgrass ataenius (Coleoptera: Scarabaeidae), pp. 113–118. *In*: H.D. Niemczyk and B.G. Joyner (Eds.) *Advances in turfgrass entomology*. Hammer Graphics, Piqua, OH.

Wegner, G.S. and H.D. Niemczyk. 1981. Bionomics and phenology of *Ataenius spretulus*. *Ann. Entomol. Soc. Am.* 74:374–384.

Dichondra Flea Beetle

McCrea, R.J. 1973. A new species of the flea beetle genus *Chaetocnema* found on dichondra in California. *Pan-Pacific Entomol.* 49:61–66.

European Chafer

Gyrisco, G.G., W.H. Whitcomb, R.H. Burrage, C. Logothetis, and H.H. Schwardt. 1954. Biology of the European chafer, *Amphimallon majalis* Razoumowsky (Scarabaeidae). *Cornell Univ. Agric. Exp. Sta. Mem.* 328.

Nyrop, J.P., M.G. Villani, and J.A. Grant. 1995. Control decision rule for European chafer (Coleoptera: Scarabaeidae) larvae infesting turfgrass. *Environ. Entomol.* 24:521–528.

Tashiro, H., G.G. Gyrisco, F.L. Gambrell, B.J. Fiori, and H. Breitfeld. 1969. Biology of the European chafer *Amphimallon majalis* (Coleoptera: Scarabaeidae) in northeastern United States. *NY State Agric. Exp. Sta. Bull.* 828.

European Crane Fly or Leather Jacket

Jackson, D.M. and R.L. Campbell. 1975. Biology of the European crane fly, *Tipula paludosa* Meigen, in western Washington (Tipulidae: Diptera). *Wash. State. Univ. Tech Bull*. No. 81. 23 pp.

Wilkinson, A.T.S. and H.R. MacCarthy. 1967. The marsh crane fly, *Tipula paludosa* Mg., a new pest in British Columbia (Diptera: Tipulidae). *J. Entomol. Soc. Brit. Columbia* 64:29–34.

Green June Beetle

Chittenden, F.H. 1922. The green June beetle. *U.S. Dept. Agric. Bull.* 891.

Davis, J.J. and P. Luginbill. 1921. The green June beetle or fig eater. *N. Carolina Agric. Exp. Sta. Bull.* 242.

Ground Pearls

Kouskolekas, C.A. and R.L. Self. 1974. Biology and control of the ground pearl in relation to turfgrass infestation, pp. 421–423. *In*: E.C. Roberts (Ed.). *Proc. 2nd Internat. Turfgrass Res. Conf.*, Amer. Soc. Agron., Madison, WI.

Japanese Beetle

Fleming, W.E. 1970. The Japanese beetle in the United States. *U.S. Dept. Agric. Handbook* 236.

Fleming, W.E. 1972. Biology of the Japanese beetle. *U.S. Dept. Agric. Tech. Bull.* 1449.

Gordon, F.C. and D.A. Potter. 1985. Efficiency of Japanese beetle (Coleoptera: Scarabaeidae) traps in reducing defoliation of plants in the urban landscape and effect on larval density in turf. *J. Econ. Entomol.* 78:774–778.

Redmond, C.T and D.A. Potter. 1995. Lack of efficacy of *in vivo-* and putatively *in vitro*-produced *Bacillus popilliae* against field populations of Japanese beetle (Coleoptera: Scarabaeidae) grubs in Kentucky. *J. Econ. Entomol.* 88:846–854.

Vittum, P.J. 1986. Biology of the Japanese beetle (Coleoptera: Scarabaeidae) in eastern Massachusetts. *J. Econ. Entomol.* 79:387–391.

May Beetles

Luginbill, P. and H.R. Painter. 1953. May beetles of the United States and Canada. *U.S. Dept. Agric. Tech. Bull.* 1060. Washington, DC.

Pfadt, R.E. 1978. *Fundamentals of applied entomology.* (3rd ed.) Macmillan Publishing Co., NY.

Mole Crickets

Brandenburg, R.L. and C.B. Williams. 1993. A complete guide to mole cricket management in North Carolina. *N. Carolina Coop. Ext. Serv. Bull.* ENT 101.

Cobb, P.O. 1993. Controlling mole crickets on lawns and turf. *Alabama Coop. Ext. Serv. Circ.* ANR-176.

Short, D.E. and J.A. Reinert. 1982. Biology and control of mole crickets, pp. 119–124. *In*: Niemczyk, H.D. and B.G. Joyner (Eds.). *Advances in turfgrass entomology.* Hammer Graphics, Piqua, OH.

Walker, T.J. (Ed.) 1984. Mole crickets in Florida. *Univ. Fla. Inst. Food Agric. Sci. Bull.* 846.

Northern and Southern Masked Chafers

Johnson, J.P. 1941. *Cyclocephala (Ochrosidia) borealis* in Connecticut. *J. Agric. Res.* 62:79–86.

Potter, D.A. 1981. Seasonal emergence and flight of northern and southern masked chafers in relation to air and soil temperature and rainfall patterns. *Environ. Entomol.* 10:793–797.

Potter, D.A. and F.C. Gordon. 1984. Susceptibility of *Cyclocephala immaculata* (Coleoptera: Scarabaeidae) eggs and immatures to heat and drought in turfgrass. *Environ. Entomol.* 13:794–799.

Oriental Beetle

Adams, J.A. 1949. The oriental beetle as a turf pest associated with the Japanese beetle in New York. *J. Econ. Entomol.* 42:366–371.

Facundo, H.T., A. Zhang, P.S. Robbins, S.R. Alm, C.E. Linn, M.G. Villani, and W.L. Roelofs. 1994. Sex pheromone responses of the oriental beetle (Coleoptera: Scarabaeidae). *Environ. Entomol.* 23:1508–1515.

Friend, R.B. 1929. The Asiatic (*sic*) beetle in Connecticut. *Conn. Agric. Exp. Sta. Bull.* 304:585–664.

9

PESTS THAT BURROW IN STEMS OR DAMAGE CROWNS

Larvae of several types of billbugs, weevils, and flies damage turfgrasses by burrowing in the stems or by damaging the crown. The crown is the most vulnerable part of the plant because it contains the growing points from which the roots, lateral shoots, and leaves arise. Because these pests begin feeding within grass stems, they are protected from conventional insecticides during part of their lives. Successful control requires knowledge of life cycles for proper timing, or use of long-residual insecticides having systemic activity.

ANNUAL BLUEGRASS WEEVIL
Listronotus maculicollis (Dietz) [formerly *Hyperodes* sp. near *anthracinus* (Dietz)]
(Plate 15)

Importance and Nature of Injury. The annual bluegrass weevil (ABW), formerly called the hyperodes weevil, is a serious pest of close-cut annual bluegrass on golf courses and tennis courts in the northeastern United States. Adult ABW chew notches or holes in grass blades and at the juncture of leaves and stems. This damage is minor compared to that caused by the larvae. Young larvae feed inside plant stems, causing the central leaf blades to turn yellow and die. Inspection with a 10x hand lens reveals the hollowed-out stem or sometimes the larva itself. Older larvae feed externally on the crowns, often partially or completely severing the stems from the root system. Each larva may kill several plants during its development.

Damage usually begins along edges of fairways, especially those bordering wooded areas or other overwintering sites, and around edges of greens or tees. It starts out as small, yellowish-brown spots or scattered dead patches that coalesce into larger dead areas as the larvae grow. The tunneled stems break off easily at the crown. Densities may exceed 450 larvae per ft^2 (nearly 500 per 0.1 m^2). Heavy infestations cause severe damage to greens, collars, tees or fairways where annual bluegrass predominates. The worst damage occurs in late May and early June, coinciding with maturation of the first brood of larvae. The second generation causes further damage in late July and early August, but the injury is usually less severe and more scattered than in May and June.

Damage from this pest is largely restricted to annual bluegrass maintained at low to moderate cutting heights. It is rarely a problem on home lawns or on golf roughs cut at 1.5 in. (4 cm) or higher. The ABW will leave patches of creeping bentgrass untouched even when the surrounding annual bluegrass has been killed. Where bentgrass greens are invaded by scattered patches of annual bluegrass, ABW damage to the bluegrass may be mistaken for symptoms of anthracnose, dollar spot, or other diseases.

Plants Attacked. Only short-cut annual bluegrass, *Poa annua* L., is damaged. Adults may nibble on clover, dandelion, plantain, and tall fescue, but do not cause serious harm.

Distribution. The worst problems with ABW have occurred around the metropolitan New York area, including southwestern Connecticut, Long Island, northern New Jersey, and southeastern New York. Damage to golf courses has also occurred in eastern and central Pennsylvania, upstate New York, and all the New England states (Figure 9.1).

Distinguishing Characteristics. Adults are small, 1/8 to 5/32 in. (3.5–4.0 mm) long, dark charcoal-gray beetles. The body is covered with fine, yellowish hairs and scales that wear off with age, so that older adults may appear shiny black. Newly emerged adults are light reddish-brown and do not darken for several days. The head is prolonged into a blunt snout. The ABW is sometimes confused with turf-infesting billbugs, which are similar in body form (Figure 9.2). ABW can be distinguished by its short, broad snout; the combined length of the snout and prothorax is less than the length of the wing covers. Billbugs, in contrast, have a longer, narrower snout, and the snout and prothorax together are about the same length as the wing covers. In ABW, the antennae are attached at the tip of the snout, although they may be folded back alongside the head. In billbugs, the antennae arise from the base of the snout.

ABW eggs are rice-shaped, about 1/32 in. (1 mm) long, yellow at first but becoming smoky black before hatching. Eggs are inserted between leaf sheaths. Larvae are creamy white and somewhat C-shaped, with a distinct brown head. They look a bit like small scarab grubs, but lack legs and have a more pointed abdomen. Larvae are about 1/32 in. (1 mm) when newly hatched and about 3/16 in. (5 mm) when full-grown. There are five larval instars, each lasting about 5–7 days. Young larvae burrow and feed inside grass stems, but older larvae feed externally, mainly on the plant crown. Pupation occurs in an earthen cell just under the soil surface. Pupae are about 1/8 in. (3.5 mm) long. They are whitish at first, becoming reddish brown before the adult emerges. The legs, wing pads, and snout are visible on the pupa, but are folded close to the body.

Life History and Habits. The ABW has two generations per year in the metropolitan New York area and southern New England. Only one generation occurs in more northern extremes of its range. Adults overwinter in leaf litter under trees, tufts of tall fescue, or other sheltered sites in roughs or along borders of golf courses. Needle litter under white pines, *Pinus strobus* L., is a favorite hibernation site. The weevils become active in spring about when forsythia (*Forsythia* spp.) is in full bloom, generally mid to late April in southeastern New York. They crawl or fly to areas of close-cut annual bluegrass and begin to feed. The adults usually hide in the foliage or thatch by day, climbing up grass stems to feed at night. Egg-laying begins in early May, just before flowering dogwood (*Cornus florida* L.) and redbud (*Cercis canadensis* L.) are in full bloom.

Eggs are laid between leaf sheaths; typically 2 or 3 eggs are placed end to end inside the sheath. Eggs hatch in 4–5 days and the young larvae burrow into the grass stems, where they feed for the first few molts. The young larva tunnels within the stem, packing it with sawdust-like frass. Small larvae may exit and reenter the same plant several times, or may move from stem to stem. When the larva becomes too large to feed within stems, it burrows out and feeds externally on the crown. Each larva may damage or kill several plants. Most of the population reaches the fifth, or final, instar by early to mid-June, the period when the most severe damage

Figure 9.1. Distribution of the annual bluegrass weevil in the continental United States.

Figure 9.2. General body form of an adult billbug (left) versus the annual bluegrass weevil (right). Note differences in the shape of the snout, where antennae are attached, and relative length of snout and pronotum compared to the wing covers (compiled from photos by D. Shetlar).

occurs. Pupation occurs in mid to late June, and adults of the second generation emerge in late June or early July to mate, lay eggs, and start the cycle anew.

Larvae of the second brood are nearly full-sized by late July or early August. Their damage usually extends farther into the center of fairways, greens, or tees than that caused by the spring generation. Most of the population pupates in late August, emerging as adults in September. In warm summers, they may emerge a bit earlier, and some of these adults may lay eggs that give rise to a partial third generation. There is considerable overlap between the generations, so that during mid to late summer all life stages may be found at any given time. The adult weevils migrate back to overwintering sites with the onset of cooler weather in the fall.

Management. Presence of holes or notches in annual bluegrass blades is a good indicator of adult ABW activity. The adults can be spotted with a flashlight as they feed on foliage at night. A standard golf hole cutter is useful for sampling ABW. Gently break apart the cores and look for larvae, pupae, or adults. Placing the soil and thatch into a dishpan with lukewarm water will float out any remaining insects. Vigorous turf with ample soil moisture may tolerate 30–50 larvae per ft^2 (3–5 per hole cutter sample). Fewer larvae may cause unacceptable damage if turf is stressed, or if they occur in sensitive locations such as greens and tees.

Conventional insecticides are presently the only available means of managing ABW infestations. Control is difficult once the eggs and larvae are inside the stems. One strategy is to treat with a short-residual insecticide in early spring, between the time that *Forsythia* is in bloom until dogwood is in full bloom. This intercepts the adults as they move into annual bluegrass, before they have laid their eggs. A light trap is useful for monitoring adult activity, especially during this spring migration from hibernation sites to close-cut annual bluegrass. If an area was damaged by the first generation, an application in early July may be warranted. This targets the emerging, second-generation adults before they have laid eggs, and will help to reduce damage from the second brood of larvae. Several organophosphates and pyrethroids are labeled for ABW control.

Another option is to apply a long-residual, systemic insecticide (e.g., imidacloprid) when the adult weevils become active in the spring, before the eggs have hatched. The systemic action kills the young larvae inside the stems, and the prolonged residual activity gives season-long control of larvae that make it to the soil. Root-feeding scarab grubs are controlled at the same time. This preventive approach should be reserved for sites with perennial ABW problems, or where heavy adult activity suggests that a damaging infestation will occur.

BILLBUGS — INTRODUCTION
(Plates 16,17)

Importance and Nature of Injury. Billbugs are among the most misdiagnosed pests of turf-grass. Many turf managers confuse billbug damage with symptoms of drought stress, diseases such as dollar spot or brown patch, or injury from greenbugs or white grubs. Several species of billbugs are major pests of lawns and golf courses in the United States.

Adult billbugs feed by chewing holes in grass stems, but adults cause only minor damage compared to the larvae. Eggs are deposited within small cavities chewed in stems, usually just above the crown. Young larvae tunnel up and down the stem and then burrow down to feed on the crown. If the stem becomes hollowed out, the young larva may exit and then bore into another stem. Older larvae migrate to the thatch and soil and feed externally on the crown, killing the whole plant. They may also feed on roots and rhizomes. Scattered dead stems are the first symptom of infestation. Soon afterward, small patches of turf, 2–3 in. (5–7.5 cm) across, begin to die out. This injury is often mistaken for dollar spot disease. Tufts of straw-colored dead grass are easily pulled out by hand, with the stems breaking off at the crown. The broken stems are hollowed out, and fine, sawdust-like frass can be seen at their base. The affected turf does not recover with watering. With heavy infestations, the scattered patches merge into large areas of brown, dead grass. Billbug damage usually shows up in mid to late summer, especially during extended dry periods. With billbugs, the grass turns a whitish-straw color rather than the burnt orange associated with greenbugs. The soil remains firm, not spongy underfoot as with white grub or mole cricket infestations.

General Description. Billbugs belong to the weevil family, a group of beetles having a long, beak-like snout with chewing mouthparts at the tip. Adult billbugs are hard-bodied and usually grayish or black, although their color may be modified by dried mud or clay adhering to the body. Most species are 5/16 to 7/16 in. (8–11 mm) long. The snout, head, and thorax are about as long as the wing covers, and the elbowed antennae are attached near the base of the snout. These features distinguish billbugs from other turf-infesting weevils (e.g., annual bluegrass weevil, vegetable weevil) in which the thorax is only about one-third as long as the wing covers, and the antennae are attached near the tip of a short, blunt snout (Figure 9.2).

Billbug larvae resemble small white grubs, but without legs. Mature larvae are about 3/8 in. (9.5 mm) long and cream colored with a brown head. The body is somewhat curved, fat through the middle and pointed at the tail end (Figure 9.3). All larval instars look the same except for size. The larvae tunnel in grass stems, or are found in the thatch or soil.

Important Species. Two species of billbugs are widespread, important pests of turfgrasses in North America (Figure 9.4). The bluegrass billbug, *Sphenophorus parvulus* Gyllenhal, attacks cool-season grasses in the northern half of the United States and southern Canada from the East Coast across to Washington State and Utah. The hunting billbug, *S. venatus vestitus* Chittenden,

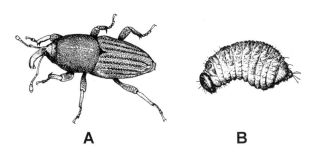

Figure 9.3. *Billbug adult (left) and larva (A, courtesy of D. Shetlar; B, from USDA).*

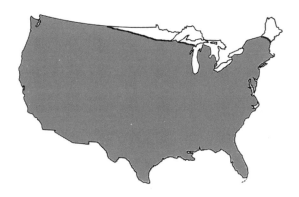

Figure 9.4. *Distribution of turf-infesting billbug species in the continental United States.*

damages warm-season grasses in the transition zone and throughout the southern states. Two other species, the Phoenix (or Phoenician) billbug (*S. phoeniciensis* Chittenden) and the Denver (or Rocky Mountain) billbug (*S. cicatristriatus* Fahraeus) are occasional pests in more restricted geographic regions. Phoenix billbugs attack bermudagrass and zoysiagrass in southern California and Arizona. Denver billbugs infest cool-season grasses in the Rocky Mountain region and northern Great Plains. All of the above species were placed in the genus *Calendra* in the early literature.

Adult billbugs can be identified by examining the patterns of pits and furrows on the back (Figure 9.5). Bluegrass billbugs have small, evenly spaced punctures on the pronotum and coarsely striated wing covers with rows of regularly spaced single punctures. Denver billbugs are shiny black and have rows of *paired* depressions resembling deer hoofprints along each groove of the wing covers. Hunting billbugs have a raised Y-shaped area on the pronotum, with a parenthesis-like curved line on either side. The Phoenix billbug has a distinct, M-shaped raised area on the pronotum. These features can be seen with a 10x hand lens. Larvae and pupae of billbugs are hard to identify to species, even by an expert. If species ID is required, try to collect some adult specimens.

BLUEGRASS BILLBUG
Sphenophorus parvulus Gyllenhal
(Plate 16)

Importance and Type of Injury. This is among the most serious pests of Kentucky bluegrass and perennial ryegrass in the northern United States and southern Canada. Damage is usually worst from late June to early August, especially when turf is under moisture stress. Light popula-

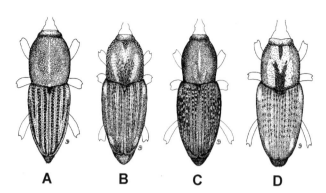

Figure 9.5. *Patterns of pits and furrows on pronotum and wing covers useful in distinguishing among billbug species; (A) bluegrass billbug; (B) hunting billbug; (C) Denver billbug; (D) Phoenix billbug (courtesy of D. Shetlar).*

tions produce scattered brown patches, while heavy infestations can completely destroy lawns or other turf areas. See Billbugs — Introduction.

Plants Attacked. Kentucky bluegrass is the favored host, followed by perennial ryegrass. Fine-leaf and tall fescues are occasionally attacked, especially when they are near heavily infested bluegrass. Bluegrass billbugs also feed on small grains and other grassy plants, including corn, rye, wheat, and timothy.

Distribution. Native to North America, the bluegrass billbug occurs throughout most of the United States and southern Canada where cool-season turfgrasses are grown.

Distinguishing Characteristics. Adults are typical-looking billbugs (see Billbugs — Introduction), about 5/6 in. (7–8 mm) long, exclusive of the length of the snout. They are slate gray to black, although they may appear brownish from dried soil adhering to the body. Newly-emerged adults are reddish-brown, but become darker after a few days. The elongate, bean-shaped, translucent white eggs are about 1/16 in. (1.6 mm) long. Eggs are inserted into small cavities chewed in grass stems. Larvae are fat, legless grubs, creamy white with a brown head (see Billbugs — Introduction). All larval instars are similar except for size. Mature larvae are about 1/4 in. (6 mm) long and found in the thatch or soil. Pupae are about 5/16 in. long and cream colored, gradually changing to reddish brown. The wing pads and legs are folded close to the body, and the elongate snout is visible. Pupae are found in the soil, about 1–2 in. (2.5–5 cm) below the thatch.

Life History and Habits. Adults overwinter in thatch, soil crevices, under bark mulch or leaf litter, or other sheltered locations. The crevice between the lawn and sidewalk is a favorite winter abode. The adults become active in late April to mid-May at the latitude of Ohio, or when soil surface temperatures reach about 65°F (18°C). They are seen crawling over driveways, curbs, or sidewalks on warm spring days as they wander in search of suitable grasses on which to feed. After mating, females begin inserting eggs into small cavities chewed in grass stems, just above the crown. Eggs are laid singly, or occasionally in groups of two or three. Each female lays 2–5 eggs per day and as many as 200 in her lifetime. Most egg-laying is completed by early July, although a few females may continue to lay eggs into August. Eggs hatch in about 6 days and the young larvae begin feeding within grass stems, later burrowing down to feed on the crown. The stem is hollowed out and packed with powdery frass. When they become too large to feed within stems, larvae tunnel out and move to the soil to feed externally on the crown and roots. Larvae leave an accumulation of fine, whitish, sawdust-like

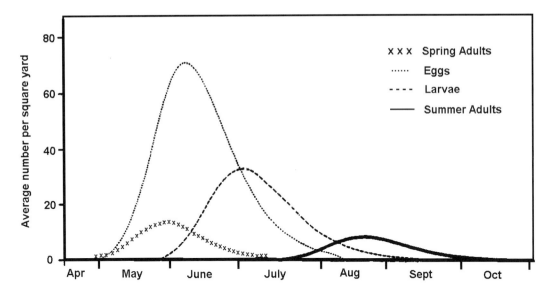

Figure 9.6. Generalized life cycle of the bluegrass billbug in central Ohio (redrawn from Shetlar, 1991).

frass near the feeding site, a good clue to their presence. Larvae are abundant in the soil from early July to early August in Ohio (Figure 9.6). They mature in 35 to 55 days, depending on temperature, and then pupate in small cells in the soil. The adult billbugs emerge about 8–10 days later. New adults are abundant in late summer and fall. They feed briefly before seeking overwintering sites when the cool temperatures arrive. The adults may be seen crawling over pavement on warm afternoons in the fall. Some early-emerging adults may begin to lay eggs for a second generation, but the resulting larvae do not grow fast enough to mature before onset of winter.

Management

Diagnosis and Monitoring. Early detection is tricky because the young larvae are hidden within stems, and their damage usually goes unnoticed until they begin feeding on crowns and roots in June or July. Adult billbugs crawling over paved areas during May and June, and again in the fall, may signal a potential problem building up in nearby turf. Watch for scattered patches of dead or dying grass near such areas, beginning in early summer. To confirm billbugs as the cause, perform the "tug test." Grasp the affected stems and pull upward. If the grass breaks off easily at the crown and the stems are hollowed out or filled with sawdust-like frass, then billbugs are the culprit. Use a knife to check the crown and roots for fat, legless billbug larvae. Tunnelled stems, feeding at the crown, and presence of fine, whitish sawdust-like frass in the stems, crown area, or root zone are sure signs of billbug activity.

Billbugs seem to prefer highly maintained bluegrass lawns; infestations are often clustered in neighborhoods where such lawns predominate. Although the adults rarely fly, they can easily crawl between adjacent lawns. Turf areas that have been damaged in the past are likely to be reinfested. Polystand lawns, and lawns planted with endophytic cultivars are usually less susceptible.

Pitfall traps are useful for monitoring first occurrence and duration of adult billbug activity in the spring. This helps you assess the abundance of adults, providing forewarning of possible damage from larvae in July and August. Standard 16 oz (473 mL) Solo® plastic drink cups make effective traps (see Chapter 3). Set the traps in holes in the turf made with a golf hole cutter. Traps can be positioned alongside plant beds, along the edge of lawns, or in other out-of-the-way spots. Check them several times per week. Pitfall traps are also useful for timing controls directed at intercepting the adults before they have laid eggs in the stems (see below).

Resistant Grasses. Perennial ryegrass cultivars with fungal endophytes are generally resistant to billbugs. Endophyte-enhanced fescues may also be somewhat resistant. When renovating billbug-damaged turf, use endophytic grasses or consider a blend of grasses containing endophytic cultivars. Research conducted in the 1970s and 1980s showed variation in susceptibility among older cultivars of Kentucky bluegrass, but comparable trials have not been done with the newer cultivars.

Masking of Damage. Low to moderate levels of billbug damage can often be masked by light fertilization and deep watering in summer to reduce plant stress from root and crown damage. The critical period is when billbug larvae are emerging from the grass stems to feed at the crown and roots, generally late June to early August. If the larva kills the main stem before the spring-formed tillers have become well-rooted, the new plants also will die.

Biological Control. Current commercial products containing entomopathogenic nematodes have provided mixed results against billbugs. More research is needed to determine the conditions under which they will work. If you try nematodes, apply them in early morning or evening out of direct sunlight, and water them in immediately. A naturally occurring fungus, *Beauveria,* helps to suppress billbug populations, especially in rainy years. Insects killed by this fungus are covered with white, cottony mycelia. A biopesticide containing *Beauveria* has been marketed under the name Naturalis®-T. There is presently little information about what level of billbug control, if any, this product may provide.

Chemical Control of Adults. One approach for controlling billbugs is to apply a short residual insecticide in spring, to intercept the overwintered adults before they can lay eggs in the stems. This breaks the cycle, preventing larval infestations from developing, and often giving season-long control. If you try this approach, treat no later than 3 weeks after adults become active. Pitfall traps can be used to pinpoint the time when adults are leaving the hibernation sites and moving into turf. This usually starts in late April at the latitude of Ohio. Several short-residual organophosphates, carbamates, and pyrethroids are labeled for control of adult billbugs. Use a liquid application where possible. Apply only a light, post-treatment watering, 1/8 in. (3 mm) or less, to keep the residues in the upper thatch where the adult billbugs reside. Because it is preventive, this approach is only justified on sites with a history of billbug problems, or where large numbers of adults were noted in spring or the preceding fall.

Chemical Control of Larvae. Billbug larvae spend much of their lives burrowing within grass stems, where they are sheltered from contact insecticides. They become more vulnerable to conventional insecticides once they have moved to the root zone. This usually occurs about 6 weeks after adults become active (around mid-June in Ohio and similar latitudes). By late June or early July, the larvae are large enough to see in the soil and thatch by cutting and laying back a flap of turf, or by taking soil cores. Once they are in the soil, you can control billbug larvae curatively, as you would white grubs. The main problem with curative control is that the plant crown may already be severely damaged. Thus, treatments targeted for summer larvae may be too late to prevent damage, especially if the turf is drought-stressed. Also, curative control is hampered by poor penetration of insecticides through the thatch.

Another approach is to apply imidacloprid or halofenozide soon after the adult billbugs become active in the spring, before the eggs have hatched in the stems. Adult activity can be monitored with pitfall traps or by visual observations of crawling adults. The systemic action of imidacloprid kills the young larvae inside the stems, and its prolonged residual activity gives season-long control of billbug larvae and white grubs in the soil. This preventive approach is best reserved for sites with a history of billbug problems, or where heavy activity of the adults indicates that a damaging infestation will occur.

Timing by Degree-Days. A system developed at Ohio State University uses accumulated degree-days to predict the seasonal occurrence of billbug activity. Degree-days are calculated from a base temperature of 50°F (10°C), using a March 1 starting date. First activity of adults can be expected between 280 and 350 degree-days, and short-residual treatments to intercept adults before they lay eggs would be effective until about 560–620 degree-days have accumulated. Preventive treatment with imidacloprid or halofenozide would also be effective at that time. Larvae begin exiting from stems between 925 and 1035 degree-days, and severe visual damage usually appears between 1330 and 1485 degree-days. Local degree-days accumulations are available from many Cooperative Extension offices. See Chapter 3 for more about forecasting with degree-days.

DENVER BILLBUG
Sphenophorus cicatristriatus Fahraeus
(Plate 17)

Importance and Type of Injury. This billbug attacks lawns in Colorado, New Mexico, and Wyoming. Damage is similar to that caused by other billbugs. This species is commonly a problem on newly established lawns, and in sod production (see Billbugs — Introduction).

Plants Attacked. Like the bluegrass billbug, Denver billbugs prefer cool-season grasses, especially Kentucky bluegrass and perennial ryegrass.

Distribution. Denver billbugs are restricted to the Rocky Mountain region and northern Great Plains where they may co-occur with the bluegrass billbug.

Distinguishing Characteristics. Adults are larger and darker than the bluegrass billbug. A key diagnostic feature is presence of rows of lighter colored, paired depressions resembling deer hoofprints along each groove of the wing covers (Figure 9.5). Larvae resemble those of other billbugs; they are about 3/8 in. (9.5 mm) long when mature.

Life Cycle and Habits. Relatively little is known about the biology of Denver billbugs. The seasonal cycle is not as well synchronized as that of the bluegrass billbug. The overwintering population consists mostly of older larvae, with some young larvae and adults also present. The relative proportions of these life stages may change from late fall to early spring, depending on temperatures. Damage may appear in the spring as the overwintered larvae resume feeding and complete their development. Overwintered adults become active by mid-May and probably begin laying eggs in stems. They are joined by increasing numbers of new adults as the overwintered larvae mature. Peak adult densities can occur from June through mid-September, often varying a month or more from year to year. Adult activity and egg-laying are less synchronized than for bluegrass billbugs, resulting in a broader period of larval damage. As with other billbugs, the young larvae tunnel inside grass stems and later move to the soil to feed on crowns and roots.

Management. See Bluegrass Billbug — Management. Emergence of larvae from stems is poorly synchronized and occurs over many weeks, so trying to control them with short-residual insecticides usually gives poor results. A more effective use of such insecticides is to target the adults in the spring, before they have laid many eggs. Because of their prolonged activity period, control of adults may require two applications, in early May and again in mid-June. Adults can be monitored with pitfall traps. Entomopathogenic nematodes have shown some promise for curative control of Denver billbug larvae.

Application of imidacloprid in the spring, before eggs have hatched, is an effective strategy. Treatment soon after adults become active in May will control the young larvae hatching within stems, as well as provide extended residual protection against billbug larvae and white grubs in the soil. This preventive approach is best reserved for sites with a history of billbug problems, or where a high level of adult activity foretells the likelihood of a damaging infestation.

HUNTING BILLBUG
Sphenophorus venatus vestitus Chittenden
(Plate 17)

Importance and Type of Injury. Hunting billbugs are sporadic, but potentially serious pests of warm-season turfgrasses in the southern United States, and in Hawaii. Damage resembles that caused by bluegrass billbugs in cool-season grasses. Warm-season turfgrass sod farms are commonly infested.

Plants Attacked. Zoysiagrass and hybrid bermudagrass are most heavily damaged. Bahiagrass, centipedegrass, and St. Augustinegrass are also susceptible.

Distribution. Hunting billbugs are widespread throughout the southern United States from Maryland across to Kansas and south into Texas, Florida, and the other Gulf states. They also occur on some of the Caribbean islands and have been introduced into Hawaii.

Distinguishing Characteristics. The adults resemble bluegrass billbugs, but are slightly larger, about 1/4 to 7/16 in. (8–11 mm) long. They are charcoal gray to black but may be covered with soil, giving them a brownish color. Clean specimens have numerous punctations on the pronotum and a distinct, Y-shaped, smooth raised area just behind the head. This area is enclosed by a shiny, parenthesis-like mark on either side (Figure 9.5). The wing covers have distinct, longitudinal furrows. Newly emerged adults are reddish brown, darkening in a few days. The adults often play dead when disturbed. Oblong, translucent white eggs are laid in cavities chewed in grass stems or leaf petioles. The plump, legless larvae are somewhat C-shaped and creamy white, with a brown head. Mature larvae are about 3/8 in. (8–10 mm) long. They are found in the crown or root zone, just below the thatch.

Life Cycle and Habits. The seasonal cycle of this species is poorly known. It overwinters as dormant adults in the northern part of its range, hiding in thatch, cracks and holes in the soil, under mulch, or other in sheltered spots. Adults become active in early spring, and may be seen crawling over sidewalks, curbs, and driveways as they wander in search of suitable grasses for feeding and egg-laying. The adults usually "play dead" for a short time when disturbed, or they may cling tightly to a stem or leaf when one attempts to pick them up. Adults are active year-round in the Gulf Coast states; they may be seen crawling or feeding on warm winter days. Most egg-laying occurs in spring after bermudagrass and zoysiagrass are well out of winter dormancy. Some females lay eggs well into the summer. Eggs are deposited in leaf sheaths, or inserted into feeding punctures in stems or leaf petioles. Eggs hatch in 3–10 days, depending on temperature, and the young larva tunnels within the stem, often boring down into the crown. The stem becomes hollowed out and filled with fine, whitish, sawdust-like frass. When the larvae become too large to feed within stems, they exit, burrow into the thatch and soil, and begin feeding externally on crowns, stolons, and roots. This is when the most severe damage is noticed, especially if the turf is stressed by drought. After 3–5 weeks, the larva is mature and pupates within a cavity in the soil under the thatch. The new adult emerges about a week later. Development from egg hatch to adult emergence takes about a month. Adults of this new generation may be noticed as they migrate over pavement in the late summer months. Adults can fly for short distances, but seem to prefer crawling. With the onset of cool fall temperatures, they seek sheltered sites in which to overwinter.

The hunting billbug has one generation per year in the northern parts of its range. There are probably several overlapping generations along the Gulf coast. Because of the extended period of egg-laying, larvae may be found throughout the growing season, and some larvae overwinter. Damage is usually worst in August in the northern zoysiagrass-growing areas, especially if the summer is hot and dry. Damage may appear earlier in the Gulf states.

Management. See Bluegrass Billbug — Management. Adults can be controlled with short-residual insecticides applied in spring, before eggs have been inserted into stems. Two applications, one soon after adults become active and again about a month later, may be needed if this approach is used. Larvae are somewhat susceptible to conventional soil insecticides once they've left the grass stems and moved to the root zone, but by then they may have already damaged the crowns. Application of imidacloprid in the spring, before eggs have hatched, is effective for preventive control. Hunting billbugs may build up in sod fields and be transported to new sites in infested sod. In southern California, this pest has been intercepted in shipments of zoysiagrass and centipedegrass sod from the southeastern states. Be sure to obtain certified pest-free sod.

OTHER BILLBUGS

The Phoenix billbug, *Sphenophorus phoeniciensis* Chittenden (Plate 17), is a pest of bermudagrass and zoysiagrass lawns and sod farms in the southwest United States, especially in California and Arizona (See Billbugs — Introduction). Little is known about its specific habits, seasonal life cycle, and number of generations per year. As with other billbug species, the young larvae feed inside the stems and crown, whereas older larvae feed underground on the crown and roots.

Recent research at Rutgers University in New Jersey suggests that the status of billbug pests of turfgrass is more complicated than was once thought. Previously, the bluegrass billbug was the only species thought to damage turfgrasses in the northeastern United States. In New Jersey, however, four different species, including *Sphenophorus parvulus*, *S. venatus*, *S. minimus* Hart and *S. inequalis* (Say), were found damaging cool-season turfgrasses. Apparent differences in their life cycles and seasonal development, including the possibility of overwintering larvae, may confound the timing of control measures. Use of management tactics that afford a degree of season-long protection, such as using grass cultivars with endophyte-enhanced resistance, is one way to reduce billbug problems until further research clarifies the differences among these closely related species.

FRIT FLY
Oscinella frit (L.)
(Plate 1)

Importance and Nature of Injury. The frit fly is a sporadic pest of golf courses, mainly on greens, collars, and approaches. The larvae damage grass plants by killing their growing points. Upon hatching, the larva moves to the base of the plant between the leaf sheath and stem. It may burrow into the stem or crown or, on rare occasions, may mine within the leaves. Rasping of the stem or crown girdles embryonic growing tissue, killing the stem from that point outward. Turf damaged by frit flies appears yellow and chlorotic. Close inspection reveals that the central leaf of one or more shoots from the crown is affected, whereas the surrounding leaves and shoots

Figure 9.7. Distribution of the frit fly in the continental United States.

remain green. As feeding progresses, the shoot dies. One or more whitish maggots may be found at the base of infested shoots.

The adult flies annoy golfers on putting greens because they are attracted to white objects, including golf balls, golf carts, and clothing. The adults also are attracted to new-mown turf, where they feed on juices exuding from the cut ends. Adult feeding does not damage the grass. Frit flies seem to prefer closely mown, irrigated turf, especially collars and approaches of golf greens. Greens with high organic matter content tend to be most susceptible. The frit fly is rarely a problem on home lawns.

Plants Attacked. The frit fly is an occasional pest of cool-season grasses, mainly close-cut creeping bentgrass and annual bluegrass. Kentucky bluegrass and ryegrasses are also susceptible.

Origin and Distribution. The frit fly is native to Europe, where it is a pest of grasses and grain crops. It occurs throughout the United States and southern Canada, and is widely distributed across the temperate Northern Hemisphere (Figure 9.7).

Distinguishing Characteristics. The adults are small, shiny black flies, about 1/16 to 3/32 in. (1.6–2.4 mm) long, with yellow markings on the legs. They have dark reddish eyes and a large triangle pattern on the top of the head. The flies are often seen hovering over golf greens or resting on the tips of grass blades. The tiny, whitish eggs are laid between leaf sheath and stem, or less commonly on leaves or the outside of the stem. The worm-like larvae, or maggots, are light yellow-white, legless, and lack a distinct head. The front end is pointed and has a pair of tiny black hooks used for rasping plant tissue. Larvae are found within the base of grass stems or between the leaf sheath and stem. They crawl actively when removed. Mature larvae are about 1/8 to 3/16 in. (3–5 mm) long. Pupae are cigar-shaped, reddish brown, and about 3/32 in. (2–3 mm) long. They are found at the base of grasses between leaf sheath and stem.

Life History and Habits. The winter is spent in the larval stage within a grass stem. The maggots pupate and adults emerge the following spring. There are two to five generations per year, depending on latitude. In Virginia, pupation occurs in late March and April, and the first brood of flies is active from April until early June. In northern Ohio, there are three full generations and a partial fourth brood; peak activity of adults occurs in mid-May, late June, late July to early August, and mid-September. These dates vary by as much as 2 weeks in warmer or cooler years. The flies emerge in the morning and mate during the warm part of the day. Egg-laying begins a few days after mating. Turf with a proliferation of new shoots and tillers seems to attract egg-laying females. Eggs hatch in 3–7 days, and the young maggots move down to the base of the plant to feed. The larvae pass through three instars before pupating, and the new adult emerges 1–2 weeks later. Individual flies live for about a week in the field.

Management. Watch for small black flies hovering close to the grass in mid to late morning. The adult flies are attracted to white surfaces and will land on a white handkerchief or golf ball dropped in the grass. They can also be sampled with a sweep net. Larval damage can be prevented by treating the foliage with a short-residual, liquid insecticide when the adults are active. Timing the application for shortly before peak adult activity will kill the flies before they have laid eggs. Targeting the first generation of adults in the spring suppresses buildup of later generations. It may be necessary to repeat the application after 14 days if the infestation is severe.

SELECTED REFERENCES

General References

Brandenburg, R.L. and M.G. Villani (Eds.). 1995. *Handbook of turfgrass insect pests.* Entomol. Soc. Am., Lanham, MD.

Tashiro, H. 1987. *Turfgrass insects of the United States and Canada.* Cornell Univ. Press, Ithaca, NY.

Watschke, T.L., P.H. Dernoeden, and D.J. Shetlar. 1995. *Managing turfgrass pests.* Lewis Publishers, Boca Raton, FL.

Annual Bluegrass Weevil

Cameron, R.S. and N.E. Johnson. 1971. Biology of a species of *Hyperodes* (Coleoptera: Curculionidae), a pest of turfgrass. *Search Agric.* (Geneva, NY) 1(7).

Vittum, P.J. and H. Tashiro. 1987. Seasonal activity of *Listronotus maculicollis* (Coleoptera: Curculionidae) on annual bluegrass. *J. Econ. Entomol.* 80:773–778.

Billbugs

Johnson-Cicalese, J.M., G.W. Wolfe, and C.R. Funk. 1990. Biology, distribution and taxonomy of billbug turf pests (Coleoptera: Curculionidae). *Environ. Entomol.* 19:1037–1046.

Kelsheimer, E.G. 1956. The hunting billbug, a serious pest of zoysia. *Proc. Fla. State Hortic. Soc.* 69:415–418.

Kindler, S.D. and S.M. Spomer. 1986. Observations on the biology of the bluegrass billbug, *Sphenophorus parvulus* Gyllenhal (Coleoptera: Curculionidae) in an eastern Nebraska sod field. *J. Kans. Entomol. Soc.* 59:26–31.

Shetlar, D.J. 1991. Billbugs in turfgrass. Ohio State Univ. FactSheet HYG 2502-91.

Frit Fly

Aldrich, J.M. 1920. European frit fly in North America. *J. Agric. Res.* 18:451–473.

Tolley, M.P. and H.D. Niemczyk. 1988. Seasonal abundance, oviposition activity, and degree-day prediction of adult frit fly (Diptera: Chloropidae) occurrence on turfgrass in Ohio. *Environ. Entomol.* 17:855–862.

10

PESTS THAT SUCK JUICES AND DISCOLOR LEAVES AND STEMS

Several types of soft-bodied insects and mites damage turfgrasses by piercing grass stems or leaves with their hollow, needle-like mouthparts and sucking out plant sap. Many of these pests also inject toxic salivary secretions during feeding which cause discoloration or death of plant tissues. Although they are small, sucking pests may occur at very high densities so that their collective feeding causes severe stress and damage to turf. Endophyte-enhanced ryegrasses and fescues are relatively resistant to many of these sucking pests.

Most of the sucking insects and mites occupy the foliar/stem target zone. When applying insecticides against these pests, the objective is to leave residues on the foliage, stems, crowns, and upper thatch. If the pest is one that lives on the foliage and stems (e.g., greenbug, bermudagrass mite), liquid applications work best. The volume of liquid applied must be sufficient for complete and uniform coverage. Mowing and irrigation should be delayed for a day or two after treatment to allow time for contact activity. If the pest lives mainly in the thatch (e.g., chinch bugs), either liquid or granular formulations can be effective. A light irrigation, done before the spray dries, may help to move the insecticide into the upper thatch, but this is usually unnecessary if high volume spray equipment is used. Most granular products require some irrigation in order to activate the insecticide. Excess irrigation, however, only reduces effectiveness by washing the residues out of the zone occupied by the target pests. Labels of some insecticides specify that post-treatment irrigation must be applied. Such products may not be a good choice if the irrigation requirements are inconsistent with the Target Principle (see Chapter 6).

BERMUDAGRASS SCALE
Odonaspis ruthae Kotinsky
(Plate 20)

Importance and Nature of Injury. Bermudagrass scales suck juices from stems and crowns, stunting the new growth and causing wilting and browning. Early symptoms resemble those of drought stress. With severe infestations, large patches of bermudagrass may be thinned and killed. The damage is worst during hot, dry periods. Crowns and nodes become encrusted with whitish shells, giving them a "moldy" appearance. In regions where bermudagrass enters win-

181

ter dormancy, infested turf may be slow to green up in the spring. Bermudagrass scales seem to prefer high-mown grass such as golf roughs or home lawns, especially areas that are heavily thatched and shaded.

Plants Attacked. This species prefers bermudagrass, but bahiagrass, centipedegrass, St. Augustinegrass, and tall fescue are sometimes attacked.

Distribution. This pest occurs worldwide in tropical and subtropical regions wherever bermudagrass is grown. In the United States it is found from Florida to California, and in Hawaii.

Distinguishing Characteristics. The scales tend to cluster on lower stems around nodes and crowns, but they may also be on leaves. Nymphs and adult females have a whitish cover, like half of a clam shell, made from waxy secretions. Usually there is a straw-yellow, raised nipple-like area near the wider end. The cover of adult females is about 1/16 in. (1.6 mm) long. Beneath the cover, the female is soft-bodied and pinkish, without wings or legs. Males are tiny, gnat-like insects that are rarely seen. The female deposits elongate, pink or reddish eggs beneath her waxy shell. The tiny, newly hatched, active nymphs are called crawlers. They are oval-shaped, flattened and pink, with short legs, antennae, and eye spots.

Life History and Habits. Relatively little is known about the life history of this pest. Development from egg to adult apparently takes about 60–70 days. There are several overlapping generations annually in Georgia and northern Florida, and year-round reproduction farther south. Settled crawlers and adults may be found throughout much of the year. In regions where bermudagrass undergoes winter dormancy, there is little development of the scales during the cold winter months.

Eggs hatch over several weeks in the spring. Crawlers move out along lower stems and stolons, insert their piercing-sucking mouthparts, and become sedentary. They often settle under old leaf sheaths at the bases of crowns, but may be elsewhere on the stolons and lower stems. They rarely infest the upper portions of the plant. They lose their legs and antennae at the first molt. The settled nymph begins secreting white, waxy filaments that eventually form a solid, shell-like cover. The cover is enlarged as the insect molts and grows. At maturity, the scales often protrude from under the old leaf sheaths where they originally settled. They may be so dense at nodes and crowns that their covers overlap like shingles.

Management. Unthrifty-looking bermudagrass should be inspected for oval, whitish scales at the nodes and bases of stems. Turf that is fertilized and irrigated to promote vigor often outgrows damage from this pest. At present, no insecticides are specifically labeled for bermudagrass scale. Contact insecticides such as pyrethroids or organophosphates applied against other pests would likely also control bermudagrass scales if applied when crawlers are active. Precise timing is difficult, however, because egg hatch is asynchronous and crawlers may be present over extended periods. You can monitor for eggs and crawlers by lifting female covers with the tip of a knife blade or pin and inspecting underneath with a hand lens. Treatments should be applied as liquid sprays when the covers are full of pinkish eggs. Use sufficient spray volume to get good coverage under leaf sheaths at the bases of stems, and on crowns. Light, post-treatment irrigation may help to reach the scales on stems and stolons in the thatch layer.

BUFFALOGRASS MEALYBUGS
Tridiscus sporoboli (Cockerell) and *Trionymus* species

Importance and Nature of Injury. Buffalograss, *Buchloë dactyloides*, a perennial, warm-season species, is becoming more widely used as a turfgrass in semiarid regions of the Great

Plains states. Two species of mealybugs cause sporadic injury to this grass. Mealybug damage resembles symptoms of drought stress, including yellowing or browning, loss of vigor, and general thinning of the stand. Mealybugs feed by withdrawing plant sap with their needle-like mouthparts. Salivary fluids are injected during feeding. These toxins weaken the plant and cause reddish or purple discoloration of plant tissues around the feeding site. With severe infestations, the plants may wilt, turn straw-brown, and die. Damage is worst during hot, dry periods in mid to late summer. Infestation levels as high as 10,000 mealybugs per ft^2 (0.1 m^2) may occur.

Plants Attacked. Buffalograss mealybugs occur in seeded and vegetatively propagated buffalograss lawns and golf roughs, as well as in natural stands.

Distribution. The geographic range of buffalograss mealybugs is presently unknown. They have been found throughout Nebraska and are probably widespread in regions where buffalograss is grown.

Distinguishing Characteristics. Buffalograss mealybugs are slow-moving, soft-bodied, oval insects that feed within leaf sheaths or behind leaf axils. Nymphs and adult females are dark pink to purple gray, but covered with a white, waxy secretion. Newly hatched nymphs are about the size of the period ending this sentence. Mature females are about 1/8 in. (3 mm) long. Clusters of pale pink eggs are laid in a white cottony mass, often within leaf sheaths. Adult males are tiny, gnat-like insects that are rarely seen.

Life History and Habits. Little is known about the biology of these pests. Females produce whitish secretions in which the eggs are laid. Egg masses appear like tufts of white cotton attached to grass stems. As the eggs hatch within 1–3 weeks, the tiny nymphs, called crawlers, disperse over the stolons and lower grass stems or onto nearby plants. They typically settle behind leaf axils enclosing the pistillate spikelets or within leaf sheaths in the crowns or nodes of plants. As the nymphs feed and grow, they become covered with white, waxy filaments. Females move about slowly as they develop through three nymphal instars, which resemble one another except for size. After undergoing two molts, male nymphs produce a white, waxy cocoon in which they transform to tiny, rarely seen, winged adult males.

Management. Buffalograss mealybugs can be detected by closely examining the plant stems and crowns. Look for tiny, white cottony masses attached to grass stems. Pull back the leaves from the stems and inspect the sheaths for nymphs or adults. Presence of predators such as big-eyed bugs (Chapter 14) and lady beetles may indicate that mealybugs are present. Close mowing and removal of clippings may eliminate some mealybugs. Watering and fertilizing tends to mask the damage and promotes recovery of infested turf. Most of the time, mealybugs are kept in check by natural enemies. Try cultural practices first to conserve predators and parasites. If the infestation is severe and damage is increasing, treatment may be warranted. Insecticides should be applied as liquids in sufficient spray volume for good coverage. Using a surfactant in the tank mix may provide better control. Do not irrigate for at least 24 hours after treatment.

CHINCH BUGS

Chinch bugs damage grasses by sucking juices from stems and crowns, causing gradually yellowing or dead patches of turf. Two closely related species are important pests of turfgrasses, especially in lawns. The hairy chinch bug attacks cool-season turfgrasses, damaging bentgrasses, bluegrasses, and fine-leaf fescues in the Northeast and upper Midwest (Figure 10.1). It also

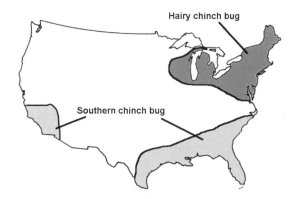

Figure 10.1. Distribution of the hairy chinch bug and southern chinch bug in the continental United States.

attacks zoysiagrass when that grass is grown in the cool-season zone. The southern chinch bug is a highly destructive pest of St. Augustinegrass lawns in Florida and the Gulf Coast region.

Two other species, the common chinch bug, *Blissus leucopterus leucopterus*, and the buffalograss chinch bug, *Blissus* sp., are occasional pests of turf, especially in the Great Plains region. The common chinch bug feeds mainly on small grains and other field crops, but it occasionally damages turfgrasses, especially stands adjacent to maturing grain fields. Kentucky bluegrass, perennial ryegrass, fescues, bentgrass, and zoysiagrass may be attacked. The buffalograss chinch bug is known to feed only on buffalograss. Both of these species resemble the hairy chinch bug in appearance and damage, and can be managed by similar methods.

HAIRY CHINCH BUG
Blissus leucopterus hirtus Montandon
(Plate 18)

Importance and Nature of Injury. The hairy chinch bug (HCB) is among the worst pests of northern turfgrasses, especially in lawns. Adults and nymphs insert their piercing-sucking mouthparts into stems and crowns and extract plant juices, while pumping toxic salivary fluids into the plant. Damage is caused both by loss of plant fluids and from clogging of the conducting tissues within the stem. HCB typically occurs in scattered aggregations rather than being evenly distributed over the turf. In its early stages, the damage appears as irregular patches of wilted, yellow-brown turf that may be mistaken for drought stress. As the infestation builds, these patches coalesce into larger areas of dead or dying grass that does not recover in spite of watering. Chinch bug damage may be masked by symptoms of summer dormancy or drought, so that the effects are not apparent until the damaged turf fails to "green up" in response to late summer rains.

Damage from HCB typically appears during hot, dry periods in mid to late summer. Under such conditions, large populations may build up and severely damage the already-stressed grass. Sunny areas are most heavily infested with populations often reaching 200–300 bugs per ft^2 (210–320 per 0.1 m^2). HCB seem to prefer open, sunny lawns with thick thatch and a high percentage of perennial ryegrass and/or fine-leaf fescue.

Plants Attacked. The HCB prefers cool-season turfgrasses, including perennial ryegrass, Kentucky bluegrass, red fescues, and creeping bentgrass. It will also feed on zoysiagrass.

Distribution. In the United States, the HCB occurs throughout the northeast and parts of the Midwest, into the mid-Atlantic states as far south as Virginia, and west to Minnesota (Figure

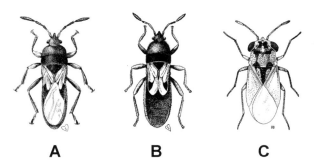

Figure 10.2. *Long-winged (A) and short-winged (B) forms of the hairy chinch bug, and (C) predaceous big-eyed bug (from USDA).*

10.1). It is also found across southeastern Canada from southern Ontario and Quebec east to New Brunswick, Nova Scotia, Prince Edward Island, and Newfoundland.

Distinguishing Characteristics. Adults are about 1/6 in. (3.1–3.6 mm) long and 1 mm wide. Adult females are slightly larger than males. The body is grayish-black and covered with fine hairs, and the legs often have a dark, burnt-orange tint. The antennae are 4-segmented, black, and easily seen. The wings are shiny white and folded flat over the back so the tips overlap. There is a distinctive, triangular-shaped black marking in the middle of the outer edge of each wing. The wings of some individuals extend to the tip of the abdomen, whereas in others the wings extend only about halfway to the tip. Local populations may consist mostly of long-winged (macropterous) or short-winged (brachypterous) individuals, or contain both wing forms (Figure 10.2).

HCB have gradual metamorphosis (see Figure 2.7). The eggs are tiny, elongate, and bean-shaped; they are whitish at first, but become orange-red a few days before hatching. Newly hatched nymphs are about half the size of a pinhead, < 1 mm long. Young nymphs are bright reddish-orange with a distinct white band across the abdomen. As the nymphs mature, their coloration gradually darkens and they gain small wing pads. The fifth-instar (oldest) nymphs are gray-black and almost as large as adults, with wing pads that extend at least to the second abdominal segment. All sizes of nymphs suck plant juices in the same manner as the adults.

Several kinds of natural enemies help to suppress HCB populations. Big-eyed bugs, *Geocoris* spp., commonly attack the nymphs and adults, sucking out their body fluids. These beneficial predators may be mistaken for HCB because of their similarity in size and shape (Figure 10.2). Big-eyed bugs are more robust, with prominent bulging eyes on either side of a large, blunt head. The head is the widest part of the body. HCB, by comparison, are slimmer, with a narrower, pointed head and small eyes. Also, big-eyed bugs are faster and more active than the slower-moving HCB.

Life History and Habits. There are two generations per year in southern New England, in the middle Atlantic states, including New Jersey and New York (Long Island), and westward through Ohio (Figure 10.3). In more northern parts of the range, including upstate New York and southern Canada, there is only one generation per year. Adults overwinter in dense thatch, leaf litter, or similarly sheltered sites. They become active in early spring as temperatures near 50°F (10°C). The adults feed and mate for about 2 weeks before females begin laying eggs in mid-April to May. Eggs are deposited in leaf sheaths or into the thatch. Each female lays as many as 20 eggs per day for 2–3 weeks. In areas where there is only one generation, egg-laying may be delayed for a few weeks and occurs over a longer period. At the latitude of New Jersey, peak egg-laying occurs from early May through early June, about the time that white clover, *Trifolium repens* L., is in early bloom. The developmental rate of eggs and nymphs depends on temperature, and

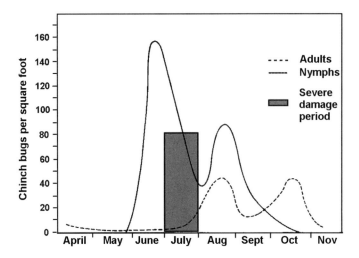

Figure 10.3. *Seasonal abundance of the hairy chinch bug in central Ohio, showing period of most severe damage (redrawn from Niemczyk, 1981).*

thus varies within the species' geographic range. Eggs laid during April may take a month to hatch, whereas those laid in midsummer may hatch in as little as 7–10 days.

Young nymphs pierce a grass stem and begin to suck sap. Where two generations occur, the first brood matures in 4–6 weeks, usually by about mid-July. At this time, swarms of older nymphs and adults may be seen crawling on leaf blades, sidewalks, and driveways, or up the sides of buildings. Emergence of first-generation adults is often synchronized with the time when sumac, *Rhus copallina* L., is in full bloom. The new adults lay eggs from mid-July through late August. These hatch into second-generation nymphs, which complete their development by September or October. As cool temperatures arrive, the second-generation adults seek out protected sites for hibernation. If the spring has been hot and dry, damage from the first generation may become obvious in June. More often, the worst damage coincides with periods of heat and drought stress in July and August, when first-generation adults are feeding and laying eggs and their second-generation nymphs are becoming active.

Predatory big-eyed bugs may be slow to build up until the HCB have reached outbreak densities. They are occasionally so effective, however, that the HCB are nearly eliminated and only the big-eyed bugs remain. In such cases, the predators may be mistaken for the cause of the damage. Other natural enemies include predatory mites, ground beetles, and a tiny wasp that parasitizes the eggs. None of these natural enemies is commercially available for release. Nevertheless, it is wise to conserve them by cutting back on nonessential insecticide treatments. The fungus *Beauveria bassiana* often drastically reduces HCB populations in warm, moist years. This pathogen may kill 90% or more of the adults and nymphs. Infected HCB appear to be coated in gray cotton wool, but this is actually the mycelia of the fungi which have sporulated on the carcass of the victim.

Management

Monitoring and Sampling. HCB are fairly easy to control if the infestation is detected early, before it gets out of hand. Lawns with a past history of HCB should be monitored for early damage symptoms, especially if the spring was warm and dry. You can check for HCB by parting the grass at the interface between healthy and damaged areas and inspecting the lower stems and thatch. However, the eggs and small nymphs are tough to spot by this method. Another sampling method is flotation (see Chapter 3). Cut off both ends of a large coffee can or similar container and remove one rim with tin snips to produce a sharp edge. Push the edge down through the thatch in areas to be checked. Flood the can with water to the brim (Figure 3.5). If the water recedes, add more to keep the level above the grass foliage. If HCB are present, they will float to the surface within a few minutes. The tiny red nymphs may be hard to see. As a rule of thumb, infestations of 20–25 nymphs per ft^2 (4–5 per 6 in. [15.5 cm] diameter can) will cause enough damage to warrant control. A more durable flotation sampler can be made from a sturdy steel cylinder, sharpened on one edge. Portable vacuum samplers, including cordless shop vacs, can also be used for sampling. A series of quick passes reveals whether HCB are present.

Cultural Control. HCB thrive in thatchy lawns, so topdressing, vertical cutting, or other tactics to reduce thatch should help to discourage infestations. Lawns that are watered during dry periods in summer are better able to tolerate HCB injury. Irrigation may drown some of the nymphs, and keeping the soil moist encourages growth of the *Beauveria* fungus that can greatly reduce HCB populations. Conversely, fungicide applications may suppress *Beauveria* fungus and favor buildup of HCB. Turf maintained on a moderate, well-balanced fertility program is more tolerant of HCB injury. If damage isn't too severe, watering and a light fertilizer application will encourage recovery. Over-fertilizing, however, may aggravate thatch and chinch bug problems.

Resistant Turfgrasses. Endophyte-enhanced cultivars of perennial ryegrass, fine-leaf fescue, and tall fescue are resistant to HCB. Consider using these resistant turfgrasses when renovating or overseeding damaged lawns, or when establishing a new lawn in neighborhoods where HCB is abundant. Bluegrass lawns with a high percentage of nonendophytic fine-leaf fescue and/or perennial ryegrass and excessive thatch are especially susceptible to HCB. Avoid planting fine-leaf (red) fescue in sunny areas.

Chemical and Microbial Control. Various short-residual insecticides are labeled against HCB. The goal is to deposit insecticide on the stems and upper thatch, so the pests are controlled by initial contact or exposure to the residues. Either liquid or granular applications can be effective. When using liquids, spray volume should be sufficient to provide good coverage. A light irrigation (about 1/8 in. or 3–4 mm), done before the spray dries, may help to move the insecticide into the upper thatch. With sufficient spray volume, post-treatment irrigation is unnecessary. If the thatch and surface soil are very dry, watering the day *before* treatment may also help the spray to move into the thatch. If granules are used, the foliage should be dry to ensure that the material reaches the upper thatch. After applying granules, irrigate lightly (1/8 in. or so) to activate the insecticide. Excess irrigation, however, is counterproductive because it may wash the residues too deep into the thatch. Check the product label, and be sure to conform with watering-in requirements. Removing excessive thatch beforehand may enhance treatment effectiveness.

There are two schools of thought regarding timing of controls for HCB. Some turf managers favor a preventive treatment in April or May, targeting overwintered females before they can lay eggs as well as any young nymphs that may already have hatched. The drawback of this approach is that the treatment is applied before the damage potential of the infestation is known. In some years, especially when there is a cool, wet spring, HCB populations are nearly wiped out by *Beauveria* fungus and may never gain a foothold. Thus, the preventive treatment is wasted because the pests would not have reached a damaging level. Unnecessary treatments eliminate natural enemies such as big-eyed bugs, and may encourage pest resistance. Thus, it is best to avoid preventive sprays unless you've sampled to confirm that a potentially damaging infestation exists.

A more selective approach is to wait until June when HCB nymphs have hatched and begun to feed. Keep a close watch for symptoms resembling early drought stress, especially on turf sites with a history of HCB problems. Warm, dry springs are especially favorable for buildup of HCB. Spot-treat infested lawns or other sites as needed.

A biological insecticide containing *Beauveria* fungus (Naturalis®-T) has been marketed for control of chinch bugs and certain other pests. This product may provide some suppression of HCB under moist conditions, but more testing is needed to say what level of control can be expected.

SOUTHERN CHINCH BUG
Blissus insularis Barber
(Plate 18)

Importance and Nature of Injury. The southern chinch bug (SCB) is a major pest of St. Augustinegrass lawns wherever that grass is grown. This pest accounts for many millions of dollars in damage to turf and control costs each year. Adults and nymphs feed by sucking plant juices from stems and crowns. As with the hairy chinch bug, the damage results from loss of sap, as well as salivary toxins that disrupt the plant's vascular system. SCB prefer open, sunny areas of St. Augustinegrass, especially lawns with abundant thatch. They typically occur in scattered aggregations, producing irregular patches of wilted, yellow-brown grass that later coalesce into larger areas of dead turf. Whole lawns or entire street blocks may be severely damaged or killed. The damage often first shows up in stressed turf alongside sidewalks or driveways, especially during hot, dry weather. Multiple applications of insecticides are often necessary to control this pest.

Plants Attacked. The SCB is the worst insect pest of St. Augustinegrass in Florida and the other Gulf States. It feeds occasionally on bermudagrass, bahiagrass, centipedegrass, and zoysiagrass, but damage to these grasses is usually not severe unless they border on St. Augustinegrass on which huge populations of SCB have developed and subsequently migrated. Crabgrass, pangolagrass, and torpedograss are also susceptible.

Distribution. SCB occur from southern North Carolina south to the Florida Keys, and west through Alabama, Mississippi, and Louisiana into central Texas (Figure 10.1). They also occur in California, Mexico, and throughout the Caribbean islands. Their geographic range generally coincides with that of St. Augustinegrass, their preferred food.

Distinguishing Characteristics. Eggs, nymphs, and adults of the SCB closely resemble those of the hairy chinch bug. In fact, an expert is needed to tell the two species apart. Both long-winged and short-winged adult forms may occur. If chinch bugs are found damaging St. Augustinegrass in Florida, Louisiana, or other southern coastal states, they are almost always the SCB. Big-eyed bugs, a common predator, are often found feeding on SCB. These beneficial bugs may be confused with SCB because they are similar in size and shape (Figure 10.2). Big-eyed bugs are more robust than SCB, however, with a wider head and bulging eyes. Also, they're more active, scurrying among the grass blades and stolons.

Life History and Habits. The SCB has seven or more generations per year in the warm climate of south Florida, where it is active year-round. Reproduction is continuous throughout the winter; three generations are produced between November and April. Many overwintered adults will die off in February, but this coincides with a surge in numbers of newly hatched nymphs, which results in rapid buildup of the population. In warm weather, the SCB completes a generation, from egg to egg, in as little as 5 weeks. By midsummer, densities of 500–1000 chinch bugs per ft^2 (0.1 m^2) are common. Outbreaks of more than 2000 per ft^2 have been reported.

In northern Florida (around Gainesville) and Louisiana, the SCB completes three or four overlapping generations per year. Adults comprise most of the overwintering population, with some nymphs also present. Egg-laying does not begin until late winter, giving rise to a first brood of nymphs that begins feeding in late March and early April. Development from egg to adult requires about 13 weeks at 70°F (21°C), and about 5 weeks at 83°F (28°C). Additional generations are produced during the summer and early fall, with peaks of nymphs emerging around late June, late August, and early October. The greatest damage occurs during hot, dry periods in mid to late summer. In the fall, the onset of cool weather causes a sharp decline in the population, and damage to turf is reduced. This seasonal pattern may be several weeks later in the Carolinas and other northern parts of the species' range.

Females begin to lay eggs about 7–10 days after mating; each produces about 100–300 eggs over several weeks. Eggs are laid singly or a few at a time. They are usually inserted into crevices at the grass nodes, between the overlapping bases of grass blades, or between the leaf sheath and stem. Eggs hatch in about 9 days at 83°F (28°C), but 24–25 days is required at 70°F (21°C). In north Florida and Louisiana, where four generations normally occur from April to October, the incubation period lasts about 4 weeks for the first generation, and about 2 weeks during the summer months. Newly hatched nymphs are about half the size of a pinhead and reddish-orange, with a white stripe across the abdomen. They often seek sheltered feeding sites under leaf sheaths, or where grass blades come together at the nodes. On St. Augustinegrass, feeding is concentrated on the tender, basal growing portion of the grass blades and the nodes of runners. Normally, there are five nymphal instars. As the nymphs molt and grow, their coloration changes in a manner similar to that described for the hairy chinch bug. Development from egg hatch to adulthood is temperature-dependent, requiring 2–3 months in the spring but only 3–4 weeks during the warm summer months.

Southern chinch bugs spread from lawn to lawn mainly by walking. Large numbers may be seen crawling over the grass blades or streaming across sidewalks and driveways that border heavily infested lawns. Although long-winged adults are capable of flight, relatively few seem to disperse by flying. SCB infestations tend to be aggregated or patchy, rather than being evenly distributed within infested lawns. These localized populations spread slowly, often completely killing the grass in the infested patch before moving on to undamaged turf.

Several kinds of natural enemies help to suppress SCB populations in nontreated areas. The black big-eyed bug, *Geocoris uliginosus* Say, is an abundant predator that sucks body fluids from its victims. Sometimes these predatory bugs are mistaken for SCB and a needless treatment is applied. A predatory earwig, *Labidura ripara*, also feeds on SCB, and a small wasp, *Eumicrosoma benefica* Gahan, parasitizes the eggs. Although none of these natural enemies is commercially available, it is nevertheless wise to conserve them by cutting back on insecticides. The fungus *Beauveria bassiana* (see Hairy Chinch Bug) attacks SCB under moist, humid conditions, but it seems to have minor impact most of the time. A product containing this fungus has recently been marketed.

Management

Monitoring and Sampling. SCB can be detected and monitored using the same methods described for the hairy chinch bug. When using the flotation technique, you may need to cut the grass runners with a sharp knife in order to push the bottom edge of the can into the soil. Several samples should be examined in suspect areas. Densities of 20–25 bugs per ft^2 (0.1 m^2) generally warrant control. With early detection, there is often time to spot-treat before a localized infestation spreads and causes extensive damage. Treat the infested areas, plus a 6 ft (2 m) border surrounding them. Recheck the infestation in 2–3 days, and spot-treat again if necessary.

Cultural Control. Excessive fertilization seems to encourage buildup of SCB populations, possibly by enhancing the nutritional value of the grass. Also, it encourages St. Augustinegrass to develop a thick, spongy thatch layer in which SCB will hide and thrive. Finally, deep thatch reduces treatment effectiveness by preventing penetration of insecticides. Lawns with excessive thatch should be mechanically dethatched or topdressed to improve the general growing conditions. Cutting back on fertilizer and increasing irrigation may help to reduce populations of SCB. Sound mowing practices (e.g., a sharp mower blade), mowing at 3–4 in. (7–10 cm) height, and removing no more than one-third of the leaf blade at each mowing will increase tolerance of St. Augustinegrass to SCB and other stresses.

Resistant Cultivars. St. Augustinegrass cultivars "Floratam," "Floralawn," and "FX10" are relatively resistant to SCB. When renovating or replacing a SCB-damaged lawn, consider using one of these cultivars. Another cultivar, "Floratine," is susceptible to feeding but tolerates the damage better than most other cultivars. Recently, the SCB has begun to damage these normally resistant cultivars in localized areas of Florida. This is believed to involve a strain of SCB that has developed immunity to the resistance factors. Other potentially resistant cultivars are being developed and tested. Check with suppliers and your local Cooperative Extension office for the most resistant cultivars of St. Augustinegrass.

Chemical Control. Once SCB infestations have reached damaging levels, insecticides are the only reliable means of control. Various organophosphates, carbamates, and pyrethroids are registered for use against SCB. General guidelines for treatment are the same as discussed for the hairy chinch bug. Use ample spray volume to wet the surface of the thatch, and/or light post-treatment irrigation. Be sure to read and follow label instructions regarding application rates and watering in.

Insecticides have been widely used against SCB in St. Augustinegrass lawns. In some parts of south Florida, neighborhoods have been treated as many as 6–12 times per year to suppress the multiple generations of SCB that occur annually. Not surprisingly, this chemical barrage has selected for resistance to insecticides, especially organophosphates, in some areas. If you experience poor control with organophosphates or carbamates, try alternating to a pyrethroid instead. Scouting and monitoring will help you to reduce the incidence of unnecessary treatments. This pays dividends in reducing the likelihood of insecticide-resistant populations.

Ideally, the best long-term strategy for managing SCB is to reduce thatch, and use resistant cultivars. To preserve natural enemies, spot-treat rather than relying on blanket applications.

GREENBUG
Schizaphis graminum (Rondani)
(Plate 19)

Importance and Nature of Injury. The greenbug is a type of aphid or "plant louse." It has long been recognized as a pest of grain crops in the United States and Canada. Since the mid-1970s, sporadic, occasionally severe outbreaks of this pest have occurred on Kentucky bluegrass lawns. Greenbugs suck sap from grass blades with their piercing-sucking mouthparts. As they feed, salivary fluids are pumped into the plant, causing the tissue around the feeding site to die (Figure 10.4). Damaged leaf blades develop yellowish, necrotic lesions that turn burnt orange, and eventually brown. Loss of sap and translocation of the salivary toxins weakens the whole plant, including the root system. Left untreated, heavy infestations of greenbug will damage the lawn to the point where reseeding or resodding is necessary. This pest seems to be more of a problem on heavily fertilized lawns than on golf courses.

On home lawns, the damage typically begins in turf under shade trees. It appears as circular or irregular patches of grass with characteristic burnt orange or yellow coloration. Damage may

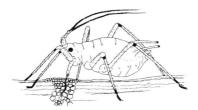

Figure 10.4. *The greenbug uses its piercing-sucking mouthparts to reach the phloem vessels and suck out plant sap. During feeding, it also injects salivary fluids into the grass blade, causing the plant tissue to die around the probed area (from Niemczyk and Moser 1982; with permission).*

also occur along foundation walls, fences, or other upright objects, or (less commonly) in open sunny parts of the lawn. As infestations spread, the greatest concentrations of greenbugs will be in the living grass just beyond the edge of damaged areas. Close examination reveals large numbers of pale-green adults and nymphs on the grass blades. In the Ohio Valley region, damage usually begins to appear in mid to late spring. Populations may build up during the growing season, reaching outbreak densities by the fall. Greenbugs may remain active into mid-November if the fall is extended. Their damage may be mistaken for early winter dormancy at that time.

Plants Attacked. Different biotypes or strains of greenbug are adapted to feed on specific types of cereal grasses. Increasing problems with this pest on lawns suggests that a new biotype has evolved that is adapted to Kentucky bluegrass. Annual bluegrass, Canada bluegrass, chewings fescue, and tall fescue are occasionally attacked. Greenbugs do not survive on most grassy or broad-leaved weeds found in lawns.

Distribution. Most outbreaks of greenbugs on turfgrasses have occurred in the midwest and north central United States (Figure 10.5). Various strains of the greenbug attack cereal grains throughout much of the world.

Distinguishing Characteristics. Adult greenbugs are tiny, soft-bodied insects, about 1/16 in. (1.5–2.5 mm) long (Figure 10.6). The body is pear-shaped, light green, with a darker-green stripe down the middle of the back. Two short tubes, called cornicles, project backward from the abdomen. The tips of the legs, cornicles, and antennae are black. Both wingless and winged forms may occur. The latter are more common when populations are crowded, such as during outbreaks. Winged adults are usually darker green, with transparent wings having an expanse of about 1/4 in. (6 mm) and dark-colored wing veins. Eggs are glued to upper surfaces of grass blades, fallen tree leaves, or other debris. The eggs are oblong and about 1/32 in. (0.8 mm) in length. They are light yellow-green when newly laid, but turn shiny black after a few days. Nymphs resemble the wingless adults, but are smaller. Nymphs destined to become winged adults develop small wing pads in the last instar. Aggregations of adults and nymphs feed along the upper surfaces of grass blades.

Life History and Habits. Nymphs and adults may be present year-round in the southern United States. Winged forms are produced in the spring and fall, or when food becomes scarce. In the transition zone and farther north, greenbugs overwinter as shiny black eggs (see above), which are laid in the late fall. These hatch in early spring, giving rise to pale-green nymphs, all of which are females. Nymphs mature to become wingless adults in 14–18 days, and begin giving birth to living, female young. These, in turn, mature and give birth within a couple of weeks and the population increases rapidly through additional generations. With the onset of cold weather, winged males and females are produced. After mating, the females deposit the overwintering eggs. By mid-December, the adults have died off and only eggs remain.

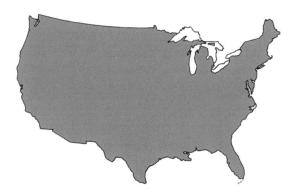

Figure 10.5. *Distribution of the greenbug in the continental United States. Most greenbug outbreaks on turf have occurred on cool-season turfgrasses.*

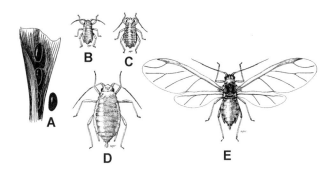

Figure 10.6. *Life stages of the greenbug; (A) eggs on leaf blade; (B) first instar nymph; (C) second instar nymph; (D) wingless adult female; (E) winged adult female (from USDA).*

The greenbug's ability to reproduce parthogenetically (without mating or fertilization) by giving birth to live young allows its populations to build at an enormous rate. Each female continues to reproduce for 20–30 days, producing as many as 60 young. During warmer weather the nymphs may mature in as little as 7 days. Even in the cool-season zones there may be 15–20 generations during the growing season, all but the last being composed entirely of females. Densities of 2000–3000 greenbugs per ft^2 (0.1 m^2) are common on heavily damaged lawns.

Infestations of greenbugs on northern lawns were once believed to originate from adults migrating northward each spring on prevailing winds from the South. This theory, however, did not explain why certain lawns were reinfested in successive years while nearby lawns were not attacked. It is now understood that infestations in the cool-season zones originate mainly from hatching of overwintered eggs, possibly augmented by annual migrations from the South. One possible explanation for why infestations tend to originate under trees is that the shade protects the tiny, soft-bodied insects from drying out in the hot sun.

Management. On home lawns, watch for burnt-orange or yellow discoloration beginning under trees or next to structures, and spreading outward. Close inspection on your hands and knees reveals numerous green aphids lined up along the grass blades. Lady beetle larvae are often found preying on the greenbugs. A sweep net (Chapter 3) is useful for assessing the extent of an infestation. Greenbugs occasionally cause damage to sod farms, but they don't seem to be much of a problem on golf courses.

Endophyte-infected cultivars of perennial ryegrass, tall fescue, and fine-leaf fescue are resistant to greenbugs. Consider overseeding with one of these resistant grasses when renovating a greenbug-damaged lawn. Creeping bentgrass, bermudagrass, and zoysiagrass are not attacked. Excessive fertilization seems to encourage greenbug outbreaks on Kentucky bluegrass.

Greenbugs can become windborne and thus spread to new sites. They may also be carried on clippings adhering to wet boots or clothing, or be spread by mowers, bagged clippings, or on infested sod. Lawn care applicators should be careful not to transport greenbugs from infested to noninfested lawns. Although the damage often shows up under trees, the greenbug is *not* a tree-feeding species. Treating the tree canopy will not prevent or eliminate a greenbug infestation.

Insecticides may be the only solution when greenbugs get out of hand. If the infestation is localized, spot treatments often are adequate. Treat the infested area as well as a 6 ft (2 m) band surrounding the damaged grass. Insecticides should be applied as liquid sprays. Granular formulations are not effective against this pest. Do not irrigate or mow the turf for at least 24 hours after treatment, because the goal is to leave the residues on the foliage. If rainfall occurs soon after an application, inspect for live greenbugs the following day and treat again if necessary.

Greenbugs are fairly easy to control with contact or systemic insecticides. Acephate (Orthene®), an organophosphate with systemic activity, has been particularly effective. Some local populations of greenbugs have become resistant to certain insecticides. Try switching to a pyrethroid if resistance is encountered. Insecticidal soaps may also provide some control. Cutting back on insecticides, especially preventive or blanket applications, helps to slow the development of resistance. Predators, including lady beetles, lacewings, and syrphid flies, and tiny parasitic wasps take a heavy toll on greenbugs. This is probably why most lawns do not suffer damage from this pest. Excessive fertilization, which stimulates growth and reproduction of aphids, coupled with destruction of beneficials by insecticides, may encourage greenbug outbreaks on high-maintenance lawns. Conserving natural enemies by cutting back on insecticides for other insects (e.g., sod webworms) may be the best preventive tactic for greenbugs.

LEAFHOPPERS
(Plate 20)

Importance and Nature of Injury. Leafhoppers are very abundant in lawns, sometimes developing populations of hundreds per ft^2 (0.1 m^2). Adults and nymphs feed on the sap of grasses with their piercing-sucking mouthparts. Most species cause some local injury to cells around the feeding site, resulting in whitish flecks or streaks. With heavy infestations, the foliage appears mottled or bleached, and the grass dries out as if under drought stress. The symptoms are rarely serious on healthy lawns because the grass readily outgrows the injury, but newly seeded lawns are occasionally damaged. Homeowners may notice clouds of leafhoppers jumping and flying ahead of the lawnmower. Although they don't bite, the tiny insects cause an annoying, "crawly" sensation when they alight on bare feet and legs.

Plants Attacked. Leafhoppers feed on all species of turfgrasses.

Distribution. These insects occur wherever grasses are grown.

Distinguishing Characteristics. Adults are tiny, wedge- or canoe-shaped insects about 1/8 to 1/4 in. (3–6 mm) long. They may be yellow, green, brown, gray, or mottled in color. The head is triangular, often pointed in front, with small bristle-like antennae. Adult leafhoppers are quite active and fly or jump short distances when disturbed. The pale, wingless nymphs are smaller than adults but similar in shape. They typically scurry sideways or backwards, and will often move to the back side of the leaf when disturbed. Tiny, white, elongate eggs are inserted into slits cut in stems, leaves, or leaf sheaths. Various species, including large green ones called sharpshooters (*Dracuelacephala* spp.), and smaller, brown or grayish leafhoppers belonging to *Agallia*, *Dikraneura*, *Endria*, *Exitianus*, *Psammotettix*, and other genera may be abundant in turf.

Life History and Habits. Leafhoppers overwinter as eggs or adults in most parts of the United States. They are active year-round in the deep South. Some species overwinter only in the Gulf States, migrating northward each year on prevailing winds to reinfest cool-season turfgrasses. Adults feed and mate, and then each female deposits 75–200 eggs over several weeks. Eggs hatch in 7–10 days. The nymphs feed on young leaves and develop through five instars, transforming to winged adults in 2–4 weeks. These new adults begin another generation, and the population explodes by midsummer. There are 1–5 generations per year, depending on latitude and the particular leafhopper species.

Management. Leafhoppers rarely do enough damage to warrant control. High densities may cause minor stunting and discoloration during hot, dry weather or on newly seeded lawns. Leafhoppers can be controlled with sprays of contact or systemic insecticides if the damage becomes unacceptable, or if they become too much of a nuisance. Repeat applications may be needed because the adults readily fly between adjacent lawns. Endophyte-enhanced ryegrasses and fescues are somewhat resistant to leafhoppers.

RHODESGRASS MEALYBUG (= Rhodesgrass Scale)
Antonina graminis (Maskell)
(Plate 20)

Importance and Nature of Injury. This pest attacks southern turfgrasses, sucking out the juices and reducing vigor and growth. The plant's vascular system is disrupted by the feeding process, causing the grass to wilt and fade from yellow to a dull, lifeless brown. Damage is worst during extended hot dry periods, and may be mistaken for drought stress. The most obvious symptom is whitish, cottony masses attached to grass stems at the crown or nodes of stolons. Heavy populations may exceed 1,000 mealybugs per ft^2 (0.1 m^2); severe infestations resemble an overdose of fertilizer that has caked around the nodes and crown. The mealybugs' honeydew attracts wasps, bees, and ants, and encourages growth of black sooty mold on the foliage.

Plants Attacked. Rhodesgrass, a coarse-textured pasture grass used in the deep South, is the main host for this pest. Among turfgrasses, bermudagrass and St. Augustinegrass are the most susceptible. Tall fescue, centipedegrass, and bahiagrass are less commonly attacked.

Distribution. Rhodesgrass mealybug is found across the southern United States from southern South Carolina to southern California. It is abundant in Texas, Florida, and other Gulf states, and also occurs in Hawaii and other tropical and subtropical regions around the world.

Distinguishing Characteristics. Adult females are covered with a white waxy secretion that looks like tufts of cotton on the grass crowns and stems. Under this waxy coat, the insect itself is soft-bodied, sac-like, and dark purplish-brown. Females are about 1/8 in. (3 mm) long, legless, with short antennae, and long, threadlike mouthparts that are inserted into the plant. The actual insect can be seen through openings at either end of the waxy coat. A long, 1/8 to 3/8 in. (3–10 mm) whitish, hairlike filament protrudes from the anus to the outside of the white, cottony mass. Droplets of sticky honeydew, the sugary excrement, may exude from the tip of the anal filament.

No males are known for this species. Females reproduce without mating, giving birth to active, six-legged nymphs called crawlers. Crawlers are flat, oval, and about 1/32 in. (0.8 mm) long, with six-segmented antennae and a pair of long tail filaments. They are mostly cream colored with a purplish tinge down the middle of the back. Crawlers settle at the grass crown or nodes, insert their mouthparts, and begin to feed. The legs and antennae are lost at the first molt. Older nymphs resemble adult females, except for their smaller size. The waxy coat is enlarged and the anal excretory tube elongates as the nymph grows. Only the threadlike mouthparts and anal filament emerge from the cottony mass.

Life History and Habits. Rhodesgrass mealybugs feed year-round, but reproduction is slowed in winter. Activity increases in early spring as the grass begins to grow vigorously. In spring, females give birth to about 150 crawlers over about 50 days. Crawlers disperse out from under the female's cover and move about the plants, settling at the crown or lower nodes. They wedge themselves under a leaf sheath, insert their slender mouthparts, and become immobile. The excretory tube and white, waxy cover are started soon afterward. The first molt occurs about 10 days after the crawler has settled. The insect molts twice more under the waxy cover, maturing in about 25–30 days. In Texas and northern Florida, where there are about five generations per year, a life cycle takes about 2 months to complete during spring, summer, and fall, and about 3.5–4 months in winter. Populations build up in May and June, peaking by July. They usually decline in late summer as the turf becomes drought-stressed, resurging again in the fall and peaking in early November. There are continuous generations in southern Florida.

Rhodesgrass mealybugs apparently cannot survive subfreezing temperatures. Thus, cold winters limit their northern movement and distribution. This pest may be accidentally spread by transport on grass clippings or infested sprigs and sod. Crawlers are dispersed by wind, or by hitching a ride on the fur or feathers of animals passing through infested grass.

Management. Mealybugs can be detected by inspecting stems and crowns for white, cottony masses. A 10x hand lens is useful for spotting crawlers. Pull leaves away from the stems, and examine the sheaths. Damage is usually not severe unless turf is under additional stress. Raising the cutting height, watering, and fertilizing to promote vigor will help turf to tolerate moderate infestations with little or no damage. Mass release of a tiny parasitic wasp, *Neodusmetia sangwani* Rao, provided effective biological control of this pest across much of its range. Normally, the rhodesgrass mealybug is rarely a problem except at sites where overuse of insecticides has killed off the parasite. Predators such as lady beetles, green lacewings, and big-eyed bugs also suppress mealybug infestations. Conserving these natural enemies by cutting back on insecticides will pay dividends in the long run.

Contact insecticides may not reach the protected life stages, especially settled crawlers, so repeated applications may be required if insecticides are used. Use liquid sprays to provide thorough coverage, and withhold irrigation for 24 hours after treatment. Use of a surfactant in the tank mix may increase control. Very few insecticides are labeled for this pest. Check with your Cooperative Extension agent for the latest recommendations.

TWO-LINED SPITTLEBUG
Prosapia bicinata (Say)
(Plate 20)

Importance and Nature of Injury. This pest causes sporadic damage to warm-season turfgrasses in the southeastern United States. Adults resemble robust, dark-colored leafhoppers with two reddish stripes across the back. Nymphs feed within conspicuous masses of frothy white spittle formed in the turf. Adults and nymphs feed by sucking juices from turfgrasses with their needle-like mouthparts. Removal of sap leads to weakened, stressed grass that turns yellow and then brown. Even worse, the adults inject a salivary toxin that is translocated up and down the stems, causing the whole plant to turn brown and die. In the field, the damage appears

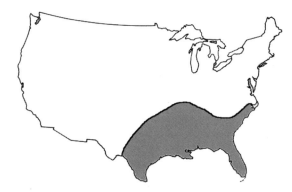

Figure 10.7. *Distribution of the two-lined spittlebug as a pest of turfgrasses in the continental United States.*

as small patches of wilted, stunted, or dead grass. With severe infestations, the stand may appear sparse and blighted. The frothy spittle masses are unsightly and unpleasant to step on with bare feet.

Plants Attacked. This pest attacks centipedegrass, bermudagrass, St. Augustinegrass, bahiagrass, ryegrasses, and various grassy weeds. Centipedegrass and bermudagrass are favored hosts. Adults also feed on various ornamental plants, especially hollies. Feeding by adults causes small dead spots on flowers or leaves of ornamentals.

Distribution. The two-lined spittlebug is most abundant in the Gulf states north to North Carolina (Figure 10.7).

Distinguishing Characteristics. Adults are wedge-shaped and about 3/8 in. (9–10 mm) long, with reddish eyes and legs. The wings are dark brown to black and held roof-like over the back in an inverted V. There are two prominent reddish-orange bands across the wings and a thinner reddish band across the thorax. Unbanded specimens sometimes occur. The abdomen under the wings is bright red; this coloration is visible when the insect is in flight. Eggs are small, less than 1/16 in. (about 1.1 mm) long, oblong, and bright orange. Nymphs are normally found at the base of grass stems, covered by frothy spittle. Nymphs are wingless, with red eyes and a brown head. Newly hatched nymphs are about 5/64 in. (2 mm) long, and pale yellow with a small orange spot on each side of the abdomen. Older, fifth-instar nymphs are about 5/16 in. (8 mm) long, with a uniformly orange abdomen. Older nymphs have well-developed wing pads marked with two transverse orange bands.

Life History and Habits. Two-lined spittlebugs overwinter as eggs deposited in the soil or thatch, behind leaf sheaths, or inserted partially into plant stems. In Florida, a few overwintering adults may also be found. Depending upon temperature and rainfall, most overwintering eggs hatch in March or April when the turf is coming out of dormancy. Newly hatched nymphs seek moist, humid feeding sites near the base of the grass plants. As they feed, the nymphs excrete a mass of frothy spittle. The spittle mass, consisting of digestive secretions and bubbles of air, is discharged from the anus. The mass completely covers the nymph, protecting it from desiccation and possibly from natural enemies. Nymphs can move about, but slowly. There may be one or several nymphs within each spittle mass. The masses are found from just below the soil surface to a few inches (5 cm) above it. Nymphs develop through five instars, maturing and molting to adults in 30–50 days. Depending upon temperature and moisture, adults of the first generation peak in late May and early June in Florida, to early July in South Carolina.

Females begin laying eggs a week or so after emergence and mating, producing about 45 eggs over a 2-week period. Eggs deposited in mid-summer hatch in 2–3 weeks, and the summer nymphs require about a month to mature. Adults peak again in August and September; this second generation deposits the overwintering eggs. Two generations occur annually in the Southeast.

Two-lined spittlebugs are most active in the morning. During the heat of the day they may hide deep in the grass. Adults, especially males, may be active at night and are sometimes attracted to lights. The adults are not strong fliers; most flights are short and occur when the insects are disturbed. A fungus, *Entomopthora grylli,* attacks the adult spittlebugs in late summer.

Management. Two-lined spittlebugs are usually most abundant in years with high spring and summer rainfall. In the Gulf Coast states, first-generation nymphs may be abundant enough to cause damage by May. The greatest injury, however, is inflicted by the second generation in mid-summer. Damage resembles that of southern chinch bugs, except it usually first appears in shady areas, rather than in full sun.

Young spittlebugs cannot survive under dry conditions, but they thrive in moist, thatchy turf. Dethatching and other cultural practices to reduce thatch buildup will help to reduce problems with spittlebugs. Withholding irrigation during periods when spittlebug nymphs are hatching in spring and midsummer also helps to suppress this pest. Avoid planting Japanese hollies near centipedegrass, as this combination seems to encourage spittlebugs.

The best way to monitor for this pest is to search for spittle masses down in the grass canopy. Sites with a history of spittlebug problems should be monitored more closely. Several contact insecticides are labeled for control of leafhoppers and spittlebugs in turf. Liquid applications work better than granules. Good coverage is essential. Mowing beforehand and disposing of clippings, and irrigating several hours before treatment, will aid in control. Treatments seem to work best if applied late in the day. Recheck the area periodically because adults may migrate in from surrounding turf.

MITE PESTS OF COOL-SEASON TURFGRASSES

Several species of mites cause sporadic damage to cool-season grasses. Others become a nuisance when they migrate into homes or other buildings adjacent to infested grass.

Mites are tiny arthropods that are more closely related to spiders than to insects. Most species are no larger than the period at the end of this sentence. Mites have two main body regions; the front portion bears the mouthparts, and the hind portion is where the legs are attached. Unlike adult insects, which typically have six legs, most mites have eight legs in the adult stage.

All mites undergo simple metamorphosis. The life cycle consists of several stages: the egg, larva (a newly hatched immature with only three pairs of legs), two nymphal instars (protonymph and deutonymph), and the adult (Figure 10.8). Nymphs resemble the adults except they are smaller. All life stages are typically found on or near the host plant, except for those species that migrate into homes. Plant-feeding mites use their needle-like mouthparts to rasp and pierce plant tissues, sucking out the cell contents. Mite-damaged turf appears speckled, purplish-tinged, or turns a bleached straw color, and/or may fail to green up in spring. Severely infested turf is weakened, stunted, or killed.

Eggs of some turf-infesting mites are deposited under leaf sheaths or beneath layers of silken webbing produced by the adults. Eggs and active stages are often present at the same time. Other species (e.g., clover mites) migrate out of the grass to lay eggs in protected places, often on upright surfaces. Eggs of most mite species are relatively resistant to chemical controls. This means that multiple applications may be necessary if there are overlapping generations. Control will also be ineffective during periods when the eggs become dormant. Even the active stages

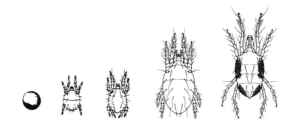

Figure 10.8. Life stages of a typical spider mite. From left: egg, larva, protonymph, deutonymph, adult (from USDA).

of many mites are relatively immune to many insecticides. Bifenthrin, chlorpyrifos, diazinon (not for use on golf courses or sod farms), dicofol, and fluvalinate are currently labeled for control of mites in turf. Other miticides may have special state registrations. Check with Cooperative Extension for local recommendations regarding products for mite control.

BANKS GRASS MITE
Oligonychus pratensis (Banks)
(Plate 21)

Importance and Nature of Injury. The Banks grass mite (BGM) is a sporadic, sometimes serious pest of both cool- and warm-season turfgrasses. It sucks juices from grass blades, causing white stippled areas and chlorosis. Heavily infested turf takes on a bleached, straw color and may fail to green up in the spring. As damage progresses, the leaves wither and die, and the blades become stiff. On St. Augustinegrass, the feeding damage and webbing may be mistaken for symptoms of mildew or St. Augustine decline. BGM is capable of causing rapid damage or death of turf. Severe damage is almost always associated with drought stress, and may be mistaken for summer dormancy. The worst injury appears on warmer, drier areas (e.g., south-facing slopes), or around the base of evergreen trees. Peak damage typically occurs in May and June in the Rocky Mountain region and northern Great Plains.

Plants Attacked. The BGM commonly attacks Kentucky bluegrass in the Rocky Mountain region and Pacific Northwest. Bermudagrass, St. Augustinegrass, and zoysiagrass are attacked in the Southern states. It is also a pest of field crops such wheat, corn, and sorghum.

Distribution. BGM is widely distributed in the western and southern United States, Puerto Rico, Mexico, Central America, Hawaii, and Africa.

Distinguishing Characteristics. BGM is smaller than the clover mite or brown wheat mite, and it lacks the elongated front legs that characterize those species. Adults are pale to deep green, with salmon-colored front legs. During the winter the green body color fades and the mites become more salmon-colored. Immature forms are pale yellow-green, becoming brighter green after they have fed. The nymphs often climb up grass blades during outbreaks, forming writhing clusters near the leaf tips. Young mites may be dispersed by the wind. BGM produce fine silk webbing at the base of turf tillers; eggs are laid on this webbing, or on the underlying foliage. The eggs are pearly white when first laid, becoming light straw-colored before hatching.

Life Cycle and Habits. Mated females overwinter at the base of grass plants or in the soil. The survivors become active in late winter or early spring and begin feeding and laying eggs. Damage to cool-season grasses may appear as early as March. The life cycle requires about 4–5 weeks during cooler periods in spring and fall, but may be completed in as little as 9 days if turf temperatures are above 70°F (21°C). BGM are more tolerant of warm weather than most other mites attacking cool-season turfgrasses. They can be found throughout most of the growing season, completing as many as six to nine overlapping generations per year. Outbreaks of this mite are almost always coupled with drought stress, and dry conditions amplify the effects of the feeding damage.

Management. BGM thrives under warm, dry conditions. Regular watering, especially of south-facing slopes and other dry areas, helps to suppress buildup of infestations. BGM may escape detection because they spend much of their time feeding and resting at the base of grass plants. This habit, together with the overlapping generations, makes them difficult to control. Because the eggs take 2–3 weeks to hatch in cooler weather, it may be necessary to reapply short-residual miticides to "mop up" any immatures that have hatched since the last application. Bifenthrin, a pyrethroid, is reportedly highly effective against this mite. Some insecticides (e.g., carbaryl, chlorpyrifos) may aggravate problems with BGM, presumably because of destruction of mite predators. Among zoysiagrasses, *Zoysia tenuifolia* is resistant, but cultivars of *Z. matrella* and *Z. japonica* are susceptible.

BROWN WHEAT MITE
Petrobia latens (Müller)
(Plate 21)

Importance and Nature of Injury. The brown wheat mite (BWM) is an occasional pest of cool-season turfgrasses grown in drier climates. BWM is a cool-season species that is most active during late winter, spring, and fall. Outbreaks are almost always associated with drought-stressed turf, especially in early to mid-spring following periods of prolonged winter drying. The mites suck juices from grass blades, producing very fine mottling, bronzing, or yellowing. South-facing slopes, highway medians, and similar hot, dry sites are especially vulnerable. Unlike injury from clover mites, damage from BWM is not so restricted to turf around buildings or trees. Damage to dry areas under trees, especially evergreens, is nevertheless common. BWM will occasionally migrate into buildings, but less commonly than does the clover mite.

Plants Attacked. BWM attacks all common cool-season turfgrasses, as well as many small-grain crops.

Distribution. This species is widespread in temperate regions throughout the world. It seems to be most damaging to turf in arid parts of the Great Plains and Rocky Mountain regions.

Distinguishing Characteristics. The BWM is similar in size and color to the clover mite. It shares the characteristic elongated front legs of the clover mite, but lacks the flattened hairs on the back. Viewed under magnification, the body shape is more rounded and less flattened than that of the clover mite.

Life Cycle and Habits. This mite seems to thrive only when conditions are very dry. Even moderate rainfall in late winter will suppress it. It typically completes two or more generations during the late winter and spring before laying eggs that will remain dormant during the summer months. Damage may also occur in the fall, especially during periods of moderate temperature and drought stress. Eggs are not deposited on foliage, but instead are laid on soil particles or other solid objects near host plants.

Management. Rainfall or watering in spring will suppress buildup of BMW populations. Irrigation to promote vigorous growth will also mask the symptoms and promote recovery of mite-damaged turf. BWM are susceptible to many organophosphate and pyrethroid insecticides.

CLOVER MITE
Bryobia praetiosa Koch
(Plate 21)

Importance and Nature of Injury. The clover mite is a relatively minor turf pest, but it becomes a real nuisance when hordes of the mites migrate into homes or offices. This mite does not bite humans or pets, or feed indoors, but it can be quite annoying. Squashing them leaves red stains on light-colored walls or curtains. Clover mites suck juices from turfgrasses, clover, and many weeds. Loss of chlorophyll and drying out of damaged cells causes silvery streaks or specks on grass blades. Peak damage usually occurs in March or April, ending by mid-May, with a secondary peak in the fall. Heavily infested turf may fail to green up in the spring. Clover mite damage is almost always concentrated in areas close to the south and west (i.e., sun-exposed) sides of buildings, trees, or shrubs. The mites are especially common in situations where a lush growth of succulent, well-fertilized turf occurs close to foundation walls.

Plants Attacked. These mites feed on a variety of plants, including Kentucky bluegrass, perennial ryegrass, clover, and many weed species.

Distribution. Clover mites occur throughout most of the United States and southern Canada, and are widely distributed in temperate regions of the world (Figure 10.9).

Distinguishing Characteristics. The adult mites are about the size of the period at the end of this sentence. They are dull reddish-brown to greenish, with eight orange-red legs. Adults have very long front legs which extend forward from the body (Figure 10.10). The body shape is oval and slightly depressed, with scattered, flattened hairs on the back. Viewed under a microscope, the skin is covered with fine, fingerprint-like ridges. Immature mites are dull red. The smooth, spherical red eggs are laid on rough bark at the base of trees, in cracks in concrete foundations, under sheathing of buildings, or in other dry, protected sites. The mites and eggs are easily seen with a 10x hand lens.

Life Cycle and Habits. Clover mites are "cool season" mites that are active mainly in the spring and fall. Eggs deposited in late spring remain dormant throughout the summer, hatching in September when cool temperatures return. The mites develop through a six-legged larval stage and two nymphal stages before maturing as adults. About a month is required to complete a generation outdoors. Feeding and egg-laying continue until freezing temperatures cause the turf to become dormant. Dormant eggs are also produced during the winter months. Overwintering eggs hatch in late winter, sometimes as early as February, and one or more generations are completed in the spring. In the southern United States, both active stages and eggs may overwinter, resulting in two or three overlapping generations in the spring. Mature mites often spend the winter within exterior walls of houses.

During even brief periods of warm weather in late winter or early spring, the mites migrate to warm surfaces and will climb up the sun-exposed sides of buildings and trees. Enormous numbers may enter under windows or doors. Migration into homes may also be triggered by overpopulation, by onset of stressful conditions such as drought, or because the mites seem to prefer vertical surfaces for egg-laying and molting. The period when mites are most likely to enter dwellings varies with climate. This may occur in April or May in Pennsylvania, but

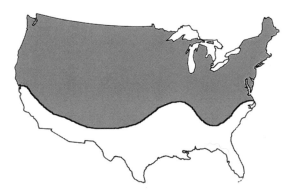

Figure 10.9. Distribution of the clover mite and winter grain mite on turfgrasses in the continental United States.

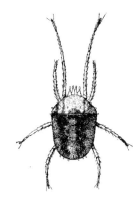

Figure 10.10. Clover mite, adult (from USDA).

earlier or later, respectively, in more southern or northern locales. Invasions may also occur during the fall.

Management. Damage to turf is sporadic and usually not severe. Infestations are typically concentrated within 6 ft (2 m) of buildings, trees, and shrubs, usually on the sun-exposed sides. Chemical controls applied to a band of turf about 15 ft (5 m) wide around the perimeter of the structure, and to the lower foundation walls and tree trunks, will reduce turf damage and migration into buildings. Several organophosphates and pyrethroids, as well as dicofol, are labeled for control of clover mites. Be sure to treat the juncture between the soil and the foundation, as this is prime harborage for eggs and overwintering mites. Repeated applications of insecticidal soaps may give some control. Summer eggs are not susceptible to miticides.

Creating a plant-free band of crushed stone or pea gravel around the foundation, at least 3 ft (1 m) wide, may help to keep clover mites away from buildings. This may be more feasible for commercial sites than for homes. Mulching around shrubs, and close-mowing of turf, clover, or other ground covers around the foundation, will discourage the buildup of clover mites. Irrigation and fertilization will help the damaged turf to recover, and watering may directly suppress the mite population. Where chronic problems exist, try to determine what plants are supporting the mites, and treat or eliminate them if practical. Inside dwellings, mites can be sucked up with a vacuum cleaner. This is less likely to squash them and cause the red smears that result when a brush or cloth is used.

WINTER GRAIN MITE
Penthaleus major (Dugès)
(Plate 21)

Importance and Nature of Injury. The winter grain mite (WGM) is a sporadic pest of lawns and golf courses in the cool-season zones. This mite is unusual because its activity and damage are restricted to the winter months. The injury is often mistaken for winter kill or snow mold. The mites feed by rasping the surface of grass blades and sucking up the cell contents. Injured blades have a silvery, scorched appearance caused by loss of chlorophyll. The damaged tissue dries out upon exposure to sun and wind, producing symptoms that resemble winter desiccation. Peak mite activity and damage occur from mid-December to mid-March in the northeastern United States. In Texas, mites are present from early November until mid-April. Damage often occurs under snow cover and goes unnoticed until patches of scorched, bleached turf appear when the snow melts. This species does not cause the yellowing associated with some other mite pests; rather, damaged turf appears silvered due to drying out of surface cells on which the mites have fed.

Plants Attacked. WGM feeds on Kentucky bluegrass, perennial ryegrass, fescues, and creeping bentgrass, as well as many small grain crops.

Distribution. The WGM is widely distributed in temperate regions of the United States and much of the world (Figure 10.9). Outbreaks on turf have been reported mostly in the midwestern and eastern United States. This pest also damages grass seed fields in the Pacific Northwest.

Distinguishing Characteristics. WGM is larger than other turf-infesting mites, about the size of a small pinhead (1 mm long), and easily visible to the unaided eye. The adults are dark greenish-black, with reddish-orange legs and mouthparts. There are two silvery eye spots, one on each side of the anterior part of the back. The anal opening, surrounded by a reddish-orange spot, is located on the back. This dorsal anus distinguishes the WGM from all other mites that infest cool-season grasses (Figure 10.11). Newly hatched, six-legged larvae are reddish-orange, becoming darker olive-black after they have fed. The eight-legged nymphs resemble the adults, but are smaller. Eggs are reddish-orange and shiny at first, becoming wrinkled and more straw-colored in a day or two.

Life Cycle and Habits. WGM has two generations per year in most areas. Summer is spent as dormant eggs attached to the base of grass plants, roots, or thatch. These hatch in October when upper soil temperatures drop to about 50°F (10°C), and the resulting fall generation develops into adults by November. Adult females live up to 5 weeks, during which they lay 30–65 eggs. WGM thrives when temperatures range from about 45–64°F (7–18°C). Populations increase rapidly during November and December, when all life stages are present. They decline slightly between generations in mid-winter, and then peak again in late February and March as the second generation matures. By late winter, heavily infested turf may have several thousand WGM per ft^2 (0.1 m^2). The mites decline in April and disappear by May after the females have laid dormant, oversummering eggs. Active mites will not be seen again until the following October.

Most feeding occurs at night, or on dark, cloudy days. On bright winter days the mites hide at the base of grass plants, or in the thatch or surface soil. They move up after dark and the same plants may be covered with feeding mites. Snow cover does not seem to inhibit feeding, and may provide protection from temperature extremes. When temperatures drop below about 40°F (4°C) or rise above 70°F (21°C), the mites stop feeding and take shelter near the ground.

Management. Damage from WGM is sporadic and unpredictable. Overuse of insecticides, especially carbamates, can aggravate WGM problems by destroying predators which normally

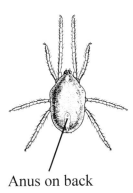

Anus on back

Figure 10.11. Winter grain mite, adult (from Swan, redrawn by D. Shetlar).

keep WGM populations in check. WGM can be spread by transport of dormant eggs on grass plants, clippings, or soil. Fortunately, feeding by WGM does not usually kill the turf. Fertilizing in late fall, or a light, spring application of fertilizer, helps to mask the symptoms of silvering and encourages the damaged turf to recover.

Little specific information exists on control for this pest. Late fall treatments for WGM have not proved very effective, although the new mite ovicides (egg poisons) being developed may provide better control in the future. WGM is susceptible to treatments made in late winter or early spring, when temperatures allow spraying. Chlorpyrifos and lamda-cyhalothrin are presently labeled for control of WGM.

MITE PESTS OF WARM-SEASON TURFGRASSES

Several species of mites in the family Eriophyidae attack warm-season turfgrasses. Eriophyids are tiny, soft-bodied, banana-shaped mites that live under leaf sheaths, or in folded leaves. They suck juices and cause growth deformities in certain grasses. Eriophyids are so small that they are barely visible with a good quality (15–20x) hand lens. Unlike most mites, which are eight-legged, eriophyids have only four legs. The body is elongate, whitish, and worm-like, with rings that look like segments (Figure 10.12). Adult eriophyids are less than 1/100 of an inch (0.2 mm) long; immatures (nymphs) resemble the adults, and are even smaller. The most important turf-infesting species are associated with bermudagrass, zoysiagrass, and buffalograss.

BERMUDAGRASS MITE (also called Bermudagrass Stunt Mite)
Eriophyes cynodoniensis Sayed
(Plate 22)

Importance and Nature of Injury. This mite is a serious pest of bermudagrass on southern golf courses, home lawns, and commercial landscapes. The mites live and feed under the leaf sheaths. Damage is first noticed in spring, when bermudagrass appears weak and off-color and does not respond to irrigation and fertilization. A closer look reveals slight yellowing of the leaf tips and twisting of the foliage. This is followed by shortening of stem internodes, resulting in tufted or rosetted growth sometimes referred to as a "witches' broom" effect. This distinctive stunting is most likely caused by a reaction to the mites' toxic saliva injected into the developing bud. With severe infestations, the tufts may resemble cabbage heads and the grass appears to not have internodes. The leaves appear shortened, and they turn brown and die back to their point of origin at the stem. If not treated, the stand becomes thin and dies out, allowing encroachment by weeds. The damage is usually worst during hot, dry weather when the grass is under stress.

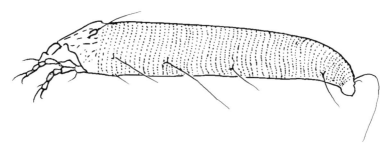

Figure 10.12. Bermudagrass mite, adult (from Arizona Cooperative Extension Service).

Plants Attacked. This mite feeds only on bermudagrass.

Distribution. Bermudagrass mite occurs throughout the southern United States wherever bermudagrass is cultivated (Figure 10.13). The mite is widely distributed in Australia, New Zealand, and North Africa.

Distinguishing Characteristics. Bermudagrass mites are typical eriophyids (see above). They are banana-shaped, light yellowish in color, and barely visible with a good hand lens.

Life History and Habits. The mites overwinter under leaf sheaths in the crown of bermudagrass. Females begin laying spherical, translucent eggs under leaf sheaths of new growth in the spring. Maturation from egg to adult requires only 7–10 days, so there are multiple generations during the growing season. This allows for rapid buildup of the population. As many as 100–200 mites, including all life stages, may live together under one leaf sheath. Mites are also abundant in the rosettes. Bermudagrass mites can be spread on grass clippings or by being transported on infested turf. They can apparently also be dispersed by wind or by hitchhiking on insects present in the turf. They cannot survive on bermudagrass seed.

Management. The improved cultivars "FloraTex," "Midiron," and "Tifdwarf" are relatively resistant, but common bermudagrass and other standard cultivars, including "Tifway," are susceptible. Damage from bermudagrass mite is seldom severe during extended wet periods. Maintaining a close mowing height seems to discourage this pest. Fertilizing and irrigating to promote turf vigor will mask the symptoms and speed up the recovery of mite-damaged grass.

Watch for plants with stunted, rosetted or tufted appearance. Pull back the leaf sheaths and examine the inside of the sheath and the exposed stem with a 10x or 20x hand lens or binocular microscope to confirm the presence of tiny, worm-like mites or eggs. Control is probably warranted if an area has 4–8 stunted tufts per ft^2 (0.1 m^2). Applications of diazinon are effective but cannot be used on golf courses or sod farms. Reapplication in 7–10 days is necessary to kill any stragglers still hatching from eggs. Dicofol or Fluvalinate are also effective. Check with your Cooperative Extension office about other products that are labeled for control of this pest.

BUFFALOGRASS MITE
Eriophyes slyhuisi (Hall)
(Plate 22)

Description, Life History, and Damage. This mite feeds exclusively on buffalograss, *Buchloë dactyloides*, which occurs in the Midwestern United States and the Great Plains. The mite's appearance, habits, and feeding damage are similar to those of the bermudagrass mite on bermudagrass. Severe infestations cause distinctive stunting and tufting, called "witches' brooms,"

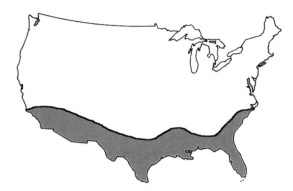

Figure 10.13. Distribution of the bermudagrass mite in the continental United States.

with thinning and loss of the stand. The damage becomes more severe in late summer when the grass is under drought stress.

Management. This species can be managed in the same manner as the bermudagrass mite.

ZOYSIAGRASS MITE
Eriophyes zoysiae Baker, Kono, and O'Neill
(Plate 22)

Description, Life History, and Damage. The zoysiagrass mite, a native of Japan and Korea, was accidentally introduced into the United States in 1982. This mite feeds only on zoysiagrass, *Zoysia* spp. It has been reported in Maryland, Texas, and Florida. Its appearance and life history are similar to the bermudagrass mite.

All life stages are present during the growing season of zoysiagrass. The tiny, worm-like mites infest the unexpanded leaves, leaf sheath, collar, and seed head. They are abundant in the rolled, expanding terminal shoots where their feeding inhibits leaf expansion. Typical damage symptoms include whitish or yellow streaks on young leaves, severe growth reduction, and lengthwise rolling to the upper leaf surface along one leaf margin. In heavy infestations, the entire leaf margin is rolled and most of the leaf is chlorotic.

New leaf tips, and occasionally panicles, are twisted and caught in partially unrolled older leaves. This results in distinctive terminal loops or arches that resemble "buggy whips." This mite can cause serious damage, and may be a limiting factor in seed crop production.

Management. Resistance has been identified in the cultivars "Emerald," "El Toro," and "Crown," and in several breeding lines. Check with your Cooperative Extension office for the ones recommended in your area. Other management tactics are similar to those for bermudagrass mites. Even when zoysiagrass is kept vigorous, it does not seem to outgrow zoysiagrass mite damage as readily as some other turfgrasses outgrow their mite pests.

SELECTED REFERENCES

General References

Brandenburg, R.L. and M.G. Villani (Eds.). 1995. *Handbook of turfgrass insect pests.* Entomol. Soc. Am., Lanham, MD.

Tashiro, H. 1987. *Turfgrass insects of the United States and Canada.* Cornell University Press, Ithaca, NY.

Watschke, T.L., P.H. Dernoeden, and D.J. Shetlar. 1995. *Managing turfgrass pests*. Lewis Publishers, Boca Raton, FL.

Hairy and Southern Chinch Bugs

Mailloux, G. and H.T. Streu. 1981. Population biology of the hairy chinch bug, *Blissus leucopterus hirtus* Montandon: Hemiptera: Lygaeidae). *Ann. Entomol. Soc. Quebec* 26:51–90.

Maxwell, K.E. and G.F. Mcleod. 1936. Experimental studies of the hairy chinch bug. *J. Econ. Entomol.* 29:339–343.

Kerr, S.H. 1966. Biology of the lawn chinch bug, *Blissus insularis*. *Fla. Entomol.* 49:9–18.

Reinert, J.A. 1978. Natural enemy complex of the southern chinch bug in Florida. *Ann. Entomol. Soc. Am.* 71:728–731.

Reinert, J.A. 1973. Bionomics and control of lawn chinch bugs. *Bull. Entomol. Soc. Am.* 19:91–92.

Reinert, J.A. 1982. A review of host resistance in turfgrasses to insects and acarines with emphasis on the southern chinch bug, pp. 3–12. *In*: H.D. Niemczyk and B.G. Joyner (Eds.). *Advances in turfgrass entomology*. Hammer Graphics, Piqua, OH.

Greenbug

Jackson, D.W., K.J. Vessels, and D.A. Potter. 1981. Resistance of selected cool and warm season turfgrasses to the greenbug (*Schizaphis graminum*). *HortScience* 16:558–559.

Niemczyk, H.D. and J.R. Moser. 1982. Greenbug occurrence and control on turfgrasses in Ohio, pp. 105–112. *In*: H.D. Niemczyk and B.G. Joyner (Eds.). *Advances in turfgrass entomology*. Hammer Graphics, Piqua, OH.

Mealybugs and Scale Insects

Baxendale, F.P., J.M. Johnson-Cicalese, and T.P. Riordan. 1994. *Tridiscus sporoboli* and *Trionymus* sp. (Homoptera: Pseudococcidae) potential new mealybug pests of buffalograss turf. *J. Kans. Entomol. Soc.* 67:169–172.

Chada, H.L. and E.A. Wood. 1960. Biology and control of the Rhodesgrass scale. *U.S. Dept. Agric. Tech. Bull.* 1221.

Shetlar, D.J. 1995. Bermudagrass scale, pp. 252–254. *In*: T.L. Watschke, P.H. Dernoeden and D.J. Shetlar. *Managing turfgrass pests*. Lewis Publishers, Boca Raton, FL.

Mite Pests

Baker, E.E., T. Kono, and N.R. O'Neil. 1986. *Eriophyes zoysiae* Baker, Kono, and O'Neil (Acari: Eriophyidae), a new species of eriophyid mite from zoysiagrass. *Int. J. Acarol.* 12:3–6.

Jeppson, L.R., H.H. Kiefer, and E.W. Baker. 1975. *Mites injurious to economic plants*. Univ. California Press, Berkeley, CA.

Reinert, J.A. 1982. The bermudagrass stunt mite. *U.S. Golf Assoc. Green Section Rec.* 20(6):9–12.

Reinert, J.A., A.E. Dudeck, and G.H. Snyder. 1978. Resistance in bermudagrass to the bermudagrass mite. *Environ. Entomol.* 7:885–888.

Reinert, J.A., M.C. Engelke, and S.J. Morton. 1993. Zoysiagrass resistance to the zoysiagrass mite, *Eriophyes zoysiae* (Acari: Eriophyidae). *Internat. Turfgrass Soc. Res. J.* 7:349–352.

Streu, H.T. and J.B. Gingrich. 1972. Seasonal activity of the winter grain mite in turfgrass in New Jersey. *J. Econ. Entomol.* 65:427–430.

Streu, H.T. and H.D. Niemczyk. 1982. Pest status and control of winter grain mite, pp. 101–104. *In*: H.D. Niemczyk and B.G. Joyner (Eds). *Advances in turfgrass entomology*. Hammer Graphics, Piqua, OH.

Two-Lined Spittlebug

Beck, E.W. 1963. Observations on the biology and cultural-insecticidal control of *Prosapia bicincta*, a spittlebug, on coastal bermudagrass. *J. Econ. Entomol.* 56:747–752.

Fagan, E.B. and L.C. Kuitert. 1969. Biology of the two-lined spittlebug, *Prosapia bicincta*, on Florida pastures (Homoptera: Cercopidae). *Fla. Entomol.* 52:199–206.

Pass, B.C. and J.K. Reed. 1965. Biology and control of the spittlebug *Prosapia bicincta* (Homoptera: Cercopidae) in coastal bermudagrass. *J. Econ. Entomol.* 58:275–278.

11

INSECTS THAT CHEW LEAVES AND STEMS

ARMYWORMS IN GENERAL

Armyworms are stout-bodied, hairless, striped caterpillars that chew the foliage of grasses and grain crops. They are so named because of their habit of crawling in large numbers from field to field when they've exhausted their food supply. Several species of armyworms may attack turfgrasses. Homeowners are understandably concerned when their lawn is literally mowed down by a moving "army" of caterpillars that seems to have appeared overnight. These pests are sporadic, but have an ever-present potential for outbreaks.

ARMYWORM
Pseudaletia unipuncta (Haworth)
(Plate 23)

This pest is sometimes called the "common" or "true" armyworm to distinguish it from other armyworm species. It can be an injurious pest in the southern states, but it only occasionally damages, cool-season turfgrasses.

Importance and Type of Injury. Young armyworms skeletonize the foliage or chew the margins of leaf blades, but the real damage is caused by the bigger ones that chew whole plants down to the crown. Armyworms are gregarious and tend to feed as a group, devouring the grass in roughly circular patches before moving on to the next available food. Every bit of green leaf and stem may be stripped by the horde of larvae. Most of the damage occurs at night. Armyworms may build up large populations in small grain crops, pastures, or other grassy areas. When these food supplies are depleted, the worms move out and may attack nearby turf.

Plants Attacked. Armyworms are especially fond of corn and small grains, but will feed on many other grassy plants including all common turfgrasses. Agricultural crops are usually more likely to be attacked than turf.

Figure 11.1. Distribution of the armyworm in the continental United States.

Distribution. The armyworm is a native species that is found throughout the United States and southern Canada, east of the Rockies (Figure 11.1). It is an occasional pest in the Southwest from northern Texas across to California. It also occurs in many other parts of the world.

Distinguishing Characteristics. Adult armyworms are uniformly pale-brown to grayish-brown moths with a wingspan of about 1-1/2 in. (38 mm). There is a small, distinct white spot in the center of each forewing (Figure 11.2). The hindwings are dirty white to light gray-brown. The tiny, greenish-white, globular eggs are laid in rows or clusters on grass foliage. Egg masses typically contain from 25 to several hundred eggs. Newly hatched larvae are pale green and about 1/16 in. (2 mm) long. They crawl by looping (in the manner of inchworms) until about half grown. Full-grown armyworms are about 1-1/2 in. (38 mm) long, of general grayish to greenish-brown color, with two pale-orange stripes along each side of the body and another pale-colored, broken stripe down the middle of the back (Figure 11.2). The head is brown and honeycombed with dark lines, and the mandibles lack distinct teeth. Like cutworms, large armyworms will often curl into a tight ball when disturbed. Pupae are reddish-brown, about 5/8 to 3/4 in. (16–19 mm) long and shaped like a skinny football, but blunt at the head end and tapering sharply at the tail.

Life History and Habits: The armyworm probably does not overwinter in the northern half of the United States. Annual infestations in the middle and northern parts of its range result from northward migrations of moths in the spring. At the latitude of Ohio, the first moths arrive in April, producing larvae that feed during May and June. A second generation occurs during June and July, and a third brood is active in late summer and early fall. Arrival of moths is later in the northern parts of the species' range, usually in May. There are only two generations per year in upstate New York and southern Canada. The number of annual broods in other regions depends mainly on latitude. In Louisiana and other southern states, armyworms reportedly overwinter mainly as pupae, with spring populations supplemented by migration of moths from farther south. First emergence of moths may be as early as late February, and the longer growing season allows time for four or more generations per year. Reproduction is continuous along the Gulf Coast, and overlapping broods may be present year-round.

The moths remain hidden by day, becoming active about dusk. They are strong fliers and are attracted to lights. Adult moths feed on flower nectar and do not themselves harm the turf. Each female may lay several thousand eggs. On turfgrasses, egg masses are usually laid on the foliage, often between the leaf sheath and blade, in a leaf fold, or covered by another leaf blade fastened about the eggs with a sticky secretion. They may also be laid on twigs, fence posts, or other objects. Eggs hatch in as little as 3 days in warm weather. Larvae from a given egg mass tend to stay together and feed in the same area until everything has been devoured. They then migrate *en*

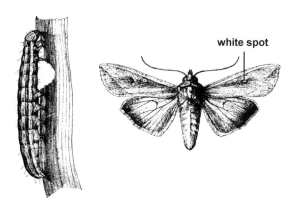

Figure 11.2. Armyworm larva and moth (from USDA).

masse to another area with fresh food. Larvae reach full size in about 3–4 weeks under summer conditions. They then burrow into the soil and transform to the pupal stage, emerging as moths in about 2–3 weeks. In middle and northern parts of the range, armyworm populations tend to build up earlier in spring and summer than do fall armyworms, a related species.

Management. Because the occurrence of armyworms is erratic, preventive treatments are rarely justified. Also, blanket sprays kill natural enemies that normally help keep armyworm populations in check. Armyworms are easy to control by spot-treating on an "as needed" basis. Still, it's best to catch them early, before they've done extensive damage. Watch for skeletonized or chewed leaves, piles of frass, or the worms themselves. Flocks of birds attracted to turf areas or holes pecked in the turf may indicate presence of armyworms or other pests. A soap or pyrethrin drench (see Black Cutworm — Management) can be used to sample for larvae hiding in the thatch. Almost any of the surface insecticides will provide good control. Liquid applications work best, because the objective is to leave residues on the foliage. Thus, irrigation and mowing should be withheld for 24 hours after application. Note that immediate irrigation is required by some insecticide labels, making those products less well suited for armyworm control. Granular formulations generally are less effective because they sift into the thatch, below the target zone, and require watering to be activated. Two new kinds of insecticides, halofenozide (MACH 2®), an insect growth regulator, and Conserve SC, a spinosad-based product, are effective against armyworms. Products containing azadirachtin (neem) or *Bacillus thuringiensis* var. *spodoptera* may provide some control of smaller larvae (see Black Cutworm — Management). Endophyte-enhanced ryegrasses and fescues may be somewhat more resistant than the same grasses without endophytes.

A synthetic sex lure is available for monitoring armyworm moths with sticky traps. Watch for larvae beginning about a week after peak flights. Armyworm outbreaks are more likely in years with a mild winter, a cool, moist spring, and early arrival of summer. Turf areas adjacent to susceptible small grain crops are at highest risk. Usually, the second or third generation causes the most damage to turf. Fortunately, armyworms usually eat only the leaves and upper stems of turfgrasses. Since the crown is undamaged, the turf will usually recover with remedial irrigation and fertilizer.

FALL ARMYWORM
Spodoptera frugiperda (J.E. Smith)
(Plate 23)

Importance and Type of Injury. The fall armyworm (FAW) is a sporadic, but occasionally severe pest of southern turfgrasses. The damage is similar to that caused by armyworms but tends to occur more uniformly over a broad area, rather than in patches. Newly hatched larvae feed gregariously at first, scraping the underside of leaf blades and leaving the clear, upper epidermal layer, or chewing the leaf margins and producing a tattered look. Older larvae devour every bit of green tissue down to the plant crown. They leave bits of chewed leaves and piles of greenish frass strewn about. Each worm devours the equivalent of a good-sized handful of grass, and the large larvae are especially voracious. That is why a lawn can be literally mowed down in just a few days. FAW tend to be less gregarious than true armyworms, so that their feeding causes progressive thinning of the turf. They feed anytime during the day or night, but move about mostly in the early morning or after dark. FAW don't usually kill well-established bermudagrass turfs; however, fescues and bentgrass may be killed if the grass plants are chewed down to the crowns.

Despite their name, FAW may damage southern turfgrasses from mid-summer until the end of the growing season. Outbreaks are most likely from July to October in the Gulf States, after populations have built up during the summer. At such times, "armies" of larvae may crawl from depleted pastures or agricultural fields into adjacent turf. This pest is only occasionally a problem on northern turfgrasses because of its inability to survive the winter in the cool-season zones. Thus, infestations originating from annual northward migrations of moths usually get started too late in the season to reach the outbreak levels experienced in the southern states.

Plants Attacked. FAW attack cotton, tobacco, legumes, and many vegetables, but small grains and grasses are preferred. Most turfgrasses, including bermudagrass, bentgrasses, ryegrasses, fescues, and bluegrasses, are susceptible. Among turfgrasses, bermudagrass is probably the most often attacked.

Distribution. The FAW is essentially a southern species which extends its range by migrating northward each summer into the temperate regions of the United States (Figure 11.3). Reproduction occurs year-round in the extreme southern parts of Texas and Florida, in tropical Mexico, and in Central and South America. The egg-laying moths may reach as far north as the Great Lakes and southern New England by late summer. Annual migrations also occur westward into southern New Mexico, Arizona, and California.

Distinguishing Characteristics. The adults are dull-colored, medium sized moths that resemble those of their close relatives, the cutworms (Figure 11.4). The wingspan is about 1-1/2 in. (38 mm). Front wings of males are dark gray, mottled with lighter and darker splotches, with a noticeable whitish blotch near the extreme tip. Forewings of females are more uniform gray, with less distinct markings. The hindwings of both sexes are grayish white. The adult moths are active mainly at night. Eggs are laid in clusters of 50–250, in two or three layers. Individual eggs are tiny, globular, and greenish-gray, becoming darker before hatching. Egg masses are covered with hairs from the female moth's body, so that the mass resembles a small patch of gray cotton or flannel. Egg masses are laid on grass blades or other green plants, twigs, fence posts, sides of buildings, or almost any light-colored object or surface near the turf. Newly hatched larvae are about 1/16 in. (2 mm) long and light grayish-green in color. Older ones range from light tan, to olive green, to nearly black, with longitudinal stripes along their sides, and are about 1-1/2 in. (38 mm) long when full grown. FAW resemble true armyworms, but can be distinguished by the more prominent, light-colored, inverted Y-shaped marking on the front of the head and by the presence of four distinct, black tubercles on the back of each abdominal segment. Unlike armyworms, FAW have well-defined teeth on their mandibles. Pupae are similar to those of armyworms.

Life History and Habits. Successive broods of moths migrate northward beginning in the spring, reaching Kentucky and North Carolina by mid-June and as far north as the northern Great Plains, Michigan, and New Hampshire by late summer. The moths can travel hundreds of

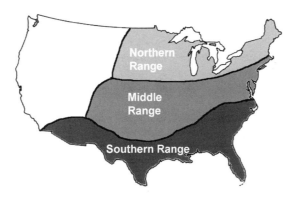

Figure 11.3. Distribution of the fall armyworm in the continental United States.

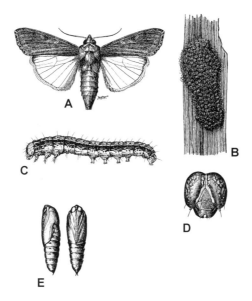

Figure 11.4. Fall armyworm (A) moth, (B) egg mass, (C) larva, (D) close-up of larval head, showing inverted Y-marking, and (E) pupa (from USDA).

miles on rapidly moving storm fronts before alighting to lay their eggs. Adult moths sip plant nectar or other sugary substances. They are active at night and are attracted to lights. If she survives, a female will lay three to five egg masses, totaling about 1000 eggs, over about a week. Eggs hatch in 7–10 days in cool weather, but in as little as 2–3 days during mid-summer. Most eggs within a mass hatch within a few hours. Larvae hatching from egg masses laid on objects other than edible plants will spin down on silk strands to reach the turf. The larvae feed gregariously at first, but begin to scatter when they're about half grown. Unlike true army-worms, FAW do not leave the plant to hide in the soil or thatch during daylight. If disturbed, the large ones will drop to the ground and remain tightly curled where they fall. They soon recover and climb back up the plant to resume feeding. Larvae require as little as 12 days to mature in mid-summer, but 4 weeks or more by October. When full grown, the sixth-instar larva burrows into the thatch or soil to pupate within some loosely spun silk webbing. New moths emerge in 9–20 days, depending on temperature. Only 23–28 days are required to complete a generation in mid-summer.

The FAW cannot survive exposure to freezing temperatures. Northern populations die off each year in the late fall. There may be nine to ten annual generations in south Texas and south Florida, four or more broods per year in Louisiana and westward, and two or three generations in Kentucky and North Carolina. There is one annual generation in the northern Great Plains, Ohio, New York, and other northern states, beginning in late summer after the moths arrive.

Management. See Armyworms — Management. A synthetic sex lure is available for monitoring flights of FAW moths with sticky traps. Begin inspecting for larvae about a week after sustained flight of moths. Most of the time, naturally occurring parasites and predators are sufficient to keep FAW populations in check. However, cold, wet springs seem to reduce the abundance of these enemies, so that in the southern states, outbreaks of FAW may be more likely during summer or fall of such years. Some state agricultural agencies release alerts when outbreaks of armyworms or FAW are imminent. Watch for these notices, because these are times when turfgrasses are most likely to be invaded. Besides scouting for damage symptoms, look for gray, cottony egg masses laid on light-colored objects and surfaces.

LAWN ARMYWORM
Spodoptera mauritia (Boisduval)
(Plate 23)

Importance and Type of Injury. The lawn armyworm (LAW) is a major pest of bermudagrass lawns in Hawaii. Injury is similar to that caused by true armyworms and fall armyworms in the southern United States. Moderate infestations produce thinning and a tattered look. With outbreak populations, hordes of hairless, smooth-skinned larvae move across the lawn, devouring all leaves and stems in their path. Usually there is a sharply defined boundary between the brown, defoliated areas and the undamaged grass. With severe infestations, the front may spread outward by about 1 ft (30 cm) each night.

Plants Attacked. Most of the damage occurs on bermudagrass lawns, but zoysiagrass may also be attacked. Other host plants include sedges, sugarcane seedlings, and various grassy weeds.

History and Distribution. The LAW, a native of the Oriental, Indo-Australian, and Pacific regions, was accidentally introduced into the island of Oahu in Hawaii sometime before 1953. It is now found on all of the Hawaiian Islands. It is not known to occur in the continental United States.

Distinguishing Characteristics. The adult moths resemble those of the fall armyworm. Males have mottled, dark gray or brownish-gray forewings. There is a white diagonal marking across each wing, followed by a kidney-shaped darker spot. Wings of females are less distinctly marked. Male moths have a wingspan of about 1-1/4 to 1-1/2 in. (34–38 mm); females are slightly larger. The upper surface of the thorax is cloaked with grayish to reddish-brown hairs. Eggs are laid in elongate, oval masses that are attached to tree leaves, buildings, or other objects overhanging or near the turf. The female moth covers her egg mass with long light-brown hairs from her abdomen, so that the eggs themselves are not visible. The body hairs become depleted as the female ages, so that her last egg masses may be nearly bare. Each mass contains about 600–700 eggs in several irregular layers. Individual eggs are tiny (0.5 mm), globular, and light tan, becoming darker before hatching. Newly hatched larvae are less than 1/16 in. (1.25 mm) long and greenish. Young larvae do not develop their darker coloration and distinctive markings until they are about half grown. Full-sized larvae are about 1-1/2 in. (38 mm) long, hairless, and vary in color from brown, to purplish-brown, to nearly black, with a dark brown head. There is a lighter stripe down the middle of the back and more prominent, longitudinal, yellowish stripes on either side. A pair of black, dash-shaped marks occurs on each body segment except the first and last ones, just inside the yellowish, lateral stripes. The pupa resembles that of the armyworm and is about 5/8 in. (16 mm) long.

Life History and Habits. The LAW is a tropical species that develops and reproduces year-round. Adult moths emerge after dark and usually mate on the first night. They sip nectar from flowers, but do not themselves cause any damage to turf. The moths are active at night and are attracted to lights. Females begin laying eggs about 4 days after emergence. Egg-laying begins at dusk and is usually finished by midnight. Egg masses are deposited on foliage of trees or shrubs, sides of buildings, or other objects, especially in areas where outdoor lights have attracted the moths. Eggs are rarely laid on the grass itself. The eggs hatch in about 3 days and the young larvae spin down on silk strands until they reach the grass. Larvae are gregarious, often feeding together on the same plant, until they are about half grown. Younger larvae feed during both day and night. Older larvae are night feeders and hide in the thatch during the day. There are seven or eight larval instars, and development from egg hatch to pupation requires about 28 days. The mature larva burrows into the thatch or soil to pupate, and the new moth emerges about 11 days later.

Management. See Armyworm — Management. Numerous natural enemies attack the LAW in Hawaii and help to suppress populations below damaging levels. Two tiny wasps, *Telenomus nawai* Ashmead and *Trichogramma minutum* (Riley), parasitize the eggs. Another wasp, *Apanteles marginiventris* (Cress.), and several species of tachinid flies parasitize and kill the larvae. Ants, lady beetles, and other predators feed on the eggs. It is wise to conserve these beneficial insects by avoiding unnecessary treatments. LAW can be sampled with a soap disclosing flush (see Black Cutworm — Management). The adult moths are attracted to lights, so be watchful for developing infestations in well-lit turf areas. Modifying outdoor lighting may help to reduce the likelihood of such infestations. Yellow-colored lights are much less attractive to night-flying insects.

CUTWORMS IN GENERAL

Cutworms are plump, smooth, dull-colored caterpillars that hide in underground burrows or coring holes during the day, emerging at night to chew off grass blades and stems close to the ground. They usually curl into a ball or tight "C-shape" when disturbed. Adults are dull-colored, night-flying moths with a wingspread of 1-3/8 to 1-3/4 in. (35–45 mm). The forewings are generally grayish or brownish and marked with nondescript light and dark spots or narrow bands. All cutworms have complete metamorphosis, passing through the egg, larval, and pupal stage before reaching adulthood. They shed their skin periodically as they grow, passing through six or seven larval instars and reaching a length of 1-1/4 to 1-3/4 in. (32–45 mm) when full grown. Pupation occurs in the soil, within the larval burrow. The adult moths have siphoning mouthparts and feed only on nectar; their feeding does not damage plants.

The black cutworm, *Agrotis ipsilon* (Hufnagel) is a major pest on golf courses because of its fondness for close-cut creeping bentgrass and its habit of infesting greens and tees. Black cutworms eat turfgrasses other than bentgrass, but they are seldom abundant enough to cause problems in higher-mowed areas where the injury is less apparent than on greens and tees. Other species, including the bronzed cutworm, *Nephelodes minians* Guenee, the variegated cutworm, *Peridroma saucia* (Hubner), and the granulated cutworm, *Felta subterranea* (Fabricius) are sporadic pests of lawns or golf roughs, but those species rarely injure greens or tees. Each species differs somewhat in appearance and habits, but tactics for sampling and controlling the different species are similar. The black cutworm is the only species that regularly requires control in turf.

BLACK CUTWORM
Agrotis ipsilon (Hufnagel)
(Plate 24)

Importance and Nature of Injury. The black cutworm (BCW) is the most destructive of all cutworms that attack turfgrasses. It is a major pest of creeping bentgrass on putting greens, tees, and sometimes fairways, throughout the United States and worldwide. BCW dig a burrow in the thatch or soil, or occupy coring holes or other cavities. The larvae emerge at night to chew down the grass blades and stems around the burrow. This results in small dead patches and sunken areas, or pockmarks, that resemble ball marks on golf greens. Cutworm damage reduces the smoothness and uniformity of the putting surface. Infested areas attract foraging birds that pull up tufts of grass, further reducing the surface quality. Leaves and stems may be dragged down into the burrow, or larvae may leave the burrow and wander over the surface, chewing down random grass blades. Inspection of damaged areas often reveals the burrow, coarse green fecal pellets (frass), or the cutworm itself. Frass pellets of cutworms are typically two to three times larger than those left by sod webworms. Flocks of birds foraging on greens or tees may indicate problems with cutworms or other insects. Numerous beak holes about the diameter of a pencil, with tufts of turf pulled up, are evidence of bird activity.

Plants Attacked. This pest feeds on most common turfgrasses, dichondra, white clover, and many weed species. It thrives on creeping bentgrass and nonendophytic perennial ryegrass and tall fescue, but fares poorly on Kentucky bluegrass. A wide range of field and garden crops also is attacked.

Distribution. The BCW occurs throughout most of North America (Figure 11.5), as well as in Europe, Asia, and Africa and elsewhere. This species was called the "greasy cutworm" in older literature; in Great Britain it is called the "dark sword grass moth."

Distinguishing Characteristics. Adult BCW are robust, hairy moths with a wingspan of about 1 to 1-3/4 in. (35–45 mm). The forewings are gray-black to dull brown, slightly paler toward the ends. There is a distinctive, black, dagger-shaped marking in the center of each forewing, about 1/4 in. (6 mm) from the tip (Figure 11.6). The hindwings are lighter and more uniformly dirty white, with darker veins. When resting, the moth usually holds its wings flat over the back in a triangular position. Males have antennae with tiny, comb-like teeth, whereas females' antennae are more slender and thread-like.

Eggs are laid singly or in small clusters attached to grass blades or weeds. The eggs are half the size of a pinhead (0.5 mm), and shaped like tiny gumdrops. They are cream colored at first, becoming darker as the embryo matures. BCW larvae are hairless except for a few scattered bristles. The upper half of the body, above the spiracles, ranges in color from gray to nearly black, while the underside is slightly lighter gray. The spiracles are black. The body is without distinct stripes or markings except for an indistinct, pale stripe down the middle of the back. Under magnification, the skin has a pebble-like surface, and a generally greasy appearance. There are three pairs of true legs on the thorax, just behind the head, and five pairs of fleshy prolegs on the abdomen. Newly hatched larvae are about 1/8 in. (3.5 mm) long. Mature larvae range from about 1-1/4 to 1-3/4 in. (30–45 mm) long and 1/4 in. (7 mm) wide. There are six or seven larval instars. If disturbed, the larvae usually curl into a C-shaped ball. Pupae are found in the soil. They are about 3/4 in. (19 mm) long and reddish brown to dark brown. The antennae, wing-pads, and legs are fused to the body, but the pupa can twist its abdomen when disturbed.

Life Cycle and Habits. The number of annual BCW broods varies with latitude and temperature. In Louisiana, there are five to six overlapping generations, with adults found every month.

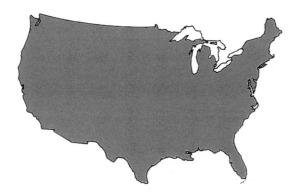

Figure 11.5. Distribution of the black cutworm in the continental United States.

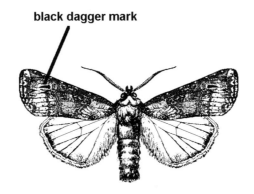

Figure 11.6. Black cutworm moth (from USDA).

There are four generations in northern Tennessee; three per growing season in Ohio, the central Great Plains, and Missouri; two to three broods in the northern Great Plains; and only two annual broods in upstate New York. In the transition zone, the BCW overwinters as pupae in the soil. In northern Tennessee, moths of the overwintering brood emerge from about mid-March to the first of May. Damage from their offspring begins showing up in early- to mid-May. Second-brood moths emerge from late May until mid-July, and third-brood moths emerge from mid-July until late August. Fourth-brood moths are active from early September until late fall and give rise to the overwintering generation. During the warm months, larvae can be expected about 1–2 weeks after peak flight activity of adults.

The BCW has trouble surviving at subfreezing soil temperatures. It apparently is unable to overwinter north of the transition zone. Spring infestations on northern golf courses begin with the arrival of migratory adults from southern states. The moths can be carried several hundred miles in just a few nights by strong southerly winds. In Ohio, the first spring migrants normally arrive in mid to late April; damage from their offspring begins to appear in mid to late May. Damage from the second brood of cutworms shows up on greens and tees from late June through July, and damage from the third brood appears in late summer. A range of larval sizes may be present at one time because the population tends to spread out its emergence and egg-laying as the season progresses. Damage from the first brood appears about a month later in upstate New York than in Ohio because of the later arrival of migrating adults.

The moths emerge around dusk and are active at night. They feed by sucking nectar from flowers, but do not themselves harm the turf. Mating occurs soon after emergence; females then lay as many as 1200–1600 eggs over 5–10 days. Eggs typically are attached to tips of grass blades, or laid on weedy plants such as curled dock or yellow rocket mustard. Eggs hatch in 3–6 days, depending on temperature, and the young larvae begin feeding on the leaf blades. Older larvae develop a subterranean habit, forming silk-lined burrows in the thatch or soil. On golf courses, they often take up residence in coring holes or in spike marks left behind by golf shoes. The larva hides in its burrow by day, venturing forth to feed at night. Larvae pass through 6 to 7 molts, maturing in 20–40 days. The young larvae don't cause much damage, but the large ones are highly destructive, eating as much as a handful of foliage in one night. Pupation occurs within the larval burrow, and the adult moth emerges about 2 weeks later. Development is slower during cooler periods of the year.

BCW larvae are nocturnal pests, doing most of their feeding from midnight until just before dawn. They may remain partially within the burrow, feeding on grass around the opening, or may leave the burrow to graze on the surface. On putting greens, wandering larvae can move 60 ft (20 m) or more in a single night. Movement of larvae from peripheral areas into close-cut creeping bentgrass may explain why greens or tees are sometimes reinfested soon after being treated with short-residual insecticides.

Management. With multiple generations per year and capacity to damage high-profile areas such as greens and tees, cutworms are often targeted for regular, preventive sprays. Nevertheless, with monitoring and knowledge of cutworm behavior, golf superintendents can maintain high-quality turf with reduced amounts of insecticides.

Monitoring and sampling. BCW moths can be monitored with commercial pheromone traps containing a synthetic female sex attractant. Only male moths are attracted, so there is no danger that traps will increase infestations. The first sustained capture of males signals that egg-laying has begun. Scouting should begin a couple of weeks later. Expect the damage to begin showing up on putting greens about 2 weeks after the peak of flight. Trap catches are not necessarily a good predictor of infestation levels on golf courses because many of captured moths may have come from nearby agricultural fields or other areas. When mowing, watch for the robust, dark-colored moths that are flushed out and fly a short distance before alighting. Black light trapping is another way to monitor flight activity of adult cutworms, but sorting the samples is time-consuming and tedious.

The best sampling method for BCW larvae on greens and tees is to use a soap flushing solution to determine population density. Mix 1 oz, or 2 tablespoon (30 mL) of lemon-scented liquid dishwashing detergent in 2 gal (7.6 L) of water. Pour the solution, or apply it with a sprinkling can, over 1 yd^2 (0.8 m^2) of turf and allow it to soak into the thatch and soil. Medium-to large-sized cutworms react quickly and will wriggle to the surface within 2–3 minutes. Smaller cutworms and sod webworms may take a bit longer (5–8 minutes) before they come up. Black turfgrass ataenius beetles, billbug adults, armyworms, mole crickets, earthworms, and other small creatures may also surface. Other liquid detergents may be equally effective, but test them first to be sure that they won't burn or discolor the turf. Two tablespoons of a commercial garden insecticide containing 1–2% pyrethins in 2 gal of water is also effective. Sampling is best done in late afternoon or evening. Water the turf after soap flushing to minimize any risk of sun scald or phytotoxicity. Presence of 5–10 cutworms per yd^2 in lawns or fairways probably warrants control. On priority areas such as golf putting greens and tees, the tolerable density may be much lower. Soap flushing is useful to confirm that cutworms are present and to determine the size range of the larvae. It can also be used after treatment to see if an application has been effective.

Regular monitoring is a key to effectively managing BCW with reduced use of insecticides. Golf superintendents usually know which greens and tees are perennial "hot-spots." Begin sampling these sites in spring after the moths have become active. Continue with weekly soap flushes, but do not treat until after the first small, 1/2 in. (12 mm) larvae are found. These cutworms will grow large enough within a week or two to cause visible damage on putting greens. Treat only if BCW are present at damaging levels. Follow up with weekly soap flushes to determine that suitable control has been achieved. A single treatment sometimes fails to provide lasting control, especially when mixed-age populations are present. This is because short-residual insecticides may not kill larvae that hatch from eggs several days after the initial treatment. Reinfestations may also occur from larvae crawling in from surrounding areas, or from moths flying in from nearby agricultural fields.

Turf managers can choose among many products for control of BCW. Conventional insecticides include organophosphates, carbamates, and pyrethroids. Two new kinds of insecticides, halofenozide (MACH 2®), a molt accelerating compound, and Conserve SC, a spinosad-based insecticide, are also effective against cutworms. Any of these choices will provide good control if the timing is right and certain guidelines are followed. Liquid formulations generally work better than granules. Don't water the material in, and withhold irrigation for 24 hours after application. This keeps the residues on the foliage where the BCW will feed during the night. Select products that do not require immediate, post-treatment irrigation. Apply treatments as late in the day as possible, ideally just before dusk. This ensures that the larvae will encounter fresh residues as they feed on the turfgrass foliage after dark. Applications in the morning or early afternoon may be less effective because most insecticides will lose activity due to photodegradation and volatilization. Treating toward dusk also reduces exposure to golfers until the residues have dried.

Female BCW moths laying eggs on putting greens or tees nearly always glue their eggs near the tips of grass blades. Research has shown that 80–90% of the eggs are removed with the clippings during each daily mowing. Furthermore, most of these eggs survive passage through the mower blades and will hatch within a few days. This implies that many of the large BCW larvae infesting tees and greens originate from surrounding areas where clippings are not removed during mowing, or from areas around greens where clippings were strewn. Kentucky bluegrass is a relatively poor host for BCW. Greens and tees surrounded by Kentucky bluegrass may be at lesser risk from BCW because a large reservoir population is less likely to build up in this grass than in other, more suitable turfgrasses such as perennial ryegrass or tall fescue. Endophytes of perennial ryegrass and tall fescue do not seem to provide much resistance against cutworms.

The capacity of BCW to crawl considerable distances may explain why greens and tees often are reinfested 7–10 days after an insecticide application. Clippings should be discarded away from putting greens and tees to reduce reinfestations. Treating a 20–30 ft (6–9 m) buffer zone around greens and tees will reduce the reservoir population developing in fairways and roughs. This may help to keep crawling larvae from reinfesting the close-cut turf.

Several so-called biological insecticides can provide satisfactory control of BCW. Products containing entomopathogenic nematodes, particularly *Steinernema carpocapsae*, have been fairly effective. Use fresh product, and check a sample of the spray mix with a 15x hand lens to be sure that the nematodes are alive and squirming. Nematode-based products are best applied in the early morning when dew is still on the greens, or just before dusk. Nematodes are intolerant of sunlight, so avoid treating during the heat of the day. Unlike conventional insecticides, nematodes should be watered in as soon as they are applied. When using nematodes, sample weekly with soap drenches and apply the product as soon as the first small larvae are found. Treating a surrounding buffer zone may be helpful, as discussed earlier. Continue sampling weekly to determine that suitable control has been achieved. Like most standard insecticides, current nematode products do not provide long-residual control. If larger cutworms are flushed up a week after the nematode application, consider switching to a conventional product.

Microbial insecticides containing *Bacillus thuringiensis* (Bt) are labeled for control of BCW. These products will provide some control of small, first- or second-instar larvae, but they are much less effective against larger cutworms. Thus, they often fail to give adequate control when a range of sizes of cutworms is present. Bt bacteria are rapidly degraded by direct sunlight. If you try Bt for cutworms, treat about 1 week after peak adult trap catches. Apply the spray in the evening, and do not water it in.

Azadirachtin, or neem, is a natural botanical insecticide with low toxicity to humans and wildlife. Azadirachtin is an insect growth regulator that acts by disrupting the molting process. It therefore is most effective against young, actively-growing larvae that must molt every few days. Azadirachtin will provide some control of BCW if applied when the larvae are small. Superintendents who use it should monitor with weekly soap flushes and apply the product when the first small BCW are noted on greens and tees. Apply the material late in the day and don't water it in. Continue weekly sampling to determine if the treatment has been effective. Azadirachtin may need to be reapplied every 2–3 weeks during peak larval feeding periods.

BCW are parasitized by several kinds of naturally-occurring wasps (*Apanteles* spp.) and tachinid flies. Unfortunately, none of these parasites is commercially available for release.

BRONZED CUTWORM
Nephelodes mimians Guenée
(Plate 24)

Importance and Nature of Injury. Bronzed cutworms are occasional pests of lawns, golf roughs and pastures. Unlike the black cutworm, they rarely damage golf greens and tees. In bluegrass, the young larvae may be found deep within the crown. When abundant, bronzed cutworms cause general thinning of lawns in mid-spring. Symptoms include clipped leaves, piles of green fecal pellets, and larvae in the thatch. Homeowners may be alarmed when the large larvae are encountered.

Plants Attacked. Bronzed cutworms are especially fond of bluegrasses (*Poa* spp.). They also feed on clover, small grains, corn, and buds and leaves of fruit trees.

Distribution. This cutworm occurs throughout the northern half of the United States east of the Rocky Mountains, about as far south as Colorado, Kansas, Missouri, Tennessee, and Virginia. It is also abundant in eastern Canada, particularly in New Brunswick.

Distinguishing Characteristics. Adults are similar in size to black cutworm moths, but lack the dagger-shaped mark on the wings that distinguishes the latter species. The forewings vary in background color from brown, to purplish gray to maroon. There is a wide, darker-brown band across the middle of each forewing. The hindwings are buff-colored. Larvae are fat-bodied, light- to dark brownish above and lighter below, with a distinct bronze sheen. A light yellow stripe runs head-to-tail down the center of the back, with another pale stripe on either side of the body. All spiracles are black. Full-sized larvae are 1 to 1-3/4 in. (35–45 mm) long. Eggs and pupae resemble those of black cutworms.

Life Cycle and Habits. This species is well-studied in field crops, but less is known about its habits as a pest of turf. Unlike other turf-infesting cutworms, the bronzed cutworm has only one generation per year. Adult moths emerge, mate, and lay eggs in the early fall, but the eggs don't hatch until the following spring. Larvae begin feeding in April and are full-sized by mid-May, when most of the damage occurs. They then burrow into the soil and form pupal cells, remaining quiescent therein until pupating around mid-August. The new moths emerge about a month later, completing the 1-year cycle.

Management. See: Black Cutworm — Management.

GRANULATE CUTWORM
Feltia subterranea (Fabricius)

Importance and Nature of Injury. See: Variegated Cutworm — Damage Symptoms.

Plants Attacked. Larvae feed on a wide range of field and garden crops, as well as many grasses.

Distribution. This pest occurs from Massachusetts and New York west to South Dakota, Arizona, and California, but it is usually common only in regions south of the latitude of the Ohio River. It is most abundant in the southern states. It is also found in the Caribbean region and in Central and South America.

Distinguishing Characteristics. Adults have yellowish-brown forewings with a span of just under 1-1/2 to 1-3/4 in. (38–45 mm). The hindwings are whitish with slightly darker veins. Mature larvae are about 1-1/4 to 1-1/2 in. (32–38 mm) long. The larva's skin is covered with small, bluntly-conical tubercles and under magnification appears pebbled. The tubercles cause a thin coating of dust to be retained on the skin when the cutworm emerges from the soil. The larva's back is ashy gray overlaid with sandy brown; the sides are darker, with black spiracles, and the underside is splotched with white. Eggs and pupae resemble those of black cutworms. Eggs are deposited singly, or in small groups, on the foliage of plants.

Life Cycle and Habits. This species has three full generations per year at the latitude of Tennessee. Moths begin to emerge in early spring and produce mature larvae by the end of May. The second brood of moths emerges in June and July, with mature larvae appearing in mid-summer. Moths of the third brood emerge in August and September. Their eggs become a final, fall brood of cutworms that passes the winter as pupae in the soil. Farther south in Louisiana, there are five or six generations and larvae are present throughout the year.

Management. See: Black Cutworm — Management

VARIEGATED CUTWORM
Peridroma saucia (Hubner)
(Plate 24)

Importance and Nature of Injury. This species is sometimes encountered in lawns or golf roughs, especially in rural areas bordered by field crops from which infestations may originate. Symptoms include clipped grass blades and deposits of green fecal pellets. Damage to turf is rarely severe.

Plants Attacked. The larvae feed on a wide range of grasses, weeds, and field and garden crops.

Distribution. This species occurs throughout North and South America, Europe and the Mediterranean region.

Distinguishing Characteristics. The adult moths have a wing span of 1-1/2 to 2 in. (38–50 mm). The forewings are yellowish to brownish, often with a row of small black dashes on the leading edge. They lack the dagger-shaped marking present on forewings of black cutworm moths. The hindwings are whitish, with dark-shaded veins. Full-grown larvae are 1-3/8 to nearly 1-7/8 in. (35–46 mm) long. Their background color ranges from pale gray to dark brownish-gray, the latter being more common. There is a row of pale yellow dots and dashes down the middle of the back, a distinct, brownish W-shaped marking on the eighth abdominal segment, and a yellowish or orange area near the tail end. Another row of indistinct, black, yellowish or orange markings runs along either side. Eggs and pupae are similar in size to those of the black cutworm, except that this species lays several hundred eggs in a single layer on foliage, twigs, fences, buildings or other objects.

Life Cycle and Habits. This cutworm has four generations per year in the Great Plains states and Tennessee. Moths emerge from overwintering pupae in March and April, and larvae from eggs deposited by these first-brood moths are full-sized by late May. Three additional broods of moths and larvae occur from June to October or November, the last one giving rise to overwintering pupae. Development from egg to adult requires 8–9 weeks. Variegated cutworms are less subterranean and nocturnal in habit than most cutworms, sometimes feeding exposed on foliage on dark or cloudy days.

Management. See: Black Cutworm — Management

SOD WEBWORMS: TEMPERATE-REGION SPECIES
(Plates 25, 26)

Sod webworms are small caterpillars that live in silk-lined tunnels in the thatch and soil (hence the name "webworms"). The adults are small, buff-colored "lawn moths" that hover over lawns at dusk. More than 20 species of sod webworms attack turfgrasses in North America, but usually only two or three species are pests in a given area. Different species are important in different geographic regions.

Some of the more common species of sod webworms that attack cool-season turfgrasses in the United States include the bluegrass webworm, *Parapediasia teterrella* (Zincken); larger sod webworm, *Pediasia trisecta* (Walker); silver-striped webworm, *Crambus praefectellus* (Zincken); striped sod webworm, *Fissicrambus mutabilis* (Clemens); and western lawn moth, *Tehama bonifatella* (Hulst). All of the aforementioned species used to be grouped together in the genus *Crambus.* Their biology and management are similar enough that they can be discussed together. Another species, the buffalograss webworm, *Surrattha indentella* Kearfott, attacks buffalograss, but its appearance, life history, and feeding habits are similar to those of other temperate-region sod webworms.

The cranberry girdler, *Chrysoteuchia topiaria* (Zeller), though technically a sod webworm, differs in habits from other common webworm species. Similarly, burrowing sod webworms, *Acrolophus* spp., have somewhat different appearance and habits than true sod webworms. These pests are discussed separately, later in this chapter.

Importance and Nature of Injury. Sod webworms hide in silk-lined burrows in the thatch and soil, emerging at night to feed on nearby foliage. Leaves and stems are chewed off just above the crown, pulled into the burrow, and devoured. Vigorous turf will often tolerate and recover from this scalping, but weak or drought-stressed plants may be killed as the hot sun beats down on the exposed crowns. Sod webworm damage begins as general thinning, followed by small patches of brown, closely-cropped grass. A close look reveals silk-lined tunnels in the thatch or upper soil. Clumps of pinhead-sized, green fecal pellets are often found around the mouth of the burrow. With severe infestations, scattered damage coalesces into large irregular patches of brown, closely-cropped grass. Injury often appears on south-facing slopes, along sidewalks, and other sunny sites where the turf is stressed. Damage is accentuated by hot, dry weather. Early symptoms of sod webworms may be masked if the turf is dormant from drought stress; the injury becomes apparent after rains come and the damaged patches fail to recover.

Figure 11.7. Sod webworms are sometimes blamed for damage from other causes, such as dog urine.

Flocks of birds may indicate a sod webworm infestation, but the birds might also be foraging on grubs, billbug larvae, adult black turfgrass ataenius, earthworms, or other caterpillar prey.

Sod webworms often "take the rap" for damage from other causes. Homeowners may mistake "doggy burn" for webworm damage (Figure 11.7), but with dogs, the grass won't be chewed down, and silk-lined burrows and fecal pellets (at least small green ones) will be absent. Except for the cranberry girdler, sod webworms don't feed on roots. Thus, turf damaged by webworms remains firmly anchored and cannot be lifted or rolled back as with white grubs. Symptoms of fungal diseases such as *Rhizoctonia* brown patch and *Fusarium* patch may also be mistaken for webworm damage, but with diseases, you won't see any burrows or chewed grass. Adult sod webworm moths feed solely on dew and do not harm turf.

Plants Attacked. Sod webworms damage cool-season turfgrasses including Kentucky bluegrass, perennial ryegrass, fine-leaf and tall fescues and creeping bentgrass. Weed grasses such as crabgrass and orchardgrass, clovers, and other grassy plants may also be eaten, but dichondra lawns are not attacked. Endophyte-infected ryegrasses and fescues are relatively resistant. The buffalograss webworm feeds mainly on buffalograss.

Distribution. Various species of sod webworms occur throughout the United States and in temperate regions worldwide (Figure 11.8). Damage seems to be greatest in the Midwest and eastern states. *Parapediasia teterrella* is probably the most common species attacking lawns and golf courses. It occurs over most of the eastern two-thirds of the United States, from Massachusetts and Connecticut west to Colorado, south through mid-Texas and eastward to Florida. It is quite abundant in Kentucky and Tennessee. *Pediasia trisecta* is widely distributed across the northern half of the United States and southern Canada, south to North Carolina and west to New Mexico and Utah. It is common in the Ohio Valley region, west to Iowa. *Crambus praefectellus* and *F. mutabilis* both occur throughout most of the United States east of the Rocky Mountains. *Surrattha indentella* attacks buffalograss golf roughs and lawns in parts of Nebraska, Kansas, and Oklahoma. *Tehama bonifatella* is a common pest of bluegrass and bentgrass lawns in coastal regions of California, as well as in parts of Nevada, Utah, Idaho, Oregon, and north into British Columbia. *Crambus sperryellus* occurs in the coastal, inland and desert valleys of California.

Distinguishing Characteristics. All sod webworms have complete metamorphosis, with life stages consisting of eggs, larvae, pupae, and adults. The adults are small, dull-colored moths with wingspans of about 3/4 to 1 in. (19–25 mm). The front wings are mostly whitish, dull gray

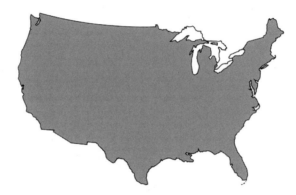

Figure 11.8. Distribution of sod webworms (various species) in the continental United States.

or tan, often with longitudinal stripes and other faint markings in silver, gold, yellow, brown and black. These markings are used for identifying the various species. The hindwings are usually lighter, whitish or light gray, with delicate fringes on the outer margin. The moths are often seen flying over lawns at dusk or after dark. They rest on grass blades or other low vegetation during the day, but are often flushed out when turf is mowed. They will fly erratically for a short distance, then dive down to rest on a grass blade. The wings are typically rolled around the body when at rest, so the settled moth resembles a tan or silver-beige sliver of wood. Two small, snout-like projections, formed by mouthparts, extend forward from the front of the head. That's why the adults are sometimes called "snout moths." This snout, together with the tube-like appearance of the rolled wings, distinguishes the adults from all other moths associated with turf (Figure 11.9).

The eggs are tiny (about the size of the dot of this "i") and oval- or barrel-shaped, with fine, longitudinal ribbing on the surface. Viewed under a microscope, the ribbing is distinctive for each species. Eggs are dropped, bomb-like, as the female moth flutters over the turf at night. The eggs are dry, nonsticky, and tend to settle in the upper thatch, so they will not ordinarily be seen. Sod webworm larvae are beige, gray, brown, or greenish, depending upon species, with a brownish head. They typically curl into a ball when disturbed. Most species have characteristic dark, circular spots and coarse hairs scattered over the body. However, at least two common species, *C. topiaria* and *Crambus caliginosellus*, lack the darker, circular spots. The length of full-grown larvae ranges from about 5/8 to 1 in. (16–25 mm); most species are about 3/4 in. (19 mm) long. The larvae construct shallow, silk-lined burrows in the thatch and upper soil — thus the name "sod webworm." Pupae are tan to dark brown, torpedo-shaped, and about 3/8 to 1/2 in. (10–13 mm) long. Pupae of most species are enclosed in a silken cocoon that is covered with bits of fecal matter, soil, and plant debris. Pupation occurs in the soil, in or near the larval tunnel.

Life Cycle and Habits. Temperate-zone sod webworms overwinter as partially grown larvae in silk-lined chambers in the thatch or soil. In spring, they resume feeding, grow rapidly, and pupate. The moths emerge in 10–20 days, depending on temperature and species. Mating occurs soon after emergence, and females usually start laying eggs the next night. Egg-laying begins at dusk and continues for a couple of hours. Females drop their eggs as they fly low over the turf, usually no higher than 12–24 in. (30–60 cm). The moths usually live less than 2 weeks, but each female may lay 60 eggs per night and as many as several hundred eggs during her lifetime. Eggs hatch in about a week in hot weather, and larvae complete their development in 4–7 weeks. There are usually six to eight larval instars. Young larvae feed by scraping surface tissues from leaf blades, but they soon drop to the ground and make a tube-like, silken tunnel in the thatch or surface soil. The tunnel may have bits of plant debris attached; piles of green fecal

Figure 11.9. Sod webworm moth showing characteristic resting position with wings folded about body. Note elongated mouthparts forming a snout (photo by D. Shetlar).

pellets are often found near the opening. Older larvae feed mainly at night, chewing down foliage around the burrow. A complete life cycle usually requires 6–10 weeks. Depending on geographic latitude, most species of sod webworms have two or three generations per year (Figure 11.10). Some, such as the cranberry girdler and buffalograss webworm, have only a single annual generation, whereas others, such as *Tehama bonifatella*, have as many as four broods per year.

Natural enemies include parasitic wasps and flies, predatory insects such as ground beetles, rove beetles and ants, and many birds. Predators and parasites often are sufficient to keep webworm populations at tolerable levels.

Management. Close examination by the "hands and knees method" is the best way to confirm a sod webworm infestation. Part the grass and look for chewed blades, small green fecal pellets, silk-lined burrows, or the larvae themselves. Be sure to check the interface between the damaged and healthy grass. If you suspect sod webworms but are unable to find the burrows or larvae, try using a soap flush (see Black Cutworm — Management). Any larvae that are present should surface within a few minutes. Damage thresholds vary for different situations, but generally 10–15 larvae per yd^2 (12–18 per m^2) may warrant control.

Healthy, vigorous turf will often tolerate and outgrow damage from sod webworms. Balanced fertility and irrigation during dry periods will enhance tolerance, whereas close mowing and drought stress will accentuate the damage. Endophyte-infected perennial ryegrasses and fescues are relatively resistant to sod webworms. When buying seed, look for the designation "endophyte-enhanced" on the label. These cultivars can be overseeded or slit-seeded into damaged lawns.

Keep a close watch if you notice swarms of sod webworm moths flying over the turf at dusk, or attracted to outdoor lights at night. Mere presence of moths, however, does not necessarily mean that a damaging infestation will occur. In healthy lawns, natural enemies take a heavy toll on the eggs and larvae and often keep sod webworms in check. Treating lawns preventively can destroy these beneficial insects and encourage outbreaks where the pest population was tolerable before. Sod webworms are fairly easy to control on a curative, or as-needed basis. In general, it's best not to treat unless you've sampled or inspected to confirm that a potentially damaging infestation is indeed present.

Controls should be directed against the feeding larvae, not the adult moths. Depending on geographic latitude, most species in cool-season zones will have one to three generations per growing season. Moth flights can be monitored with black light traps, but sorting the samples is usually too tedious to be practical. Commercial sex attractant lures are available for the bluegrass webworm and cranberry girdler; such baits can be used in sticky traps for monitoring

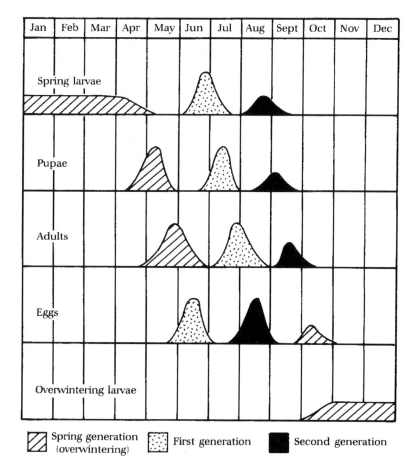

Figure 11.10. *Life history of the bluegrass webworm,* Parapediasia teterrella, *in Tennessee (from Tashiro, 1987; with permission).*

purposes. The simplest monitoring tactic is to walk the turf at sunset after daytime temperatures warm to 80°F (26°C) and nights are above 55°F (13°C). When you first see adults skittering in low, zig-zagging flight over the grass, egg-laying has begun. Note the abundance of moths, and the date when the flight starts to decline. Most of the larvae should have hatched by 10–14 days after peak flight, and that's the best time to treat.

Sod webworms are fairly easy to control with insecticides. Because most feeding is at night, try to treat in late afternoon or evening. This will reduce the amount of active ingredient lost to volatilization and photodegradation, as well as potential for exposure by turf users. Liquid sprays often work better than granules. Don't water the treatment in, and withhold deep irrigation and mowing for at least a day so that the residues remain on the leaves, stems, and upper thatch. Choose insecticides that do not require immediate watering in. Light syringing, about 1/8 in. (3 mm) of water, is necessary to activate the insecticide if granules are used. Light syringing may help to move liquid applications to the lower leaf blades, crowns, and upper thatch, but is usually unnecessary if adequate spray volume was used. Various organophosphates, carbamates, and pyrethroids are labeled for use against sod webworms. Two new kinds of insecticides, halofenozide (MACH 2®), a molt accelerating compound, and Conserve SC, a spinosad-based product, are effective against sod webworms.

Several so-called "biorational" products can also be used against sod webworms. Entomopathogenic nematodes (*Steinernema carpocapsae*) have given satisfactory control. Apply the nematodes in early morning or late in the day to avoid heat and direct sunlight. Irrigate beforehand to moisten the thatch and soil, and immediately after application, before the spray droplets dry. Azadirachtin (neem), a botanical insecticide, is somewhat effective against small and medium-sized larvae. Products containing *Bacillus thuringiensis* (Bt) are also labeled for webworms, but like neem, they work best against the young larvae. By the time that damage shows up, the webworms may be too large to be very susceptible to these products. Azadirachtin or Bt sprays should not be watered in.

SOD WEBWORMS: TROPICAL-REGION SPECIES
(Plate 27)

Two introduced species, the grass webworm and the tropical sod webworm, are important pests of warm-season turfgrasses in Hawaii, and in the southern states, respectively. These pests differ from the temperate-zone sod webworms in that the moths do not roll their wings around their bodies. Also, the eggs are glued to vegetation rather than being dropped into the grass.

GRASS WEBWORM
Herpetogramma licarsisalis (Walker)
(Plate 27)

Importance and Nature of Injury. The grass webworm is among the worst pests of turf-grasses in Hawaii. Grass webworms damage turf by chewing the blades, stems, and crowns. Young larvae feed on the upper layers of leaf blades, leaving the lower epidermis intact. Mid-sized larvae chew notches in leaf margins, whereas older larvae devour whole blades while leaving large amounts of webbing and green fecal pellets. Severe infestations result in irregular patches of brown, chewed turf. In kikuyugrass, densities of 50 larvae per ft^2 (0.1 m^2) can occur.

Plants Attacked. This pest attacks all of the important turfgrasses in Hawaii, including bermudagrasses, centipedegrass, and St. Augustinegrass. Kikuyugrass is an especially favored host.

Distribution. The grass webworm is found throughout Hawaii, but is not known to occur in the continental United States. It is widely distributed in Japan, Australia, and throughout much of southeast Asia and the Pacific Islands.

Distinguishing Characteristics. The adult moths are uniformly fawn colored to light brown and have a wingspan of about 1 in. (24 mm). The forewings are unmarked except for a faint, slightly darker, zigzag line across the wing about one-fifth the way in from the outer edge. The wings slant backwards, so that in outline the resting moth resembles a swept-wing jet. Eggs are flat, elliptical, and about 1/32 in. (0.9 mm) long, whitish at first but becoming dark orange when ready to hatch. They are usually laid on the upper surface of grass blades, near the base and typically along the midvein. Eggs are deposited singly or in small clusters, overlapping each other like shingles. Newly hatched larvae are translucent amber to green, with a black head. Larger larvae are brownish to greenish, depending on the amount of fresh grass they have eaten, with a brown head. There is a conspicuous ring of dark brown spots on each body segment. Full-grown larvae are about 3/4 in. (19–20 mm) long. The brown, fat cigar-shaped pupae are about 7/16 in. (11 mm) long. Pupation occurs in a loosely woven, silken cocoon covered with bits of plant debris and frass.

Life Cycle and Habits. Feeding, mating, and egg-laying occur at night. The moths rest in tall grass during the day. If disturbed, they will fly erratically for a short distance before dropping back into the grass. Large numbers of moths can be flushed out by walking through high grass bordering turf areas. The moths sip flower nectar but do not damage turf. Egg-laying begins a few days after mating; each female deposits an average of 250 eggs over 1–2 weeks. Eggs hatch in about 5 days, and young larvae begin feeding on upper leaf surfaces. Larvae develop through five instars, maturing in about 2 weeks. Large larvae make tunnels leading from the surface of the turf into the thatch. They remain curled up and inactive by day, emerging after dark to feed. When ready to pupate, the mature larva webs together bits of plant debris and frass to form a crude cocoon. The adult moth emerges about a week later. A complete life cycle takes about 32 days at 76°F (24°C), and there are continuous generations throughout the year.

Management. Damage can occur at any time, but outbreaks seem to be more common following periods of rainy weather. Watch for chewed grass blades, webbing, and frass beginning about a week after adults are abundant. Larvae can be sampled by flushing them to the surface with a detergent or pyrethrin drench (see Black Cutworm — Management). Control may be justified if 10–15 larvae per yd^2 (12–18 per m^2) are found. *Trichogramma semifumatum* (Perkins), a tiny parasitic wasp that was introduced into Hawaii, kills more than 95% of the grass webworm eggs at some sites. Several other natural enemies also attack grass webworms. These beneficials can be conserved by cutting back on unnecessary insecticides. Common and Tifway bermudagrasses seem to be somewhat less susceptible than Sunturf and Tifdwarf bermudgrasses, centipedegrass, or St. Augustinegrass. (See Temperate-Region Sod Webworms — Management).

TROPICAL SOD WEBWORM
Herpetogramma phaeopteralis (Guenee)
(Plate 27)

Importance and Nature of Injury. The tropical sod webworm (TSWW) is among the most destructive pests of highly maintained bermudagrass and other turfgrasses in Florida and other Gulf States. Young larvae feed by rasping the leaf tissues between the veins. They often work along the midrib in the V-shaped trough formed by the leaf blade. Damage often begins near flower beds and shrubbery, possibly because the moths rest in such vegetation and lay eggs in the nearby grass. Mid-sized larvae chew notches in edges of leaf blades, causing a ragged appearance. Older larvae devour whole portions of leaves, and may completely strip the foliage in the manner of armyworms. Infested turf appears to have been severely scalped. Damaged areas may join together into large yellowish or brown patches. Vigorous lawns often outgrow the damage, but weak or drought-stressed turf may be killed outright. The older larvae hide underground by day and feed only at night. In south Florida, damage from TSWW usually begins in May or June and continues until late fall. In north Florida, the injury is usually not apparent until late July or August and is greatest in the fall. Much of the turf damage attributed to armyworms is actually caused by TSWW.

Plants Attacked. This pest damages St. Augustinegrass, bermudagrass, and centipedegrass; zoysiagrass and bahiagrass are less commonly attacked.

Distribution. The TSWW occurs along much of the Gulf Coast from the upper coastal region of Texas across to southern Georgia. It also occurs in the Caribbean region and apparently is widespread in tropical regions of the world. It is unable to overwinter north of central Florida in most years.

Distinguishing Characteristics. Adult TSWW are dingy brown moths with a wingspan of about 3/4 in. (20 mm). There are several darker, indistinct wavy lines across each wing, and the wings slant backwards so that a resting moth resembles a swept-wing jet. Eggs are flattened, oval-shaped, and just under 1/32 in. (0.6–0.7 mm) long. They are whitish at first, becoming brownish red before hatching. Eggs are laid on blades and stems of grass, either singly, or more often in clusters of 6–15 overlapping eggs. Larvae are a dark, translucent amber, but they appear greenish after they have fed. The head is dark yellowish brown. Full-grown larvae are about 3/4 in. (19 mm) long. Pupae are brown, fat cigar-shaped, and about 3/8 in. (9 mm) long. They may lie free or partially buried in the duff on the soil surface, or may be enclosed in a shapeless, silken bag that incorporates bits of plant debris and soil.

Life Cycle and Habits. The moths rest in shrubbery or high grass during the day. When disturbed, they flutter a short distance before settling down again. They become active at dusk, hovering over the surface of lawns and alighting periodically to lay eggs on the grass. TSWW are fairly strong fliers and can easily move between adjacent lawns. Eggs hatch in about a week at 78°F (26°C) and the larvae complete their development in about 25 days. They grow more slowly at cooler temperatures, requiring 45–50 days to mature at 73°F (23°C). There are seven or eight larval instars. Pupation occurs on the soil surface, and the adults emerge after 1–2 weeks, depending on temperature. A complete cycle from egg to adult requires 5–6 weeks at 78°F (26°C), or about 11 weeks at 73°F (23°C). TSWW cannot survive subfreezing conditions, so they don't overwinter above the latitude of central Florida in most years. The number of generations per year varies by geographic location. There are typically four generations per year in south Florida, where all life stages are present throughout the winter. Damage to turf usually begins in May or June, with outbreaks most common from mid-summer until late fall. In north Florida, there are two generations in most years. Larval populations usually do not build up to damaging levels until August, with the greatest injury occurring in late summer and fall.

Management. Grass blades with notched edges are a tipoff that TSWW are active. Infestations can be confirmed by the "hands and knees method" — part the grass and examine the soil surface for tightly curled larvae or frass. Larvae leave trails of silk as they crawl through the grass. These strands are easiest to spot in mornings when there is dew. Flocks of foraging birds may indicate that TSWW are present. Larvae can be sampled by flushing them with a soap or pyrethrin drench (see Black Cutworm — Management). Turf areas should be monitored weekly beginning about 2 weeks after peak numbers of moths are observed. Spot-treat as necessary, targeting the damaged areas and a 6 ft (2 m) buffer zone around the infestation. Reinspect for living larvae in a few days, and spot-treat again as necessary. Watering and light nitrogen fertilization will encourage recovery of damaged grass. Multiple applications may be needed because there are overlapping generations, and the moths may continually fly in to deposit new eggs. Nevertheless, try to avoid calendar-based cover sprays, in order to conserve natural enemies. Some bermudagrass cultivars are somewhat less susceptible — consult your Cooperative Extension agent for local recommendations. Guidelines for treatment are the same as for other sod webworms (see Temperate-Region Sod Webworms — Management).

VARIOUS TURF-INFESTING CATERPILLARS

Several other kinds of caterpillars are occasional pests of turfgrasses within a restricted geographic range. Most of these pests can be managed by the same tactics used for sod webworms, armyworms, and cutworms.

BURROWING SOD WEBWORMS
Acrolophus spp.
(Plate 26)

Importance and Nature of Injury. Burrowing sod webworms (BSWW) are not often serious pests, but their habit of leaving white silken tubes scattered across a lawn can cause concern by homeowners. The larvae make vertical burrows in the thatch and soil, deeper than the surface burrows of temperate-zone sod webworms. Burrows of mature larvae are about as wide as a pencil and may go down 4–12 in. (10–30 cm). The opening may be covered by a flap of silk and grass clippings; it may not be visible unless this flap is brushed off. The tubular, white silken lining of the burrow may extend above ground level onto stems and lower leaf blades. The larvae are active at night, chewing down grass foliage and pulling it into the burrow to feed. The damage resembles that caused by cutworms or temperate-zone sod webworms, but is rarely severe. After the moths emerge, the burrow lining often comes loose and may be sucked out by lawnmowers. These white silken tubes are about 1-1/2 to 2 in. (3.8–5 cm) long and resemble empty cigarette papers. They often have bits of soil, frass or plant debris clinging to the outside. Birds also may pull out the burrow lining, eat the larva or pupa, and leave the white tube on the surface.

Plants Attacked. The feeding preferences of BSWW are poorly known. They occur in Kentucky bluegrass, tall fescue, bermudagrass, and other lawn grasses.

Distribution. Several species of BSWW are found in turfgrasses. They are most common east of the Rocky mountains, especially in the transition and warm-season turf zones.

Distinguishing Characteristics. Adults are rather nondescript, small to medium-sized, active moths with a wingspan of 1 to 1-3/8 in. (25–35 mm). The forewings are grayish, reddish brown or yellow-brown, with irregular darker markings. Most species have large, tusk-like, hairy mouthparts (palps) that curve back over the head, almost touching the thorax. The tiny, spherical eggs are dropped into the grass and thatch. Larvae are velvety grayish, brownish, or dirty-white caterpillars with a brown head. They lack the distinctive dark spots of most temperate-zone sod webworms, but are distinguished by having a wide, leathery-brown collar on the first segment of the thorax, just behind the head. Depending on species, full-sized larvae range from 7/8 in. to about 1-3/4 in. (22–44 mm) long. Pupae are torpedo-shaped, dark brown, and found in silk-lined burrows in the soil.

Life Cycle and Habits. The adult moths emerge from mid-June through July. Mating and egg-laying start around dusk and continue for several hours. The moths move swiftly, and upon landing will quickly crawl into the grass. Eggs hatch in 1–2 weeks, and the larvae soon burrow down into the thatch and soil. The larva feeds and grows until late fall, overwinters in the burrow, and then resumes feeding and completes its development in the spring. In June, the mature larva spins a heavier silken lining in the upper 2 in. (5 cm) of the burrow and pupates therein.

Management. BSWW are rarely abundant enough to warrant control. Should it be necessary, they can be managed in the same manner as temperate-region sod webworms.

CRANBERRY GIRDLER (= Subterranean Webworm)
Chrysoteuchia topiaria (Zeller)
(Plate 26)

Importance and Nature of Injury. The cranberry girdler is common in the cool-season and transition turfgrass zones. It is especially damaging to turfgrasses grown for seed production in the Pacific northwest. This species is more subterranean in habit than other webworms. It rarely feeds on grass blades, preferring instead the crowns and roots. Damage results in small patches of dead turf. Heavy infestations can kill grass by severely pruning the roots in a manner similar to white grubs. Peak injury occurs in late summer and early fall.

Plants Attacked. This species feeds on roots and crowns of cool-season grasses such as Kentucky bluegrass, bentgrasses, and fine-leaf fescues, as well as roots of cranberries and coniferous seedling plants.

Distinguishing Characteristics. Larvae are dirty white in color, with an orange-brown head. They lack the prominent dark spotting typical of most other sod webworms found in lawns. Mature larvae are about 3/4 in. (19 mm) long. The adult moths have a wingspan of about 3/4 in. (19 mm). The front wings are generally buff colored, with delicate brown and cream stripes following the wing veins, a silver chevron and three black spots near each wing tip, and a tip fringe of silvery scales. Eggs and pupae resemble those of other webworm species.

Life Cycle and Habits. The moths emerge in early summer and are active from late June until mid-August. Flight and mating occur at night. Unlike other sod webworms, which drop eggs while in flight, females of this species usually do so while resting on a grass plant. Each female lays several hundred eggs over about a week. Eggs hatch in 9–11 days at 72°F (22°C), and the young larvae move to the thatch or upper soil to feed. As they grow, the larvae may burrow into grass crowns as well as feed on the roots. Older larvae construct silk-lined tunnels in the soil or thatch. Development takes about 2 months under normal field conditions, with larvae becoming nearly mature by late September or October. Feeding ceases with the onset of cool weather. Overwintering occurs as a full-grown, dormant larva (pre-pupa) within a tough silken case. Pupation occurs the following spring, in May or early June, and the moths appear 2–4 weeks later.

Management. Because larvae of this species burrow into crowns and also feed underground, they are more difficult to control than surface-feeding sod webworms. A synthetic sex attractant is available. Sticky traps baited with this lure can be set out in June to monitor activity of the adult moths. Treatments made about 2 weeks after peak adult trap captures will coincide with presence of young larvae. There have been few studies on control of this pest in turf. Post-treatment irrigation would presumably help to move the insecticide residues into the thatch and upper soil. Nematode-based products have given some control of this pest. Watering and fertilizing in fall will help turf to tolerate and recover from the damage. (See Temperate-Region Sod Webworms — Management.)

FIERY SKIPPER
Hylephila phyleus (Drury)
(Plate 27)

Importance and Nature of Injury. The fiery skipper is an occasionally serious pest of turfgrasses in Hawaii, especially bermudagrass golf fairways and lawn bowling greens. It also causes sporadic damage to lawns and golf courses in California and the Gulf Coast states. The injury begins as localized brown spots about 1–2 in. (2.5–5 cm) across, each marking where a larva has chewed down the grass. With severe infestations, the spots merge into irregular patches of dead turf.

Plants Attacked. Bermudagrass is preferred, but St. Augustinegrass, bentgrasses, and various weedy grasses, particularly crabgrass, are also attacked. Lawns contaminated with crabgrass may be especially attractive.

Distribution. This species occurs throughout most of North and South America, and has been transported to Hawaii. Most reports of damage are from Hawaii, California, and the Gulf Coast states.

Distinguishing Characteristics. The adults are stout yellow butterflies marked with orange and brown. The name "skipper" refers to their fast, erratic flights. They have large dark eyes and a wingspan of about 1 in. (25 mm). Pinhead-sized (0.7 mm), globular eggs are laid singly on the undersides of leaf blades. Eggs are white at first, changing to a light blue-green in a couple of days. Larvae have a distinctive form. The neck is strongly constricted behind the large coal-black head, and there is a strap-like, dark-colored shield across the first body segment, just behind the head. The body is plump and covered with tiny bristles, and the surface of the skin appears pebbled. Newly hatched larvae are pale greenish yellow and just under 1/8 in. (3 mm) long. Mature larvae are about 1 in. (25 mm) long and yellow-brown to gray-brown, with an indistinct stripe down the middle of the back. Even fainter stripes may be present on either side. Pupae are found in the thatch or near the soil surface, either exposed or partially enclosed in a cocoon of loosely webbed plant debris. The pupa is about 5/8 in. (15–18 mm) long, with the head and abdominal regions covered with sparse, bristly hairs. The head and thorax change from light green to brown as the pupa matures.

Life History and Habits. This pest is active year-round in tropical and subtropical regions. There are apparently 3–5 generations per year in Florida and Hawaii. Farther north, only 2–3 generations are completed, with adults most abundant in mid to late summer. Adult fiery skippers feed on nectar. They are attracted to flowers of latana, honeysuckle, alfalfa, clover, and other plants. The males perch near flowers to await visiting females, and then vigorously chase after them in flight. After mating, females lay eggs on grass blades. The female alights on the turf, attaches a single egg to the underside of a leaf, and then flies a short distance to repeat the process. Most egg-laying takes place on warm, sunny days. Each female deposits 50–150 widely scattered eggs over about a week. Eggs hatch in about 3 days at 80°F (27°C). Young larvae chew notches in the edges of leaf blades. Later, they move to the thatch and spin a lightly woven, silken shelter. They emerge after dark to chew off and devour whole leaves, causing the scattered spots of damage. Pupation occurs in a loosely woven shelter formed from silk and plant debris, or free in the thatch or soil. Development from egg to adult takes about 7 weeks at 75°F (24°C), and less than 4 weeks at 81–84°F (28–29°C).

Management. (See Armyworms, Cutworms, and Sod Webworms — Management.) This pest is rarely abundant enough to cause extensive damage. Control may be warranted when the feeding spots occur on putting greens, tees, and other high-profile sites. Larvae can be sampled with a soap disclosing solution (see Black Cutworm — Management). Products containing *Bacillus thuringiensis*, neem, or entomopathogenic nematodes that are registered for other turf-infesting caterpillars should have similar activity (and limitations) against fiery skipper larvae. Because the large larvae feed only at night, apply treatments late in the day, and withhold irrigation for 24 hours.

LUCERNE MOTH
Nomophila noctuella D. & S.

Importance and Type of Injury. Larvae chew the leaves and stems of clovers and similar legumes, but will occasionally feed on turfgrasses and dichondra. Damage typically appears in late summer, but is usually slight. Control measures are seldom warranted.

Distribution. This species is regarded as a minor lawn pest in California. It has not been reported as a turf pest in other states.

Distinguishing Characteristics. The adult moths have mottled gray-brown forewings with two pairs of indistinct spots, and a wingspan of just over 1 in. (25–30 mm). The hind wings are uniform grayish white. Larvae are slender, dull-colored, spotted caterpillars with a dark brown head. They resemble sod webworms, but larger. The first segment of the thorax, behind the head, bears a dark brown, leathery shield. Full-grown larvae are about 1 in. (25 mm) long and tend to wriggle actively when disturbed.

Life History and Habits. The adult moths are active at night. Females lay eggs on clover and other legumes, and sometimes on turfgrasses and dichondra. Activity is greatest during warm months. Larvae construct small, horizontal silken tubes near the base of plants. They venture forth to feed at night. There reportedly are two to four generations per growing season.

Management. Little specific information exists regarding control of this pest. (See Armyworms, Cutworms, and Sod Webworms — Management.)

STRIPED GRASSWORM (= Grass Looper)
Mocis latipes (Guenée)
(Plate 27)

Importance and Type of Injury. This is an occasional pest of warm-season grasses in the Gulf Coast states from Texas across to Florida. Damage resembles that caused by armyworms, fall armyworms, and tropical sod webworm. Young larvae feed on leaf surfaces, removing the upper cell layers in lengthwise strips along leaf blades. Mid-sized larvae chew on leaf margins, producing a tattered appearance, whereas large larvae devour entire leaves and tender stems. Light infestations cause general thinning, but heavy, unchecked infestations can chew the grass down to the stolons. Striped grassworms sometimes build up in pastures and migrate into adjacent lawns when their food supply becomes depleted.

Plants Attacked. Striped grassworms feed on many pasture grasses, as well as bahiagrass, bermudagrass, and St. Augustinegrass. Corn, sugarcane, rice, and other grassy plants are also attacked.

Distribution. This pest reportedly occurs throughout the United States and southern Canada east of the Rocky Mountains, south into Mexico, Central and South America, and the West Indies. It is rarely a turf pest except for sporadic problems in the Gulf Coast states.

Distinguishing Characteristics. The adult moths are about the same size as cutworm moths, but with broader wings and a less robust body. The forewings are mottled gray to brown, with a darker brown stripe across each wing, about two-thirds of the way toward the tip and parallel to the outer margin. The wingspan ranges from 1-1/4 to 1-3/4 in. (30–45 mm). Tiny, globular eggs are deposited singly on grass blades. The eggs are light green at first, changing to mottled brown before hatching. Newly hatched larvae are about 3/16 in. (5 mm) long, with faint brown and cream-colored longitudinal stripes. Full-sized larvae are about 1-3/4 in. (40–45 mm) long. They are easily recognized by the slender, cylindrical body, conspicuous yellow and brown stripes, and habit of looping, inchworm-like, when moving about. Larvae have three pairs of fleshy prolegs on the abdomen. Pupae are chestnut brown and enclosed in a spindle-shaped, silken cocoon that has grass blades incorporated into it. Cocoons are found in the thatch or duff under the turf canopy.

Life History and Habits. Striped grassworms are present year-round in south Florida and southern Texas, with several generations per year. Adult activity peaks in the fall. The moths emerge, mate, and lay eggs at night. Each female may lay 300 or more eggs, mostly within the first week after emergence. Eggs hatch in about 3 days under warm conditions. Newly hatched larvae spin webbing over the V-shaped trough formed by a leaf blade. They then feed by stripping surface tissues from the upper leaf surface. Larvae grow rapidly, molting every 2–3 days and becoming full-sized in about 3 weeks. Feeding damage becomes more severe with successive molts. Mid-sized larvae feed on the leaf margins, but damage may not become obvious until older larvae begin devouring whole leaves and stems. Development from egg hatch to pupation requires about 3 weeks in warm weather. Before pupating, the larva fastens leaf blades about itself with silk to form a cocoon. Cocoons are sometimes attached at the base of grass stems. New moths emerge about 9 days later. A complete life cycle from egg to adult requires about a month. Striped grassworms feed during both day and night. They may climb grass plants, or may remain on the ground while feeding. When the grass is destroyed in one spot, they crawl to adjacent areas with fresher food. The adults rest in tall grass by day and will fly up when disturbed.

Management. (See Armyworms, Cutworms, and Sod Webworms — Management.) Striped grassworms are easy to control by methods described for these other turf-infesting caterpillars.

VEGETABLE WEEVIL
Listroderes difficilis Germar (= *L. costirostris obliquus* [Klug.])
(Plate 14)

Importance and Type of Injury. This is an occasional pest of dichondra lawns in California. Both adults and larvae chew small holes in the leaves. With high infestations, leaves may be skeletonized or completely removed, so only bare stems remain. Damage appears from early fall to mid-spring. Since the adults do not fly, infestations are usually localized or spotty, and are slow to spread to new areas.

Plants Attacked. Besides dichondra lawns, adults and larvae feed on vegetables such as carrots, turnips, and spinach. Turfgrasses are not attacked.

History and Distribution. A native of Brazil, this introduced pest occurs in Gulf states and in southern and central California.

Distinguishing Characteristics. The slow-moving, brownish to grayish "snout" beetles are about 3/8 in. (9.5 mm) long and have a light gray, V-shaped marking across the wing covers. The wing covers are rough and punctate, with sparse, short hairs, and each one has a short, pointed tubercle on the dorsal surface toward the hind end. The antennae are attached near the tip of the short, blunt snout. Adults often "play dead" when disturbed. Larvae are light green, legless, fat-bodied grubs about 3/8 in. (9.5 mm) long when fully grown.

Life History and Habits. Females of this species reproduce without mating; males are not known to occur. Eggs are laid on plants or in the underlying soil, from September to March. Each female deposits 300–1500 eggs. Larvae develop during the winter and most are full-sized by early spring. They then burrow into the soil, pupate, and transform to adults which feed during the spring and summer. There is one generation per year. The adult weevils disperse by crawling, but do not fly. They may crawl to nearby lights at night. Both adults and larvae feed mainly at night. Larvae hide in the soil or debris under the plants during the day. A few adults are sometimes seen during the day, but usually they remain hidden within the plant canopy.

Management. Infestations can be confirmed by looking for fat-bodied, legless grubs in the soil under damaged plants. Soap or pyrethrum drenches (see Black Cutworm — Management) can be used to flush adults to the surface. Vegetable weevils can be controlled with insecticide sprays applied during the larval feeding period, generally from early December until mid-March. To avoid burning the foliage, certain insecticides should not be applied to water-stressed dichondra, or when the temperature exceeds 90°F (32°C). Always read and follow the label directions. Another pest, the dichondra flea beetle, is more likely to be the cause of severe damage to dichondra.

SELECTED REFERENCES

General References

Brandenburg, R.L. and M.G. Villani (Eds.). 1995. *Handbook of turfgrass insect pests.* Entomol. Soc. Am., Lanham, MD.

Tashiro, H. 1987. *Turfgrass insects of the United States and Canada.* Cornell Univ. Press, Ithaca, NY.

Watschke, T.L., P.H. Dernoeden, and D.J. Shetlar. 1995. *Managing turfgrass pests.* Lewis Publishers, Boca Raton, FL.

Armyworms

Breeland, S.G. 1958. Biological studies on the armyworm, *Pseudaletia unipuncta* (Haworth) in Tennessee (Lepidoptera: Noctuidae). *J. Tenn. Acad. Sci.* 33:263–347.

Guppy, J.C. 1961. Life history and behavior of the armyworm, *Pseudaletia unipuncta* (Haw.) (Lepidoptera: Noctuidae) in eastern Ontario. *Can. Entomol.* 93:1141–1153.

Pond, D.D. 1960. Life history studies of the armyworm, *Pseudaletia unipuncta* (Lepidoptera: Noctuidae) in New Brunswick. *Ann. Entomol. Soc. Am.* 53:661–665.

Burrowing Sod Webworm

Banergee, A.C. 1967. Injury to grasses in lawns caused by *Acrolophus* sp. *J. Econ. Entomol.* 60:1173–1174.

Cranberry Girdler (= Subterranean Webworm)

Kamm, J.A. 1973. Biotic factors that affect sod webworms in grass fields in Oregon. *Environ. Entomol.* 2:94–96.

Cutworms

Crumb, S.E. 1929. Tobacco cutworms. *U.S. Dept. Agric. Tech. Bull.* 88.

Rings, R.W. 1977. An illustrated field key to common cutworms, armyworms and looper moths in north central states. *Ohio Agric. Res. Dev. Circ.* 227.

Walkden, H.H. 1950. Cutworms, armyworms, and related species attacking cereal and forage crops in the Central Great Plains. *U.S. Dept. Agric. Circ.* 849.

Williamson, R.C. and D.J. Shetlar. 1994. Black cutworms: Where are they coming from? *U.S. Golf Assoc. Green Section Record* 32(5):5–7.

Williamson, R.C. and D.A. Potter. 1997. Oviposition of black cutworm on creeping bentgrass putting greens and removal of eggs by mowing. *J. Econ. Entomol.* 90:590–594.

Fall Armyworm

Barfield, C.S., J.L. Stimac, and M.A. Keller. 1980. State-of-the-art for predicting damaging infestations of fall armyworms. *Florida Entomol.* 63:364–374.

Luginbill, P. 1928. The fall armyworm. *U.S. Dept. Agric. Tech. Bull.* 34.

Grass Webworm

Tashiro, H. 1976. Biology of the grass webworm, *Herpetogramma licarsisalis* (Lepidoptera: Pyraustidae) in Hawaii. *Ann. Entomol. Soc. Am.* 69:797–803.

Lawn Armyworm

Tanada, Y. and J.W. Beardsley. 1958. A biological study of the lawn armyworm, *Spodoptera mauritia* (Boisduval), in Hawaii (Lepidoptera: Phalaenidae). *Proc. Hawaiian Entomol. Soc.* 16:411–436.

Sod Webworms

Ainslie, G.G. 1927. The larger sod webworm. *U.S. Dept. Agric. Tech. Bull.* 31.

Ainslie, G.G. 1930. The bluegrass webworm. *U.S. Dept. Agric. Tech. Bull.* 173.

Bohart, R.M. 1947. Sod webworms and other lawn pests in California. *Hilgardia* 17:267–307.

Sorensen, K.A. and H.E. Thompson. 1979. The life history of the buffalograss webworm *Surattha indentella* Kearfott, in Kansas (Lepidoptera: Pyralidae). *J. Kans. Entomol. Soc.* 52:282–296.

Tolley, M.P. and W.H. Robinson. 1986. Seasonal abundance and degree-day prediction of sod webworm (Lepidoptera: Pyralidae) adult emergence in Virginia. *J. Econ. Entomol.* 79:400–404.

Striped Grassworm

Reinert, J.A. 1975. Life history of the striped grassworm, *Mocis latipes*. *J. Econ. Entomol.* 68:201–204.

Vickery, R.A. 1924. The striped grass looper, *Mocis repanda* Fab. in Texas. *J. Econ. Entomol.* 401–405.

Tropical Sod Webworm

Kerr, S.H. 1955. Life history of the tropical sod webworm *Pachyzancla phaeopteralis* Guenee. *Florida Entomol.* 38:3–11.

Short, D.E. 1993. Insects and related pests of turfgrass in Florida. *Univ. Florida Coop. Ext. Serv. Bull.* SP 140, Gainesville, FL.

12

BITING AND STINGING PESTS IN THE TURFGRASS ENVIRONMENT

INTRODUCTION

Biting or stinging arthropods can be a significant hazard in and around the turfgrass environment. Encounters with wasps, chiggers, ticks, red imported fire ants, and other pests can be annoying, painful, or even debilitating or life-threatening. Knowledge of these pests will help you to safeguard the health and safety of employees, golfers, and other turf users.

CHIGGERS
(Order Acari; Family Trombiculidae)

Larvae of mites in the family Trombiculidae, sometimes called "chiggers," "red bugs," or "harvest mites," are medically important pests around the world. The maddening itch that accompanies their bite must be experienced to be fully appreciated. Several species are encountered in the United States, the most common being *Eutrombicula alfreddugesi* (Oudemans) and *E. splendens* (Ewing). Chiggers are most common in the southern United States, but they may become abundant during summertime in the northern states.

Description, Life History, and Habits. Adult chiggers are 8-legged, about 1/32 in. (1 mm) long, with a bright red, velvety appearance. The waist is constricted, giving the mite a "figure-eight" shape. Adults and nymphs live on or in the soil, where they prey upon small arthropods and their eggs. These older life stages do not bite humans. Adults overwinter in the soil, becoming active and laying eggs in the spring. The eggs hatch into tiny, six-legged larvae, the stage which attacks humans (Figure 12.1). Larval chiggers are so small that they are barely visible to the unaided eye. The body is hairy and red to reddish orange in color.

Larval chiggers crawl up grass blades, weeds, or other low vegetation, and soon grab onto a passing vertebrate host. They normally feed on rodents, ground-dwelling birds, and other wild hosts, but will also attack poultry, domestic animals, and people. After feeding for a few days the engorged larva drops to the ground and transforms into the free-living, soil-dwelling nymph. Later, after another molt, the adult emerges. The entire life cycle from egg to adult is completed

Figure 12.1. Chigger (from USDA).

in 30–60 days. There are one to three generations per year in temperate regions — as many as six in subtropical areas. In the northern half of the United States, chiggers are active from about May to September, but in the South they may be active almost year-round.

Medical Importance. On humans, chiggers tend to crawl upward until they reach a place where clothing is pressed against the skin, such as under belts, underwear, and socks. Bites most commonly occur around the ankles, waistline, armpits, back of the knee, or groin area. Chiggers do not feed on blood, nor do they burrow under the skin. The larva feeds by sinking its mouthparts into the host, often at the base of a hair, injecting saliva that partially digests the host's tissue, and then sucking up the resulting soup. Most people react to chigger bites by developing dome-shaped, reddish welts within 24 hours. Reaction to the chigger's saliva causes intense local itching and extreme discomfort for a week or more. Scratching usually removes the chigger but can result in secondary infection, sometimes accompanied by fever. Chiggers in the genus *Leptotrombidium* transmit the agent of scrub typhus in Japan, Southeast Asia, and parts of Australia. Fortunately, chiggers in North America are not known to transmit human diseases.

Management. People are most likely to encounter chiggers in vegetational transition zones, such as high grass at the edge of lawns, or weedy and brushy areas bordering picnic grounds or golf roughs. Regular, close mowing of weeds and high grass, and removal of overgrown vegetation, makes such areas less suitable for chiggers and their wild hosts. This is important in reducing chigger populations in parks and outdoor recreation areas. Populations can be reduced by treating infested areas with a residual miticide. High grass should be mowed before treatment to enhance penetration and performance of the miticide. Although chiggers occasionally occur in lawns, most closely-cut, well-maintained lawns do not get chigger problems.

Personal protection using tick repellents is recommended for those working in chigger-infested areas. Products containing permethrin can be applied to clothing either as a band around socks, cuffs, waist, fly, sleeves and neck, or as a light spray over the surface of the entire clothing. *Do not apply permethrin-based repellents directly to skin.* Diethyl toluamide (DEET) can be applied to clothing or skin around the ankles, waist, and other favored chigger feeding sites. Be sure to read and follow label directions. Wearing long pants tucked into socks or boots provides some protection. Persons who suspect they have been exposed to chiggers should take a hot soapy bath or shower as soon as possible. This will help to remove any chiggers, attached or unattached. Antiseptic, hydrocortisone, and/or anesthetic (benzocaine) ointments will provide temporary relief from itching and reduce chances of secondary infection.

CICADA KILLERS AND SAND WASPS
Sphecius speciosus (Drury) and *Bembix* spp., respectively
(Plate 29)

Cicada killers are very large wasps that evoke a good deal of fear and attention because of their burrowing habits in lawns and golf courses, and their buzzing flights that alarm homeowners and golfers. Despite their menacing appearance, they very rarely sting. Sand wasps can be a nuisance when their colonies occur in bunkers on golf courses.

Description, Life History, and Habits. Cicada killers are very large wasps, up to 1-5/8 in. (40 mm) long, that resemble gigantic hornets or yellowjackets. They have a rusty red head and thorax, amber-yellow wings, and a black abdomen with pale yellow stripes. Cicada killers occur in all states east of the Rocky Mountains and south into Mexico. They prefer to nest in areas of full sun, scant vegetation, and light-textured, sandy, well-drained soils. The wasps feed on flower nectar, whereas the larvae feed on cicadas that are brought to the burrow by the mother wasp.

Cicada killers overwinter as larvae within cocoons, 3/4 to 1 in. (2–2.5 cm) deep in the soil. Pupation occurs in the spring and the wasps emerge from mid-June through July. The female feeds, mates, and digs soil burrows for several weeks before stocking them with cicadas. The burrows are about 1/2 in. (12.5 mm) across, 6–9 in. (15–23 cm) deep, vertical or slightly angled, with several secondary tunnels, each ending in a brood chamber. Excess soil is pushed out of the burrow, forming a small, U-shaped mound around the entrance. Each female excavates and provisions numerous burrows.

Once the burrows are prepared, the female begins her hunt for cicadas. She ambushes an adult cicada on a tree trunk or lower limb, knocks it to the ground, overturns it, and stings it with paralyzing venom. She then climbs part way up a tree or plant with her burden and glides through the air in the direction of a burrow, covering as much distance as possible. She does this repeatedly until finally dragging the paralyzed, still-living victim down the hole. She stuffs the cicada into one of the brood chambers, lays a greenish-white egg on it, backs out, and seals the cell. The female continues hunting and provisioning additional chambers until the cicada population wanes in late summer. The egg hatches in 2–3 days and the hungry wasp larva quickly devours the zombified victim, leaving only the empty shell. Sometimes two cicadas are placed in one cell, supporting development of an even bigger wasp. In fall, the wasp larva spins a brown, spindle-shaped cocoon, becomes shrunken and leathery, and prepares to overwinter. Only one generation occurs each year.

Cicada killers may form nesting aggregations, with numerous individuals nesting in the same area. However, they are not social wasps like hornets or yellowjackets, which live in a communal nest and cooperate to rear the young. Each female excavates and provisions her own burrows. Males usually emerge before females and patrol the nesting area, awaiting the emergence of virgin females and fighting off any rival males. They buzz-bomb any intruder, occasionally hovering about or flying into a person's head or back. Fortunately, males cannot sting. Females are quite docile and do not defend their burrows. They can give a painful sting, but will rarely do so unless they are handled, stepped upon with bare feet, or otherwise provoked.

Sand wasps are related to cicada killers, but are smaller. The fast-flying adult wasps are about 13/16 to 1 in. (20–25 mm) long and dark colored, often with pale green markings. Sand wasps nest in sandy areas, usually in colonies, and stock their nests with various kinds of insect prey. Unlike cicada killers, their brood burrows are not completely provisioned before egg-laying, and the young are fed as they grow. These wasps can be quite a distraction when they nest in bunkers. Although they are not aggressive, golfers hesitate to enter bunkers where the low-flying males are patrolling in search of mates, or where the females are digging burrows or provisioning their nests.

Management. Cicada killers and sand wasps are beneficial insects, except when their behavior interferes with human activity. The mounds thrown up by females can be unsightly or smother patches of grass. Infestations may occur in bunkers, playground sand boxes, or sand-based volleyball courts. These wasps prefer sandy areas with sparse vegetation for nesting. Thus, cultural practices (e.g., watering, fertilizer) to promote a thick growth of turf will discourage their burrowing activity. Cruising males can be captured with an insect net or whacked with a tennis racket. This may suffice to end complaints by golfers. Replacing sand under play structures with mulch or bark chips will discourage the wasps from nesting. In some situations, insecticide treatment may be warranted to allay anxiety and fears of stings. When only a few wasps are involved, dusting the burrow openings with carbaryl or bendiocarb will kill the females as they engage in nesting activities. Where large numbers of nests are present, broadcast applications of labeled carbamates or pyrethroids will often eliminate the problem.

FLEAS
(Order Siphonaptera; Families Pulicidae, Ceratophyllidae, and Leptopsyllidae)
(Plate 29)

Fleas are common worldwide in and around homes with pets. Flea bites result in irritation and severe discomfort to both pets and humans. The cat flea, *Ctenocephalis felis* (Bouché), which attacks both cats and dogs as well as humans, is by far the most common pest species in suburban areas in the United States. The dog flea, mouse flea, and oriental rat flea are also sometimes encountered, especially when a structure has been infested with rodents, squirrels or other wild hosts. Most flea problems in suburban areas can be eliminated by treating the pet and the interior of the home. Spot-treatment of the yard may also be necessary in cases where pets spend much of their time outdoors.

Description, Life History, and Habits. Adult fleas are small, brown or reddish brown, wingless insects, about 1/16 to 1/8 in. (1.6–3.2 mm) long. The body is covered with backward-pointing spines and is flattened from side to side, allowing the flea to move easily through fur or hair. Fleas have powerful legs that enable them to jump 16 in. (40 cm) or more. Adult fleas have piercing-sucking mouthparts and feed exclusively on blood.

Because the cat flea is the main pest of dogs and cats, its life cycle is presented here (Figure 12.2). Adult fleas (the biting stage) spend virtually all of their time on the host, taking periodic blood meals and laying all of their eggs *on the animal.* The eggs are not attached and soon fall off into carpeting, bedding, or other areas frequented by the pet. Eggs are oval, pearly white, and about the size of a grain of sand. Each female may produce several hundred eggs in her lifetime. Larvae are whitish, spiny, legless, and about 1/16 to 1/5 in. (1.5–5 mm) long. They remain hidden deep in carpet fibers, beneath furniture cushions and in other protected places. They may occur outdoors in moist, shaded grassy areas frequented by pets. Flea larvae feed on dried blood defecated by adult fleas, dead skin and hair, and other grunge that accumulates, along with the eggs, in animal resting and bedding areas. Before becoming an adult, the larva transforms to a pupa within a silken cocoon interwoven with bits of organic debris.

Medical Importance. Fleas account for more than half of the dermatological problems seen by veterinarians. Humans typically are bitten on the lower legs and ankles. Flea bites produce an itchy red welt with a single puncture point in the center. In sensitized persons the reaction may persist for a week or more. Oral antihistamines may help relieve the itching, and corticosteroid can be applied to treat the welts. Certain flea species, most notably the oriental rat flea, can transmit plague and murine typhus to humans. Fleas become carriers of these diseases after feeding on infected rodents such as rats. Fortunately, these flea-borne diseases are uncommon in the United States. Fleas are, however, capable of transmitting tapeworms from dogs to people.

Management. The best way for pet owners to manage fleas is through prevention. By acting in spring, before fleas become active, you can prevent fleas from becoming established and avoid severe infestations later in the summer. The preventive approach reduces the need to apply insecticides within the home. Ridding a home of an established flea infestation is much harder

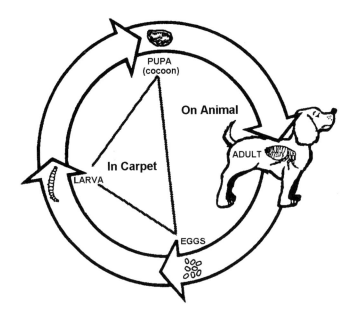

Figure 12.2. *Life cycle of the cat flea (from Potter and Beavers, 1995).*

and more time-consuming, requiring a systematic program that includes treatment of the pet *and* the premises.

Preventive approach. Pet owners can break the flea's life cycle and prevent a massive infestation in the home by killing the eggs as they are laid on the pet. *The best way to accomplish this is to treat the dog or cat with a long-lasting insect growth regulator (IGR) during the spring, before flea season begins.* Two types of products, one a collar and the other a tablet, are especially effective and easy to use. Flea collars containing methoprene or pyriproxyfen are available through veterinarians and pet supply stores. Unlike the ingredients in conventional flea collars, these IGRs rapidly distribute over the pet's fur, killing flea eggs on contact. These collars are extremely effective at preventing new flea eggs from hatching for 6–9 months on dogs, and year-long on cats. These collars will not, however, control stray adult fleas that the pet may pick up. Another product, available through veterinarians, is administered orally once a month as a tablet or liquid. When a female flea bites a treated animal, she ingests the active ingredient (lufenuron) which then passes into her eggs and prevents them from hatching. Both of these IGR-based products are essentially nontoxic to people and pets, and they are compatible with other pet medications. Be sure to read and follow label directions, and the advice of your veterinarian.

Curative approach. Once fleas become established in a home, treatment of the premises is almost always necessary to control them. *Having the pet dipped or installing a flea collar after the fact will not, in itself, eliminate fleas in an infested home.* Failure to treat the pet's environment will result in missing more than 90% of the developing flea population — the eggs, larvae and pupae.

Curative flea control should begin with thorough vacuuming, especially in areas where pets rest or sleep. Vacuuming removes many of the eggs, larvae, and pupae developing in the home. It also raises the nap of the carpet, enhancing penetration of insecticides to the base of the fibers where the developing fleas live. Be sure to vacuum along the baseboards and beneath furniture, cushions, and throw rugs. Seal the vacuum bag in a garbage bag when finished and discard it in an outdoor trash container. Wash, dry-clean, or destroy all pet bedding at the same time.

The next step is to apply an approved insecticide to the infested premises. Various flea control products are available for home treatment. The most effective ones contain both an adulticide (e.g., permethrin) effective against the biting adults, and an IGR (e.g., methoprene, pyriproxyfen) for long-term suppression of the immature stages. Check the label to determine if these ingredients are present. Most people will find aerosol formulations easier to use than liquids. The application should be thorough and include all likely areas where fleas may be developing, such as carpets, throw rugs, under and behind beds, and beneath cushions upon which pets sleep. Pets and family members should be out of the house during treatment, and should remain off treated surfaces until the spray has dried. Expect to see some adult fleas for a few weeks following treatment. Provided that treatment was thorough, these are probably late-hatching survivors that have not yet succumbed to the insecticide. Continue to vacuum, but do not retreat the premises (and pet) unless fleas continue to be a problem after 2–4 weeks. Always read and follow directions on the label.

The pet should be treated in conjunction with the premises, preferably on the same day. Otherwise, the pet will continue to be bitten by adult fleas which live on the animal, and it may continue to transport fleas in from outdoors, eventually overcoming the residual effectiveness of the insecticide applied inside the home. A variety of on-animal formulations are available by prescription from veterinarians. The most effective ones contain an IGR to prevent eggs laid on the animal from hatching, or a long-lasting adulticide (e.g., imidacloprid or fipronil). Certain products can be used only on dogs, and some list specific procedures for puppies and kittens. *Carefully follow instructions on the label.*

In cases where pets spend substantial amounts of time outdoors, it may also be necessary to spot-treat the yard with an insecticide. Presence of fleas can be confirmed by walking the area wearing white athletic socks pulled to the knee. Fleas are attracted to and can be easily seen against the white fabric. Outdoor flea treatments should focus on spots frequented by pets, including doghouses and kennel areas, under decks and porches, and favored resting spots next to the foundation. Flea larvae are very susceptible to heat and desiccation. Thus, it is usually unnecessary to treat large expanses of turf exposed to full sun. Short-term control of fleas infesting outdoor areas can be obtained with conventional insecticides. Long-term suppression can be enhanced with formulations containing a light-stable IGR (e.g., pyriproxyfen). Products containing entomopathogenic nematodes (*Steinernema carpocapsae*) may provide some control of larval and pupal fleas in lawns. Mowing, raking, and thatch removal will aid penetration of the insecticide and make the turf less hospitable for fleas. In most cases, indoor treatment of the home and pet will also be necessary.

Opossums, raccoons, and feral (stray) cats and dogs may be a source of fleas around homes, golf course maintenance buildings, or other sites where no pets are present. These wild hosts are also the main reservoir for fleas overwintering out-of-doors in temperate areas. See Chapter 15 for tips on eliminating nuisance wildlife in such situations.

HARVESTER ANTS
Pogonomyrmex species
(Plate 28)

Harvester ants are dangerous insects that will inflict painful stings if their nest is disturbed. They become pests when they nest near areas of human activity. They also create bare spots in turf by their nest-building activities. Harvester ants are found in the southern and western United States (Figure 12.3). The Florida harvester ant, *Pogonomyrmex badius* (Latreille), which occurs in the Coastal Plain, states from Louisiana to North Carolina, is the only species found east of the Mississippi River. About 20 species occur in the western states. Among the most common are the red harvester ant, *P. barbatus* (F. Smith), the western harvester ant, *P. occidentalis* (Cresson), and the California harvester ant, *P. californicus* (Buckley).

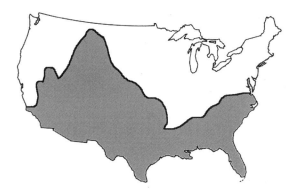

Figure 12.3. Distribution of harvester ants in the continental United States.

Description, Life History, and Habits. Harvester ants are soil-inhabiting ants that build nests in open areas, usually in full sun. Their colonies consist of a single reproductive queen and thousands of worker ants. The workers forage for food, tend to the queen and young, and defend the colony from outside invaders. Depending upon the species, the workers range from red to black in color, and from 1/5 to 3/8 in. (5–9.5 mm) in length. Harvester ants have two segments or nodes comprising the narrow section between the thorax and main part of the abdomen (Figure 12.4). They are further distinguished by the presence of rows of long hairs on the underside of the head. The end of the abdomen bears a stinger. These identifying features are visible with a 10x hand lens. Most species of harvester ants have workers of only one size, as opposed to having small and large workers as is common in other types of ants. The Florida harvester ant is an exception, having several sizes of workers, including some with enormous heads and powerful jaws used for cracking seeds.

Harvester ants are so-named because of their habit of gathering plant seeds as part of their diet. They also prey upon other insects or act as scavengers. Seeds and other foods are carried back to the nest and stored in underground chambers. The workers use their powerful jaws to clear out a large, vegetation-free, crater-like area on the ground surface around the entrance to the nest. These bare spots may be 3–10 ft (1–3 m) or more in diameter. There are one or more holes leading down into the nest. Workers may forage as far as 200 ft (60 m) or more out from the nest. Thus, ants foraging in a lawn may be from a nest in an adjacent yard, field, or wooded area. Colonies may persist for several years before producing winged queens and males that swarm out of the nest in summer. After mating, the male dies and the female sheds her wings, searches for a suitable nesting site, and starts a new colony.

Harvester ants are larger than red imported fire ants, and the size and shape of their mounds also differs. Harvester ant mounds are usually flat or only slightly elevated and surrounded by an area of no vegetation. Red imported fire ant mounds are rounded or conical, distinctly elevated, and composed of excavated soil.

Medical Importance. Harvester ants inflict painful stings that produce localized swelling and inflammation. The reaction to stings may spread along lymph vessels, resulting in intense, persistent pain in the lymph nodes of the armpits and groin. First aid for stings includes washing the wound with soap and water, and ice packs to reduce pain and swelling. Persons who show signs of allergic reaction from ant stings should get medical attention. Allergic reactions may require administration of epinephrine or antihistamines.

Management. The most effective way to control harvester ants is through use of ant baits containing avermectin, hydramethylnon, or an insect growth regulator such as fenoxycarb. Spread

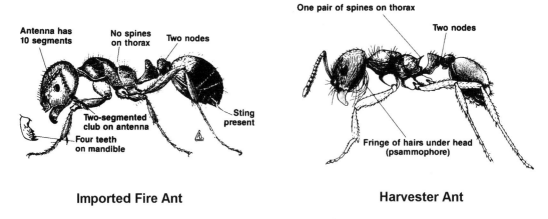

Imported Fire Ant

Harvester Ant

Figure 12.4. *Distinguishing features of harvester ants (right) and the red imported fire ant (from Hedges, 1992; with permission).*

the bait around the entrance to the mound, where it will be collected by the workers and carried into the nest. It may take several weeks for the bait to kill off the colony. Other methods of control can be used, although they are often less effective than baits. Insecticidal dusts labeled for ant control can be puffed over the mounds and into each of the nest entrances, or residual insecticides can be injected into the mounds using a compressed air sprayer. Drenching with an insecticide is often ineffective because the tunnels in the nest may extend deep into the soil.

RED IMPORTED FIRE ANT
Solenopsis invicta Buren
(Plate 28)

Two aspects of red imported fire ant (RIFA) infestations are especially troublesome: the unsightly mounds produced on golf courses, home lawns, parks, playgrounds, and athletic fields; and the painful stings that are inflicted when the mounds are disturbed. RIFA are a particular hazard to children and persons with hypersensitivity to their venom. A number of human deaths have been attributed to their stings. Economic losses from RIFA amount to many millions of dollars annually. It is not practical to eradicate these ants, but their populations can be suppressed and the chance of contact with people reduced.

Origin and Distribution. The RIFA, a native of southern Brazil, was accidentally brought to Mobile, Alabama about 1930. Since then it has spread throughout the southeastern United States (Figure 12.5). The species continues to expand its range northward and westward into areas with mild climates and adequate moisture and food. Infested areas are currently under federal and state quarantine to regulate shipments of nursery stock and sod that might carry RIFA to other parts of the United States.

Three other related species, the black imported fire ant, *Solenopsis richteri* Forell; southern fire ant, *S. xyloni* McCook; and native fire ant, *S. geminata* (Fabricius) also occur in the southern states. These species are far less important than the RIFA. The black imported fire ant currently occurs in the United States only in northeastern Mississippi, northwestern Alabama, and parts of southern Tennessee. The southern fire ant ranges from California to South Carolina and northern Florida. The native fire ant was originally found across the southern states but has been displaced by the RIFA. Colonies are still scattered from Texas to South Carolina. These other fire ants can be managed in the same manner as the RIFA.

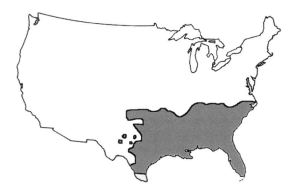

Figure 12.5. Present distribution of the red imported fire ant in the continental United States.

Description, Life History, and Habits. Adult RIFA are reddish to dark brown and occur in five forms: minor workers, about 1/8 in. (3.2 mm) long; major workers, about 1/4 in. (6.4 mm) long; winged males and winged females, each about 1/3 in. (8.5 mm) long; and wingless queens, about 1/3 in. (8.5 mm) long. Figure 12.4 shows distinguishing characteristics of RIFA workers.

RIFA build elevated mounds, usually in open, sunny locations. Mounds constructed in clay soils are usually symmetrical and dome-shaped; mounds built in sandy soils tend to be lower and more irregularly shaped. The size of the mounds varies, usually in proportion to the size of the colony. A large mound that is 2 ft (60 cm) in diameter and 18 in. (45 cm) high would typically contain 100,000 to 500,000 workers, several hundred winged adults, and one or sometimes several egg-laying queens. Active colonies also contain whitish eggs, grub-like larvae, and pupae, collectively called the brood. These immature stages will eventually develop into workers or winged adults. The underground portion of the nest is a series of tunnels and chambers that may extend 3–4 ft (0.9–1.2 m) into the soil.

During spring and summer, winged males and females leave the mound and mate in the air. Males die soon after mating. Fertilized females become queens and may fly or be blown by wind for several miles, although most will land much closer to the parent colony. A mature mound can produce as many as 2,000 new queens per year. Fortunately, only a few will survive to start a new colony. Most queens are killed by predators, especially other RIFA, soon after landing. If she survives, the young queen sheds her wings, burrows into the ground, and makes a small depression in which she lays her first group of about 30 eggs. For about a month, the queen is self-sufficient and relatively vulnerable as she must provide food for her first offspring. As the worker ants mature, they take over mound construction, food gathering, and protection of the queen and brood. The ants prey upon other insects or scavenge for dead insects, seeds, carrion, or other foods. The workers forage aboveground for considerable distances, or travel in underground tunnels that radiate from the nest. The queen continues laying eggs, as many as 200 per day, and the mound grows. Typically, the colony is mature in about 9 months and begins producing reproductives that leave the mound to begin the cycle anew. Individual queens may live 5 years or more.

The mound of a new colony may not be noticeable until several months after the young queen begins laying eggs. Numerous small colonies of RIFA ants will appear in the late fall. Many of these will perish over the winter unless the weather is mild. The ant expands its range mainly through the mating flights. These flights are the reason why eradicating the RIFA from a specific area is unlikely, if not impossible. Even with good pest management, areas are reinfested by newly mated queens from surrounding areas.

Damage to Turf. RIFA do not feed upon turf, but their mounds are eyesores when they occur on lawns, golf courses, playgrounds, and athletic fields. The mounds interfere with golf course maintenance and may disrupt play. Mowers can be dulled or broken by the high mounds of soil. Turf managers must be concerned with possible liability for turf users who are stung by uncontrolled ants.

Medical Importance. RIFA are highly aggressive and will attack anything that threatens their nest. If the mound is disturbed, hundreds of worker ants will stream out to the surface to defend the colony. Children at play are not likely to notice fire ant mounds and may be stung repeatedly before they can get away (Figure 12.6). Golfers and athletes are at risk when they inadvertently stand or fall on RIFA mounds, some of which are hard to see in the early stages. Such persons may be swarmed and stung many times. Each ant can sting repeatedly, gripping the flesh with its mouthparts and swinging its stinger around to inflict multiple wounds. The ant injects a venom that causes an intense burning itch. Within 24 hours, a pustule-like sore develops which may persist for a week or more. Scratching the pustules may lead to secondary infection and scarring. While painful, RIFA stings are not life-threatening for most persons. Ice packs, antibiotic ointments, or hydrocortisone creams are often used to treat local reactions. People who suffer chest pains, nausea, or other allergic reactions to RIFA stings should seek immediate medical attention.

Management. Because RIFA cannot be eradicated over wide areas, the goals of management are to eliminate the mounds in areas where people are at risk, and to reduce infestations to tolerable levels. Successful control requires a long-term commitment to periodic treatments. If you don't stick to the program, RIFA are very likely to reinfest the site as newly mated queens fly in from surrounding areas. There are two approaches to chemical control of RIFA. An insecticide can be applied to individual mounds, or it can be broadcast over a larger infested area containing many RIFA colonies. Often, the most effective approach is to use both tactics together. Regardless of the method followed, the objective is to kill the queens, because they are the only ants capable of laying eggs.

Mound Treatments. Mound-specific treatments require only a fraction of the insecticide needed for broadcast treatments. This approach is reasonable when only a few mounds are present, but it may be too labor-intensive for golf courses, large commercial sites, or other widely infested areas. Also, it's difficult to see mounds which are developing — for every one that you notice, there may be several more that are overlooked. Mound treatments are usually attempted when the objective is to quickly eliminate colonies from high-risk areas. Mounds can be treated with baits, contact insecticides, or injectable products.

Baits. Baits are the slowest-acting method for treating mounds, but are often the most effective. Another advantage is their low mammalian toxicity. Baits containing fenoxycarb, an insect growth regulator, are formulated on compressed corn grits coated with soybean oil as a feeding attractant. Worker ants carry the bait back to the mound and dispense it as food to the rest of the colony, including the queen. After eating the bait, the queen stops producing workers and any winged reproductives that hatch out will be sterile. Existing larvae that are fed the bait will not develop into adults. Without replacement workers to forage for food, the colony starves and gradually dies out. Similar baits containing avermectin work by halting egg production and sterilizing the queen. Ant activity in bait-treated mounds may continue for 1–2 months after treatment. A different, somewhat faster-acting bait product containing hydramethylnon kills RIFA by interfering with their ability to convert food into energy.

The active ingredients in ant baits are rapidly degraded by moisture, high temperature, and intense sunlight. Moisture also makes the bait's attractant oils less appealing to foraging workers. Baits should be applied when the ground and grass are dry and no rain is expected for 24

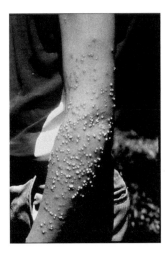

Figure 12.6. Arm of a child who received multiple stings after rolling on a fire ant nest (courtesy Texas Department of Agriculture).

hours, avoiding excessively hot periods. RIFA do not forage for food when soil temperatures are less than 68°F (20°C). Because foraging workers are most active in the early evening, baits are best applied in late afternoon, on warm, dry days. For individual mound treatments, sprinkle the bait around each undisturbed mound, but not on the mound itself.

Drenches. Some RIFA insecticides are formulated as liquid concentrates that are diluted with water and applied as a drench. To be effective, mound drenches must trickle down through the mound and contact most of the ants, including the queen and her brood. Pour the drench on top of the undisturbed mound and about 2 ft (30 cm) around the perimeter, using sufficient water to thoroughly wet the soil. Larger mounds may require up to 2 gal (7.6 L) of drench. Drenches can eliminate a colony when the nest is near the surface, but they often fail because they do not reach the queen(s). If the colony is not completely killed off, the surviving ants will move the queen and brood and construct a new mound near the parent colony. Several days after treatment, search the surrounding area for new mounds and treat them with the drench.

Granular products and dusts. Products containing contact insecticides formulated as granules can be sprinkled on and around individual mounds. When instructed, water the granules into the mound without disturbing the colony. Some dust products are also labeled for treating individual mounds. As with drenches, problems occur if the queen is not killed.

Injectable products. Products containing certain fast-acting insecticides are formulated as vapors or aerosols that can be injected into individual mounds. These products are often more expensive and time-consuming to use, but tend to give better results than mound drenches. Injectable products have the advantage of depositing the insecticide underground, out of reach of children.

Broadcast Applications. Areas of high public use can be protected from RIFA by spring and fall broadcast applications of ant baits (see above). With broadcast treatments, detection of individual nests is unnecessary because the foraging ants will encounter the bait and carry it back to the nest. Broadcast applications are the most cost-effective method for treating large areas with many mounds. This approach also eliminates mounds that may be too young to be visible above the turf. A fast-acting contact insecticide can be used to treat individual mounds that become established between bait applications. Golf superintendents should map their courses to locate heavily infested sites in high traffic areas, and target those areas. RIFA baits are applied at very low rates and require a properly calibrated spreader. The oily baits tend to cake up during treatment and cannot be used with some equipment. Note the guidelines for timing suggested above for single-mound bait treatments.

Products containing residual, contact insecticides are also labeled for broadcast applications against RIFA. These products may temporarily reduce activity of foraging workers, but they are rarely effective in eliminating established colonies because they fail to reach the queen.

Nonchemical Options. Individual colonies can sometimes be eliminated by pouring about 3 gal (11 L) of boiling water on the mound. A few "organic" insecticides (pyrethrins, diatomaceous earth) are available, but they are not very effective. Disturbing, knocking down, or digging up mounds does not eliminate the ants, and may result in multiple stings. Various home remedies, such as sprinkling grits, gasoline, etc. on the mound, are ineffective and may be downright dangerous. Various mechanical, electrical, or explosive products that have been marketed for RIFA control are ineffective.

TICKS
(Order Acari; Family Ixodidae)
(Plate 29)

Ticks are blood-sucking parasites of mammals, birds, reptiles, and amphibians. They are abundant in tall grass, weeds, and brushy or wooded areas where wild hosts such as rodents, rabbits, and deer occur. Ticks are seldom a problem in well-maintained turf. They may, however, be abundant in overgrown vegetation along edges of yards, golf roughs, and picnic areas. In addition to creating annoyance and discomfort, ticks can transmit several serious diseases. Common species include the American dog tick, *Dermacentor variabilis* (Say); the lone star tick, *Amblyomma americanum* (L.); the Rocky Mountain wood tick, *Dermacentor andersoni* Stiles, and the black-legged tick, *Ixodes scapularis* Say. Ticks are widely distributed across North America and worldwide. Many species are regional in occurrence.

Description, Life History, and Habits. Ticks are more closely related to mites and spiders than to insects. They have eight legs, and lack wings or antennae. The body is oval and flattened, usually reddish brown to brown, often with whitish, grayish, or silvery markings. The mouthparts project forward and are equipped with tiny barbs that help to anchor the feeding tick in the skin of its host. All of the important ticks encountered in turf environments belong to a group called hard ticks (family Ixodidae) which have a hard shield, or scutum, on the back. In males the scutum covers all of the abdomen, whereas females have the scutum extending only partway down the back.

The life cycle of ticks includes four stages: egg, larva, nymph, and adult (Figure 12.7). All stages except eggs are solely blood-feeding. Although some ticks feed on and complete their development on one or two hosts, most species have a three-host life cycle. Mating usually takes place on the body of the host. The female then drops to the ground and lays a mass of eggs which hatch into thousands of tiny, six-legged larvae. These so-called "seed ticks" crawl about and attach themselves to a rodent or other small animal. After feeding, the blood-engorged larvae drop off and transform to eight-legged nymphs. These nymphs seek another host, feed, and drop to the ground to transform to adults. Adults crawl up low vegetation and wait for another host to pass. Males search for females on the animal and mating occurs after both sexes have fed. The length of the life cycle (egg to egg) varies from 3 months to more than 1 year. Depending upon the species, ticks may overwinter as larvae, nymphs, or adults. Ticks are generally active from about the end of March until mid-September.

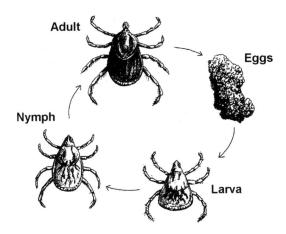

Figure 12.7. Life cycle of a tick (from Potter and Beavers, 1995).

Because they cannot jump or fly, ticks often climb up low vegetation to await a passing host. Initial contact with humans is usually made on the foot, ankle, or lower leg. The tick then crawls upward until constricted by skin folds or clothing. Ticks often attach behind the knee, waist, armpit, or base of the scalp.

Medical Importance. Tick bites can result in anxiety, irritation, and itching. The likelihood of infection is increased if the tick is removed incorrectly (see below). Ticks also transmit a number of diseases, including Lyme disease, Rocky Mountain spotted fever, tularemia, relapsing fever, and others. Fortunately, most tick encounters do not involve disease-carrying specimens. Some ticks can also cause tick paralysis, a neurotoxic reaction to the tick's saliva.

Lyme Disease is a potentially dangerous bacterial infection, transmitted mainly through the bite of a small tick called *Ixodes scapularis* (formerly called *Ixodes dammini*). *Adults of this tick are less than 1/8 in. (2 mm) long, about the size of a sesame seed.* They are less than half as large as common dog ticks (Figure 12.8). Adult females appear orange-brown with a black spot near the head. The nymphs are even smaller (Figure 12.8). About 20% of human Lyme disease is contracted from infected adult *Ixodes* ticks. It is the infected nymphs that transmit 80% of human cases of Lyme disease, probably because they easily escape detection.

Most of the reported cases of Lyme disease have been in the Northeast, upper Midwest, and California, but the incidence of the disease is spreading. The disease manifests itself in many ways and if left untreated may progress through several stages. It is hard to diagnose clinically because the early symptoms mimic the flu (fatigue, headache, fever, swollen glands, pain or stiffness in the neck, muscles, or joints). The most definitive early sign is a gradually expanding circular or oval-shaped red rash at the site of the bite. However, this rash only develops in about two-thirds of infected persons, and it may be overlooked. In its early stages, Lyme disease can be successfully treated with antibiotics, but therapy becomes more difficult as the disease progresses. Left untreated, Lyme disease may result in chronic arthritis, heart disease, and neurological disorders. Persons experiencing any of the above symptoms after being bitten by a small tick should consult a physician immediately.

Rocky Mountain Spotted Fever (RMSF) is a potentially fatal disease caused by a bacterium-like microorganism, *Rickettsia rickettsii*. The primary vector is the American dog tick, although lone star ticks can also transmit the pathogen. Symptoms of RMSF begin 2–12 days after tick attachment and include headache, chills, muscle aches, and a very high fever (104–106°F [40–41.1°C]). The most characteristic symptom of RMSF is a rash that appears on about the second to fifth day on wrists and ankles, later spreading to other regions of the

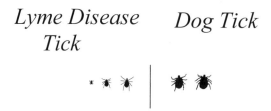

Lyme Disease Tick   *Dog Tick*

Figure 12.8. *Actual size, left to right, of nymph, adult male, and adult female* Ixodes *(Lyme Disease) ticks, and adult male and female* Dermacenter variabilis *(dog tick).*

body. In its early stages, RMSF can be successfully treated with antibiotics. Left untreated, the victim may die.

In the case of both Lyme disease and RMSF, the infected tick must remain attached for at least 12–24 hours for the disease pathogens to be transmitted. Periodic body checks for ticks greatly reduces one's chance of becoming infected.

Management. Human encounters with ticks can be reduced by trimming grass, weeds, and overgrown vegetation, thus creating a less favorable habitat for ticks and their wild hosts. Remove clutter and debris to eliminate hiding places for tick-bearing rodents. A good way to determine if ticks are present is to drag a 3 ft by 3 ft (1 m^2) white flannel or cotton sheet through suspected areas. Ticks will attach to the cloth and are easily spotted.

Various insecticides are labeled for tick control in outdoor vegetation. Pay particular attention to high grass and weeds along edges of lawns or golf roughs, beside footpaths, and around ornamental plantings or doghouses. A single application in the spring, when ticks are first detected, is often all that is required. The treatment may need to be repeated in summer. Thoroughly wet the ground and vegetation up to a height of 3 ft (1 m) with the insecticide. Treating the entire lawn is of little benefit because ticks avoid direct sunlight and normally will not infest close-mown turf.

Personal protection can be gained by wearing long pants tucked into boots or socks, shirts tucked in, and by periodically inspecting clothing and the body for ticks to remove them before they become attached. Tick repellents containing diethyl toluamide (DEET) or permethrin are effective when applied to shoes, cuffs, socks, and pant legs. *Permethrin-based repellents should not be applied to skin.* Avoid walking through overgrown areas during tick season, and walk in the center of mowed trails to avoid brushing up against vegetation.

Removing attached ticks. Ticks should be removed promptly to reduce the chance of disease transmission. *The best way to remove an attached tick is to grasp its head with tweezers as close to the skin as possible and pull slowly and steadily until the tick is dislodged* (Figure 12.9). Don't jerk or twist because the head and mouthparts may break off and remain embedded in the skin, increasing likelihood of infection. If tweezers are unavailable, grasp the tick with a piece of tissue, placing fingernails on or just behind the mouthparts. Be careful not to squeeze, crush, or puncture the tick, as this could force disease organisms into the wound. Avoid handling ticks because infected tick secretions on the hands can be transmitted via contact with eyes or mucus membranes. After removing the tick, wash the bite site and your hands with soap and water, apply antiseptic, and cover with an adhesive bandage. Itching can be relieved by applying topical ointments such as those containing hydrocortisone. Place the tick in a bottle, preferably with alcohol, and save it for at least 3 weeks. Should any disease-related symptoms appear, the identity of the tick may help the doctor with diagnosis.

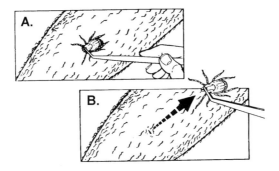

Figure 12.9. *To remove an attached tick, grasp it with tweezers close to the skin, and pull slowly and steadily until it is dislodged (from USAF Publ. USAFSAM-SR-89-2).*

Avoid "folk" remedies for tick removal. Coating a tick with nail polish or petroleum jelly will generally not cause it to let go. Touching it with a hot match may cause the tick to burst or to regurgitate infected fluids into the wound, increasing risk of disease transmission.

WASPS (PAPER WASPS, HORNETS, AND YELLOWJACKETS)
(Order Hymenoptera; Family Vespidae)
(Plate 29)

Wasps, hornets, and yellowjackets are a common nuisance and hazard on golf courses and in outdoor landscapes. Numerous people in the United States die each year from allergic response to their painful stings. These insects are far more dangerous and unpredictable than honeybees. Worker wasps foraging away from the nest are usually not aggressive, but the process of eliminating nests should be undertaken with great care and in a specific manner. "Folk" remedies such as dousing nests with gasoline or a garden hose will seldom work, and may result in multiple stings.

General Biology and Habits. Wasps, hornets, and yellowjackets are social insects that live in nests or colonies. Mated queens overwinter under bark or in other sheltered locations. They emerge in spring and begin constructing a small nest in which the first eggs are laid. The nest is made of paper-like material consisting of chewed wood fibers and salivary secretions. The queen forages for insect prey with which to feed her developing larvae. The first brood of wasps matures in about a month, emerging as nonreproductive females called workers. The workers assume all nest activities except egg-laying. Thereafter, the nest is enlarged and the colony grows rapidly, reaching maximum size by summer's end. Males and new queens are produced in the late summer or early fall. After mating, the young queens seek out overwintering sites and the main colony dies off.

Wasps, hornets, and yellowjackets are generally beneficial because they prey on other insects, including pest species. There is usually no need to control a hornet nest located high in a shade tree or a paper wasp nest on a remote eave of a house. If the nest does not pose an immediate hazard, the best option is usually to leave it alone. The colony will die off naturally once the weather turns cold, and the paper nest disintegrates over the winter months. Nests are not reused the following season. Control may be warranted, however, when the nest is located near areas of human activity.

Medical Importance. Wasps, especially hornets and yellowjackets, will usually sting if the nest is disturbed. Attacking wasps release a chemical "alarm pheromone" that causes nestmates to swarm to the defense. Unlike honeybees, the stinger is barbless, so that each wasp can inflict multiple stings. In most people, stings result in localized redness and swelling. Treatment for mild local reactions involves washing the wound to prevent infection, using an ice pack and/or oral pain relievers to reduce pain, and taking oral antihistamines. In the case of large, local reactions, elevation of the affected limb and rest may also be needed.

Some people are hypersensitive to wasp and bee venom, so that stings can be life-threatening. *People who have been stung and who experience a general allergic reaction (e.g., hives or rash) away from the site of the sting, dizziness, or difficulty breathing or swallowing should seek immediate medical attention.* Such persons may be at even greater danger should they receive additional stings, regardless of whether these occur weeks, months, or even years later. Sting-allergic persons should ask their doctor about prescribing an insect sting kit containing syringes with epinephrine. In the case of a sting, they can give themselves an injection that may well save their life. Allergic persons should also consider immunotherapy, a series of injections to increase their tolerance to insect venom.

Paper Wasps. Paper wasps typically build their umbrella-shaped nests under eaves and ledges of buildings. Adults are narrow-bodied, brownish with yellow or reddish markings, and about 5/8 to 3/4 in. (16–20 mm) long. Paper wasps are less aggressive than hornets or yellowjackets. They are fairly easy to eliminate with the wasp and hornet sprays sold at grocery or hardware stores. These products can often be sprayed from as far away as 20 ft (6 m). Although it is safest to treat all wasps at night, paper wasps can be controlled during the daytime *provided that you do not stand directly under the nest during treatment.* Most wasp sprays cause the insects to drop instantly. Standing directly under the nest increases the chance of being stung. Wait a few days after treatment to ensure that the wasps have been killed, then scrape or knock down the nest. This will prevent secondary problems with carpet beetles and other insects that feed on the remains of the nest and may later invade the building.

Persons trimming ornamental shrubs or hedges should be wary of paper wasp nests because the wasps are likely to attack if the nest is disturbed. Check for and eliminate any paper wasp nests before proceeding.

Hornets. Hornets are far more dangerous and difficult to eliminate than paper wasps. Baldfaced hornets, the most common species, are 5/8 to 3/4 in. (15–20 mm) long and black, with white markings on the face, thorax, and end of the abdomen. Hornet nests are made of gray, paper-like material and resemble a large bloated football. Nests are typically built in trees or shrubs, on overhangs, or attached to the outside of sheds or other structures. Hornet nests may contain thousands of wasps which become extremely aggressive when disturbed. The nests are often located out of reach. When deemed necessary, *their removal is best accomplished by a professional pest control firm.*

Hornet nests should be treated *only at night,* when most wasps are inside the nest and the colony is less active. Wear a full wasp suit, secured at the wrists, ankles, and collar. Hornet nests have a single opening, usually at the bottom of the nest, through which the wasps enter and exit. Apply an aerosol-type wasp and hornet spray, or a dust formulation (e.g., carbaryl or bendiocarb) directly into the nest opening. An extension pole that allows application of the dust or aerosol from the ground or from a considerable distance away gives added safety to the applicator. Only background lighting should be used (*do not shine a flashlight into the nest opening during treatment*). Be especially careful not to break the paper envelope of the nest, as this will cause the angry wasps to scatter in all directions. Following treatment, wait several days to ensure that all of the wasps are dead before removing the nest. If active hornets are still observed, the application may need to be repeated.

Yellowjackets. Yellowjackets are likely the most dangerous stinging insects in the United States. The common name is based on their distinctive black and yellow color pattern. Like hornets, yellowjackets become extremely aggressive when their nest is disturbed. Nests are often located underground in old rodent burrows or beneath rocks or landscape timbers. Yellowjackets also build nests in rock walls, or in walls, attics, crawlspaces, garages, sheds, or other structures. If the nest can be located, the colony can usually be eliminated by carefully applying an aerosol wasp spray into the nest opening. Dust formulations (e.g., carbaryl, bendiocarb) are also effective, provided a hand duster or similar type of applicator is used to puff the insecticide into the nest opening. A dry, empty detergent bottle filled no more than halfway with dust, and shaken before dispensing, works well. A few pebbles can be added to the bottom of the container to prevent caking.

Elimination of colonies should be done only at night, when most of the yellowjackets are in the nest and less active. Locate the nest opening during daylight so you will know where to direct the treatment after dark. As with hornets, a full protective wasp suit should be worn. Approach the nest carefully, using indirect light. Do not shine your flashlight into the nest opening, as this will startle the wasps. If possible, place the light on the ground, to one side, rather than holding it, because the angry wasps tend to fly toward light. A long string attached to the handle is helpful for recovering the flashlight when the job is done. Olympic sprinting skills may be called for if some wasps leave the nest. It is often best to call an experienced pest control operator, especially when access to the nest is difficult.

The yellowjackets' tendency to scavenge for food causes them to become pests around outdoor food concessions, picnic sites, parks, and similar areas. Contact with humans peaks in late summer and fall, when the colonies are nearing maturity and thousands of workers are out foraging for food for the developing queens. At that time, feeding preferences shift in favor of sugary foods which include fruits (e.g., sliced watermelon), beer, soft drinks and other sweets. Golf superintendents and grounds managers can take steps to reduce hazards of people being stung:

Sanitation and Avoidance. The best way reduce problems with foraging yellowjackets is to reduce their access to attractive food sources. Trash cans should be equipped with a tight-fitting (preferably self-closing) lid, fitted with a plastic liner, and emptied and cleaned frequently. Dumpsters and trash cans should be located away from picnic and concession areas to the extent that it is practical. Clean up spills and leftovers promptly. Maintaining good sanitation earlier in the summer will make areas less attractive to foraging yellowjackets later on. This tactic is especially useful for parks and recreation areas.

People eating outdoors should keep food and beverage containers covered. Yellowjackets foraging away from the nest are usually not aggressive and will seldom sting unless provoked. People should resist the urge to swat at the wasps — and be especially careful when drinking from beverage cans that may contain a foraging worker wasp. Diet drinks seem to be less attractive to wasps than drinks with sugar.

Repellents and Traps. A dilute solution of ammonia (6 oz of ammonia per gal of water (50 mL per L) sprayed in and around trash cans, and sponged onto outdoor tables and food preparation surfaces, may help to repel yellowjackets from these areas. Use household ammonia, not bleach. Traps are available that will catch large numbers of yellowjackets when properly baited and positioned. Although generally of questionable benefit, traps placed around the perimeter of an area may help to reduce numbers of foraging workers when used in combination with other approaches. Braunschweiger liverwurst spread, jelly, and fruit juice are effective attractants.

SELECTED REFERENCES

Apperson, C.S., L. Garcia, and M. Waldvogel. 1993. Control of the red imported fire ant. *N. Carolina Coop. Ext. Bull.* AG-486.

Bennett, G.W., J.M. Owens, and R.M. Corrigan. 1988. *Truman's scientific guide to pest control operations.* Edgell Communications, Duluth, MN.

Ebeling, W. 1978. *Urban entomology.* Division of Agricultural Science, Univ. Calif., Berkeley, CA.

Goddard, J. 1993. *Physician's guide to arthropods of medical importance*. CRC Press, Inc., Boca Raton, FL.

Hedges, S.A. 1992. *Field guide for the management of structure-infesting ants*. Franzak & Foster, Cleveland, OH.

James, M.T. and R.F. Harwood. 1969. *Herm's medical entomology*. Macmillan, New York, NY.

Mallis, A. 1990. *Handbook of pest control*. Franzak & Foster, Cleveland, OH.

Potter, M.F. and G. Mark Beavers. 1995. Public health pest management. *Univ. Kentucky Coop. Ext. Bull.* ENT-63.

Sparks, B. 1993. Controlling fire ants in urban areas. *Univ. Georgia Coop. Ext. Bull.* 1068.

13

NUISANCE PESTS AND INNOCUOUS INVERTEBRATES

Besides the familiar pest species, turf is inhabited by a multitude of other small creatures. Even though they don't damage the grass, these innocuous invertebrates may attract attention or cause concern. Sometimes they are mistaken for pests and treated unnecessarily. Ants are a nuisance when they produce small mounds on putting greens. Other turf inhabitants may become an annoyance when they accidentally invade homes. This chapter discusses some of the common innocuous and nuisance arthropods encountered in turfgrass environments.

ANTS — NUISANCE SPECIES
(Order Hymenoptera; Family Formicidae)
(Plate 28)

Importance and Nature of Injury. In addition to the more troublesome fire ants and harvester ants (Chapter 12), several other kinds of ants can be a nuisance when they nest in turfgrass areas. These species construct small, volcano-shaped mounds of granulated soil around the openings of their underground nests. Ant mounds are especially troublesome on golf greens, approaches, and fairways, where maintaining a smooth, uniform surface is essential. The mounds can smother the surrounding short grass, especially after being compacted by tires of golf carts or mowing equipment. Grass may become weak and thin as the soil around the roots dries out from the effects of the ants' digging and burrowing. Some ants forage on grass seeds and can reduce the rate of establishment of newly seeded grasses. Most ants, however, are beneficial — they prey upon eggs and young larvae of sod webworms, white grubs, and other pests.

Distribution. Ants are found practically everywhere, although the predominant species vary from region to region. Ants may nest near sidewalks, foundations, and driveways, as well as out in the open turf. They can be a nuisance when the workers forage around homes or picnic areas.

Distinguishing Characteristics. Adult ants have a constricted waist, elbowed antennae, and may be winged or wingless. They may be black, brown, red, or light tan. Common species range in length from less than 1/16 to 3/8 in. (1–10 mm). Winged ants have two pairs of wings.

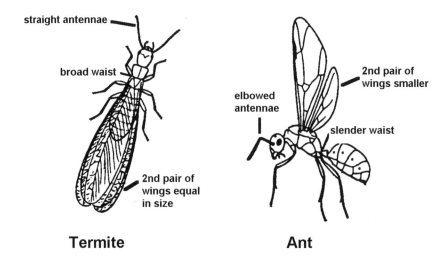

straight antennae

broad waist

2nd pair of
wings equal
in size

Termite

elbowed
antennae

2nd pair of
wings smaller

slender waist

Ant

Figure 13.1. How to distinguish a winged ant from a termite (from University of Kentucky Cooperative Extension Service).

Ant eggs are tiny, white or cream colored, and vary in shape depending on species. Larvae are soft, whitish, and legless, with a light colored head. The larvae are small enough to be carried by the worker ants. Ant pupae are small and translucent; the structures of the adult ant (legs, antennae, etc.) are visible but closely appressed to the body. Pupae of some species are enclosed in a tough, papery, yellow to tan cocoon. The pupae are often mistaken for eggs when the nest is dug up.

When they swarm, winged ants may be mistaken for reproductive termites, causing homeowners concern in homeowners. Ants and termites are easy to tell apart (Figure 13.1). The body of a winged termite is black, whereas ants may be black, brown, reddish, or tan. Termites have a broad "waist," whereas ants have a narrow constriction between the thorax and abdomen. Ants have elbowed antennae; those of termites are straight, like a string of beads. The front and back wings of termites are of equal size and shape. In ants, the front wings are much larger and longer than the hind wings.

Life History and Habits. Ants live in colonies consisting of hundreds or thousands of individuals. Ant colonies contain several kinds of ants. There are two types of reproductives — winged males, and the queen. The queen ant lays all of the eggs, from which the colony gets its new members. Most species of ants have only one queen, but some may have multiple queens in the nest at the same time. The most abundant ants, by far, are workers — wingless, sterile females that do all of the work in the colony. Worker ants forage for food, enlarge the nest, tend to the queen and the young, and defend the colony from enemies.

Each colony is started by a fertile, winged female (i.e., a young queen). Most ant species initiate new colonies by a process called swarming. A mature ant colony will produce winged reproductives which fly out of the colony and mate. Males die soon after mating, and the females disperse to start a new colony. Upon finding a suitable nesting site, the young queen sheds her wings, excavates a small underground burrow, and lays a few eggs. She feeds and cares for the first brood of larvae, which develop into workers. The workers then take over the routine maintenance, while the queen concentrates on egg-laying. Ant nests most often occur in sunny locations with well-drained soils. Colonies are usually initiated in the spring, and are built up during the warm months when food is abundant. The underground tunnels and galleries of a mature nest may extend for 3 ft (1 m) or more beneath the surface. A colony may persist for two or more years before producing swarmers. Depending upon the species, swarming may occur from early spring until early fall. In fall-swarming species, the queen may overwinter in a sheltered spot and start her new colony the following spring.

Most turf-infesting ants scavenge or prey upon the eggs, nymphs, or small larvae of other insects. Ants can be very important in suppressing pest insects. Some ant species feed on seeds, whereas others eat the sugary honeydew excreted by aphids, scales, and mealybugs.

Management. Harvester ants and red imported fire ants are dangerous pests that often require control (see Chapter 12). Because most other ants are beneficial predators, controlling them in turf is not recommended unless their nests occur on golf putting greens or other sensitive sites. The key to eliminating an ant colony is to kill the queen or queens. If the queen and a small number of workers are left alive, the colony may survive the treatment. In most cases, ant control requires one or more applications of a liquid or granular insecticide. When only a few mounds are present, apply the insecticide directly to the colony openings, and to the area immediately around the mounds. If colonies are numerous, broadcast treatments over the infested area may be more practical. Liquid applications should be made in sufficient spray volume to thoroughly wet the soil surface. Granular treatments should be irrigated to activate the insecticide and move it into the soil. Early spring treatments, when ants are first noticed on greens and tees, seem to work the best. This may be due to the weakened condition of colonies following overwintering.

CENTIPEDES
(Class Chilopoda)
(Plate 30)

Importance. Centipedes are mostly beneficial because they prey upon insects and other small arthropods. They usually live outdoors under leaves, stones, boards, mulch, or other moist places. When such prime haunts occur close to a home's foundation, centipedes occasionally may wander indoors and cause alarm. Smaller centipedes found in the northern states are harmless to people, but a few of the large, southern species can inflict a painful bite if handled. Fortunately, these large species are unlikely to enter houses.

Distribution. Various species are common throughout the world.

Distinguishing Characteristics. Centipedes are fast-moving, elongate, flattened animals with long antennae and 15 or more pairs of long legs. They are usually brownish and range in length from 1–6 in. (2.5–15 cm). Each body segment bears one pair of legs. The last two pairs are directed backward and often differ in shape from the other legs. The "bites" of centipedes are not inflicted by their mouthparts, but by specially modified front legs which function like jaws and contain venom glands. By comparison, millipedes are slower-moving, with short antennae. Millipedes have a more cylindrical body, with two pairs of short legs on most body segments (Figure 13.2).

Life History and Habits. Most centipedes overwinter as adults in sheltered sites. Females lay eggs in moist soil during spring and summer. The eggs are usually sticky and become covered with soil. Like the adults, young centipedes prey upon insects and other small arthropods.

Management. Centipedes do not cause any damage indoors, but many people are afraid of these fast-moving creatures and want them controlled. Occasional centipedes found indoors can be squashed, vacuumed, or swept up. Chronic problems with centipedes entering buildings are best managed by reducing the types of habitats that encourage their presence. This includes

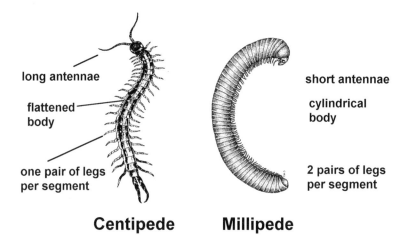

long antennae

flattened body

one pair of legs per segment

short antennae

cylindrical body

2 pairs of legs per segment

Centipede   **Millipede**

Figure 13.2. Distinguishing characteristics of centipedes versus millipedes (from USDA).

removal of accumulated leaves, compost, rocks, boards, mulch and other hiding places close to the foundation. Caulking cracks, installing door sweeps and thresholds on outside doors, and other exclusion techniques will keep centipedes from entering homes. These tactics alone are often sufficient to resolve the situation. Where problems persist, various residual insecticides are registered for outdoor applications. Treat thoroughly around the foundation, including the mulch in flower and shrub beds close to the structure.

CRAYFISH
(Class Crustacea; Order Decapoda)
(Plate 30)

Importance and Nature of Injury. Crayfish, also called crawfish, normally live in fresh water. They occasionally invade wet, poorly drained turfgrass areas, especially near waterways. They build up muddy, knobby, hollow "chimneys" of mud with a hole about 1 in. (2.5 cm) in diameter. The chimneys are unsightly and can interfere with mowing.

Distribution. There are about 100 species of crayfish in North America; some species are common in most areas.

Distinguishing Characteristics. Crayfish resemble miniature lobsters. They have five pairs of legs, the first of which usually bears large claws. There are two pairs of antennae and two distinct body regions.

Life History and Habits. Most crayfish are strictly aquatic but a few live in nonpermanent water or semiaquatic situations. They burrow into the soil to get to water when free water is not available on the surface. Some crayfish burrow into the soil even when surface water is available. Crayfish are most often found in heavy, low-lying soil, especially near ponds and streams.

Management. No pesticides are registered for crayfish control, and attempting to control them with chemicals may contaminate nearby waterways. Drying out the surface soil by contouring surface drainage may discourage their burrowing.

EARTHWORMS
(Phylum Annelida; Class Oligochaeta: Family Lumbricidae)

Importance and Nature of Injury. Earthworms are beneficial in most situations because of their role in enriching the soil, alleviating soil compaction, and decomposing thatch (see Chapter 14). They can be a nuisance, however, on sites where maintaining a smooth, uniform playing surface is essential. Earthworms deposit soil-rich fecal matter, or castings, at the soil surface. These mar the surface of putting greens or tees, and dull mower blades. On clay soils, the piles of castings may harden during dry weather or in winter, causing the turf to feel lumpy or crunchy underfoot.

Distribution, Distinguishing Characteristics, and Life History. (See Earthworms — Chapter 14.)

Management. Some insecticides and fungicides are highly toxic to earthworms (see Chapter 7), but none is labeled for earthworm control. Mounds of castings on golf greens, tees, or other closely cut turf can be raked down, rolled down, or picked up during mowing. Lumpy lawns can be smoothed with a heavy lawn roller.

EARWIGS
(Order Dermaptera)
(Plate 30)

Importance. Earwigs are mostly beneficial because they feed on pest insects, as well as dead and decaying plant material. One species, *Labidura riparia* Pallas, preys upon southern chinch bugs in the Gulf states. Although some earwigs will occasionally gnaw on living plants, they do not damage turf. They can be a nuisance, however, when they build up in mulch and other debris and then find their way into homes. Their forceps-like tails are used for defense; larger ones can inflict a sharp pinch. The forceps are not poisonous, but some species emit a foul odor if handled or squashed. The name "earwig" comes from the old myth that they will enter sleeping people's ears and burrow into their brain. In reality, the only harm done by earwigs around homes is the annoyance caused when they wander indoors.

Distribution and Species. The European earwig, *Forficula auricularia* L., is an introduced species that has become widespread in the United States. The ring-legged earwig, *Euborellia annulipes* (Lucas) is also widely distributed, whereas the striped earwig, *L. riparia*, is especially abundant in the southern states.

Distinguishing Characteristics. Earwigs are elongate, slender, somewhat flattened insects that range from about 5/8 to 1 in. (16–25 mm) long. They are easily recognized by the pair of large pincers, resembling forceps, at the tip of the abdomen. Forceps of females are almost straight; those of males are curved. Adults are mostly brown to black, but may be marked with yellow or orange. Adults may be winged or wingless. The front wings, when present, are short and leathery, with the hind wings folded up underneath. Earwigs are fast runners, but they rarely fly. Nymphs resemble the adults, but are smaller, with thinner forceps and without wings.

Life History and Habits. Earwigs are mainly active at night. During the day they hide in cracks and crevices, or under boards, stones, mulch, or other debris. All life stages overwinter in the southern and central states. They seek shelter as cold weather approaches, sometimes invading greenhouses or sheds, or entering under doors or along windowsills of homes. The oval, white eggs are laid in clusters in brood chambers in the ground. The mother guards her eggs, protecting them from predators. Eggs deposited in the fall usually overwinter; those laid during the warm months hatch in a few weeks. Young nymphs leave the nest after a few days. They feed and develop through five instars, maturing in about 6–7 weeks during summer, but requiring longer during cold weather. Each female may lay several clutches of eggs per year. Because the broods overlap, all life stages are present at a given time.

Management. Earwigs don't need to be controlled unless they are entering homes and causing annoyance. Habitat removal and exclusion tactics described for managing millipedes will work for earwigs. With high infestations, an insecticide can be applied outdoors around the foundation, to flower beds, around window wells and other openings, and to turf within 6 ft (2 m) of the building.

MILLIPEDES
(Class Diplopoda)
(Plate 30)

Importance. Millipedes normally live outdoors in moist places, such as under decaying leaves, mulch, or in thick thatch of lawns. They feed on decaying plant material. They occasionally damage young seedlings by gnawing on the fine roots, but damage to turf or outdoor ornamentals is negligible. Indeed, millipedes are mostly beneficial by helping to break down and recycle plant debris. In dry weather, millipedes will migrate out of plant litter as the leaves or mulch dry out. They may enter basements or garages at such times. Migration into buildings may also occur during cool, wet periods in the spring and fall. Millipedes do not bite, nor do they damage food supplies or household furnishings. Still, many people consider them a nuisance, and won't tolerate them indoors.

Distribution. Various species of millipedes are found throughout the world.

Distinguishing Characteristics. Millipedes, or "1000-leggers," are elongate, gray or brownish, worm-like animals. Most species found in yards and gardens are less than 1-1/4 in. (32 mm) long. The body is cylindrical or slightly flattened, with a distinct head bearing a pair of short antennae. Most millipedes have 30 or more pairs of legs; most body segments bear two pairs each. This feature distinguishes millipedes from centipedes, which have only one pair of legs per body segment (Figure 13.2). Millipedes are slow-moving and typically curl up when disturbed. When walking, the many legs move with a wavelike motion. Newly hatched millipedes have only three pairs of legs. Additional segments and legs are added with each molt.

Life History and Habits. Millipedes reproduce by laying clusters of 20–100 smooth, round, sticky eggs in moist soil. Eggs hatch in 1–3 weeks, and the young take about 6 months to mature, molting about seven times in the process. Adults may live for several years. The various species overwinter as either immatures or adults.

Management. Millipede invasions of homes are usually seasonal and will typically subside in a week or two. Millipedes don't reproduce or survive for very long inside homes, so the problem usually resolves itself without intervention. Occasional millipedes in basements or garages can simply be squashed, vacuumed, or swept up and discarded outside. Because they feed and reproduce in decaying organic matter, clearing away plant mulch, accumulated leaves, and other debris from the foundation will help to reduce invasions. Cracks in foundation walls or around doorways and window wells can be repaired or caulked to discourage entry. Install door sweeps and thresholds on basement and garage doors. Millipedes are less troublesome in properly ventilated basements and crawl spaces than in damper areas. If outdoor cleanup doesn't resolve the problem, you can try a residual insecticide. When spraying, treat a 6–15 ft (2–5 m) wide barrier around the foundation. Treat thoroughly so the insecticide reaches the soil surface. It may also be necessary to treat the mulch in flower and shrub beds.

PERIODICAL CICADA
(Order Homoptera; Family Cicadidae)
(Plate 30)

Importance and Nature of Injury. Cicadas are large, robust, sucking insects that are most evident from the shrill mating calls of males within trees. The common dog-day cicadas (*Tibicen* spp.) are an annoyance with their loud singing in summer, but they are seldom abundant enough to warrant control. In contrast, nymphs of periodical cicadas (*Magicicada* spp.) cause sporadic damage to turf when enormous numbers emerge simultaneously from the ground beneath trees. Fortunately, these mass emergences usually occur only once every 13 or 17 years in a given area. As the nymphs burrow out of the soil to transform to adults, they leave behind numerous emergence holes about 1/2 in. (13 mm) in diameter, or mud "chimneys" similar to those produced by crayfish in water-soaked ground. These mud tubes may extend as much as 3 in. (7.5 cm) above the soil surface. The sudden appearance of hundreds of holes or mud chimneys under a tree may be quite striking.

Distribution. Periodical cicadas occur throughout most of the eastern United States. There are two forms — the 13-year and the 17-year. Each form has a number of different broods; each brood emerges as a group at a particular location on a predictable, prolonged cycle. Although particular broods appear only once every 13 or 17 years, a brood appears somewhere in the eastern United States every summer. Adding to the confusion is the fact that some areas have more than one brood.

Distinguishing Characteristics. Periodical cicadas have a fat, wedge-shaped, nearly black body with clear wings. They are about 1-1/2 in. (3.8 cm) long, including the wings. The eyes are red, and the legs and wing veins are distinctly orange. The more familiar, less damaging, dog-day cicada is somewhat larger, 2 to 2-1/2 in. (5–6.4 cm) long from snout to wing tips, with green eyes and wing veins.

Life History and Habits. The life cycle of a periodical cicada is prolonged but simple. Nymphs live underground, feeding on sap from tree roots with their piercing-sucking mouthparts. They usually cause little harm. In years when a brood matures, swarms of adults will exit from the ground in May or early June. Nymphs burrow out of the soil and crawl up tree trunks, posts, or other upright objects. The shell-like, nymphal skin splits down the back, and the adult cicada emerges. These empty, brown skins remain attached to bark or are left lying about. The adult remains near the shed skin for several hours until its wings have expanded and hardened. Males then congregate in trees where they "sing" to attract females. The shrill mating call is produced by vibrating membranes on the underside of the abdoment. After mating, females disperse to lay eggs. Using their sword-like ovipositor, they slit the bark of twigs on hardwood or fruit trees and insert a row of eggs into the wound. Damaged twigs often wilt and die, or are broken off by winds. The eggs hatch in 6–8 weeks and the young nymphs drop to the ground and burrow down to the tree roots, where they remain for the next 13 or 17 years.

Management. It is impractical to control cicada nymphs because they live at least 12 in. (30 cm) underground. Nothing can be done to prevent the exit holes or mud chimneys once the cicadas begin to emerge. Take comfort in the fact that damage from periodical cicadas is unlikely to occur at the same site for another 13 or 17 years. Small trees can be sprayed or covered with netting during peak emergence periods to prevent damage to the twigs.

SHORT-TAILED CRICKET
Anurogryllus muticus (DeGeer)
(Order Orthoptera; Family Gryllidae)
(Plate 30)

Importance and Nature of Injury. This cricket is a minor pest only because it occasionally nests in turfgrass soils. As the cricket excavates its burrow, mounds of soil pellets are thrown out around the entrance. Mounds of older burrows may be nearly 2 in. (5 cm) high and 2-3/4 in. (7 cm) across. Usually there is a flurry of digging and mound-making during warm periods following a rain or prolonged cold weather.

Distribution. In the United States, short-tailed crickets occur mainly along the Atlantic Coast from New Jersey to Florida and west to Louisiana and southeastern Texas.

Distinguishing Characteristics. The adults resemble common field crickets, but with shorter wings and light brown coloration. Females lack the long ovipositor that is typical of other crickets. Adults range in length from 9/16 to 2/3 in. (14–17 mm). Eggs are shiny, oblong, and whitish, averaging about 1/10 in. (2.5 mm) long. The nymphs are light brown; older ones have well-developed wing pads.

Life History and Habits. These crickets overwinter as large nymphs, maturing in the spring. Adults begin to appear in April. After mating, each male or female excavates an individual, multichambered burrow. Most burrows are less than 12 in. (30 cm) deep, but in sandy soils they may extend down to 20 in. (50 cm). The cricket hides in its burrow by day, coming to the surface at night to feed. Food reserves are stored within the burrow. The female lays eggs and rears her young nymphs within the burrow. After about a month, the young disperse to construct their own burrows. Adult females live for 8–10 weeks. Not all crickets are active at the same time. New burrows may continue to appear for several weeks. The crickets feed on forbs, grasses, pine seedlings, or seeds of these plants. Direct feeding damage to turfgrasses is negligible.

Management. This pest is rarely abundant enough to warrant treatment. If necessary, the mounds can be raked down. Various surface insecticides are labeled for controlling crickets in turf.

SLUGS AND SNAILS
(Phyllum Mollusca; Class Gastropoda)
(Plate 30)

Importance. Slugs and snails are mainly plant-feeders, preferring broad-leaved weeds such as clovers and ground ivy, flowers, bedding plants, and vegetables. They do not damage turfgrasses. Some people complain because they leave glistening, slimy mucus trails on grass blades, sidewalks, and walls as they move about at night. They are unpleasant to step on with bare feet. Slugs are attracted to beer, and may crawl into cups, cans or bottles of beer set down at picnics. At times, they become a nuisance by wandering into damp basements or crawl spaces.

Distribution and Species. Slugs and snails occur worldwide in temperate and tropical regions. Common species include the gray garden slug, *Agriolimax reticulatus* (Muller); spotted garden slug, *Limax maximus* L.; tawny garden slug, *L. flavus* L.; and brown garden slug, *Helix aspersa* Muller.

Distinguishing Characteristics. Slugs and snails are molluscs, and so are more closely related to clams and octopuses than insects. Slugs are soft-bodied, gray, brown, or mottled, slimy creatures with stalked eyes and two small feelers. Some large species may grow to 3 in. (8 cm), or longer. They do not have a shell. Snails are similar, but are easily recognized by their prominent shell. Common land species are usually brown or gray and 1 to 1-1/2 in. (2.5–4 cm) long. The giant African snail, found in Florida, California, and Hawaii, has a shell that may be 5 in. (12.5 cm) long. Both slugs and snails creep on a flat "foot" that secretes a mucus trail. Young slugs and snails resemble the adults, only smaller.

Life History and Habits. Adult slugs and snails may lay eggs any time during the growing season. Clusters of 20–30 or more eggs are laid in moist, sheltered spots such as soil crevices, or under boards, stones, or leaf litter. Eggs hatch in a few weeks, depending on temperature and moisture, and the young slugs feed on decaying organic matter as well as succulent plant tissues. They grow slowly, taking as long as a year to mature. Slug damage on foliage usually appears between the veins, and on leaf margins. They use their rasp-like mouthparts to scrape away plant tissues and suck up the residue. Small ones just rasp streaks in the surface, but larger ones rasp streaks or holes, or sometimes eat whole leaves or petals. A silvery slime trail is left behind wherever they crawl. Slugs are most active at night, especially during warm, humid weather. During the day they usually seek moist hiding places under debris, mulch, or in the soil.

Management. Slug infestations can be reduced by eliminating their breeding and hiding places. Remove rotting boards, empty flowerpots, dead leaves, and other plant debris that provides dark, moist shelter. Clean up old plant residues from flower beds, and trim high grass and weeds near infested sites. Mulched areas that stay moist are ideal haunts for slugs. Try to create landscaped areas which allow the surface to dry out following watering or rains. Slugs can be excluded from basements, crawl spaces, and garages by the same tactics described for millipedes. Bait formulations containing either metaldehyde or methiocarb (Mesurol®) are effective for controlling slugs. Apply the baits to infested areas (under shrubs, in plant beds, outside crawl spaces, etc.) according to label instructions. Baits work best on warm, humid nights without rain. Baits can be placed under boards set out as traps. A single treatment often provides satisfactory control in plant beds.

SOWBUGS AND PILLBUGS
(Class Crustacea; Order Isopoda)
(Plate 30)

Importance. Sowbugs and pillbugs feed on decaying plant material and are found under mulch, accumulated leaf litter, boards, stones, or other debris on damp ground. They often get into damp basements and crawl spaces, but they do no harm. They do not bite. Although mainly scavengers, they may seek refuge under and in potted plants, where they can cause minor damage to roots. They do not injure lawns; in fact, they are beneficial because they help to break down and recycle plant debris. The only problem with sowbugs is the unfounded alarm they cause when they enter homes.

Distribution. Sowbugs and pillbugs are found worldwide in moist soils.

Distinguishing Characteristics. Sowbugs and pillbugs are crustaceans, so they are more closely related to crabs and crayfish than to insects. They are oval-shaped, about 3/8 to 1/2 in. (10–12.5 mm) long, and solid or mottled gray. They have a pair of conspicuous antennae and seven pairs of legs. Sowbugs (*Porcellio* spp.) are flattened, have a pair of tail-like structures at the tip of the abdomen, and are incapable coiling up. Pillbugs (*Armadillidum* spp.) are similar-looking, but lack the tail-like structures and curl into a protective ball or "pill" when disturbed. Some people call them "roly-polies."

Life History and Habits. Females carry their small, white eggs in a brood pouch for several weeks until they hatch. The immatures remain in the pouch for 1–2 months, apparently obtaining food from their mother. Each brood consists of about 50 young. After emerging from the pouch, immature sowbugs and pillbugs molt several times, becoming full-sized in a few months to a year. Many of the young perish after leaving the pouch, mostly due to desiccation. Adults, however, can live for two or more years under ideal conditions. There are one to three broods per year, depending on species and temperatures. Pillbugs and sowbugs spend the day hiding and feeding under cover. During rainy periods, however, they are often seen crawling about or climbing walls, and may wander into homes. They rarely survive for more than a few days indoors unless the conditions are quite damp.

Management. Problems with sowbugs and pillbugs migrating indoors usually means that a large population has built up in plant debris or mulch surrounding the foundation. These occasional invaders can be managed in the same manner as millipedes (see Millipedes — Management).

SELECTED REFERENCES

Bennett, G.W., J.M. Owens, and R.M. Corrigan. 1988. *Truman's scientific guide to pest control operations.* Edgell Communications, Duluth, MN.

Davidson, R.H. and W.F. Lyon. 1979. *Insect pests of farm, garden, and orchard* (7th ed.). John Wiley & Sons, New York, NY.

Ebeling, W. 1978. *Urban entomology.* Division of Agricultural Science, Univ. Calif., Berkeley, CA.

Mallis, A. 1990. *Handbook of pest control.* Franzak & Foster, Cleveland, OH.

Shetlar, D.J. 1995. Turfgrass insect and mite management, pp. 171–343. *In*: Watschke, T.L., P.H. Dernoeden, and D.J. Shetlar. *Managing turfgrass pests.* Lewis Publishers, Boca Raton, FL.

14

BENEFICIAL INVERTEBRATES: PREDATORS, PARASITES, AND THATCH BUSTERS

This chapter concerns the role of natural enemies and earthworms in the turfgrass environment. Conservation of these naturally occurring beneficial species is important for maintaining healthy lawn and golf course turfs, so it is important to recognize them. Some common, nonpest arthropods often encountered in turfgrass also are covered in this section.

In addition to the familiar pests, such as grubs and webworms, lawns and golf courses are inhabited by a multitude of other insects and related small creatures. Some of these are natural enemies of pests, preying upon or parasitizing the plant-feeders. Others, especially earthworms, help to aerate and enrich the soil, alleviate soil compaction, and break down thatch. Springtails and oribatid mites feed mainly on organic matter or fungi and are relatively innocuous from our perspective.

All of these plant-feeding, predatory or parasitic, and soil-inhabiting invertebrates are part of a complex food web. They interact with the living grass, thatch, and soil, and contribute to the stability of the turfgrass system. Have you noticed that pest outbreaks and excessive thatch accumulation rarely occur in low-maintenance turf? This implies that such turfgrass is a relatively stable habitat. Pests are held in check by natural enemies, and production of thatch is balanced by decomposition. Unfortunately, these checks and balances are sometimes upset when large areas of one or a few grass species are maintained under intensive management.

Invertebrates that are mostly beneficial or innocuous may be viewed as pests in some situations (see Chapter 13). Earthworms cause problems when they leave mounds or castings on golf putting greens. Common turf-inhabiting spiders are beneficial predators, but many people fear them because they mistakenly believe them to be poisonous species. Millipedes and earwigs are harmless to humans, but they often cause concern when they wander into basements. Professional turf managers need to be able to distinguish between the true pests and the innocuous or beneficial species. Knowing a bit about beneficial and nonpest species will help you to answer clients' questions, and to educate them to be more tolerant of these harmless turf inhabitants.

IMPORTANCE OF NATURAL ENEMIES

Reproductive powers of insects can be enormous. Greenbugs, for example, can produce 60 young per female. In the Midwest, there may be 15 or more generations per year. Starting with one female under these conditions, and assuming that all of her offspring survive and reproduce, you'd have to deal with 470,184,980,000,000,000,000,000,000 aphids, the equivalent of 77 quadrillion tons of aphids, by the end of one year! Most other insects don't reproduce quite as quickly as greenbugs, but sod webworms and armyworms can lay hundreds of eggs. Japanese beetles and other scarabs can each leave 60 or more offspring. Why, then, are lawns and golf courses not uniformly overwhelmed by pest insects?

The fact that outbreaks of turfgrass insects are uncommon in golf roughs and low-maintenance lawns suggests that most pests are normally are held in check by natural factors. Environmental stresses such as drought take a heavy toll on some pests, as do diseases caused by bacteria, fungi, and other microbes. But natural enemies can also play an important role in suppressing populations of pest insects in turf. Evidence for this comes from numerous accounts of pest outbreaks on sites where natural enemies were inadvertently eliminated by insecticides. Such a phenomenon is called a **pest resurgence** if the outbreak pest was targeted with the original treatment, or a **secondary pest outbreak** if another pest was the original target. Similar problems are common in orchards and other agricultural systems that receive intense insecticide use.

Insect natural enemies are of two general sorts: predators and parasitoids. A **predator** feeds on smaller and weaker insects, usually using one or more for a single meal. It typically subdues and consumes its prey immediately, and feeds on a number of victims during its lifetime. A **parasitoid** is an insect that parasitizes other insects. Parasitoids feed in a more insidious manner (Figure 14.1). The adult female lays one or more eggs on, or in, the host insect. When the egg hatches, the larval parasitoid slowly consumes the host, feeding either externally or internally (like the juvenile monster in the movie *Alien*). The host typically remains alive, albeit barely, until the parasitoid has almost completed its development, but it dies soon thereafter. The parasitoid emerges from the host's body and spins a silken cocoon before pupating, or else it pupates inside the remains of the host. Then, the adult parasitoids emerge and seek new hosts to resume the cycle.

Practically every turfgrass pest is attacked by various predators and parasitoids. Probably no tactic that we employ to manage insect pests is more important than the control exerted by these natural enemies, yet the public has little awareness of these benefits. *Professional turf managers should try to conserve these natural buffers whenever possible. The best way to accomplish this is to cut back on use of broad-spectrum insecticides unless the treatment is truly needed.*

ANTS
(Order Hymenoptera; Family Formicidae)
(Plate 28)

Importance and Beneficial Aspects. Ants are among the most abundant insects in turf. A few species are serious pests because of their mound-building activities, or their vicious stings (see Chapters 12, 13). Most ants, however, are very beneficial because they prey on eggs and small larvae of pests such as sod webworms and white grubs. Most turf-inhabiting ants build small, underground nests with inconspicuous mounds. A typical lawn may harbor millions of ants which are constantly patrolling the soil and thatch in search of food to bring back to the nest. A healthy ant population is an important buffer against pest outbreaks.

Distribution, Description, and Life History. (See Ants, Chapter 13.)

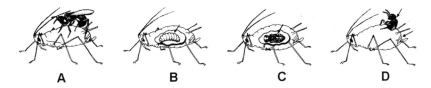

Figure 14.1. *Life cycle of a parasitoid of the greenbug. (A) Adult wasp lays an egg into a live greenbug. (B) The wasp larva feeds within the greenbug; as the larva nears pupation, the greenbug dies. (C) The parasitoid pupates within the dry shell of the dead greenbug. (D) The adult wasp cuts an exit hole in the back of the greenbug and flies off, leaving behind the empty greenbug "mummy" (adapted from Weinzierl and Henn, 1994; with permission).*

Management. Most species of ants are beneficial predators. Control is not recommended unless you are dealing with dangerous pest species such as red imported fire ants or harvester ants (Chapter 12), or when ant mounds become a nuisance on putting greens (Chapter 13).

BIG-EYED BUGS
(Order Hemiptera; Family Geocoridae)
(Plate 18F)

Importance and Beneficial Aspects. Big-eyed bugs are common predators of chinch bugs, greenbugs, mites, insect eggs, young caterpillars, and other small arthropods. Adults and nymphs move rapidly among the grass blades and stolons in search of prey. Victims are captured, speared with the needle-like mouthparts, and sucked dry. Big-eyed bugs sometimes build up in chinch bug–infested lawns after damage has occurred. At such times, the big-eyed bugs may be mistaken for chinch bugs because of their similarity in size and shape (Figure 10.2). Big-eyed bugs are part of a group of natural enemies whose combined impact helps to suppress chinch bug populations at most sites.

Species and Distribution. Several species of big-eyed bugs are widely distributed in the United States. *Geocoris bullatus, G. uliginosus,* and *G. punctipes* are the ones most often associated with chinch bug infestations in turf. The former two species occur coast to coast and in southern Canada. The latter species occurs south of a line from southern New Jersey west to southern Indiana and Colorado, and southwest through Arizona and California.

Distinguishing Characteristics. Adult big-eyed bugs are about 1/8 in. (3–4 mm) long, flattened, and somewhat oval-shaped. The blunt head is much broader than it is long (Figure 10.2). The eyes are widely spaced, conspicuous, and curve back around the front of the thorax. Adults of *G. uliginosus* are mottled tan or straw colored, with numerous punctures. Adults of *G. bullatus* are nearly black, with lighter-colored margins. Nymphs of big-eyed bugs resemble those of chinch bugs, except for having obviously bigger eyes and lacking the orange and white coloration of younger chinch bug nymphs. Nymphs of *G. bullatus* and *G. punctipes* are straw colored with darker spots. Those of *G. uliginosus* have a blackish-brown head, thorax, and wing pads.

Life History and Habits. In the northern states, *G. uliginosus* and *G. punctipes* apparently overwinter as adults in cracks in the soil, litter around plants, or other sheltered places. They become active in spring when daytime temperatures warm to about 75°F (24°C). The bugs feed mainly on small arthropod prey. They may also pierce plant tissues to obtain moisture, but this does not damage the plants. Females attach their small, oval eggs to plant leaves and stems in areas with abundant prey. Eggs hatch in 11–23 days at 70–80°F (21–27°C), and the young nymphs begin feeding on mites, small insects, and insect eggs. Nymphs develop through five instars, maturing in about a month at warm summer temperatures. After mating, females deposit 100–300 eggs during a 40–80 day adult life span. Thus, there are several overlapping generations during the growing season. In contrast, *G. bullatus* usually overwinters as eggs that hatch in spring, giving rise to several successive generations.

Management. Big-eyed bugs are beneficial predators. Be careful not to mistake them for chinch bugs when scouting lawns. Using spot-treatments for chinch bugs and webworms rather than blanket sprays will help to conserve these and other natural enemies.

GREEN LACEWINGS
(Order Neuroptera; Family Chrysopidae)
(Plate 31)

Importance and Beneficial Aspects. Both adults and larval lacewings feed on aphids, mealybugs, and other small, soft-bodied prey. They can be important in helping to suppress greenbug populations in turf.

Distribution. Green lacewings are found worldwide in open, grassy habitats.

Distinguishing Characteristics. Adults are delicate, greenish insects with golden or coppery eyes and long antennae. The wings have a net-like appearance, with many cross-veins, and are held roof-like over the back. Eggs are laid at ends of tiny stalks, usually on foliage. Larvae are flattened and tapered toward the tail, with long sickle-shaped mouthparts used for grabbing prey. They pupate in small pea-shaped cocoons.

Management. Lacewings are beneficial predators, so no controls are needed. Eggs can be purchased for small-scale biological control in greenhouses; however, augmenting lacewings in this manner probably has little value in turf.

GROUND BEETLES AND TIGER BEETLES
(Order Coleoptera; Families Carabidae and Cicindellidae, respectively)
(Plate 31)

Importance and Beneficial Aspects. Ground beetles and tiger beetles are fast-moving, beneficial insects that are abundant in turf. Both the adults and larvae prey upon eggs or larvae of insects. Many species help to reduce populations of sod webworms, white grubs, or other pests. Some ground beetles feed on seeds and pollen, or have mixed feeding habits. Ground beetles and tiger beetles do not feed upon or otherwise harm the turf. Homeowners may be upset when one of these swift-moving beetles mistakenly gets indoors.

Distribution. Many species of ground beetles and tiger beetles inhabit turfgrasses worldwide.

Distinguishing Characteristics. Most ground beetles are shiny and dark colored, with long legs and forward-pointing jaws for grabbing prey. Common species range in length from less than 1/4 to 1 in. (6–25 mm). Some species have a metallic sheen. The wing covers are broad and hard, and their upper surfaces are typically marked by longitudinal grooves (like corduroy cloth). The prothorax is usually narrower than the abdomen, and the head is narrower still. Ground beetle larvae are elongated and slightly flattened, tapering toward the hind end. They are usually light brown with darker spots, with long legs and formidable-looking mouthparts. They often have a pair of pointed projections at the tip of the abdomen.

Tiger beetles are elongate, long-legged, metallic green, blue, or bronze-colored beetles, typically 3/8 to 3/4 in. (10–20 mm) long. The head is large, with sickle-shaped mandibles that are directed forward. Tiger beetle larvae are somewhat S-shaped when viewed from the side, and there is a hump with hooks on the fifth segment of the abdomen. The head is large and dark, with prominent jaws.

Life History and Habits. Most ground beetles have one generation per year, overwintering as either larvae or adults. Eggs are laid singly in the soil. The larvae are found in soil, grass, or under stones and debris. Adults are mainly active at night, prowling through the grass in search of prey. They are often attracted to outdoor lights.

Most tiger beetles require 2–3 years to complete a life cycle. Tiger beetle larvae live in vertical burrows in the soil. They lie in the mouth of the burrow with the head and jaws out, ready to grab victims that wander by. The hooks on the fifth abdominal segment keep the larva from being pulled out of the burrow by the struggling prey. Adult tiger beetles are daytime feeders. They prefer bright, sunny areas with dry or sandy soil.

Management. Ground beetles and tiger beetles are beneficial predators, so no controls are needed.

LADY BEETLES
(Order Coleoptera; Family Coccinellidae)
(Plate 31)

Importance and Beneficial Aspects. Like lacewings, presence of lady beetles (also mistakenly called ladybugs) in turf often indicates an infestation of aphids or mealybugs. Lady beetles are important predators of greenbugs.

Distribution. Many species are found throughout the United States and worldwide.

Distinguishing Characteristics. Lady beetles are familiar, small, rounded bright-orange or reddish beetles, usually with black spots. Most species are less than 3/8 in. (9 mm) long. The larvae are somewhat flattened and alligator-shaped, often slate gray to bluish, with orange markings. Larvae are found on plants, usually feeding on aphids.

Management. Some species of lady beetles are mass-reared and sold for biological control in greenhouses and gardens. These types generally prefer crop habitats, so releasing them in turf provides little or no benefit. Conserving lady beetles by reducing insecticide use helps to reduce the risk of greenbug outbreaks.

ROVE BEETLES
(Order Coleoptera; Family Staphylinidae)

Importance and Beneficial Aspects. Rove beetles are common inhabitants of turfgrass thatch and soil. Many species are predaceous, feeding on eggs and small larvae of sod webworms, grubs, and other turf pests. Others feed on decaying organic matter, molds, or fungi. Rove beetles occasionally burrow into golf putting greens, leaving tiny mounds of soil on the surface. This damage is rarely conspicuous.

Distribution. Dozens of species occur wherever turfgrasses are grown.

Distinguishing Characteristics. Adults are small to medium-sized beetles, usually 1/8 to 3/4 in. (3–20 mm) long, and brown or black in color. The distinctive body is elongate, slender, and parallel-sided, with the head and mouthparts directed forward. The front wings are reduced to short leathery pads that rarely extend more than halfway down the abdomen. The hind wings, when not in use, are folded and tucked under the short wing covers. Larvae are slender, with a tapering fleshy body and a darker head.

Life History and Habits. Not much is known about the habits of rove beetles. Adults run quickly, usually with the tip of the abdomen bent upwards, and they are good fliers. They may be attracted to outdoor lights at night. Some species produce a foul odor when handled or crushed. Like the adults, the larvae prey on small insects. Most species overwinter as adults or larvae and have several generations per year.

Management. No controls are needed.

SCOLIID WASPS
(Order Hymenoptera; Family Scoliidae)
(Plate 10)

Importance and Beneficial Aspects. Scoliid wasps are considered beneficial because they parasitize grubs of the green June beetle, and certain other turf-infesting white grubs. The adult wasps feed on flower nectar. They do not sting people unless handled or greatly provoked. Still, their presence and activity tends to alarm homeowners and golfers.

Distribution. Scoliid wasps occur from New England to Florida and west to the Rocky Mountains. *Scolia dubia,* the most common species, is abundant wherever the green June beetle is found.

Distinguishing Characteristics. Adults of *Scolia dubia* are relatively large, dark colored, robust wasps about 3/4 in. (20 mm) long, with a wingspan of about 1-1/4 in. (32 mm). The wings are purplish black, and the antennae, head, thorax, and front part of the abdomen are shiny black. There is a pair of yellow spots about midway down the abdomen, one on each side. These may appear as a band across the abdomen when the wasp flies. The tip of the abdomen is brownish and somewhat fuzzy. The wasps attract attention as they fly several inches (6–12 cm) above grub-infested soil in a more or less figure-eight pattern. The larva is a legless, cream-colored grub with a brown head. It is found at the bottom of burrows made by green June beetle grubs, feeding on the paralyzed grub.

Life History and Habits. Scoliid wasps are most abundant in late summer, when they are observed hovering over lawns and golf fairways. The female wasp locates a grub burrow, enters it, and stings the grub to paralyze it. She then attaches an egg to the grub's underside. The grub provides a fresh food supply for her developing larva. The wasp larva passes the winter in a cocoon at the bottom of the burrow, pupating in the spring. A new generation of wasps emerges in August. These wasps can be very abundant, and are important natural agents in control of green June beetle grubs.

Management. Scoliid wasps are not at all aggressive. They will not sting unless handled or stepped on with bare feet. Try to reassure golfers and homeowners that the wasps are harmless and beneficial, and that they will disappear on their own in a few weeks. Presence of large numbers of these wasps usually means that there is a sizeable grub population that may be only partially controlled by the parasitoids.

SPIDERS
(Class Arachnida, Order Araneida)
(Plate 31)

Importance and Beneficial Aspects. Many kinds of spiders are abundant in turfgrass. All of these species are beneficial, since they prey on pest insects. Some kinds of spiders trap their prey in webs or snares; others are active hunters that stalk or ambush their food. All spiders kill their prey by biting and injecting venom. In the United States, the black widow and the brown recluse spider are the only spiders that are potentially dangerous to humans. Neither of these species is likely to be encountered in turf.

Distribution. About 2,500 different species of spiders are found in North America; as many as 1 million individuals may inhabit a single acre (0.4 hectare) of grassy field. Dozens of different species may be found in turf.

Distinguishing Characteristics. All spiders have two main body regions, a cephalothorax bearing the eyes, mouthparts, and four pairs of legs; and an abdomen, bearing the reproductive structures, spiracles, anus, and spinnerets for spinning silk. The abdomen is nearly always unsegmented, and is strongly constricted at its base. Eggs are generally laid in a silken sac attached to vegetation, crevices, or carried around by the female. Young spiders resemble the adults except for size.

Common Spiders in Turf. **Wolf spiders** (Family Lycosidae) are among the more common turf-inhabiting spiders. These are medium to large, active spiders, usually grayish to brownish, with darker stripes on the back. They actively hunt their prey and do not use webs or snares, although they may dig a burrow in the ground. They may be active by day or night. The female carries on egg sac on her abdomen, and the young spiderlings ride on her back after they hatch. Wolf spiders look fierce and their rapid movements make them seem aggressive. They have strong fangs and could inflict a bite if handled. Their bite is painful, but not dangerous. Wolf spiders do not live indoors, but may be accidental invaders.

    Funnel-web spiders (Family Agelenidae), also called grass spiders, resemble wolf spiders, but have a pair of long, distinctive spinning tubes at the tip of the abdomen. They construct a horizontal, sheet-like web that ends in a funnel-shaped tunnel which leads to a burrow. These spiders live in grass or shrubbery and seldom come indoors. **Sheet-web spiders** (Family Liniphiidae) are probably the most abundant spiders found in turf. These tiny spiders, 5/32 to 3/8 in. (4–10 mm) long, spin a bowl-shaped web between grass blades and irregular webbing over the bowl. Webs of funnel-web and sheet-web spiders are most apparent when covered with morning dew. **Orb-weaving spiders** (Family Araneidae) weave large, sheet-like orb webs that consist of rays and spirals of silk. They rarely occur indoors, but are common on or near the outer walls of buildings. The large, black and yellow garden spider is a familiar member of this group. This striking spider tends to build its webs in open, sunny places in gardens, tall grass, and weeds.

Management. Turf-inhabiting spiders are beneficial predators. Controlling them is unnecessary. If spiders are abundant around homes, they can be prevented from entering by applying a narrow band of insecticide around the foundation.

    A Note About Venomous Spiders (see Plate 29). When a spider is encountered in a home, garage, or outbuilding, the usual question is: "Is it a black widow or a brown recluse?" The black widow spider, *Lactrodectus mactans*, is fairly common in the southern states. Females are jet black with a bright red hourglass marking on the underside of the abdomen (Figure

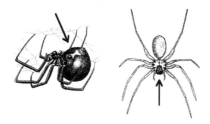

Figure 14.2. *Venomous spiders, showing characteristic hourglass-shaped marking on underside of black widow (left) and dark violin-shaped mark on brown recluse (right). These spiders are not ordinarily found in turfgrass (adapted from USDA).*

14.2). The brown recluse spider, *Loxoceles reclusa*, occurs east of the Rocky Mountains. Known also as the fiddle-back spider, it has a brown, inverted violin-shaped marking on its back (Figure 14.2). These spiders are sometimes encountered in woodpiles, sheds, garages, basements, or outdoor privies. People are rarely bitten unless these spiders are inadvertently handled. *Neither of these venomous species is likely to occur in or around turf.*

TIPHIID WASPS
(Order Hymenoptera; Family Tiphiidae)
(Plate 31)

Importance and Beneficial Aspects. Small to medium-sized wasps in the genus *Tiphia* are parasitoids of root-feeding white grubs. Soon after the Japanese beetle was discovered in the United States, several species of *Tiphia* were purposefully imported from the Orient in an effort to establish biological control. Two species, *Tiphia vernalis* and *T. popilliavora*, became established and spread throughout much of the beetle's range. Although parasitism rates are generally below 20%, these wasps do contribute, along with native natural enemies, to suppression of Japanese beetles. Other, native species of *Tiphia* attack grubs of masked chafers and May beetles. These wasps occasionally account for 60% or better mortality at particular sites.

Distribution. Various species of *Tiphia* are associated with white grubs (Scarabaeidae) wherever these pests are found.

Distinguishing Characteristics. Tiphiid wasps are about the size of a large ant, generally 1/2 to 5/8 in. (12–15 mm) long. They are slender, narrow-waisted, and black with clear to smoky wings. The whitish larvae are somewhat curved, legless, and worm-like, with a light-colored head. They are found attached to a white grub, usually on the back. *Tiphia* cocoons are distinctive, resembling a tan-colored, fuzzy jelly bean found in a cavity in the soil.

Life History and Habits. Adult *Tiphia* wasps feed on flower nectar and on the sugary honeydew excreted by aphids. The female burrows into the soil, locates a white grub, and paralyzes it with a sting. It then deposits an egg on the host's thorax or abdomen. The parasitoid larva hatches and feeds externally by sucking body fluids from the living grub. The weakened victim finally dies, and the wasp larva completes its development by consuming the dead host. All that remains of the grub is its hardened head capsule. The wasp larva then spins a silken cocoon within the earthen cell that was formed by its host. The adult wasp emerges the following year in spring or fall, depending on the *Tiphia* species.

Management. Tiphia wasps are usually most numerous in areas with abundant flowering plants. These wasps are beneficial and do not need to be controlled.

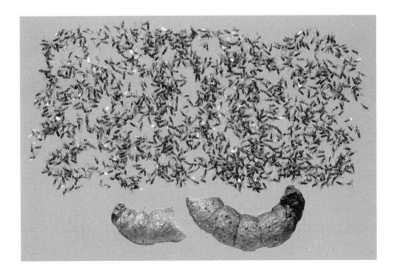

Figure 14.3. *Parasitic wasps that killed and then emerged from a black cutworm collected on a golf course. A total of 1667 wasps emerged from this one cutworm.*

OTHER PREDATORS AND PARASITOIDS

In addition to the aforementioned groups, other kinds of natural enemies can be abundant in turf. Long-legged predatory mites (Mesostigmata and Prostigmata) feed on plant-feeding mites (e.g., winter grain mite, clover mite), as well as on eggs of sod webworms and other pests. Many species of parasitic wasps and flies have been reared from turfgrass pests. All life stages of pests are vulnerable to attack. For example, eggs of black cutworms are parasitized by tiny wasps (family Trichogrammidae), larvae are attacked by several types of wasps or flies (Figure 14.3), and pupae are parasitized by yet other species. Much remains to be learned about the habits of these natural enemies. We understand little about why they are able to suppress pest populations at some sites, but not at others, or how to manipulate them for our benefit. All of these predators and parasitoids are quite vulnerable to broad-spectrum insecticides.

THATCH BUSTERS

Thatch is a tightly intermingled layer of living and dead roots, stems, crowns, and organic debris that accumulates between the green vegetation and the soil surface (Figure 6.4). Thatch accumulates when organic debris is produced more quickly than it can be broken down and recycled. Excessive thatch can lead to long-term problems: reduced water infiltration, shallow rooting, reduced stress tolerance, and restricted penetration of fertilizers and insecticides. This weak turf is prone to all manner of pest problems. A heavily thatched lawn may require expensive mechanical dethatching. Thatch is mostly a problem in highly cultivated turf, especially when a high rate of fertilizer is applied for several years. Use of certain fertilizers or pesticides can encourage thatch accumulation, both by increasing production of organic matter and by killing off earthworms and other soil fauna that help to decompose plant debris (See Chapter 7).

Earthworms are sometimes viewed as nuisance pests by turf managers because their surface castings create a roughened surface. This can disrupt the smoothness and uniformity of putting greens and other fine turf (see Chapter 13). Also, because earthworms are preferred food for moles, insecticides are sometimes applied in the hope that eliminating worms will cause the moles to go away (probably won't work — see Chapter 15). Thus, some turf managers consider a healthy earthworm population to be more of a problem than a blessing. These nuisance problems are generally more than offset, however, by the benefits that earthworms and other soil fauna provide by breaking down thatch, alleviating soil compaction, and maintaining a healthy, fertile soil (see Chapter 7).

EARTHWORMS
(Phylum Annelida; Class Oligochaeta; Family Lumbricidae)

Importance and Beneficial Aspects. Aristotle, the Greek philosopher and scientist, called earthworms "the intestines of the earth." Indeed, earthworms play a key role in breaking down plant litter, such as the thatch layer, and in recycling of nutrients. Burrowing by earthworms reduces soil compaction, allowing air and water to better infiltrate the soil. Earthworm tunnels may account for two-thirds of the total pore space in soils. Earthworms also mix the soil and enrich it with their fecal matter, called **castings**. As much as 18 tons per acre (> 40,000 kg/ha) of earthworm castings, equivalent to a uniform layer of enriched topsoil 1/4 in. (6.4 mm) deep, may be deposited on the surface every year.

Thatch is rarely excessive where earthworms are abundant. Earthworms feed on decaying thatch and leaf litter, fragmenting and mixing it into the soil, and stimulating microbial decomposition. Earthworms also incorporate large amounts of soil into the thatch layer. This enhances its suitability as a medium for turfgrass growth, such as is accomplished by mechanical topdressing.

Negative Aspects. Earthworm castings deposited on the soil surface can blemish the uniform appearance of golf greens, dull mowers, and interfere with ball roll. In lawns on clay soils, the piles of castings may harden during dry weather or winter, causing the turf to feel lumpy or crunchy underfoot.

Distribution and Species. Earthworms are found worldwide wherever turf is grown. Certain species may be more or less abundant in different areas. In the United States, the common nightcrawler, *Lumbricus terrestris* L., and the red earthworm, *L. rubellus* Hoffmeister, are abundant large species. Species of *Allolobophora* and *Eisenia* are among the more common smaller earthworms in turf.

Distinguishing Characteristics. Earthworms or nightcrawlers are familiar to everyone. All species have slender, legless bodies composed of many ring-like segments. Earthworms differ from roundworms (nematodes) in having many tiny hairs, called setae. These can be felt by running your finger along the underside of a good-sized worm. Earthworms move by constricting and expanding the body, creating a wavelike pulse that pushes the setae against the soil and propels the animal forward. Nematodes, by comparison, move by wriggling. Immature earthworms resemble adults; growth is accomplished by adding segments to the body. Sexually mature worms have a swollen, band-like organ, the clitellum, between the head and middle of the body.

Life History and Habits. The sex life of earthworms is rather bizarre. Not only are they hermaphroditic (having both male and female sex organs), they are also homosexual. Although each worm is both a male and a female, only one sex is operational at a time. When two worms come together for a sexual liaison, they join by attaching to each other by mucus bands. During mating, both partners function as males and they exchange sperm. Sperm from each worm travels down ducts to enter the female pores of their current mate. They do not fertilize themselves. Later, the eggs mature and the worm becomes functionally a female. The clitellum swells and secretes a nutritive mucus band. This nutritive material is pushed forward on the body by muscular contractions. As it passes over the egg ducts it picks up the eggs and then continues forward to the organ where sperm from the mating partner is stored. Sperm is added to the band and then it continues to be pushed forward until it sloughs off over the tip of the worm. The band closes into a cocoon which gradually hardens, and in which fertilization finally occurs. Cocoons are deposited in the soil and if moisture is sufficient, the young worms will hatch out in 2–3 weeks. They feed on organic matter in the soil and become sexually mature in 2–3 months under favorable conditions.

Earthworms prefer loose, moist soil with plenty of organic matter on which to feed. They are generally intolerant of acidic soils (pH less than 6). They are concentrated in the upper soil during the spring and fall. They go deeper during the dry part of the summer, but may emerge from the ground when their burrows are flooded by heavy rains. On warm nights when the turf is moist, they come to the surface to feed partly out of their burrows, or to crawl about in search of mates.

Management. No pesticides are registered for control of earthworms, nor is chemical control recommended. Indeed, the benefits provided by earthworms generally far outweigh whatever nuisance that they may cause. Certain insecticides and fungicides are highly toxic to earthworms (see Chapter 7), and use of these compounds will suppress or nearly eliminate their populations. As discussed above, this may aggravate thatch accumulation and soil compaction. Controlling earthworms will not eliminate moles (see Moles, Chapter 15). Mounds of castings on golf greens, tees, or other closely cut turf can be raked down, rolled down, or picked up during mowing. Lumpy lawns can be smoothed with a heavy lawn roller.

ORIBATID MITES
(Order Acari; Suborder Oribatida)

Importance and Beneficial Aspects. Oribatid mites and springtails are probably the most abundant arthropods that inhabit turf. They occur mainly in the thatch and soil, where they feed upon decaying organic matter and fungi. Ecologically, oribatid mites serve as tiny shredders, fragmenting and conditioning plant debris in their guts before it is further decomposed by microorganisms. These mites are important in recycling of organic matter and nutrients in turf.

Distribution. Oribatid mites are common in turfgrasses throughout the world.

Distinguishing Characteristics. Oribatid mites are tiny, dark-brown, hard-shelled arthropods that resemble minute beetles (Figure 14.4). Most species are rounded or pear-shaped. Adults have eight legs, and some species have tiny, wing-like projections on either side of the back (although they cannot fly). Tens of thousands of oribatids representing a half-dozen or so species may occur in a few shovelfuls of rich topsoil. These mites are seldom noticed because they are as small as the dot of this "i," and because they feed in the thatch and upper soil.

Life History and Habits. As is typical for mites, the immature stages consist of eggs, six-legged larvae and eight-legged nymphs. Larvae and nymphs are smaller and more soft-bodied than adults, and usually whitish in color. Like adults, they feed on decomposing organic matter.

Management. Oribatid mites are beneficial and no control is needed. These mites seem to be tolerant of most insecticides.

SPRINGTAILS
(Order Collembola)

Importance and Beneficial Aspects. Like oribatid mites, springtails feed on decaying plant material and fungi. They help to break down dead plant litter into smaller pieces that are then

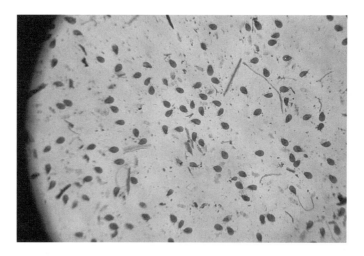

Figure 14.4. Oribatid mites from a handful of turfgrass soil, greatly magnified.

decomposed by microbes. Springtails are extremely abundant in thatch and soil, and many millions occur in an average lawn.

Distribution. Springtails are found in turfgrasses worldwide.

Distinguishing Characteristics. Despite their abundance, springtails are seldom noticed because of their small size, 1/100 to 1/4 in. (0.25–6 mm) long, and their habit of living under soil or leaf litter. The name "springtail" comes from the forked structure on the abdomen that catapults these tiny creatures through the air. This structure is reduced or totally atrophied in many of the soil-inhabiting species. Most springtails are whitish, but some are grayish or purple. Viewed without magnification, springtails look like white or purple-gray powder that jumps and moves.

Management. Springtails are beneficial, so control is unnecessary.

SELECTED REFERENCES

Cockfield, S.D. and D.A. Potter. 1983. Predation on sod webworm eggs as affected by chlorpyrifos application to turfgrass. *J. Econ. Entomol.* 77:1542–1544.

Potter, D.A., A.J. Powell, and M.S. Smith. 1990. Degradation of turfgrass thatch by earthworms and other soil invertebrates. *J. Econ. Entomol.* 83:205–211.

Potter, D.A. 1991. Earthworms, thatch, and pesticides. *U.S. Golf Assoc. Green Section Record* 29(5):6–8.

Potter, D.A. 1992. Natural enemies reduce pest populations in turf. *U.S. Golf Assoc. Green Section Record* 30(6):6–10.

Potter, D.A. 1994. Effects of pesticides on beneficial invertebrates in turf, pp. 59–70. *In*: A.R. Leslie (Ed.). *Integrated pest management for turfgrass and ornamentals.* Lewis Publishers, Boca Raton, FL.

Reinert, J. 1978. Natural enemy complex of the southern chinch bug in Florida. *Ann. Entomol. Soc. Am.* 71:728–731.

Terry, L.A., D.A. Potter, and P.G. Spicer. 1993. Insecticides affect predatory arthropods and predation on Japanese beetle eggs and fall armyworm pupae in turfgrass. *J. Econ. Entomol.* 86:871–878.

Weinzierl, R. and T. Henn. 1994. Beneficial insects and mites, pp. 443–453. *In*: A.R. Leslie (Ed.). *Integrated pest management for turfgrass and ornamentals.* Lewis Publishers, Boca Raton, FL.

15

MANAGING NUISANCE WILDLIFE PROBLEMS IN THE TURFGRASS ENVIRONMENT

This chapter discusses how to resolve nuisance wildlife problems in the turfgrass environment. As urban and suburban areas are expanded into undeveloped wooded areas and fields, we continue to displace animals that previously occupied these areas. Often, these animals are adaptable enough that they continue to survive and thrive on golf courses and in suburban neighborhoods.

For most people, presence of birds and other urban wildlife is a desirable and aesthetically important part of their environment. Nevertheless, when certain animals damage lawns or golf courses, injure property, or cause a nuisance, they become pests, and management may be required. Solving problems with animal-inflicted damage to turf is challenging because, as a professional, you must sometimes resolve the situation without harming the animal involved. In some cases (e.g., moles), destroying the animal pest may be warranted, but in a manner that ensures that other wildlife, pets, and children will not be harmed.

Armadillos, opossums, raccoons, skunks, foxes, wild pigs, and various birds may damage turf by digging in search of webworms, cutworms, white grubs, earthworms, or other juicy prey. Often, you can put a stop to this by eliminating the food supply — that is, controlling the insect infestation. Skunks, raccoons, and opossums occasionally take up residence in outbuildings on golf courses, under porches or crawl spaces, or in similar locations from which they must be removed. I've therefore included guidelines in this chapter for doing so in a safe and humane manner. Other pests, such as moles and pocket gophers, damage turfgrasses by burrowing and pushing up ridges and unsightly mounds of soil. Getting rid of these pests requires patience, persistence, and knowledge of their habits.

Note that in most areas, urban wildlife is protected under state and local laws. Some species (e.g., raccoons) are regarded as protected furbearers in most states, with specific seasons set for when they can be hunted or trapped. Landowners are usually allowed to control these animals without a permit when they damage property or create a nuisance. Professional pest control operators or nuisance wildlife control specialists, however, often need a permit to control such wildlife, even when the animal is live-trapped and removed unharmed. Even such varmints as moles, voles, and pocket gophers are considered native, nongame mammals and may receive some protection under state or local laws. These animals can usually be controlled without permits, but some states, cities, or townships have special ordinances that prohibit the use of certain methods (e.g., poison baits). *Thus, professional turf managers should always check with the local conservation officer or state wildlife agency before controlling nuisance wildlife, especially if lethal methods are to be used.* It is usually far better from a public relations stand-point, and more humane, to manage nuisance wildlife by nonlethal methods whenever possible.

BIRDS IN GENERAL
(Class Aves, various species)
(Plates 11, 25, 32)

Various species of birds are attracted to turf to feast on white grubs, turf-infesting caterpil-lars, black turfgrass ataenius, and other insects.

Value as Indicators. Flocks of birds frequenting a particular spot should provide warning that destructive insects may be present. Crows often concentrate on white grubs, and star-lings have an almost uncanny ability to locate cutworm and sod webworm infestations. Savvy golf superintendents make note of what the birds may be telling them, and follow up with closer inspections.

Types of Damage. Starlings (*Sturnus vulgaris*), grackles (*Quiscalus quiscala*), and red-winged blackbirds (*Agelaius phoeniceus*) leave numerous probe holes when searching for caterpillars or other surface- or thatch-dwelling insects. The holes look as if a pencil was repeatedly jabbed into the ground. Birds foraging on cutworms may pull up tufts of grass on golf greens or tees, causing as much damage as the insects themselves. Flocks of starlings or blackbirds that gather in spring or fall may damage turf by scraping away the surface vegetation, like chickens scratch-ing, as they search for insects. Crows (*Corvus brachyrhynchos*) scratching for white grubs may rip up patches of the weakly rooted turf.

Waterfowl, mainly ducks and geese, are often abundant in turf areas surrounding ponds or lakes (see Canada Geese). Their abundant droppings, often laden with weed seeds, can become a major nuisance. In coastal areas, gulls may be attracted to grassy areas, where they gorge on Japanese beetles and similar prey. They can be so numerous near airport runways that they pose a hazard to aircraft.

Management. Except for starlings and a few other pest species, birds are considered benefi-cial and are protected by federal and state laws. The only appropriate or effective tactic for reducing bird damage to turf is to eliminate the insect pests that are attracting them. This invari-ably causes the birds to move on. Be careful to select insecticides that are not harmful to birds (see Chapter 7).

CANADA GEESE
Brant canadensis (L.)

Importance and Type of Injury. Canada geese (Figure 15.1) are the cause of most water-fowl-related problems in urban and suburban areas. If left undisturbed, these large birds will establish nesting territories around ponds or lakes on golf courses, city parks, cemeteries, corporate settings, shopping malls, or residential areas. Most people enjoy watching a pair of geese and their young, but after a few years, two geese can easily become dozens of birds that pose a significant nuisance. Their grazing damages grass, and their unsanitary droppings can pose health problems. Ponds and surrounding turf may become so fouled with goose drop-pings that they are unfit for human use. Adult geese aggressively defend their nests and

Figure 15.1. *Canada geese (from University of Nebraska Cooperative Extension Service).*

young, startling, chasing, or pecking unsuspecting persons who come too close. The grazing behavior of Canada geese makes them susceptible to poisoning by certain insecticides applied to turf (see Chapter 7).

Distribution. Canada geese breed throughout most of North America. They are migratory, flying long distances in spring and fall between northern breeding grounds and wintering areas. Most geese using the Central, Mississippi, or Atlantic Flyways winter in the southern Great Plains, Texas, Louisiana, and Mississippi coastal marshes, or in the coastal regions of Chesapeake Bay and the mid-Atlantic states. However, geese may find life around urban ponds and lakes so agreeable that they become year-round residents even as far north as southern Minnesota.

Distinguishing Characteristics. Adult Canada geese are 25–43 in. (64–109 cm) long, weighing 11–15 lb (5–7 kg), with a wingspan of 5–6 ft (1.5–2 m). They have a grayish brown coat and white patches on the cheeks. The head, neck, and tail are black, and the underparts are gray. Nests are constructed of twigs, weeds, reeds, or grass, and lined with down. Nests typically hold five to seven pale-green, yellowish, or buff-white eggs.

Life History and Habits. Geese generally take up residence around ponds in early spring after returning with their mates from southern wintering grounds. A pair will typically establish a territory, build a nest, and raise a brood by mid-summer. Eggs hatch in about 4 weeks, and the young goslings begin foraging soon thereafter. The nest site is abandoned 1 to 2 days after hatching. Canada geese have a varied diet that includes insects, grasses, water plants, and sometimes corn and wheat. They readily feed on grass surrounding ponds, and in time can cause significant damage.

Management. Canada geese can be tough to get rid of once they've become established around a pond or feeding site. It's best to discourage them before they become acclimated. Geese avoid nesting in areas where they cannot easily walk in and out of the adjacent water. Steep-sided ponds are less attractive to them than ones with shallow shorelines or open beaches. They can be deterred from using existing ponds by vertically straightening the banks, or by using large boulder rip-rap which the geese cannot easily climb over. Alternatively, geese can be excluded by erecting a 3 ft (90 cm) woven wire fence around the pond at water's edge. For sites where aesthetics preclude use of wire fencing, try a two- or three-strand fence made from 20 lb test (9 kg) or heavier monofilament fishing line. String the first strand 6 in. (15 cm) above the ground, with each successive strand 6 in. above the preceding one. Hang narrow strips of aluminum foil every 3–6 ft (1–2 m) along the strands to make the barrier more visible. It's best to have the monofilament line fence in place before the geese start grazing. Half-inch (12 mm) Mylar® tape can also be used to make multi-stranded, goose-resistant fencing.

Geese prefer certain grass species over others as food. Kentucky bluegrass is among their favorites, whereas tall fescue is much less preferred. Planting tall fescue may therefore discourage their grazing and nesting around ponds and lakes. Where practical, plant tall trees to block the birds' flight paths, and shrubs to reduce their on-ground visibility.

A bird repellent called ReJeX-iT® AG-36 is registered for use on turfgrass and is effective for repelling geese and other waterfowl from priority areas on golf courses or around privately owned ponds (see Appendix 3). It contains methylanthranilate (grape soda flavoring), an FDA-approved food product that is aversive to birds while being harmless to humans and pets. When geese and other birds graze and taste grass treated with ReJeX-iT, they spit out the food and avoid the treated area. They usually head for the nearest water to rid themselves of the bad taste. A related repellent product, ReJeX-iT® TP-40, is EPA-registered for use in nonfish-bearing water. Treating both the turf and the adjacent water causes geese to leave the area more quickly. Follow label directions, and reapply as needed.

Geese can sometimes be frightened from ponds and surrounding turf areas by using visual repellents such as scarecrows, flags, or balloons, or noise-making devices such as pyrotechnics, sirens, or recorded distress calls. General guidelines are to start early, be persistent, and use a variety of presentations and scare tactics. Be aware that local laws may restrict your use of loud devices such as firecrackers or sirens.

Local flocks of problem geese can be live-trapped and relocated to another area. Trapping works best in late June or early July when the adults are molting and have lost the ability to fly, and the goslings have not yet fledged. The flightless geese can be herded into a large, walk-in funnel trap constructed from 50 ft (15 m) lengths of woven-wire fencing narrowing to a 15 ft (5 m) square holding pen made from 5 ft (1.5 m) high welded turkey wire. The captured birds can be loaded into turkey crates and transported in covered pickup trucks to a site where they will not pose a nuisance. Federal and state permits are required before geese can be live-trapped, and a suitable release site must be approved by federal and state wildlife authorities.

CHIPMUNKS
(Order Rodentia; Family Sciuridae)

Importance and Type of Injury. Chipmunks (Figure 15.2) are cute little varmints whose antics are enjoyed by most people. But chipmunks can become troublesome around homes and gardens. Their burrowing activity can cause structural damage by undermining foundations, retaining walls, concrete patios and steps, and sidewalks. They may also damage flower beds and gardens when they dig up and eat newly planted bulbs and seeds, or attack fruits.

Species and Distribution. The eastern chipmunk (*Tamias striatus*) is common throughout the eastern United States. The western chipmunk (*Eutamias* sp.) is found from Michigan westward to the Pacific, but is most common in the Rocky and Sierra Nevada Mountains.

Distinguishing Characteristics. Chipmunks are small members of the squirrel family. Eastern chipmunks are 5–6 in. (13–15 cm) long, excluding the tail. They have dark-chocolate or reddish-brown fur with five dark stripes and two light stripes on the back. There are two pale and two brownish stripes on either side of the face. The tail is flattened and bushy, 3–4 in. (7.5–10 cm) long, and held upright when they scurry about. Western chipmunks have an additional pair of dark stripes on the back, and are slightly smaller.

tus

Figure 15.2. A chipmunk (from University of Nebraska Cooperative Extension Service).

Life History and Habits. Chipmunks usually live in underground burrows. They are also found in building walls and woodpiles. Burrows may extend for 20 ft (6 m) or more and be as deep as 2–3 ft (0.6–1 m). Burrow entrances are about 2 in. (5 cm) across. Burrows are easily overlooked because there are no obvious mounds; the chipmunk carries away the soil in its cheek pouches and scatters it away from the entrance. A burrow system usually has more than one entrance and includes a nest chamber lined with leaves, one or two food storage chambers, and several escape tunnels. Chipmunks feed mainly on nuts, seeds, bulbs, and berries. They are most active from spring to fall, but spend most of the winter in their burrows. They are especially busy collecting and storing food in the fall. As winter approaches, they enter a restless hibernation, awakening every few days to feed on stored seeds and nuts. They are sometimes seen above ground on warm, sunny days in winter. Most chipmunks have emerged from hibernation by early March.

Chipmunks are generally loners, defending their territories except during courtship and breeding. They come together to mate in early spring, and again in July and August. Litters of 2–5 young are born in the underground nest chamber after a prenatal period of about a month. The young emerge from the nest when they are about two-thirds grown and can breed the first year. Adults may live as long as 3 years. Chipmunks have limited ranges, generally less than 100 yards (90 m). There are usually no more than 2–4 chipmunks per acre (5–10 per ha), although as many as 10 per acre may occur when food and cover are plentiful.

Management. In heavily wooded, suburban neighborhoods where chipmunks are abundant, trapping them becomes a never-ending exercise. In such situations, excluding them from sensitive areas is often a better long-term solution. Hardware cloth is effective for exclusion. Use 1/4 in. (4.2 mm) material, and bury it 6–8 in. (15–20 cm) deep to keep chipmunks from burrowing under sidewalks, in gardens, and other sensitive sites. Hardware cloth or caulking can be used to close openings where chipmunks may gain entry to structures. A clear, well-kept yard will probably have fewer chipmunks.

Trapping can eliminate small numbers of chipmunks around homes. Wire mesh live-traps can be purchased, or sometimes rented from animal shelters. Good baits include a mixture of peanut butter and oatmeal, nutmeats, pumpkin or sunflower seeds, raisins or prune slices, or grain-type breakfast cereals. Place the trap close to the burrow entrance or along pathways where chipmunks are active. Pre-bait the trap for several days by wiring the doors open. This allows the chipmunks to get used to entering the trap. Set the trap after they get cocky about taking the bait. Check live traps often to remove captured animals. Live chipmunks can be transported several miles and released in areas where they will not cause a nuisance. Common rat snap-traps can also be used to eliminate problem chipmunks. Use the same baits as for live traps, but tie the bait to the trap trigger. Pre-bait the traps by not setting them until the chipmunks get used to stealing the baits safely for several days. Small amounts of bait can be scattered around the traps to make them more attractive. Set the traps crosswise to the chipmunks' runway. Snap-traps can be shielded from birds by placing them under cardboard shoe boxes with 2 in. (5 cm) holes cut in the ends. Never use snap-traps in areas where children or pets may encounter them. When handling chipmunks or any other wild animal (dead or alive), use gloves or tongs to avoid bites, and because the animal or its parasites (e.g., fleas) may carry disease.

There are no poison baits available to homeowners to kill chipmunks. Certified applicators can use poison grain baits, but chipmunks that die inside structures may create an odor problem for several days. If grain baits are used, bait stations are recommended because they keep the bait dry and away from birds and other wildlife. Bait stations can be purchased from feed and farm supply stores, or made from an old crate or box with several 2 in. (5 cm) holes cut at the base. Don't use poison baits where there are pets or children. Fumigants are not effective because of the extensive burrow system. Once the chipmunk problem is under control, you can repair any structural damage and put hardware cloth or some other barrier there to prevent further burrowing.

MOLES
(Order Insectivora; Family Talpidae)
(Plate 32)

Importance and Type of Injury. Moles (Figure 15.3) can be a real headache for turf managers. These varmints push up unsightly mounds or ridges as they burrow through the soil in search of earthworms or insects. Their tunneling activity dislodges grass plants and damages roots. Mole mounds also provide a medium for the germination of weed seeds.

Species and Distribution. The eastern mole (*Scalopus aquaticus*) causes most of the mole problems on lawns and golf courses in the eastern United States. The Townsend's mole (*Scapanus townsendii*), is troublesome in coastal areas of Oregon and Washington, and the broad-footed mole (*Scapanus latimanus*) is a pest in California. The following account is based on biology and control of the eastern mole. Other mole species can be managed by similar methods.

Distinguishing Characteristics. Moles belong to a group of mammals called insectivores, meaning "insect-eaters." They are thus closely related to shrews. Eastern moles have pointed snouts, large front feet with stout digging claws, and a short, nearly hairless tail. Fully grown moles are 5–8 in. (13–20 cm) long, with velvety fur that varies from brownish to grayish with silver highlights. They have small eyes and ears that are concealed in the fur, and sharp, pointed teeth used for catching and eating their prey.

Life History and Habits. Moles are found in pastures, meadows, and woodlands, as well as suburban lawns and golf courses. They feed mainly on earthworms, white grubs, crickets, and invertebrates that live in the soil. Moles may supplement their diet with small amounts of seeds and vegetable matter, but they do not eat roots of turfgrasses or garden plants.

Moles construct extensive underground runways or tunnels of two types: **surface runways** and **deep runways**. Certain runways of both types are used as main avenues of travel; these so-called **main runways** may be shared by several moles. Surface runways appear as raised ridges

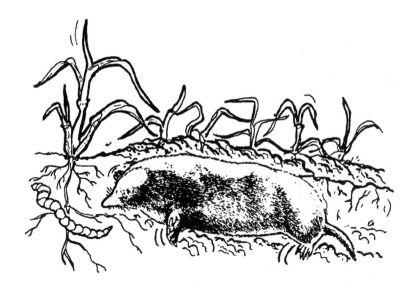

Figure 15.3. A mole (from University of Nebraska Cooperative Extension Service).

running through turf areas. They are constructed in the spring, summer, and fall. Some surface runways are used as daily travel lanes, whereas others are used infrequently or abandoned soon after they are dug. Most often, they serve as temporary feeding burrows. Moles have a high energy requirement, which dictates a large feeding territory. A single mole may extend its surface runways at a rate of 100 feet per day! Surface tunneling is greatest in spring and fall, and after warm rains. Moles are most active from 4 to 7 a.m., and from 6 to 9 p.m., although they may tunnel at any time of night or day. During winter or dry periods in summer, prey becomes scarce in the surface soil and the moles move into the deeper burrows in search of food. At such times, surface tunneling is reduced and control measures may be less effective.

Deep runways are more permanent than surface runways, and more likely to be used as main runways. These are used daily as the mole travels to and from the surface runways and its nest. The only evidence that deep runways exist may be volcano-like mounds of soil, so-called mole-hills, pushed to the surface through short vertical tunnels. Dens and nest cavities, 6 in. (15 cm) across and lined with vegetation, are located 12–18 in. (30–46 cm) underground and connect to deep runways. Moles tend to construct their main runways along the edge of sidewalks, drive-ways, fence rows, or other man-made borders, or around the woody perimeter of a yard. Temporary surface runways often branch off these main runways toward the center of the yard (Figure 15.4). An acre of turf generally supports no more than two or three moles at one time. The number of mounds or surface runways observed in an area is a poor indicator of how many moles are present.

Moles are antisocial animals that live alone except to breed. The sexes come together for a brief period in late winter to mate. In spring, after a 6-week gestation period, a single litter of 3–5 hairless young is born in the underground nest chamber. Young moles grow quickly and leave the nest to fend for themselves when about 6 weeks old. They become sexually mature by the following spring. Moles live for 3–4 years in the wild, unless they're eaten by owls, foxes, skunks, or other predators.

Management of Moles

Control by Trapping. *Trapping is the most effective method for controlling moles.* Mole densities are not as great as it would appear. An infested lawn usually supports only a few

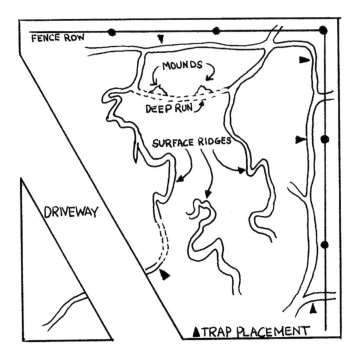

Figure 15.4. *Typical network of mole runways in a yard. The triangles show good locations to set traps. Avoid the winding surface ridges, and do not place traps on top of mounds (from Corrigan, 1993).*

moles, so it is practical to eliminate them by trapping. Furthermore, moles reproduce at a low rate, so they're slow to repopulate an area. Because a particular mole may use more than one lawn for its feeding territory, neighbors may need to cooperate for successful control. Turf areas surrounded by woodlots, pastures, or weedy fields may be continually reinfested because such areas support a large, residual population of moles.

The design of mole traps is based on the moles' habit of quickly opening and repairing damaged runways. If a mole encounters a foreign object, such as a mouse trap, in its runway, it will burrow around it. It is not suspicious, however, of soil blocking the runway. When it encounters such a blockage, the mole immediately pushes its way into the blocked area, reopens it, and continues on its daily rounds. If mole traps are carefully placed, the mole does not suspect that sudden death awaits. A poorly set or poorly positioned trap, however, is an obvious danger signal that will cause every mole to detour around it. Avoid tearing up large amounts of soil or disturbing the burrow excessively when setting a trap. Successful trapping takes knowledge of mole habits, patience, and persistence.

When and Where to Trap. Trapping is usually most effective in the spring or fall, when moles are active near the surface. Trapping in the early spring helps to prevent much of the damage. You'll also eliminate pregnant females, reducing the odds of having to deal with an extended family of moles later on. To trap effectively, you must first locate the active, main surface runways. Main runways are usually the ones that: (1) follow a relatively straight course for some distance; (2) connect two mounds or two runway systems; (3) follow sidewalks, fence rows, or other man-made boundaries; or (4) run along the perimeter of a lawn or field (Figure 15.4). Don't waste time trapping surface burrows that end abruptly or that are highly twisted; these are most likely abandoned or rarely used. To confirm which runways are active, tramp down a small section of the runway with your foot, or poke small holes with your finger into several locations throughout the system. Mark these locations with a stick or wire flag beside the burrow, so you can find them later. Moles will repair the flattened sections or holes in their

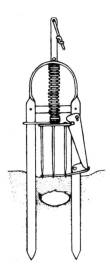

Figure 15.5. A harpoon trap properly set on a surface runway. A narrow portion of the runway (1–1.5 in.) is tamped one-half way down, the trap is inserted so that the support prongs straddle the runway, and the trigger rests lightly on top of it (from Corrigan, 1993).

main runways within a day or two. You can then put a trap near that spot. Runways not repaired within that time aren't worth trapping. Usually, you'll get better control by setting multiple traps. Use 3–5 traps per acre (7–12 per ha) for faster results. Ideally, traps should be set in each of the main runway areas.

How to Trap. Of the several types of mole traps available, the Victor® harpoon- or plunger-type mole trap (Figure 15.5) is probably the simplest to use. This trap uses sharp spikes to skewer the mole as it passes underneath. Such traps are available from hardware and garden stores, or from distributors (Appendix 3). To set a harpoon trap on a surface runway, carefully follow this procedure (adapted from Corrigan, 1993):

1. Use the side of your hand to lightly compress a narrow section, about 1 in. (2.5 cm) in length, of an active runway ridge so the tunnel is collapsed to one-half of its original dimension.
2. Center the trap (with the safety catch in place) over the runway, and push the supporting legs into the soil until the trigger pan just touches the flattened area. Be sure the supporting legs do not cut into the tunnel below.
    Note: In very hard soils, it may be helpful to form guide holes by raising and lowering the spears into the ground several times. Hold the trap firmly in place during this pumping operation to prevent the trap legs from riding up and down.
3. Set the trap and leave it. Be careful not to step on or disturb any other part of the mole's runway system. A plastic pail can be placed over the trap to discourage children or pets from tampering with it.
4. Check the trap daily. If it has not captured a mole within 3–4 days, move it to a different part of the main runway system.

Another type of trap (e.g., Victor Out O'Sight® mole trap) is set into the burrow and uses spring-loaded scissor arms to capture the mole. These traps are a bit trickier to use because they require that you partially excavate a section of burrow, but they offer the advantage of being less conspicuous than plunger-type traps to passers-by. Carefully follow the setting instructions that accompany the trap.

Other Approaches to Mole Control

Direct Removal. As an alternative to trapping, try a "mole watch" in the spring or fall on days when moles are active near the surface. Golf course superintendents can assign a few scouts to watch the surface runways for movement. One tactic is to poke small holes in runways each morning with the objective of later catching the mole in the act of repairing them. Or, you can flatten small sections of main runways with your foot and mark these with a thin wire marker flag placed on top of the compressed tunnel. A moving flag alerts the mole watcher to an active mole. To dispatch a mole "caught in the act," quietly sneak up and insert the blade of a shovel or spade behind it to prevent it from retreating back into the open tunnel. A pitchfork or a hard stomp directly on top of the mole can be used to kill it. Or else, you can capture the mole by scooping it out of the ground with a shovel, placing it in a pail, and then releasing it in a woodlot or weedy field away from the turf site.

Reducing Invertebrate Prey. It is often stated that eliminating white grubs from lawns will "starve out" the moles and cause them to go elsewhere. But remember — moles feed on earthworms and other soil invertebrates in addition to grubs. Thus, moles may be present in relatively grub-free turf. If you could really eliminate all of the grubs, earthworms, and other potential food by treating with insecticides, then the moles would be forced to seek other areas, at least temporarily. More likely, however, any benefits would not be evident for several weeks, and damage might even increase during this time as the moles work harder to find food. Also, the moles may simply move to an adjacent area or neighboring lawn, from which they will later reinvade the original site in search of food or mates. The displaced moles may live for several more years, producing additional broods that will become established in the area. In short, it's doubtful that insecticide treatments will provide much long-term relief from moles. Also, eliminating earthworms encourages problems with soil compaction and thatch buildup (see Chapter 14).

Poison Gases. Attempting to control moles with poison gases (fumigants) is rarely successful. Cartridge, tablet, or pellet-type fumigants generally don't penetrate through the moles' extensive runway system, or else the fumigant is lost through the top of the surface runways. Although you'll hear occasional success stories about fumigants repelling moles out of an area, any benefits are temporary at best because there is no residual effect. As soon as the fumigant has dissipated, the moles are free to return to their burrows. Fumigation is relatively expensive and, to date, the benefits don't justify the costs.

Poison Baits. Do not use poison peanuts or other poison baits. Remember, moles eat insects and earthworms, not nuts. Also, poison baits may be hazardous to pets or wildlife which may dig up and consume them.

Home Remedies. There are no known "silver bullets" or shortcuts to mole control. The old "remedy" of placing chewing gum in the burrow is ineffective — gum has no effect on moles even if they do eat it (which they won't). Some tabloid advertisements claim that the so-called mole plant, *Euphorbia lathyris*, or castor bean plants repel moles. This is quite doubtful. Also, these plants are poisonous to children, and because they easily escape cultivation, they may become a weed. Flooding tunnels with a water hose or directing automobile exhaust down the burrows is ineffective. Do not put broken glass, razor blades, rose branches, bleach, diesel fuel, gasoline, lye, sheep dip, or human hair down the burrow system. These misguided practices pose greater hazards to the environment than they do to moles.

Figure 15.6. *Nine-banded armadillo (from University of Nebraska Cooperative Extension Service).*

NINE-BANDED ARMADILLO
Dasypus novemcinctus texanus Bailey
(Damage, Plate 12)

Importance and Type of Injury. Like skunks and raccoons, armadillos (Figure 15.6) can damage turf by digging in search of earthworms, white grubs, and other tasty soil invertebrates.

Distribution. In the United States, armadillos are found in Texas, New Mexico, Arkansas, Oklahoma, Missouri, Kansas, and all of the Gulf States. On the eastern coast, they range from Florida into Georgia and South Carolina.

Distinguishing Characteristics. This odd-looking beast is so unique that it is easily recognized. Armadillos are covered head-to-tail with a protective "armor" of tough, horny material. The head, neck and shoulders, and hindquarters are covered with large plates, and nine narrower, flattened plates protect the rib section. The tail and outside of the legs are also armored; only the ears and underside are without a horny covering. The armadillo is the only mammal in the United States with such protective armor. Adults measure about 15–17 in. (38–43 cm) long, excluding the tail, and weigh about as much as an average cat. The front feet of armadillos are modified for digging, and their tracks appear to have been made by a three-toed animal.

Life History and Habits. Although armadillos are sometimes seen by day, they are mostly nocturnal. They prefer dense, shady cover, such as brush, woodlots, or pine forest. Den burrows are normally dug beneath rock piles, brush piles, tree stumps, or trees, but they occur occasionally under sheds or similar structures. Burrows are about 7–8 in. (17–20 cm) across and may be 15 ft (4.5 m) long. Each animal digs several burrows and may occupy different ones from day to day. Young are born in a breeding burrow lined with grass and leaves. Armadillos produce one litter per year, usually in February or March. It always consists of four offspring. Young armadillos look like small adults, but their protective plates are soft and leathery. They accompany their mother on her nightly rounds, often following in single file. Armadillos have poor eyesight, but compensate with a keen sense of smell and hearing. Although they can move rapidly when alarmed, they tend to "freeze" in a bright spotlight or automobile headlights. They are good swimmers. Armadillos are active year-round where they occur. They are intolerant of freezing temperatures, which restricts their northern range.

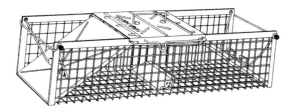

Figure 15.7. *Havahart®-type live trap (from University of Nebraska Cooperative Extension Service).*

Armadillos become pests when they dig and root in lawns and gardens in search of worms, white grubs, and other soil insects. They also feed sparingly on plant material, including fungi, young roots and shoots, berries, and fruits. Armadillos can be infected with several diseases transmissible to humans, including leptospirosis and Chagas' disease.

Management. Unlike raccoons and skunks, armadillos will usually move on after a night of feeding. Eliminating soil insects with an insecticide usually encourages them to go elsewhere. Persistent armadillos can be live-trapped with Tomahawk®, Havahart®, or similar traps (Figure 15.7). Place the traps near burrows or on trails along a fence or beside a building, and bait them with overripe fruit such as pears or apples. Marble-sized portions of ground meat, or an egg, may also be good bait. Traps can be made more effective on some trails by placing two long boards on edge to form a funnel that herds the quarry into the trap.

OPOSSUMS
Didelphis virginiana (L.)

Importance and Type of Injury. Opossums (Figure 15.8) sometimes damage turf by digging for grubs. They can become a nuisance by taking up residence in crawl spaces, garages, and outbuildings. Very few cases of rabies have been reported in opossums.

Distribution. Opossums are widespread east of the Rocky Mountains. Because of introductions, they also occur along the Pacific coast.

Distinguishing Characteristics. Opossums are sluggish animals that are active mainly at night. Adults are long-haired, light gray, and about the size of a large domestic cat. The tail is scaly, hairless, and about 12 in. (30 cm) long.

Life History and Habits. Opossums prefer living near streams, lakes, or swamps, or in woodlots where they can find suitable cover. They nest in almost any sheltered location — hollow logs and trees, abandoned woodchuck burrows, culverts, crawl spaces beneath buildings, and outbuildings to which they can gain access. Opossums typically produce one litter per year, averaging seven to nine young. Newborn opossums are quite small, naked, and undeveloped at birth. They continue to develop while nursing in their mother's pouch for about 3 months after birth. Opossums aren't picky eaters. They'll devour grubs, other insects, crawfish, fish, frogs, snakes, mushrooms, fruits, vegetables, eggs, carrion, garbage, or almost anything else they can find. They often raid uncovered garbage cans and rip open plastic garbage bags set out for disposal.

Management. Opossums are considered game or furbearers in many states, so check with local conservation officials before trying to control them. Controlling white grubs and other soil insects will usually stop their digging in turf. To prevent them from becoming unwelcome

Figure 15.8. Opossum (from University of Nebraska Cooperative Extension Service).

guests under porches or outbuildings, close off burrows or openings to deny access (see Raccoons and Skunks — Management). Opossums are readily taken in live traps set in trails or at entrances to dens. Raw red meat, poultry, fish, or canned pet food are good baits. Captured animals can be released unharmed, several miles from the trap site.

POCKET GOPHERS
(Order Rodentia; Family Geomyidae)
(Plate 32)

Importance and Type of Injury. Pocket gophers (Figure 15.9) dig underground burrows in turf and pastures, pushing up ridges and throwing up unsightly mounds of soil. Unlike moles, which eat soil insects and earthworms, pocket gophers feed mainly on plant roots and tubers. Pocket gophers make distinctive mounds with a *horseshoe-shaped or fan-shaped* pile of soil around the burrow opening. A plug of soil is placed in the entrance hole. In contrast, molehills are volcano-shaped. Besides being unsightly, pocket gopher mounds interfere with normal turf mowing practices, and the burrowing activity can disrupt plastic irrigation pipes on golf courses. Gophers are fond of bulbs and may root around in flower beds and gardens.

Species and Distribution. Several species of pocket gophers in the genus *Thomomys* are found in the western United States, from North Dakota to western Texas, and across to Oregon and California. Two other species in the genus *Geomys* are common pests east of the Rockies. The plains pocket gopher, *G. bursarius*, occurs in prairie areas from Wisconsin to eastern North Dakota, down into eastern New Mexico and eastern Texas. The southeastern pocket gopher, *G. pinetis*, damages lawns and golf courses in Alabama, Georgia, northern Florida, and southern South Carolina.

Description. Pocket gophers are stout-bodied, medium-sized rodents so named because of their large, fur-lined cheek pouches. These pouches open outside of the mouth and are used for carrying food. The pouches are reversible, like a pants pocket, and are emptied by squeezing with the front legs. Most pocket gophers are 8–14 in. (20–36 cm) long, excluding the tail. The fur is short and very soft, ranging in color from nearly black, to brown, to almost white. Gophers are well-adapted for burrowing, with powerful forequarters, a short neck, and a flattened head with small eyes and ears. The forepaws are enlarged and have stout claws used for digging. Another distinctive feature is their large, yellowish incisor teeth. These "buck teeth" are always exposed in front, even when the mouth is closed.

Figure 15.9. *Pocket gopher (from University of Nebraska Cooperative Extension Service).*

Life History and Habits. Pocket gopher burrow systems may be several hundred feet long, ranging from just under the surface to several feet deep. A gopher working a suitable area will excavate extensive surface tunnels while collecting roots and tubers. Periodically, it digs deeper tunnels and chambers for food storage, shelter, and rearing young. Excess soil from the burrows is pushed into mounds on the surface. Extra food is tucked into the cheek pockets, and then deposited in chambers within the burrow.

Pocket gophers are solitary animals except when breeding and rearing young. The males are especially aggressive and fight over disputed territory. Mating occurs in the spring, and females give birth to 2 to 11 young. After 2 months, the young disperse and begin to dig their own tunnels. At 3 months old, they are ready to breed. Some females produce a second litter later in the summer. Pocket gophers are active year-round, but the greatest tunneling activity occurs in the spring and fall when the soil is moist and most suitable for digging. During the winter, the gopher becomes less active, subsisting on stored food when fresh roots and tubers are scarce.

Management. Trapping is the most effective means of dealing with small numbers of pocket gophers. Two of the most commonly used and effective traps are the Macabee® Trap and the Victor Easy Set® gopher trap (Figure 15.10). Both of these traps are sprung when the gopher pushes soil against a flat vertical pan or grabs bait attached to the trigger. The key to success is locating the main tunnels and then placing the traps properly. Traps are most effective when they are used in main tunnels. Main tunnels connect to the fresh surface mounds via short, lateral tunnels (Figure 15.10). The main tunnel can be found by probing with a sharp stick or rod, 1–2 ft (25–50 cm) from the mound on the side opposite the burrow plug. Once the runway is located, open it with a shovel to position the traps. Place the traps in pairs facing in opposite directions so they will intercept gophers coming from either direction. Work each trap back and forth in the tunnel to loosen the soil. Be sure to exclude light from the trap site by covering the excavation with turf clods, cardboard, or some other material. Additional traps can be set in lateral tunnels leading to fresh mounds. Wire all traps to stakes to allow for easier recovery and removal of victims. Check the traps daily, and move them to a new location if you haven't caught a gopher within 3–4 days. Trapping can be done year-round, but spring is usually best because gopher activity is high and the soil is moist and easily worked. Trapping in the spring also eliminates females before they can breed.

Poison grain baits can also be used to control pocket gophers. Baits can be placed directly into the burrows by using a stick or probe to make an opening into a main burrow, and then dropping in the bait. Avoid handling the bait with bare hands, as human scent may repel gophers. Place the baits at three or four locations within active main tunnels. Openings into baited tunnels should be closed with clumps of sod or soil. Fumigants are generally not very effective because of the extensive burrow system. Also, the gophers can detect toxic gases and quickly

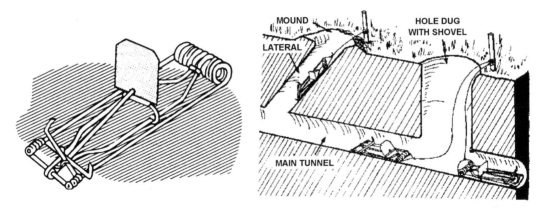

Figure 15.10. Pocket gopher trap and set (from University of Nebraska Cooperative Extension Service).

seal off portions of burrows to exclude the fumigant. As with moles, home remedies are not effective against gophers, nor are any of the sound or ultrasound-producing gadgets marketed to gullible homeowners. Chewing gum, pumping car exhaust or water down the burrow, and planting of supposedly "repellent" plants (e.g., *Euphorbia lathyris*) will not get rid of gophers.

RACCOONS
Procyon lotor (L.)
(Plate 5)

Importance and Type of Injury. Raccoons (Figure 15.11) become turf pests when they tear up large sections of lawns and golf courses while digging for white grubs. Often, they return to the same spot night after night to feast on these "land shrimp." Raccoons also raid garbage cans, and will occasionally take up residence in attics, crawl spaces, and various outbuildings. They are common carriers of rabies, and have been implicated in several other infectious diseases transmissible to humans.

Distribution. Raccoons are found over the most of the United States, except for parts of Wyoming, Utah, Nevada, and Montana.

Distinguishing Characteristics. This familiar animal has shaggy, grayish-brown and black fur, a distinctive black "mask" around the eyes, and a black and white, ringed bushy tail. Adults vary in size from 24–46 in. (60–115 cm) in total length and from 12–25 lb (5.5–11 kg).

Life History and Habits. Raccoons may be quite abundant on golf courses and in suburban areas, but they are rarely seen because of their nocturnal habits. They prefer to live near streams, lakes, or marshes, but many venture away from natural water. Raccoons are not picky eaters. During spring and early summer, their diet consists mainly of earthworms, insects, crawfish, mussels, fish, and frogs. In late summer and fall, they add fruits, berries, nuts and grains to the menu. Raccoons do not dig dens of their own, preferring to nest in hollow trees or logs, abandoned burrows of other animals, or other natural shelters. They mate in mid-winter, and a litter of two to eight (average four) young is born in the spring. Only one litter is produced each year. When the young are about 2 months old, they begin accompanying their mother on her nightly rounds. Family groups remain together for the first summer, often foraging together for food.

Management. Controlling white grubs reduces the food supply and usually discourages raccoons from digging. Unlike moles, raccoons like a varied diet and can easily forage elsewhere.

Figure 15.11. Raccoon (from University of Nebraska Cooperative Extension Service).

Managing the habitat is another option. Removing large hollow trees or logs, and sealing access to crawl spaces or outdoor structures forces the raccoons to go elsewhere for their cover and, hopefully, for their meals.

Raccoons are considered protected furbearers in most states. Thus, you can hunt or trap them only during specified seasons set by local regulations. Because these laws vary from state to state, *consult your game warden or state wildlife agency before implementing any control measures.* Often, a permit is required even for live-trapping an animal.

Live-trapping is the most effective nonlethal method of getting rid of raccoons. Use Toma-hawk®, Hav-a-hart® or similar type traps of the appropriate size. Effective baits include chunks of corn-on-the-cob in the milk stage, sardines and other fish, and fish-flavored canned cat food. Melon, prunes, fried bacon, or peanut butter, syrup, or honey on bread may also work. Raccoons are often quite wary about entering a trap. They can often be made less cautious by providing a natural footing on the trap floor. Do this by pushing the wire cage back and forth on the ground until the bottom mesh is covered by soil. Twist-tie the door(s) open for several days so that the raccoon can get used to the "metal object that gives free food."

Once the bait is being taken, set the trap. If the trap has a door on each end, set it so only one end is open. Place the bait near the closed end, positioned so the animal cannot reach it through the wire mesh. Make a small trail of bait leading into the open end. Raccoons are attracted to shiny objects, so adding a small wad of aluminum foil near the bait may stimulate their curiosity. Logs or stones can be piled beside wire cage traps to prevent them from reaching in and stealing the bait. Wire the trap to a tree, fence post, or stake to prevent the raccoon from tipping it over and shaking out the bait. Traps should be checked each morning. Those containing an animal should be placed in a burlap sack or similar covering. The raccoon will remain more calm if kept in darkness, and if the cage is handled gently. Live-trapped raccoons should be transported at least 5 miles from the point of capture before being released. Keep in mind that while raccoons are normally shy, they can be fierce when cornered. Don't approach or handle any raccoon that looks sick, or that shows no fear of humans. *If you are bitten by a raccoon, seek medical care immediately.* Try to capture and cage the animal, but don't shoot it in the head because the health department will require the head to determine if it was rabid. Leg-hold traps should *not* be used in urban or suburban areas — children or pets may encounter them.

Raccoons raiding garbage cans may be discouraged by securing the lids to prevent removal, and by placing the cans in a rack or otherwise anchoring them so they can't be tipped over. Commercial raccoon repellents aren't particularly effective. There are no known home-made repellents that work.

Figure 15.12. Shrew (from University of Nebraska Cooperative Extension Service).

SHREWS
(Order Insectivora; Family Soricidae)

Shrews (Figure 15.12) are mouse-sized mammals with an elongated snout, needle-pointed front teeth, small beady eyes, and five toes with claws on each foot. They differ from mice and voles in having no external ears. Also, mice have four-toed front feet, larger eyes, and a shorter snout. Both shrews and moles are insectivores, whereas mice are rodents. Shrews are generally smaller than moles, and do not have the moles' greatly enlarged front feet. The short-tailed shrew, *Blarina brevicauda*, is a common species in the eastern United States and southern Canada. Shrews feed mainly on earthworms, crickets, beetles, caterpillars, grubs, spiders, and other soil invertebrates. Seeds, roots, and other vegetable matter round out the diet. Unlike moles, shrews do not make raised surface burrows, and they are not harmful to turf. Control is unnecessary.

SKUNKS
(Order Carnivora; Family Mustelidae)
(Plates 11, 32)

Importance and Type of Injury. Like raccoons, skunks (Figure 15.13) damage turf when they dig for white grubs, cutworms, or other insects as food. They may tear up or roll back large patches of grub-infested turf, or leave golf ball–sized, cone-shaped pits when digging out individual larvae. Once a suitable feeding area is found, skunks will return night after night until the food supply is depleted. Their digging activities are worst during early spring and fall, when large white grubs are close to the surface. Skunks can dig under foundations or take up occupancy beneath porches, patio decks, or outbuildings. They sometimes damage beehives as they feed on adult and larval bees. The persistence of skunk odor on objects that have been sprayed is remarkable. More often than any other species of wild carnivore, skunk bites are implicated in human exposure to rabies. When skunks are not troublesome, they should be left alone because they help to suppress populations of small rodents, moles, and shrews.

Species and Distribution. Three species of skunks may damage turfgrasses in North America: the striped skunk (*Mephitis mephitis*), and the eastern (*Spilogale putorius*) and western (*S. gracilis*) spotted skunks. Striped skunks are found throughout the United States except for desert areas of the Southwest. Eastern and western spotted skunks occur over much of the

Figure 15.13. Striped skunk (from University of Kentucky Cooperative Extension Service).

country, but are absent along most of the Atlantic coast, the Northeast, the southern Great Lakes region, and Montana.

Distinguishing Characteristics. Striped skunks are short, stocky mammals about the size of a domestic house cat. They have a triangular-shaped head tapering to a blunt nose, a large bushy tail, and large feet equipped with well-developed claws. They typically have two prominent white stripes down the back in a coat of jet black fur. The amount of white fur varies. Spotted skunks are about half the size of striped skunks. They are mostly black, with white spots in front of each ear and on the forehead, and four to six broken white stripes down the back. The tail is usually tipped with white. Spotted skunks are the more active species and are better climbers. The habits of the two species are similar in most other respects.

Life History and Habits. Favored haunts for skunks include woodland edges, woody ravines, brush land, weedy fields, rocky outcrops, and drainage ditches. Skunks are nocturnal, becoming active from sunset to slightly after sunrise. During the day, they sleep in dens which are usually below ground, but which are sometimes located in hollow logs or tree stumps, brush, or lumber piles. Skunks sometimes take up residence under porches or in crawl spaces of buildings. They are most abundant in wooded or brush areas close to streams, but may be common in suburban areas within a half mile (0.8 km) of their natural habitat. During the winter months, skunks may remain inactive in the den for days or weeks. They do not hibernate, but become inactive during cold weather, relying on stored body fat to get them through the winter. Several skunks may share the same den during winter to conserve body heat. Striped skunks mate in late winter and litters of four to seven young are born in May and June. Spotted skunks breed in early spring and produce litters of two to six young in early summer. Both types of skunks may produce a second litter in late summer or fall.

Skunks eat both animal and plant material. Favorite skunk foods are white grubs, cutworms, grasshoppers, crickets, and other plump insects. They will also eat small rodents, moles and shrews, reptiles, amphibians, bird eggs and nestlings, fish, fruits, and garbage. Most of a skunk's diet consists of small mammals and insects considered injurious to humans. Thus, when skunks are not causing a nuisance they should be left alone because on the whole they are beneficial.

Skunks are renowned for their ability to discharge a very foul-smelling scent when provoked. The chemical bomb, produced by two internal glands located near the base of the tail, is used for self defense. Angry skunks usually stamp their front feet, growl or hiss, and raise their tail as a warning before spraying. The fluid, consisting of a thick, oily, volatile, sulfur-containing compound, is released in a fine spray directed accurately up to 10 ft (3 m) and less accurately for 20 ft. The fluid is acrid enough to cause nausea, and causes severe irritation or temporary blindness if it strikes the eyes.

Management. As skunks are furbearers, hunting or trapping them is regulated in many states. It is usually legal to trap or kill skunks where a health threat exists or where damage occurs. Controlling white grubs, a favorite food, will generally put a stop to their digging, although perhaps not immediately. Presence of skunks near homes or on golf courses can be discouraged by removing wood or brush piles, stacked lumber, hollow trees and logs, and similar nesting sites.

Problems with skunks under structures are best prevented by exclusion. Use sturdy wire mesh (1/4-in. hardware cloth or similar materials) to screen vents or openings near ground level, and close off spaces beneath porches or sheds. To locate areas where skunks are entering or leaving, sprinkle a smooth layer of flour or fine sand, about 1/8 in. (3 mm) thick, on the ground at the suspected access. Examine these "tracking patches" shortly after dark. When tracks lead out of the entrance, it is a good bet that the skunk is gone and you can then seal up the entrance. Stubborn skunks can sometimes be driven out by scattering 1–2 lb (0.45–0.9 kg) of mothballs or moth flakes (naphthalene or paradichlorobenzene) or placing a pan of ordinary household ammonia in the den area. Rigging floodlights under the floor of the building on the opposite side of the skunks' normal entrance for a few nights may also drive them out. Be sure that all skunks are gone before sealing up the entrance!

Skunks can be live-trapped with Hav-a-hart®, Tomahawk®, and similar type traps. For bait, use fish (canned or fresh), fish-flavored cat food, chicken parts, bacon, or peanut butter on bread. Place the trap immediately in front of the burrow's main entrance, and leave both doors open. To deal with a live-trapped skunk without being sprayed, slowly approach and cover the trap with an old blanket, plastic tarp, or piece of thick burlap. Covering the trap before it is set is simpler, and may even encourage the skunk to enter. Keeping the animal in the darkened trap makes it less fearful, and less likely to spray. Gently transfer the covered trap to the back of a pickup truck for transporting elsewhere. Striped skunks are unlikely to release scent if handled in this manner. Spotted skunks are more unpredictable. Trapped skunks can be dispatched via drowning by submerging the covered trap in water for 5 minutes or longer. Because of the potential for spreading rabies, trapped skunks should not be released elsewhere. *Be extremely careful when dealing with skunks because of the possibility that they are rabid.* If you are bitten by a skunk, cleanse the wound with warm soapy water and seek immediate medical attention. Try to capture and cage the animal, but don't shoot it in the head because the health department will require the head to determine if the skunk was rabid. Be especially wary of skunks that seem tame or listless, that wander around in the daytime, or that show no fear of humans — there is a good chance that such animals are rabid.

Shooting skunks is not recommended, as it often results in release of odor. Commercial deodorizing products containing the chemical neutroleum-alpha are effective for neutralizing and getting rid of skunk odor. These products can be used in a water bath to decontaminate dogs or humans, used to scrub walls, floors, or outdoor furniture, or sprayed on the ground in contaminated areas.

VOLES (MEADOW MICE)
(Order Rodentia; Family Cricetidae)
(Plate 32)

Importance and Nature of Injury. Voles (Figure 15.14) make narrow, 1–2 in. (2.5–5.0 cm) wide surface runways through the grass. They prefer pastures and meadows, but occasionally invade lawns and golf courses. During winter, presence of round openings to the surface may

Figure 15.14. Vole or meadow mouse (from University of Nebraska Cooperative Extension Service).

indicate that they are active under the snow. After the snow melts, homeowners are dismayed to find the lawn ragged, chewed up, and traversed by runways that are devoid of grass. The voles themselves usually leave with the melting snow, but the trails may not fill in for many weeks. This injury is sometimes blamed on moles, but moles tunnel underground and do not make surface runways through the grass. Voles may also gnaw the bark and girdle young trees and shrubs, especially where snow cover is present.

Distribution. Voles are widely distributed throughout North America wherever dense grassy habitat occurs.

Distinguishing Characteristics. Voles (*Microtis* sp.), sometimes referred to as meadow mice, are small, chunky rodents that resemble mice in size and general appearance. They have a blunt nose, small furry ears, and a short, thinly haired tail. Their dense fur is blackish-brown to grayish brown. Adults measure about 4–5 in. (10–18 cm) long, with a 1-3/4 to 2-3/4 in. (4.4–7 cm) tail. They are sometimes mistaken for moles and shrews, but moles have greatly enlarged front feet with stout digging claws, and shrews have a long, pointed snout with needle-pointed front teeth. Voles have normal-sized feet, and a rounded snout with chisel-shaped front teeth.

Life History and Habits. Voles prefer dense grassy areas, but sometimes move from pastures and meadows into adjacent home landscapes or golf courses. Nests, made from grass or other vegetation, may be on the surface or below ground. Voles are prolific breeders. Each female may give birth to as many as 10 litters per year, averaging five young per brood. Young voles are sexually mature in a month or two. Populations fluctuate greatly from year to year; when they are abundant there may be several hundred voles per acre (0.4 ha). Their usual foods are grasses and herbaceous plants, but they may gnaw bark near the base of young trees when other foods are scarce. Since they are mainly plant-feeders, grubs or other insects need not be present before they will damage turf.

Management. Keep grassy and weedy areas close-mowed to reduce the protective cover for voles. In many states, zinc phosphide baits and anticoagulant rodenticides are registered for control of meadow voles. These may be broadcast for large infestations on golf courses, or placed in bait stations or teaspoon amounts in vole runways or near burrow openings. Vole burrow systems have so many openings that fumigants are rarely effective. Ordinary snap-back mouse traps can be used to combat small numbers of voles in backyard settings. Bait the traps with a pinch of oatmeal mixed with peanut butter, and place them at right angles to the runways, with the trigger in the runway.

SELECTED REFERENCES

Corrigan, R.M. 1993. Moles. *Purdue Univ. Coop. Ext. Serv. Bull.* ADC-10, West Lafayette, IN.

Bennett, G.W., J.M. Owens, and R.M. Corrigan. 1988. *Truman's scientific guide to pest control operations.* Edgell Communications, Duluth, MN.

Hygnstrom, S.E., R.M. Timm, and G.E. Larson. 1994. *Prevention and control of wildlife damage.* Univ. Nebraska Coop. Ext., Lincoln, NE.

Marsh, R.E. and W.E. Howard. 1990. Vertebrate pests, pp. 771–831. *In*: A. Mallis (Ed.). *Handbook of pest control.* Franzak & Foster Co., Cleveland, OH.

Watschke, T.L., P.H. Dernoeden, and D.J. Shetlar. 1995. *Managing turfgrass pests.* Lewis Publishers, Boca Raton, FL.

APPENDIX 1
SOURCES OF LOCAL INFORMATION

For help or local information about turfgrass insects, contact the extension entomologist or agronomist at the College of Agriculture of your land-grant university, or at your State Agricultural Experiment Station. Bulletins, "fact-sheets," spray schedules, and other written materials are often available free, or at nominal cost. Many land-grant universities now offer such information over the Internet. Most state universities also offer pesticide certification training and educational workshops for professional turf and landscape managers. The following is a list of land-grant institutions and Agricultural Experiment Stations in the United States:

ALABAMA: Extension Hall, Auburn University, Auburn, AL 36849-5413; (334) 844-6392, FAX (334) 844-5002

ALASKA: University of Alaska–Fairbanks, Fairbanks, AK 99775-0500; (907) 474-7083

ARIZONA: Department of Entomology, University of Arizona, Tucson, AZ 85721; (520) 621-7209, FAX (520) 621-7196

ARIZONA: Maricopa Agricultural Center, 37860 W. Smith Enke Rd., Maricopa, AZ 85239; (520) 568-2273, FAX (520) 568-2556

ARKANSAS: Department of Entomology, 321 Agriculture Building, University of Arkansas, Fayetteville, AR 72701; (501) 575-3376, FAX (501) 575-3348

CALIFORNIA: Department of Entomology & Parasitology, 201 Wellman Hall, University of California, Berkeley, CA 94720; (510) 642-5565, FAX (510) 642-4879

CALIFORNIA: Department of Entomology, University of California, Davis, CA 95616-8584; (1-916)-225-2847, FAX (916) 752-9464

CALIFORNIA: Department of Entomology, University of California, Riverside, CA 92521; (909) 787-3231, FAX (909) 788-2615

COLORADO: Department of Entomology, Colorado State University, Fort Collins, CO 80523; (970) 491-6781, FAX (970) 491-0564

CONNECTICUT: Department of Entomology, Connecticut Agricultural Experiment Station, 123 Huntington Street, Box 1106, New Haven, CT 06504; (203) 789-7239, FAX (203) 789-7232

DELAWARE: Department of Entomology & Applied Ecology, University of Delaware, Newark, DE 19717-1303; (302) 831-8883, FAX (302) 831-3651

FLORIDA: Department of Entomology & Nematology, P.O. Box 110620, University of Florida, Gainesville, FL 32611; (352) 392-1901, FAX (352) 392-0190

GEORGIA: Department of Entomology/Extension, 200 Barrow Hall, University of Georgia, Athens, GA 30602; (706) 542-1765, FAX (706) 542-3872

GEORGIA: Department of Entomology, Box 1209, University of Georgia, Tifton, GA 31793; (912) 386-3424, FAX (912) 386-7133

GEORGIA: Department of Entomology, Georgia Experiment Station, College of Agriculture & Environmental Sciences, University of Georgia, Griffin, GA 30223; (770) 228-7236, FAX (770) 228-7287

HAWAII: Department of Entomology, 3050 Maile Way, Gilmore 310, University of Hawaii at Manoa, Honolulu, HI 96822; (808) 956-7076, FAX (808) 956-2428

IDAHO: Plant, Soil & Entomological Sciences, University of Idaho, Moscow, ID 83843-2339; (208) 885-5972, FAX (208) 885-7760

ILLINOIS: Office of Agricultural Entomology, University of Illinois, Illinois Natural History Survey, 607 East Peabody Drive, Champaign, IL 61820; (217) 333-6650, FAX (217) 333-4949

INDIANA: Department of Entomology, Purdue University, 1158 Entomology Hall, West Lafayette, IN 47907-1158; (317) 494-4570, FAX (317) 494-2152

IOWA: Department of Entomology, 104 Insectary, Iowa State University, Ames, IA 50011-3140; (515) 294-1101, FAX (515) 294-8027

KANSAS: Department of Entomology, 123 Waters Hall, Kansas State University, Manhattan, KS 66506-4004; (913) 532-5891, FAX (913) 532-6258

KENTUCKY: Department of Entomology, S225H Agricultural Science Center North, University of Kentucky, Lexington, KY 40546-0091; (606)-257-2398, FAX (606)-323-1120

LOUISIANA: Department of Entomology, Louisiana State University, P.O. Box 25100, Baton Rouge, LA 70803-1710; (504) 388-2180, FAX (504) 388-2478

MAINE: Department of Entomology, University of Maine, Orono, ME 04469; (207) 581-2963, FAX (207) 581-3881

MARYLAND: Department of Entomology, 1300 Symons Hall, University of Maryland, College Park, MD 20742-5575; (301) 405-3920, FAX (301) 314-9290

MASSACHUSETTS: Department of Entomology, Fernald Hall, University of Massachusetts, Amherst, MA 01003; (413) 545-0268, FAX (413) 545-5858

MICHIGAN: Department of Entomology, 243 Natural Science Building, Michigan State University, East Lansing, MI 48824; (517) 355-3385, FAX (517) 353-4354

MINNESOTA: Department of Entomology, 219 Hodson Hall, 1980 Folwell Avenue, University of Minnesota, St. Paul, MN 55108-6125; (612) 624-7785, FAX (612) 625-5299

MISSISSIPPI: MSU Extension Entomology, P.O. Box 157, Decatur, MS 39327; (601) 635-3642, FAX (601) 635-2146

MISSOURI: Department of Entomology, University of Missouri, Columbia, MO 65211; (573) 882-3446, FAX (573) 882-1469

MONTANA: Entomology Research Laboratory, Montana State University, Bozeman, MT 59717; (406) 994-3872, FAX (406) 994-6029

NEBRASKA: Department of Entomology, 210 Plant Industry, University of Nebraska–East Campus, Lincoln, NE 68683-0816; (402) 472-2123, FAX (402) 472-4687

NEVADA: Division of Agriculture, 350 Capitol Hill Avenue, University of Nevada, Reno, NV 89502; (702) 784-6611

NEW HAMPSHIRE: Department of Entomology, Nesmith Hall, University of New Hampshire, Durham, NH 03824-3597; (603) 862-1159, FAX (603) 862-1713

NEW JERSEY: Department of Entomology, Rutgers University, New Brunswick, NJ 08903-0231; (908) 932-9324, FAX (908) 932-7229

NEW MEXICO: Department of Entomology, Plant Pathology & Weed Science, New Mexico State University, Box 30003, Dept. 3BE, Las Cruces, NM 88003-0003; (505) 646-3225, FAX (505) 646-8087

NEW YORK: Department of Entomology, Comstock Hall, Cornell University, Ithaca, NY 14853; (607) 255-3250, FAX (607) 255-0939

NEW YORK: Department of Entomology, NYS Agriculture Experiment Station, Barton Lab, Geneva, NY 14456; (315) 787-2342, FAX (315) 787-2326

NORTH CAROLINA: Department of Entomology, North Carolina State University, Raleigh, NC 27695-7613; (919) 515-2703, FAX (919) 515-7746

NORTH DAKOTA: Department of Entomology, 202 Hultz Hall, Box 5346, University Station, North Dakota State University, Fargo, ND 58105-5446; (701) 231-7581, FAX (701) 231-8557

OHIO: Department of Entomology, Ohio State University, 1991 Kenny Road, Columbus, OH 43210; (614) 292-3762, FAX (614) 292-9783

OHIO: Department of Entomology, OARDC, Wooster, OH 44691; (216) 263-3730, FAX (216) 263-3686

OKLAHOMA: Department of Entomology, 127 Noble Research Center, Oklahoma State University, Stillwater, OK 74078; (405) 744-5531, FAX (405) 744-6039

OREGON: Department of Entomology, Cordley Hall, Room 2046, Oregon State University, Corvallis, OR 97331-2907; (541) 737-5499, FAX (541) 737-3643

PENNSYLVANIA: Department of Entomology, Penn State University, 501 Agric. Science & Industries Building, University Park, PA 16802; (814) 865-3008, FAX (814) 865-3048

RHODE ISLAND: Department of Plant Sciences, University of Rhode Island, Kingston, RI 02881; (401) 792-5998, FAX (401) 792-4017

SOUTH CAROLINA: Department of Entomology, 109 Long Hall, Clemson University, Clemson, SC 29634; (864) 656-5043, FAX (864) 656-5065

SOUTH DAKOTA: Department of Plant Sciences, South Dakota State University, Brookings, SD 57007; (605) 688-4603, FAX (605) 688-4602

TENNESSEE: Department of Entomology & Plant Pathology, University of Tennessee, Knoxville, TN 39701; (423) 974-7138, FAX (423) 974-8868

TEXAS: Department of Entomology, Texas A&M University, P.O. Box 2150, Bryan, TX 77806; (409) 845-6800, FAX (409) 845-6501

TEXAS: Texas A&M University Research and Extension Center, 17360 Coit Rd., Dallas, TX 75252-6599; (214) 231-5362, FAX (214) 952-9216

UTAH: Department of Biology, Utah State University, Logan, UT 84322-5305; (801)797-2515, FAX (801) 797-1575

VERMONT: Plant & Soil Science Department, Hills Building, University of Vermont, Burlington, VT 05401; (802) 656-5440, FAX (802) 658-7710

VIRGINIA: Department of Entomology, 216 Price Hall, Virginia Polytechnic Institute & State University, Blacksburg, VA 24061-0319; (540) 231-4045, FAX (540) 231-9131

WASHINGTON: Department of Entomology, FSHN Building 166, Washington State University, Pullman, WA 99164-6382; (509) 335-2830, FAX (509) 335-2959

WEST VIRGINIA: Division of Plant and Soil Sciences, West Virginia University, P.O. Box 6108, Morgantown, WV 26506-6108; (304) 293-6023, Fax (304) 293-3740

WISCONSIN: Department of Entomology, University of Wisconsin, Madison, WI 53706; (608) 262-3228, FAX (608) 262-3322

WYOMING: Department of Plant, Soil & Insect Sciences, P.O. Box 354 University Station, University of Wyoming, Laramie, WY 82071-3354; (307) 766-5124, FAX (307) 766-3998

APPENDIX 2
REFERENCE BOOKS AND PERIODICALS

The following general texts and periodicals provide additional information about destructive and beneficial turfgrass insects.

General Texts

Brandenburg, R.L. and M.G. Villani (Eds.). 1995. *Handbook of Turfgrass Insect Pests*. Entomological Society of America, Lanham, MD.

Fermanian, T.W., M.C. Shurtleff, R. Randell, H.T. Wilkinson, and P.L. Nixon. 1997. *Controlling Turfgrass Pests* (2nd ed.). Prentice Hall, Upper Saddle River, NJ.

Leslie, A. (Ed.). 1994. *Handbook of Integrated Pest Management for Turf and Ornamentals*. Lewis Publishers, Boca Raton, FL.

Niemczyk, H.D. 1981. *Destructive Turf Insects*. HDN Books, Wooster, OH.

Short, D.E. 1993. *Insects and Related Pests of Turfgrass in Florida*. Univ. Florida Coop. Ext. Serv. Bull. SP 140, Gainesville, FL.

Tashiro, H. 1987. *Turfgrass Insects of the United States and Canada*. Cornell Univ. Press, Ithaca, NY.

Watschke, T.L., P.H. Dernoeden, and D.J. Shetlar. 1995. *Managing Turfgrass Pests*. Lewis Publishers, Boca Raton, FL.

Periodicals

Golf Course Management. GCSAA Communications, Inc.; 1421 Research Park Drive; Lawrence, KS 66049-9908; 1-800-472-7878.

Green Section Record. United States Golf Association, Golf House, Far Hills, NJ 07931; (908) 234-2300.

Grounds Maintenance. P.O. Box 12901, Overbrook Park, Kansas 66282-2901; 1-800-441-0294.

Lawn and Landscape Maintenance. 4012 Bridge Ave., Cleveland, OH 44113; (216) 961-4130.

Landscape Management. 7500 Old Oak Blvd., Cleveland, Ohio 44130; (218) 723-9477.

Southern Turf Management. P.O. Box 16706, Memphis, TN 38186.

Turfgrass Trends. 131 W. First Street, Duluth, MN 55802-2065; (800) 346-0085 Ext. 477, FAX (218) 723-9437.

APPENDIX 3
SOURCES OF PEST MANAGEMENT EQUIPMENT

Entomological Supplies

BioQuip Products, 17803 LaSalle Ave., Gardena, CA 90248-3602; Phone: (310) 324-0620; FAX: (310) 324-7931; e-mail bioquip@aol.com (note: BioQuip specializes in entomological supplies)

Carolina Biological Supply Co., 2700 York Rd., Burlington, NC 27215; Phone: 1-800-334-5551; FAX: 1-800-222-7112

Gempler's, P.O. Box 270, 211 Blue Mounds Road, Mt. Horeb, WI 53572; Phone: 1-800-382-8473; FAX: 1-800-551-1128; email: 103065.3001@compuserve.com

Great Lakes IPM, 10220 Church Road, NE, Vestaburg, MI 48891; Phone: (517) 268-5693; FAX: (517) 268-5311

Ward's Natural Science Establishment, Inc., P.O. Box 92912, Rochester, NY 14692-9012; Phone: 1-800-962-2660; Fax: 1-800-635-8439

Golf Course Hole Cutters

Standard Golf Co., 6620 Nordic Dr., P.O. Box 68, Cedar Falls, IA 50613; Phone: (319) 266-2638; FAX: (319) 266-9627

Par Aide Products Co., 3565 Hoffman Road East, St. Paul, MN 55110-5376; Phone: (612) 779-9851; FAX: (612) 779-9854

Personal Protective Equipment for Pesticide Applicators

Forestry Suppliers, Inc., P.O. Box 8397, Jackson, MS 39284-8397; Phone: 1-800-647-5368; FAX: 1-800-543-4203

Gempler's, P.O. Box 270, 211 Blue Mounds Road, Mt. Horeb, WI 53572; Phone: 1-800-382-8473; FAX: 1-800-551-1128; email: 103065.3001@compuserve.com

Insect Pheromone Lures and Traps

Great Lakes IPM, 10220 Church Road, NE, Vestaburg, MI 48891; Phone: (517) 268-5693; FAX: (517) 268-5311

Trécé, Inc., P.O. Box 6278, Salinas, CA 93912; Phone: (408) 758-0204; FAX: (408) 758-2625

Traps for Moles and Other Vertebrate Pests

Tomahawk Live Trap Co., P.O. Box 323, Tomahawk, WI 54487; Phone: 1-800-272-8727

Wildlife Management Supplies, 640 Starkweather, Plymouth, MI 48170; Phone: 1-800-451-6544; FAX: (313) 453-6395

Woodstream Corp., 69 N. Locust St., P.O. Box 327, Lititz, PA 17543-0327; Phone: 1-800-800-1819; FAX: (717) 626-1912

Waterfowl Repellent for Use on Turf

RJ Advantage, Inc., 501 Murray Road, Cincinnati, OH 45217; Phone 1-800-423-2473; FAX: (513) 482-7377

APPENDIX 4
WEIGHTS AND MEASUREMENTS

Weights and measurements for insecticide rates and dosages may be expressed in either the metric or United States' systems. Scientific work is usually done in the metric system, whereas most turfgrass managers are more accustomed to the United States' system. For this reason, one may need to convert the information found in the literature from one system to the other. Where temperatures are involved, they may be expressed in either the Fahrenheit or Celsius scale.

LINEAR MEASURE

U.S. Units	U.S. Units
1 inch (in.)	= 0.0833 foot (ft)
1 foot	= 12 inches
1 yard (yd)	= 3 feet
1 mile (mi)	= 5,280 feet

Metric	Metric
1 centimeter (cm)	= 10 millimeters (mm)
1 meter (m)	= 100 centimeters
1 kilometer (km)	= 1000 meters

U.S. Units	Metric
1 inch	= 25,400 micrometers (μm)
1 inch	= 2.54 centimeters
1 foot	= 30.48 centimeters
1 foot	= 0.3048 meter
1 yard	= 0.91 meter
1 mile	= 1.61 kilometers
1 mile	= 1,610 meters

Metric	U.S. Units
1 millimeter	= 0.03937 inch
1 centimeter	= 0.3937 inch
1 meter	= 39.37 inches
1 meter	= 3.281 feet
1 kilometer	= 3,281 feet
1 kilometer	= 0.6214 mile

To convert: inches to centimeters, multiply the number of inches by 2.54; centimeters to inches, multiply the number of centimeters by 0.3937

AREA MEASURE

U.S. Units	U.S. Units
1 square foot (sq ft)	= 144 square inches (sq in.)
1 square yard (sq yd)	= 9 square feet
1 acre (ac)	= 43,560 square feet
1 square mile (sq mi)	= 640 acres

U.S. Units	Metric
1 square inch	= 6.45 square centimeters
1 square foot	= 929 square centimeters
1 acre	= 4,047 square meters
1 square mile	= 2.59 square kilometers

Metric	U.S. Units
1 square centimeter	= 0.155 square inch
1 square meter	= 10.76 square feet
1 square meter	= 1.196 square yards
1 hectare	= 2.471 acres
1 square kilometer	= 0.3861 square mile

WEIGHTS

Avoirdupois	Metric
1 ounce (oz)	= 28.35 grams
1 pound (lb)	= 453.59 grams

Metric	Avoirdupois
1 gram	= 0.03527 ounce
1 kilogram (kg)	= 2.205 pounds

When it is necessary to convert ounces to grams, multiply the number of ounces by 28.35. To convert grams to ounces, multiply the number of grams by 0.03527

LIQUID MEASURE

U.S. Units	Metric
1 fluid ounce (oz)	= 29.57 milliliters (mL)
1 pint (pt)	= 0.47 liter (L)
1 quart (qt)	= 0.95 liter
1 gallon (gal)	= 3.78 liters

Metric	U.S. Units
1 milliliter	= 0.0338 ounce
1 liter	= 2.113 pints
1 liter	= 1.057 quarts
1 liter	= 0.2642 gallon

VOLUMETRIC MEASURE FOR LIQUIDS OR POWDERS

Measure	U.S. Units	Metric Units
1 teaspoon	= 1 fluid drams (fl dr)	= 5 milliliters
1 tablespoon	= 3 teaspoons	= 15 milliliters
1 fluid ounce (fl oz)	= 2 tablespoons	= 30 milliliters
1 cup	= 16 tablespoons	= 237 milliliters
1 pint	= 2 cups or 16 fluid ounces	= 437 milliliters
1 quart	= 2 pints or 32 fluid ounces	
1 gallon	= 4 quarts or 128 fluid ounces	

TEMPERATURE

On the Celsius thermometer the freezing point of water is 0°C and the boiling point is 100°C, in contrast to the Fahrenheit thermometer where the freezing point is 32°F and the boiling point is 212°F. Temperatures can be converted from one scale to the other by using the following formulas:

To Convert from Centigrade to Fahrenheit
°F= (°C × 9/5) + 32
Example: Convert 10° Centigrade to °F
°F= (10 × 9/5) + 32
°F= 18 + 32
°F= 50; or 50°F

To Convert from Fahrenheit to Centigrade
°C= (°F – 32) × 5/9
Example: Convert 86° Fahrenheit to °C
°C= (86 – 32) × 5/9
°C= 54 × 5/9
°C= 30; or 30°C

Glossary of Terms

Abamectin — An insecticidal toxin derived from fermentation of *Streptomyces* bacteria.

Abdomen — The third, or most posterior, of the three major body regions of an insect.

Absorption — The process by which a chemical passes from one system *into* another, such as from the soil solution into a plant root.

Accelerated microbial degradation — See *enhanced microbial degradation.*

Accessory gland — A secretory organ associated with the reproductive system; in males, they produce the seminal fluid; in females, they produce substances used to protectively coat the eggs or to glue them to an object.

Acetylcholine — The chemical substance that transmits nervous impulses across a synapse.

Acetylcholinesterase — See *Cholinesterase.*

Action threshold — The density of pests that will cause unacceptable injury if no control measures are taken, often expressed a number per unit area.

Active ingredient — The actual toxic material present in a pesticide formulation.

Acute poisoning — Illness or death from a single dose of a poison.

Adaptation — The ability to adjust to and perform well under certain environmental conditions.

Adjuvant — Any ingredient that improves the properties of a pesticide formulation.

Adsorption — The binding of a chemical to the surface of soil particles or plant parts.

Aedeagus — The copulatory, or mating, organ of a male insect.

Aeration — The practice of enhancing the movement of air, water, and nutrients into the soil by making holes or slits in it. Specialized equipment is commonly used to remove plugs or to cut slices in the soil.

Alkaloids — A group of toxic or bitter-tasting compounds containing nitrogen that occur naturally in plant tissues. Endophytic fungi also produce alkaloids that are involved in resistance of ryegrasses and fescues to certain insects.

Antenna — One of a pair of segmented sensory organs located on the head above the mouthparts.

Antennal club — The enlarged segments at the end of an insect's antenna.

Anterior — Front; in front of; toward the front.

Anus — The posterior opening of the alimentary tract.

Aphid — A type of small, soft-bodied sucking insect belonging to the order Hymenoptera.

Apical — At the end, tip, or outermost part.

Approach — In golf, the fairway area immediately in front of a putting green.

Apterous — Wingless.

Arid regions — Regions where the soil is usually very dry because of the lack of rainfall.

Arthropod — An invertebrate animal with jointed body and appendages; a member of the phylum Arthropoda. Some common examples are insects, spiders, mites, ticks, centipedes, millipedes, and crustaceans.

Arthropoda — The phylum of animals that includes the arthropods.

Augmentation — Any biological control practice designed to increase the number or effectiveness of existing natural enemies.

Axil — The upper angle between a leaf and the stem from which it grows.

Axon — The part of a neuron that carries impulses away from the cell body.

Axonic poisons — A chemical that interrupts normal transmission of impulses along the axon of a neuron.

Azadirachtin — A botanical insecticide extracted from seeds of the neem tree, *Azadirachta indica*; deters feeding and interferes with growth, development, and reproduction of some insects; also called *neem*.

Bacillus popilliae — A spore-forming bacterium; causal agent of milky disease in grubs of the Japanese beetle and certain other scarabs.

Bacillus thuringiensis (often referred to as **Bt**) — A spore-forming bacterium that produces toxins which, upon ingestion, cause rapid gut paralysis and death of caterpillars and certain other insects; Bt is widely used as a microbial insecticide.

Bacterium — A one-celled organism that has no chlorophyll and multiplies by simple division.

Bait — A pesticide formulation that combines an edible or attractive substance with a pesticide.

Basal — Toward or at the base.

Base temperature — A threshold temperature (usually 50°F) used in calculating degree-days for the purpose of forecasting periods of insect activity. Daily degree-days are computed by subtracting the base temperature from the average daily temperature.

Beak — The protruding mouthpart structures of a sucking insect.

Bilobate — Divided into two lobes.

Biological control — The use of any living agent — often another insect — to suppress pest populations.

Biotype — A population or race of a pest species that differs from other populations of the species in its ability to attack a particular plant species or cultivar.

Blade — The flat portion of the leaf blade above the sheath.

Botanical insecticide — An insecticide produced from a plant, plant extract, or plant product (e.g., neem).

Brachypterous — With short or abbreviated wings; as in some forms of chinch bugs.

Bract — In botany, a modified leaf, small and scalelike or large and showy, growing at the base of a flower; for example, in flowering dogwood, *Cornus florida* L.

Broad-spectrum insecticides — Insecticides that kill many different types of insects.

Brood — The individuals that hatch from eggs laid by one mother; individuals that hatch at about the same time and normally mature at the same time.

Bt — See *Bacillus thuringiensis*.

Carbamate — A pesticide derived from carbamic acid; includes several synthetic insecticides used on turf (e.g., carbaryl, bendiocarb).

Castings — Soil-rich mounds or clumps excreted by earthworms.

Caterpillar — The larva, or active immature stage of a butterfly or moth.

Cephalothorax — The united head and thorax of the arachnids (e.g., spiders) and crustaceans.

Cerci — Paired, segmented sensory appendages or "feelers" at the posterior of the abdomen.

Certified applicator — A person who has been approved by his or her state to apply restricted-use pesticides; special training and testing are required for certification.

Chafer — A type of beetle belonging to the family Scarabaeidae; larvae of some species are root-feeding turf pests (e.g., European chafer, masked chafers).

Chemophobic — Having an excessive and irrational fear of chemicals.

Chewing-type mouthparts — Mouthparts modified for biting off pieces of solid food with paired jaws, or mandibles.

Chloronicotinyls — A new class of synthetic insecticides having both contact and systemic activity, and relatively low mammalian toxicity; represented by imidacloprid.

Chlorophyll — The green, light-sensitive pigment of plants that in sunlight carries out photosynthesis to produce carbohydrates.

Chlorosis — The yellowing of normally green plant tissue because of the loss of chlorophyll.

Chlorotic — In plant leaves, having a faded, washed out, or yellowed appearance due to loss of chlorophyll.

Cholinesterase (= acetylcholinesterase) — An enzyme that catalyzes the breakdown of acetylcholine; cholinesterase "clears" the synapses after transmission of a nervous impulse. Certain insecticides (e.g., organophosphates) work by inhibiting cholinesterase, causing the nervous system to malfunction.

Cholinesterase inhibitors — Insecticides that work by tying up cholinesterase causing a malfunctioning of the insect's nervous system; also called *synaptic poisons*.

Cholinesterase test — A blood test administered to pesticide applicators as a means of monitoring possible overexposure to organophosphate or carbamate insecticides.

Class — In scientific classification of organisms, a subdivision of a phylum containing a number of related orders.

Clitellum — A swollen, band-like sexual organ on earthworms, located between the head and the middle part of the body.

Cocoon — A silken case in which the pupa is formed.

Coleoptera — The order of insects comprising the beetles.

Collar — In golf, a narrow area surrounding the putting green that is mowed at a height intermediate between that of the fairway and the putting surface; in botany, a narrow band marking the junction of the leaf blade and leaf sheath.

Compaction soil — An unfavorable soil condition caused by intense traffic or other mechanical forces. The soil particles are pressed closely together and pore space is eliminated from the soil.

Complete metamorphosis — A type of development in which there are four stages — egg, larva, pupa, and adult — each entirely different from the others.

Compound eye — An eye composed of many individual units, each of which is represented externally by a hexagonal facet.

Constricted — Narrowed.

Contact insecticide — An insecticide that enters the body when an insect walks or crawls over a treated surface, or through treated soil; insecticide that is absorbed through the body wall.

Cool-season turfgrass — A turfgrass species that grows best when temperatures are in the 60–75°F (15–24°C) range.

Cooperative Extension Service — This national service helps to distribute agricultural knowledge throughout rural areas through Extension Service offices and agents in each county of the United States.

Cornicles — A pair of dorsal, tubular structures on the rear part of the abdomen of aphids.

Coxa — The basal (first) segment of an insect leg.

Crawler — Newly emerged, active immature form of a scale insect or mealybug.

Crochets — Hooks or tiny claws on the tips of the prolegs in caterpillars (Lepidoptera).

Crop — The expanded portion of an insect's foregut, just behind the esophagus; used for food storage.

Crown — The major meristematic area of a grass plant, from which all growth is initiated. It is located at the base of the plant near the soil surface.

Crustacea — The arthropod class that includes crayfish, lobsters, crabs, shrimp, sowbugs, and pillbugs; characterized by having two pairs of antennae, one pair of mandibles, two pairs of maxillae, and gills for breathing.

Cultivar — In botany, a plant that differs from others in the same species and retains these distinguishing features when reproduced.

Cultural control — Suppression of pest populations through normal or slightly modified cultural practices (e.g., by modifying irrigation frequency).

Cuticle — The noncellular, multilayered portion of the exoskeleton that overlies the epidermis.

Cyst — A sac-like or bladder-like structure.

Dactyls — Digging claws on the front legs of a mole cricket.

Degradation — The chemical or biological transformation of a pesticide or other substance into one or more different compounds.

Degree-day — An accumulation of heat units above some threshold temperature for a 24-hour period; used in forecasting seasonal phenology of insects and plants.

Dermal — Of or pertaining to the skin.

Desiccation — Loss of moisture from a plant because of hot, dry weather, chemicals, or pest injury.

Dethatch — To reduce an excessive thatch accumulation, usually with a machine such as a vertical cutter.

Deutonymph — An immature life stage (the third instar) of a mite.

Developmental threshold — The minimum temperature required for an insect's development to proceed.

Diapause — A period of arrested development and reduced metabolic rate; a period of dormancy usually associated with onset of winter.

Dichondra — A low-growing, broadleaf plant used as a lawn or ground cover in California and other parts of the warm-season turfgrass zones.

Diplopoda — The arthropod class that includes the millipedes.

Diptera — The order of insects that is comprised by the true flies; characterized by having only one pair of wings in adults.

Disclosing solution — A dilute solution of dishwashing detergent, pyrethrins, or some other irritant that, when sprinkled or poured on turf, causes thatch- or soil-dwelling pests to come to the surface where they can be counted or observed.

Dislodgeable residues — Pesticide residues left on turfgrass foliage following an application that could potentially be physically removed or dislodged by human contact.

Distal — Farthest from the point of attachment or origin.

Diurnal — Active during the daytime.

Dorsal — Pertaining to the back or upper side of the body.

Dorsal blood vessel — Tube running along the back of an arthropod that forms the primary organ of the circulatory system of arthropods.

Dorso-lateral — At the top and to the side.

Dorsum — The back or top (dorsal) side of the body.

Drift — Movement of pesticides by wind away from the intended target area.

Ecdysis — Molting; the process of shedding the exoskeleton.

Ecdysone — Hormone secreted by the prothoracic glands that initiates the process of molting in insects.

Economic injury level — The lowest number of insects that will cause economic damage; i.e., the minimum pest density that justifies the cost of applying control measures.

Elytra — A thickened, leathery forewing, as in beetles (Coleoptera).

Emergence — The act of the adult insect leaving the pupal case or the last nymphal skin.

Emulsifiable concentrate — A concentrated pesticide formulation containing organic solvent and a detergent-like emulsifier to facilitate mixing with water.

Emulsion — A suspension of microscopic droplets of one liquid in another.

Endocuticle — The innermost layer of the cuticle.

Endophyte — A fungus that lives between the cells of another plant, such as within certain turfgrasses. Endophytes do not harm the host plant, but may produce toxins that help to protect the plant from being eaten by insects.

Enhanced microbial degradation — Unusually rapid breakdown of soil pesticides by micro-organisms.

Entomopathogenic nematodes — Microscopic roundworms that attack and kill insect larvae, reproducing within the dead hosts; several strains have been marketed for control of turfgrass insect pests.

EPA (Environmental Protection Agency) — The federal agency responsible for registering and regulating pesticides; the EPA also regulates many other issues pertaining to the environment.

Epicuticle — The very thin, outermost layer of the exoskeleton.

Epidermis — The cellular layer of the body wall, which secretes the exoskeleton.

Eradication — Complete and total elimination of a group of organisms from an area.

Erosion — Loss of soil from the action of water or wind.

Esophagus — Part of the alimentary tract; the narrow tube that connects the mouth and the crop.

Excavated — Hollowed out.

Exocuticle — Outer, hardened layer of the insect's exoskeleton.

Exoskeleton — A skeleton or supporting structure on the outside of the body.

Exotic — Introduced from another country or continent.

Extravaginal growth — Young, vegetative stems that grow outside the basal leaf sheath by penetrating through the sheath. Rhizomes and stolons are examples of extravaginal growth.

Exuvium (plural = exuviae) — The cast, or shed, skin of an arthropod.

Fairway— In golf, the grass area between the tee and putting green of variable lengths from about 100 to more than 500 yards and mowed at heights of 1/2 to 1-1/4 in. (1.3–3 cm).

Family — In scientific classification, a subdivision of an order containing a group of related genera. Family names of animals end in *-idae*.

Fauna — Animals present in a given region, or at a particular time.

Fecundity — The reproductive capacity, or average number of eggs laid by an insect.

Femur — The third leg segment of an insect, located between the trochanter and the tibia; functionally analogous to the thigh in mammals.

Flotation — A method of sampling wherein a metal cylinder is driven into the soil and flooded with water; small insects then float to the surface.

Flowable — A pesticide formulation in which the active ingredient is wet-milled with a clay diluent and water; has a pudding-like consistency, and can be mixed with water for spraying.

Foregut — The anterior region of an insect's digestive tract.

Formulation — The form in which a pesticide is offered for sale, consisting of a mixture of active and inert ingredients. Examples include granules, wettable powders, emulsifiable concentrates, and flowables.

Frass — Solid, cellulose-rich fecal matter of a plant-feeding insect, usually in the form of pellets or sawdust-like material.

Fungicide — A substance that kills fungi.

Ganglia — A mass or bundle of nervous tissue.

Gastric caecae — Sac-like outpocketings of the anterior portion of the midgut.

Genera — Plural of *genus*.

General-use pesticides — Pesticides that can be purchased and used by persons who are not certified applicators, as opposed to restricted-use pesticides.

Genus — A group of closely related species. The first name in the binomial scientific name of an organism. Names of genera are capitalized, and when printed are italicized.

Gradual metamorphosis — A type of development in which there are three life stages — egg, nymphs, and adult — wherein the nymphs are somewhat similar to adults in appearance and habits. Sometimes called *simple* or *incomplete* metamorphosis.

Granular — A type of pesticide formulation in which the active ingredient is incorporated onto coarse particles of porous material like clay, ground corncobs, or ground walnut shell.

Green — In golf, the putting green; the area of turf mowed at 1/8 to 1/4 in. height.

Groundwater — Water that saturates cracks, caverns, sand, gravel, and other porous subsurface rock formations.

Grub — A thick-bodied larva, or immature stage, of various species of beetles, especially scarabs. Grubs typically have a well-developed head and lack abdominal prolegs.

Haltere — In Diptera (true flies), a small, knobbed structure on each side of the thorax, formed from a modified hindwing.

Hazard — The danger or risk that use of a pesticide will cause injury or other adverse side effects; hazard depends on both toxicity and exposure.

Head — The anterior body region; bears the eyes, antennae, and mouthparts, and houses the brain.

Head capsule — The fused sclerites of the head that form a hard, compact case, not unlike a football helmet.

Hemiptera — The order of insects with sucking mouthparts comprising the true bugs.

Herbicides — Pesticides used to kill weeds or other unwanted vegetation.

Hibernation — Dormancy during winter.

Hindgut — The posterior portion of an insect's alimentary tract, between the midgut and the anus.

Homoptera — The order of sucking insects that includes aphids, cicadas, mealybugs, leafhoppers, and scale insects.

Honeydew — Sugary, sticky liquid discharged from the anus of certain sucking insects, such as aphids and mealybugs.

Host — The organism on or in which a parasite lives; the plant on which an insect feeds.

Hydrolysis — A chemical degradation process resulting from the reaction of a pesticide with water under acidic or alkaline conditions.

Hymenoptera — The order of insects that includes bees, wasps, hornets, ants, and sawflies; characterized by chewing mouthparts and two pairs of membranous wings.

Hypersensitivity — A condition wherein a person is especially sensitive or allergic to levels of a substance to which a normal individual does not react.

Indicator plant — A plant whose seasonal phenology (bud break, flowering, etc.) coincides with that of particular insect pest, and that can be used to predict occurrence of the pest's life stages for purposes of treatment timing.

Insect — An arthropod characterized by having three main body regions, six legs, and one pair of antennae.

Insect growth regulator (IGR) — An insecticide that works by upsetting or modifying normal insect growth processes.

Insecta — The class of animals that contains the insects; characterized by having three main body regions and, usually, one pair of antennae and three pairs of legs.

Insecticide — A substance, usually a chemical, that is used to kill insects.

Instar — The insect between successive molts; the first instar being between hatching and the first molt.

Integrated pest management (IPM) — An effective and environmentally responsible approach to pest control that relies on a combination of preventive and corrective measures to keep pest densities below levels that would cause unacceptable damage.

Internode — In botany, the section of a plant stem between two successive nodes or joints.

Intravaginal growth — Vegetative stems that grow upward within the enveloping basal leaf sheath. A tiller is an example of intravaginal growth.

Invertebrate — An animal without a backbone.

Juvenile hormone — Hormone that suppresses development of adult characteristics; produced by a pair of glands just behind the brain (the corpora allata).

Label — The printed information on or attached to a pesticide container; federal regulations stipulate the information that must be included on it.

Labeling — The pesticide label itself, plus any brochures, leaflets, or other information provided by the manufacturer that accompanies a pesticide when you buy it.

Labial palp — One of a pair of small feeler-like structures arising from the labium.

Labium — One of the mouthpart structures; the lower lip of an insect.

Labrum — The upper lip of an insect.

Land-grant university — A college or university developed in response to the federal Morrill Act of 1862, which designated tracts of public land for development of higher education systems for rural people and to increase agricultural productivity. Each state has at least one land-grant university.

Larva (plural = larvae) — The immature stage, between egg and pupa, of insects that undergo complete metamorphosis. Examples include grubs, caterpillars, and maggots. Also refers to the six-legged first instar of a mite.

Lateral — Of or pertaining to the side (that is, the left or right side).

LC$_{50}$ — The concentration of a pesticide in some medium (air, water, soil) that will kill 50% of the test organisms to which it is administered; generally expressed as parts per million or parts per billion in the medium. The lower the LC$_{50}$, the more toxic the pesticide.

LD$_{50}$ — The dose or amount of a pesticide that will kill 50% of the test organisms to which it is administered; generally expressed as milligrams of pesticide per kilogram of body weight. The lower the LD$_{50}$, the more toxic the pesticide.

Leaching — The downward movement by water of dissolved or suspended pesticides, fertilizers, or other substances through the soil.

Leaf sheath — Basal portion of a grass leaf that surrounds the stem.

Leafhoppers — A group of small, canoe-shaped, sucking insects in the order Homoptera.

Lepidoptera — The order of insects that includes moths, butterflies, and skippers.

Life cycle — The chain or sequence of events that occurs during the lifetime of an individual organism.

Ligule — A thin outgrowth membrane attached to a grass leaf at the point where the blade meets the leaf sheath.

Lyme disease — A potentially serious bacterial infection transmitted through the bite of an infected tick.

Macropterous — With full-sized wings, as opposed to brachypterous.

Maggot — A worm-like insect larva without a well-developed head capsule, as in Diptera (flies).

Malpighian tubules — Excretory tubes that arise near the anterior end of the hindgut and extend into the body cavity; somewhat analogous to kidneys in humans.

Mandibles — Jaws; paired mouthpart structures, usually toothed, used for chewing food.

Maxilla (plural = maxillae) — One of the paired mouthpart structures immediately behind the mandibles, used for manipulating food into the mouth.

Maxillary palp — A small, feeler-like structure arising from the maxilla.

Mealybugs — A group of slow-moving, soft-bodied, sucking insects in the order Homoptera.

Membranous — Like a membrane; thin and more or less transparent (wings).

Meristem — Undifferentiated plant tissue with cells capable of division at the tip of a stem or root, or at the base of a leaf.

Metamorphosis — A change in form during development, such as when an insect transforms through the egg, larval, and pupal stages before becoming an adult.

Microbial insecticide — A biological preparation of bacteria, viruses, fungi, or other microorganisms or their products, applied and used in ways similar to conventional chemical insecticides.

Microorganism — A living organism, microscopic in size, such as a bacterium, fungus, or virus.

Midgut — The middle portion of an insect's alimentary tract, where much of the digestion of food occurs.

Milky disease — A fatal disease of Japanese beetle and other scarab grubs caused by the bacterium *Bacillus popilliae;* the blood of diseased grubs becomes milky white in color.

Minute — Very small; an insect a few millimeters or less in length would be considered minute.

Mite — A member of the class Arachnida, order Acari; this group includes tiny arthropods characterized by having two body regions, no antennae, and four pairs of legs.

Miticide — A pesticide that kills mites and ticks.

Mode of action — Means by which a pesticide exerts its toxic effects on an organism.

Molt Accelerating Compounds (MACs) — A new class of insecticides which kill target pests by inducing a premature, lethal molt.

Molting — The process of shedding the exoskeleton; to shed the exoskeleton.

Molting hormone — See *ecdysone*.

Monitoring — See *scouting*.

MSDS (Material Safety Data Sheet) — Sheets prepared by chemical manufacturers that provide information about the potential hazards and safe handling of a particular pesticide. MSDS sheets can be obtained for every labeled pesticide and must be made available to every person selling, storing, or handling that pesticide.

Mutualism — A living together of two species of organisms in such manner that both species benefit, as with endophytic fungi within certain turfgrasses.

Mycelium — A mass of branching, threadlike filaments that compose the vegetative part of a fungus.

Natural enemies — Living organisms found in nature that kill insects outright, weaken them, or reduce their reproductive potential; includes predators, parasites, and pathogens.

Necrosis — The death of plant tissue. Dead plant tissue is said to be necrotic.

Nematicide — A substance that kills nematodes.

Nematodes — Small (often microscopic), unsegmented roundworms with threadlike bodies. Many species of nematodes attack plant roots, whereas others are parasitic on insects. See *entomopathogenic nematodes*.

Neuron — A nerve cell.

Nocturnal — Active at night.

Node — In insects, a knob-like swelling. In botany, a joint of a grass stem; an enlarged area at which buds and leaves are attached.

Nymph — The active, immature stage of an insect with gradual metamorphosis (chinch bugs, scales, aphids, crickets, etc.). Unlike larvae, nymphs are similar in appearance to the adult stage. Also refers to the 8-legged, immature stage of a mite.

Ocelli — Single-faceted, simple eyes of an insect.

Ocular — Pertaining to the eyes.

Oral — Pertaining to the mouth.

Order — In scientific classification, a subdivision of a class containing a group of related families. In insects, names of orders usually end in the letters *ptera* (e.g., Coleoptera).

Organophosphate — An insecticide containing phosphorus; includes many important synthetic insecticides (e.g., diazinon, chlorpyrifos, trichlorfon).

OSHA (Occupational Safety and Health Administration) — The federal agency responsible for enforcing regulations that ensure safety in the workplace.

Ovary — The egg-producing organ of the female.

Overseeding — Seeding into an existing turf.

Overwinter — To survive the winter.

Ovicide — A pesticide that kills eggs of the target pest.

Oviparous — Egg-laying.

Oviposit — To lay or deposit eggs.

Ovipositor — The egg-laying structure of a female insect.

Palp — A segmented "feeler" borne on an insect's mouthparts that has sensory functions.

Panicle — In grasses, a type of inflorescence in which the flowers are born on lateral branches rather than on the main axis.

Parasite — An animal that lives on or in the body of another animal (its host), at least during part of its life cycle, feeding on the tissues of the host.

Parasitoid — An insect that parasitizes another insect. Parasitoids lay one or more eggs on, or in, the body of the host (victim). Upon hatching, the parasitoid larva slowly devours the host while completing its own development.

Parthenogenesis — Development of the egg without fertilization; a type of reproduction whereby young are produced without fertilization.

Parthenogenetic — Reproducing by parthenogenesis.

Pathogen — A disease-causing organism; usually a microorganism.

Peripheral — Relating to the outer margin, or the surrounding area or region.

Persistent — A pesticide that retains its toxicity for a relatively long time, also called residual.

Personal protective equipment (PPE) — Clothing and other gear (e.g., goggles, respirator) worn to protect oneself from exposure when handling or applying pesticides.

Pest resurgence — A situation in which a pest population, after a pesticide application, rebounds to numbers higher than before the application, often because of destruction of natural enemies.

Pesticide — Any substance for controlling or repelling a pest.

pH — A numerical measure of acidity used to distinguish acidic, neutral, and alkaline solutions. The scale is 1 to 14; neutral is pH 7; values below 7 are acidic, and above 7 are alkaline.

Pharynx — The anterior part of the foregut, between the mouth and the esophagus, modified into a pump in sucking insects.

Phenology —The practice of relating recurring biological events, such as flowering or first emergence of an insect pest in the spring, to climate and other events that are happening at the same time.

Pheromone — A chemical substance given off by one individual that causes a specific reaction upon reception by another individual of the same species (e.g., sex pheromones).

Phloem — In botany, the food-conducting tissue of the vascular system.

Photodecomposition — Breakdown of a pesticide when the residues are exposed to direct sunlight.

Photosynthesis — The process by which green plants manufacture carbohydrates using carbon dioxide, water, chlorophyll, and light.

Phylum — In scientific classification, one of the dozen or so major divisions of the animal kingdom. Insects and their relatives belong to the phylum Arthropoda.

Phytophagous — Feeding on plants.

Phytotoxic — Injurious to plants. The term usually refers to chemicals that can be toxic to plants.

Piercing-sucking mouthparts — Mouthparts with mandibles and maxillae modified into long, needle-like stylets used for piercing plant or animal tissues and sucking out fluids.

Posterior — Hind or rear.

ppb (parts per billion) — An abbreviation indicating parts or mass of a pesticide or other substance in a billion parts water or soil.

ppm (parts per million) — An abbreviation indicating parts or mass of a pesticide or other substance in a million parts water or soil.

Precipitate — To separate in solid form a substance that had previously been dissolved or suspended in a solution.

Predaceous — Feeding as a predator.

Predator — An animal that attacks and feeds on other animals (usually smaller and less powerful than itself) and consumes more than one prey animal in its lifetime.

Prepupa — A quiescent stage between the larval period and the pupal period.

Prolegs — Fleshy, unjointed walking legs found on the abdomen of certain insect larvae, especially caterpillars.

Pronotum — The dorsal surface of the prothorax.

Prothorax — The first, or anterior, segment of the thorax.

Protonymph — The second instar, usually the 8-legged nymph of a mite.

Proventriculus — The grinding organ and valve between the foregut and the midgut.

Pubescent — Downy, covered with short, fine hairs.

Punctate — Pitted or covered with punctures.

Pupa (plural = pupae) — The stage between the larva and adult in insects with complete metamorphosis; a nonfeeding and usually inactive stage.

Pupate — To transform to a pupa.

Pyrethroid — An organic synthetic insecticide with a structure based on that of pyrethrum.

Pyrethrum — A natural botanical insecticide derived from *Chrysanthemum* flowers.

Queen — In social insects such as ants or wasps, the reproductive female who lays all of the eggs that give rise to new members of the colony.

Quiescence — Inactivity induced by unfavorable environmental conditions.

Raster — In white grubs, a grouping of definitively arranged hairs, spines, and bare spaces on the underside of the last abdominal segment, in front of the anus.

Rastral pattern — The distinctive pattern of hairs, spines, and bare spaces on the raster, used in distinguishing among species of white grubs.

Recuperative potential — The ability of a plant to recover from injury, often referring to how rapidly a particular turfgrass can spread and fill in injured spots.

Residual — Pertains to length of time that pesticide residues remain active on treated surfaces or in the soil; long-residual pesticides are persistent and provide extended control, short-residual ones break down quickly into nontoxic by-products.

Residue — Deposits of pesticide left on foliage, thatch, or soil following an application.

Resistance — In insects, refers to the ability of a pest to survive being treated with an insecticide; in plants, refers to the ability of a plant to avoid, tolerate, or outgrow a level of pest pressure that would be much more damaging to nonresistant plants.

Respirator — A mask with replaceable cartridges worn over the nose and mouth that filters dusts or mists and protects against harmful inhalation of pesticides.

Restricted-use pesticide — A pesticide that may be used only by applicators certified by the state in which they work.

Rhizome — A jointed underground stem that arises from the crown and can produce roots and shoots at each node.

Risk — The probability that a pesticide will cause harm.

Rodenticide — A pesticide or other substance used to control rodents.

Root zone — The area of soil where plant roots develop and grow.

Rosette — A cluster of leaves in crowded circles or spirals arising basally from a crown or apically from an axis, with greatly shortened internodes.

Rough — The area of a golf course surrounding the fairway and green which is mowed higher than the fairway and has a less desirable playing surface.

Sampling — The process of counting or surveying a portion of a pest population for the purpose of estimating overall population density.

Sanitation — A tactic for managing insects by removal of dead plant material or other debris so as to eliminate hiding places and overwintering sites, and to reduce the spread of pest infestations.

Scale insect — A type of sucking insect in the order Homoptera; some scale insects secrete a waxy shell over their back.

Scarab (or scarabaeid) — A member of the beetle family Scarabaeidae; larvae of this group include the root-feeding turf pests commonly called white grubs.

Sclerite — A hardened plate forming part of the exoskeleton of an insect or other arthropod.

Sclerotized — Hardened.

Scouting — The watch kept on a pest for detection of the species' presence, and determination of the severity and extent of an infestation.

Scutum — A hardened plate on the back of a tick.

Secondary pest outbreak — A situation wherein treating for a primary pest results in destruction of natural enemies; this allows a secondary pest that is normally held in check by those enemies to quickly multiply and reach outbreak densities.

Seedhead — An elongated grass stem with a flower at its apex.

Seminal vesicles — A saclike storage organ that holds seminal fluid of males prior to discharge during mating.

Seta (plural = setae) — A bristle or hairlike structure on an insect.

Sex pheromone — A chemical emitted by one sex that attracts the opposite sex for mating.

Sheath, leaf — The tubular, nonexpanded lower portion of a grass blade which surrounds the stem.

Signal plant — See *indicator plant*.

Signal word — A word required on every pesticide label to denote the relative toxicity of the material. In order of increasing toxicity, signal words are "Caution," "Warning," and "Danger-Poison."

Skeletonize — To feed by chewing away plant tissue, leaving only a network of leaf veins.

Sod — Pieces or strips of live grass and adhering soil which are used for vegetative planting.

Solubility — A measure of the amount of a chemical that can be dissolved in a liquid.

Soluble powder — A pesticide formulation consisting of finely ground solid material that dissolves in water in the spray tank.

Sooty mold — An unsightly black fungus that often grows on the honeydew of sucking insects, coating the surface of leaves.

Species — A group of organisms with common characteristics and capable of interbreeding to produce fertile offspring which are like the parents.

Spermatheca — A saclike structure in female insects in which the sperm are received and often stored.

Spinosad — A natural insecticide derived from the bacterium *Saccharopolyspora spinosa*.

Spiracle — An external opening of the insect's respiratory system; a breathing pore.

Spittle — A frothy fluid secreted by insects; saliva.

Spot-treatment — Treating a small area infested with a pest rather than applying the pesticide to the entire turf area.

Stand — A group of plants growing together in the same area.

Stipes — The second segment or division of the maxilla.

Stippled — With yellowish or whitish specks caused by loss of chlorophyll, as with leaves that have been fed upon by mites or certain sucking insects.

Stolon — A spreading stem that grows along the surface of the ground and produces new shoots and roots at the nodes.

Striated — Marked with parallel, fine, impressed lines or grooves.

Stylet — One of the piercing structures in piercing-sucking mouthparts.

Subsurface application — Injection or incorporation of a pesticide application directly into the soil.

Subterranean — Underground.

Surfactant — A material that reduces surface tension between two unlike materials, such as water and oil. Surfactants as spray additives help to improve the spreading, wetting, sticking, and emulsifying properties of a pesticide formulation.

Swarming — The process by which a large group of insects (e.g., ants) departs from a nest or breeding habitat, usually to form a new colony.

Sweep net — A heavy-duty insect net that is swung through vegetation to sample for insects.

Synapse — The juncture between two neurons, or between a neuron and another cell.

Synaptic poisons — A chemical that interrupts normal transmission of nervous impulses across synapses.

Systemic insecticide — An insecticide that is taken up and translocated within plants or animals.

Target principle — The concept of applying an insecticide in a manner that places the residues in the zone (foliage, thatch, or soil) where they are most likely to be encountered by the target pest.

Tarsus — The "foot" of an insect, usually consisting of several segments.

Tee — The closely mowed, usually elevated area from which the first shot on each golf hole is hit.

Testis (plural = testes) — The sex organ in males that produces sperm.

Thatch — A tightly intermingled layer of living and dead roots, crowns, rhizomes, stolons, and organic debris that accumulates between the zone of green vegetation and the soil surface.

Thorax — The body region between the head and abdomen that bears the legs and wings.

Tibia — The fourth segment of the leg, between the femur and the tarsus.

Tiller — Erect, vegetative stems that arise from the crown and grow next to the original shoot of the parent plant.

Tolerance level — The maximum density of pests that can be tolerated before control actions are warranted.

Topdress — Spreading a thin layer of soil mix over a turf area and working it into the turf to stimulate thatch decomposition and to smooth the surface.

Toxicity — The inherent, poisonous potency of a pesticide or other substance.

Toxin — A poisonous substance.

Trachea — A tube of the insect's respiratory system that opens to the outside at a spiracle, or breathing pore.

Transition zone — A relatively narrow belt between the cool-season and warm-season zones where both cool-season and warm-season turfgrasses can be grown, but where the climate is not optimal for either.

Translocate — The movement of materials from one part of a plant to another.

Trochanter — The second segment of the leg, between the coxa and the femur.

Turf — A covering of mowed vegetation, usually a turfgrass, growing intimately with an upper soil stratum of intermingled roots and stems.

Turfgrass — A species or cultivar of grass, usually of spreading habit, which is maintained as a mowed turf.

Vascular system — The tissue that transports materials such as water and nutrients within the plant.

Vector — An organism that is the carrier of a disease-causing pathogen.

Ventral — Pertaining to the underside of the body.

Ventral nerve cord — Paired nerves lying along the underside of the body cavity, containing segmentally arranged ganglia. Analogous to the spinal cord of mammals.

Vertical cutting — Cutting slices in the turf with a machine that has vertically rotating blades; this is an important method of reducing thatch.

Virulence — Quality of being poisonous; the relative infectiousness of a pathogen causing disease.

Viviparous — Giving birth to living, active young (as opposed to laying eggs).

Volatilization — The process by which a solid or liquid changes to a gaseous state; loss of chemicals from plant and/or soil surfaces by evaporation into the atmosphere.

Warm-season turfgrass — A cold-intolerant turfgrass grass species that grows best when temperatures are in the 80–95°F (27–35°C) temperature range.

Weed — A plant growing where it is not wanted.

White grub — Whitish, C-shaped larva of beetles belonging to the family Scarabaeidae.

Wing pads — The undeveloped wings of nymphs of insects with gradual metamorphosis, which show behind the thorax as two lateral, flat structures.

Witches' broom — An abnormal brush-like growth of weak, tightly clustered plant shoots.

Worker Protection Standard — A federal regulation designed to protect agricultural workers and pesticide handlers from pesticide injury.

INDEX

T

344 • DESTRUCTIVE TURFGRASS INSECTS: BIOLOGY, DIAGNOSIS, AND CONTROL

White grubs (continued)
  management
    biological control   113–137
    chemical control   94–95, 137–139, 140
    cultural control   135–136
    sampling and monitoring   42, 44,
      134–135
  pest species
    Aphodius grubs   140–141
    Asiatic garden beetle   141–143, plate
      7
    black turfgrass ataenius   143–146,
      plate 8
    European chafer   146–149, plate 9
    green June beetle   149–152, plate 10
    Japanese beetle   152–157, plate 11
    May beetles   158–160, plate 12
    northern and southern masked
      chafers   160–163, plate 5, plate 13
    Oriental beetle   163–164, plate 7
Wild pigs   275
Wildlife problems   275–294
Wildlife protection laws   107
Winter grain mite (*Penthaleus major*)   38,
  202–203, plate 21
  distinguishing characteristics   202

distribution   202
life cycle and habits   202
management   202
nature of injury   202
plants attacked   202
Witches' broom   203, 204, 322, plate 22
  definition   322
Wolf spiders   269, plate 31
Worker Protection Standard   72, 322
  definition   322

Y

Yellowjacket wasp   39, 249–251, plate 29
  traps   251

Z

Zoysiagrass (*Zoysia*)   11
Zoysiagrass mite (*Eriophyes zoysiae*)   205,
  plate 22
  damage   205
  description   205
  life history   205
  management   205